12.15.91

Happy Birthday,

Love,

Jack + Barbara

ALSO BY WARREN G. HARRIS

GABLE & LOMBARD
CARY GRANT: A TOUCH OF ELEGANCE
NATALIE & R.J.
THE OTHER MARILYN: A BIOGRAPHY OF MARILYN MILLER

Warren G. Harris

Lucy & Desi

THE·LEGENDARY·LOVE·STORY·OF
TELEVISION'S·MOST·FAMOUS·COUPLE

SIMON & SCHUSTER

NEW YORK LONDON TORONTO SYDNEY TOKYO SINGAPORE

SIMON & SCHUSTER
Simon & Schuster Building
Rockefeller Center
1230 Avenue of the Americas
New York, New York 10020

Designed by Karolina Harris
Manufactured in the United States of America

1 3 5 7 9 10 8 6 4 2

Library of Congress Cataloging-in-Publication Data
Harris, Warren G.
Lucy & Desi :
the legendary love story of television's most famous couple /
Warren G. Harris.
p   cm.
Includes index.
1. Ball, Lucille, 1911–   . 2. Arnaz, Desi, 1917–1986.
3. Entertainers—United States—Biography.   I. Title.   II. Title:
Lucy and Desi.
PN2287.B16H34   1991
791.45′028′0922—dc20
[B]   91-19840 CIP
ISBN 0-671-74709-6

All photographs courtesy of:
Personality Photos
P.O. Box 50
Midwood Station
Brooklyn, NY 11230

FOR BARRY CONLEY,

"THIS TIME THE DREAM'S ON ME"

Contents

Warren G. Harris

Lucy & Desi

THE·LEGENDARY·LOVE·STORY·OF TELEVISION'S·MOST·FAMOUS·COUPLE

SIMON & SCHUSTER

NEW YORK LONDON TORONTO SYDNEY TOKYO SINGAPORE

SIMON & SCHUSTER
Simon & Schuster Building
Rockefeller Center
1230 Avenue of the Americas
New York, New York 10020

Designed by Karolina Harris
Manufactured in the United States of America

1   3   5   7   9   10   8   6   4   2

Library of Congress Cataloging-in-Publication Data
Harris, Warren G.
Lucy & Desi :
the legendary love story of television's most famous couple /
Warren G. Harris.
p   cm.
Includes index.
1. Ball, Lucille, 1911–   . 2. Arnaz, Desi, 1917–1986.
3. Entertainers—United States—Biography.   I. Title.   II. Title:
Lucy and Desi.
PN2287.B16H34   1991
791.45′028′0922—dc20
[B]   91-19840 CIP
ISBN 0-671-74709-6

All photographs courtesy of:
Personality Photos
P.O. Box 50
Midwood Station
Brooklyn, NY 11230

1

Tears and Laughter

LUCY and Desi. Lucy and Ricky. As far as the public knew, the private life of the Arnazes closely resembled that of the Ricardos on the TV screen; a camera crew just dropped by once a week to film a half hour of slapstick and tender kisses.

But in truth, the marriage between Lucille Ball and Desi Arnaz, which had been tempestuous from the start, became unadulterated hell during the eight years that *I Love Lucy* was on the air. The romantic flame had all but gone out.

"The last two or three years of the show, everybody connected with it knew the problems we were having," Lucy recalled. "The writers must have thought twice about some of the scenes, but they put them in and we did them. We could forget about our troubles while we were working. It really made it seem almost like nothing *was* wrong."

Desi's boozing and philandering, plus their incompatible ego tempers, were pulling the marriage apart. Two young children, as well as joint business commitments worth $20 million, were the main reason they stayed together. Their Desilu Productions company was the colossus of the TV industry, involved not only in *I Love Lucy* but in a total of nearly thirty shows on all three major networks.

The marriage had endured for almost two decades, confounding all those who predicted it would last six months at the most. "In the beginning, Desi needed me and I wanted him. Then I very much wanted his children. That's why I stayed so long. First I hung on wanting kids; then I hung on because I did have kids. But it got to the point where it was bad for the children to witness what was happening," Lucy said.

"I was hoping in my heart that maybe everything would change, that a miracle might happen, maybe, maybe, maybe. But people don't change. Desi was self-destructive. Whenever he built something, he couldn't wait to tear it down. Like our lives. The man had everything, but he couldn't handle it."

For two such unhappy people, there had to be a breaking point. It finally came in November 1959, just days before their nineteenth wedding anniversary. This time, hell broke loose while Lucy and Desi were discussing some production matters in his office at Desilu Studios. Desi, as usual these days, had drunk too many daiquiris, but Lucy ignored it until he belched loudly, not once, but twice.

"You pissy-eyed bastard," she screamed. She picked up an empty cocktail glass from the desk, hurled it against the wall, and stormed out.

Desi wavered a bit getting to his feet, then chased after his wife. He caught up with her in the hallway as she stopped to sip at the water fountain.

"Lucy, I want a divorce," he said. "I just can't take it anymore."

Lucy's huge blue eyes glared murderously at him, but she said nothing. She just turned her back on Desi and walked away. A studio corridor was no place for an argument. But when Desi got home . . .

The Arnazes resided in a white Colonial mansion at 1000 North Roxbury Drive, in the flatland of Beverly Hills. Desi's duties as chief executive officer of Desilu kept him late at the studio, so eight-year-old Lucie and six-year-old Desi Jr. had long gone to bed by the time he returned around midnight.

Lucy was sitting in the living room waiting for him. Wearing a dressing gown, she looked up from a dog-eared copy of Norman Vincent Peale's The Power of Positive Thinking, which had helped her through many a crisis over the years. The last cigarette from a pack opened after dinner dangled from her lips.

"Did you really mean what you said this morning?"

"Yes, I'm very sorry, but I did," Desi replied. "I cannot keep on living this way."

Lucy flew into a tantrum. "Why don't you die then? That would be a better solution. Better for the children. Better for everybody."

Desi tried to remain calm. "I'm sorry, but dying is not on my immediate schedule."

He started upstairs. Lucy trailed after him, shouting insult after insult. "You cheat! You drunken bum! I've got enough on you to hang you. By the time I get through with you, you'll be as broke as when you left Cuba. You goddam spic . . . you wetback!"

Lucy and Desi no longer shared the master bedroom. He had moved into the dressing room that adjoined it. With Lucy still breathing down his neck, he went to his bureau and took out a cardboard matchbook.

Just as Desi was about to light a cigarette, Lucy reached into the pocket of her robe, pulled out a pistol, and squeezed the trigger.

Although she seemed angry enough to kill, the gun was actually a cigarette lighter used for comic effect in one of the early episodes of *I Love Lucy*. Desi calmly lit a cigarette on the flame and then showed Lucy the matchbook in his hand.

Scrawled inside it, in Lucy's own hand, was a man's name, address, and telephone number. Whatever the writing proved (Desi may have been saving it for years), it was enough to make Lucy blush as red as her flamboyantly dyed hair.

"I know you didn't mean everything you said, but for the sake of the children let's try to make this as amicable as possible," Desi said. "We'll get a good lawyer for you and you'll be the one to sue for divorce. We'll have no trouble arriving at a fair financial settlement, and all that other stuff. But please, Lucy, don't ever threaten me again."

Desi packed some clothes in a suitcase and left. The couple never lived under the same roof again. "That was a blessing in itself, because when we weren't together, we couldn't yell at each other," Lucy recalled.

With considerable help from the PR image polishers at CBS and Desilu, Lucy and Desi kept the separation secret until production was completed on their final program of the season. They couldn't risk getting involved in a public scandal that might cause their ultraconservative sponsor, Westinghouse Electric, to cancel their contract.

By this time in its history, *I Love Lucy* had evolved into a series of one-hour specials that were shown periodically as part of the weekly anthology series *Desilu Playhouse*. The finale to the 1959–60 season was entitled "Lucy Meets the Mustache," with comedian Ernie Kovacs and his singer wife, Edie Adams, as guest stars.

It happened to be the 193rd "Lucy and Ricky" script since the series started in 1951. The filming became a highly emotional experience for Lucy and Desi, who realized it was probably the very last time that they would ever enact those characters. Even now it became a strain as both tried to conceal the hurt and disappointment over their failed marriage.

Desi was also directing "Lucy Meets the Mustache," so that compounded the problem. "By that point, Lucy and Desi weren't speaking to each other. Someone would come over and say, 'Miss Ball, Mr. Arnaz would like you to do so-and-so.' Every time they wanted to film a funny scene, Lucy would break down and cry. Nobody could stand to watch it," Edie Adams recalled.

The plot had Lucy masquerading as a male chauffeur in order to get Ricky a job on Ernie Kovacs's TV show. In the traditional kiss-and-make-up fadeout, Ricky forgives Lucy's meddling, and they go into a passionate clinch after she first removes her fake mustache.

"We looked at each other, embraced, and kissed," Desi remembered. "This was not just an ordinary kiss for a scene in a show. It was a kiss that would wrap up twenty years of love and friendship, triumphs and failures, ecstasy and sex, jealousy and regrets, heartbreaks and laughter. And tears. The only thing we were not able to hide was the tears."

Following the kiss, the couple just stood there staring at each other. Finally, Lucy said, "You're the director. You're supposed to say 'cut.' "

"I know," Desi said. "Cut, goddam it!"

Ironically, Lucy and Desi played out their last love scene only yards away from where they first met in June 1940. The place was called RKO Studios then. Who could have known that fifteen years later they'd wind up buying the fourteen-acre site for $6 million and renaming it after themselves as Desilu?

It wasn't a case of love at first sight. Desi Arnaz, then all of twenty-three years old, was having lunch in the commissary with director George Abbott, who had guided him to a big success on the Broadway stage in the musical *Too Many Girls*. While they were in the midst of discussing the imminent filming of the Rodgers and Hart extravaganza, a disheveled woman suddenly approached their table.

"She looked like a two-dollar whore who had been badly beaten by her pimp," Desi recalled. "She had a black eye, her hair was hanging down in her face, and her skin-tight dress was coming apart at the seams."

Desi sat there in stunned silence. His dark brown eyes bulged as he watched the woman exchange a few words of greeting with George Abbott and then saunter off on her dilapidated high-heeled shoes.

"What the hell was that?" Desi asked.

"That's Lucille Ball," George Abbott replied. "She'll be working with us, playing the ingenue part."

Desi couldn't believe it. He turned indignant, knowing that the ingenue in *Too Many Girls* was supposed to be an innocent, virginal college freshman. "I think you've blown your top," he told Abbott. "There's no way they can change that tough broad back into anything resembling an ingenue."

Desi couldn't have known that Lucille Ball shared his opinion. Nearly twenty-nine, she considered herself too old to pass for a college freshman. But RKO forced her to accept the part when negotiations to "borrow" Mary Martin from Paramount fell through.

Lucille couldn't sing very well, so her voice would have to be dubbed for the musical numbers. But rather than be suspended without pay, she took whatever roles RKO handed her, suitable or not. *Too Many Girls* would be the sixth movie she'd made in the past twelve months.

Lucille expected to meet the rest of the cast later that afternoon during rehearsals. Following lunch in the commissary, she returned to the set of her current assignment, *Dance, Girl, Dance.*

The backstage melodrama about the rivalry between a burlesque star and an aspiring ballerina in the chorus was the reason for Lucille's tawdry getup as a stripteaser. She had spent the morning and part of the afternoon in a vicious cat fight with her considerably younger co-star, Maureen O'Hara. It was, of course, only a scene from the script, but director Dorothy Arzner goaded the two actresses into such a frenzy that shooting finally had to be halted for the day to avoid serious injuries.

An hour later, Lucille Ball headed for the studio's rehearsal hall looking more like her usual self. Her lustrous strawberry blonde hair had been rearranged in soft waves that framed her porcelain complexion and blue eyes. She wore a yellow cashmere sweater and tight-fitting beige slacks that made no secret of her shapely legs.

Meanwhile, most of the main cast of *Too Many Girls* were already milling around on the bare stage of the Little Theatre. The group was composed of two contingents. Desi Arnaz, comedian Eddie Bracken, and tap dancer Hal LeRoy were the only principals from the original Broadway cast. The new Hollywood additions included singer Frances Langford, dancer Ann Miller, and leading man Richard Carlson.

Off to one corner of the stage, Desi was running through his show-stopping number, "She Could Shake the Maracas," with a piano player. In the middle of the performance, Lucille Ball strolled in and stood watching him.

Desi couldn't help noticing her. He sang and danced with wild abandon, shaking his hips and pounding on air in lieu of the conga drum that he would normally play in the scene.

"Man, that is some hunk of woman," Desi told the pianist when they finished. He still didn't know who she was. Certainly not the tough cookie he'd seen in the commissary. But the accompanist assured him that it was Lucille Ball.

Desi remained skeptical when she came over to introduce herself. "Miss Ball?" he said.

"Why don't you call me Lucille and I'll call you Dizzy," she said.

"Okay, Lucille, but it's not Dizzy."

"Oh? How do you say it? Daisy?"

"No. Daisy is a flower. It's Desi." He spelled it out for her. Never tongue-tied around women, he then asked Lucille if she knew how to rumba.

"No, but I bet that you do," she replied, amused.

Desi did a quick demonstration of the rumba, explaining the steps as he went along. Fascinated, Lucille leaned against the side of the piano and asked for a repeat performance.

This time Desi finished with a flourish, landing face-to-face with Lucille. Putting one arm on each side of her, he pinned her against the piano.

"You're going to have to rumba in this picture," Desi said. "I can teach you quickly, but only on condition that you go out with me tonight."

Lucille knew a fast operator when she met one, but his guileless approach amused her. "I *dun't* have *anythin'* else planned, and I'd love to," she said, affectionately poking fun at his Cuban accent.

That evening, Desi took her to El Zerape, a Mexican-Cuban nightspot close to downtown Los Angeles and the current rage for slumming Hollywood celebrities. It turned out to be a group excursion organized by George Abbott, a fanatic ballroom dancer. Nearly the entire cast of *Too Many Girls* was there, including the fourteen singing and dancing choristers that RKO had hired from the New York production at a weekly salary of forty dollars each.

Desi introduced Lucille to one of the latter, a freckle-faced redhead named Van Johnson. "Believe it or not, Van doubled as my understudy on Broadway," Desi said.

The three of them had a good laugh as Desi told of the time when he developed an ulcerated toe and George Abbott ordered the understudy to go on. "Van looked so ridiculous made up to look like me that I insisted on going on anyway. The house doctor injected my foot with Novocain to deaden the pain," Desi said.

Desi had no such handicap that night. But before he could keep his promise to teach Lucille the rumba, Ann Miller walked over and pulled him onto the dance floor. Their torrid performance received so much applause that Lucille decided it would be an impossible act to follow. There was no way she would risk dancing with someone as expert as Desi until she'd first had a chance to bone up on the Latin repertoire. Instead, the couple ended up in a cozy booth for two opposite the kitchen.

Desi asked for another date the following evening. She said she had to go to Ventura to promote the opening of her latest movie, *You Can't Fool Your Wife*. She couldn't very well refuse when Desi offered to drive her there. He loved showing off his new Buick convertible, which he'd purchased wholesale through a friend at General Motors. With its silver-gray paint job, black leather upholstery, and whitewall tires, it looked as if it had been designed for Clark Gable or Gary Cooper.

Ventura is situated about seventy-five miles northwest of Los Angeles, on the narrow and treacherous Pacific Coast Highway. With the car's top down to take advantage of the splendid weather, Desi drove at his own speed, rarely less than seventy-five miles per hour and often at the engine's limit of 103. Lucille shrieked with fright at the start, but quickly calmed down when Desi began serenading her with "Besame Mucho." He followed with every other romantic number that he could remember, both in Spanish and in English.

When Desi finally ran out of songs, Lucille started screaming again. This time, it was Desi's turn to become frightened, but she assured him that it had nothing to do with his driving. Friend and co-worker Katharine Hepburn advised her that her speaking voice was pitched too high, but that she could easily lower it by screaming at the top of her lungs whenever possible.

On the trip back to Los Angeles, Desi alternated his singing with Lucille's yelling. Passing motorists probably took them for fugitives from a lunatic asylum, but they had a marvelous time. So much so that they made a date for the following night at Ciro's, the newest and swankest club on the Sunset Strip.

"We were in love almost immediately," Lucy recalled. "We spent a

great deal of time talking about our pasts, what we'd done with our lives, and our goals for the future. Some of it was very painful, neither of us were angels, but it had to be faced before we became too involved."

2

The Jamestown Hussy

CAUGHT up in the illusion, many viewers of *I Love Lucy* believed that Lucy Ricardo's maiden name was an inside joke, that the actress playing the role actually started life as Lucille McGillicuddy. She didn't.

Her real name was Lucille Desiree Ball, which in retrospect does seem untypical for a small-town girl from upstate New York. She was born in Jamestown, a farming and manufacturing community near Lake Chautauqua, on August 6, 1911. That also happened to be the year that Roald Amundsen discovered the South Pole, that a Marmon Wasp racing car averaging seventy-five miles per hour won the first Indianapolis 500, and that Irving Berlin wrote "Alexander's Ragtime Band."

Never a natural redhead, Lucille arrived in the world with blondish hair that gradually darkened to a brunette shade best described as chestnut. She was a beautiful child, with huge blue eyes and a cupid's mouth. She never lost that "little girl" quality, which became one of her main appeals as a comedian.

The family nicknamed her "Lucyball," but she preferred to be known as Lucille; her mother told her that the name was French in origin and meant "shining light." She disliked the short form "Lucy" —also a complete and more prevalent name in its own right—and successfully avoided it for forty years. But after a certain television series debuted in 1951, she was rarely called anything but Lucy.

Lucy was the first child of Henry Dunnell Ball and the former Desiree Evelyn Hunt, both still in their teens and married scarcely a year when she was born. With roots that could be traced back to seventeenth-century settlers from France, England, Scotland, and Ireland, the Ball and Hunt families were long established in northwestern New York State as farmers and tradesmen.

Lucy's paternal grandfather, Jasper Ball, broke family tradition by becoming involved in the newfangled telephone business. He ran a contracting firm that installed the poles and wiring for some of the small independent companies that later became part of the nationwide Bell Telephone system.

Lucy's father worked for Grandpa Ball as an electrical lineman. For that time, it was considered a daring and dangerous occupation, with the constant threat of electrocution or falling from high places. Many of Henry Ball's assignments took him to remote areas, where he also had to contend with frigid weather and primitive living conditions.

Like most women of her generation, Desiree Ball (known familiarly as "DeDe") had been raised to become a wife, housekeeper, and mother hen. When DeDe married Henry Ball, it was taken for granted that she—and eventually the family—would accompany him wherever his job took him. As a result, Lucy spent her early years far from Jamestown, first in the copper-mining territory around Anaconda, Montana, and then in Wyandotte, Michigan, a factory town dependent on the automotive industry in nearby Detroit.

Lucy was a gregarious, mischievous child. Her mother would tie a rope around her waist and hook it by a pulley to the clothesline to keep her from straying out of the backyard. One morning, the pulley stopped jingling, and DeDe looked out the window to find Lucy tangled up in the branches of a tree and begging the milkman to help her get free. That might have been the birth of *I Love Lucy*, Plot Number One—Lucy Ricardo trying to talk her way out of trouble.

In November 1914, DeDe Ball was pregnant again. Since she and her husband had failed in previous attempts to have another child, they were overjoyed. Nineteen fifteen promised to be the couple's happiest year, but it didn't turn out that way.

In February, twenty-three-year-old Henry Ball came down with typhoid fever and died. "Doctors with black leather satchels hovered around us like moths," Lucy recalled.

No one knew exactly how Ball contracted the then incurable disease, but it was most likely from some contaminated food or drinking water. Fortunately, it proved to be an isolated case. Neither Lucy, now three and a half, nor the pregnant DeDe was affected. Only time would tell about the unborn baby.

The distraught widow took her husband's body back to Jamestown by train for burial. "We went to live with my maternal grandparents in Celoron, which is a suburb of Jamestown. It was near a fantastic amusement park, with a huge zoo and a bandstand where John Philip Sousa often conducted. What a marvelous place to grow up," Lucy remembered.

Lucy's grandparents, Frederick and Florabelle Hunt, were eccentric but respected local characters. A portly bon vivant and jack-of-all-trades, Grandpa Hunt was also a fanatical Socialist, and at one time or another had worked as a wood turner in a furniture factory, letter carrier, quack doctor, and hotel manager. Florabelle, a practical nurse and midwife, had been orphaned at thirteen and raised five pairs of younger twin sisters and brothers all by herself.

The Hunts' small white clapboard house was always filled with relatives and friends. Although they were lucky to be able to pay the bills each month, they believed in sharing whatever they had. The couple maintained a large vegetable garden in the backyard where the needy from the neighborhood were encouraged to pick food for their tables.

Named in honor of his grandfather, an apparently healthy Frederick Ball was born on July 3, 1915. Previously the center of attention, Lucy resented her baby brother terribly. Even into adult life, she suspected that Fred was their mother's favorite.

As it turned out, Lucy's doubts were groundless. DeDe Ball dedicated her life to her daughter, but she was hardly the manipulative "stage mother" who tries to fulfill her own frustrated career ambitions through her children. Married at seventeen and widowed at twenty-two, DeDe was still young enough to want a life of her own. Toward Lucy and Fred, she was always encouraging but never pushy.

DeDe had studied piano as a child and was an accomplished musician. Before marrying Henry Ball, she had been considering a professional musical career. Perhaps if young Lucy had been some sort of performing prodigy, DeDe *would* have been tempted to turn her daughter into a star. But the little girl showed no aptitude for anything musical despite DeDe's efforts to teach her.

While DeDe took odd jobs and looked for another husband (the field narrowed considerably when America entered World War I in 1917), Lucy was left in the care of the Hunts, who instilled in her a deep family loyalty and a commitment to hard work. "That's where I found out what was right and what was wrong and that you have a responsibility to people who love you. The values you get as a child, they open the door," she recalled.

Grandpa Hunt was the only father that Lucy ever knew. Not a religious man, he still encouraged his grandchildren to attend Sunday school at the local Baptist and Methodist churches because he felt it might do them some good. Socialism in its pure, non-political form appealed to him more. He subscribed to labor journals and led the cheering whenever reformer Eugene V. Debs came to town. It was a local joke that Grandpa could not so much as get two people together without trying to organize them into a union.

He had an insatiable, if curmudgeonly, love of life that expressed itself best through the children. "Grandpa got us up early, otherwise we might miss something," Lucy said. "Sunsets, he loved 'em. Made us love 'em. He wore an old cardigan sweater and a wide-brimmed hat always on the tilt, played ricky-tick piano and sang naughty songs. He was always building things—playhouses in trees, teeter-totters, doll houses, tents, bobsleds, stilts. In the winter it was skating and sliding and fishing through the ice. In the summer, boat rides and groaning picnic baskets."

Grandpa was the strongman who held things together during Lucy's early life, playing father figure to all the family orphans. In addition to DeDe and her brood, there were the Hunts' younger daughter, divorcée Lola Mandicos, and her child, Cleo; Uncle Ned Orcutt, who kept all his money in his shoe because he didn't trust banks; and many other relatives from Grandma's side of the family who were also permanent or transient residents.

Lucy got her first taste of show business with Grandpa Hunt. "He loved the three-a-day vaudeville that played in Jamestown, and used to take us every Saturday. In the summer, we went to the silent flickers that were shown outdoors at Celoron Park. I loved the Pearl White serials and couldn't wait until the following week for the next episode. Wow! I knew I had to be part of it," Lucy remembered.

After she saw a vaudeville show or movie, Lucy loved to go home and re-enact it. "We were forever playing theater together," said childhood friend Pauline Lopus. "We'd experiment with makeup, which even our mothers didn't use then. We used to dress up in Grandmother Hunt's old clothes. The big chicken coop in the Hunts' backyard became our ranch house, mansion, or whatever setting the plot called for."

Lucy and her friends often put on one-act plays and revues, for which they made their own tickets, posters, and props. "Lucille loved to dress up as a boy and perform a routine about how disgusting it was to wait for a girl to get ready for a date—then she'd open this huge overcoat she was wearing and begin to fiddle with a razor, mirror, comb, and bath towel. When the audience began howling, she'd start to improvise, which was disastrous for our cues," Pauline Lopus recalled.

Grandpa and DeDe encouraged Lucy to participate in the plays staged at school, the neighborhood churches, and fraternal organizations. Whenever they'd audition children, Lucy turned up. She was so enthusiastic that she once dislocated her shoulder while performing an apache dance with an equally overzealous boy partner in a Masonic revue. (Decades later, she spoofed the Parisian dance specialty in an episode of *I Love Lucy*.) Lucy's skill as a male impersonator also won her the lead in a school production of *Charley's Aunt,* the classic British farce in which an Oxford scholar poses as his maiden aunt. It was quite a stunt for a child—a girl impersonating a man impersonating a woman—but she pulled it off with aplomb.

Amid her early successes, however, Lucy had a traumatizing experience that interrupted the happy times. In 1920, DeDe Ball married Ed Peterson, a handsome factory worker. DeDe fell so wildly in love that she agreed to leave the children temporarily and move to Detroit with Peterson.

"Ed was quite a gambler and liked to drink. He promised he'd give up those things if I went with him and we made a fresh start. Once we got settled, we intended to send for the kids," DeDe said later. In the meantime, Peterson insisted that Lucy and Fred move in with *his* parents, who had a big empty house where the children would get better care than at the overcrowded Hunts'.

A puritanical Swedish couple, the elder Petersons were so opposed to frivolity that they banished all mirrors from the house, save for one over the bathroom sink. Caught admiring herself in it, Lucy was severely chastised for being so vain.

"Grandmother Peterson was the sort of woman who made *sure* of spoiling a surprise party in your honor by telling you about it in advance. While all the other kids were out playing in the summer evenings, I had to be in bed at six-thirty. They did that to discipline me, but for me it was the wrong way to bring up a child. It gave me a feeling of frustration and of reaching-out-and-trying-to-please. I found the quickest and easiest way to do that was to make people laugh. I suppose you could say it led to my wanting to be an actress," Lucy remembered.

The separation from her mother and the Hunts affected Lucy so deeply that in later life she claimed that it lasted seven or eight years, but in reality, it was probably less than one.

"We didn't stay long in Detroit, because Ed didn't keep his promises," DeDe said. "We moved in with the Petersons, but I sent Lucille and Fred back to my folks because Ed could be very difficult when he got drunk and I didn't want them exposed to that."

In his sober moments, Ed Peterson had a good side, encouraging Lucy's interest in performing. "My stepfather introduced me to the Chautauqua circuit, then at its height as a showcase for lecturers, musicians, actors," she recollected. "One night he took me to see Julius Tannen, a lanky, ugly-handsome giant who was a great monologist. There sat this man with one light bulb, a little table, and a glass of water, simply talking and creating a whole world out of nothing. He was magic. Just this voice, and this magnificent man enthralling you with his stories and his intonations.

"He changed my life. I realized it was a very serious, wonderful thing to be able to make people laugh and/or cry, to be able to play on their emotions."

Although Lucy and her brother had returned to living with the Hunts, it was no longer such a cheery household. In 1921, Grandma Florabelle was diagnosed with cancer. As the malignancy grew, even morphine failed to relieve her pain. She suffered an agonizing death a year later at age fifty-one.

Her grandmother's prolonged illness was almost too much for Lucy to bear. With her dramatic nature, Lucy tended to be overly emotional about everything, so she was forbidden to attend the funeral. She followed the procession to the cemetery anyway, dragging her little brother along with her by the hand.

Since Grandpa Hunt's other daughter, Lola, worked full-time as a practical nurse, Lucy replaced Grandma in supervising brother Fred and their cousin Cleo. "Lucille took us over completely, particularly me, who was eight years younger," Cleo recalled. "She was always wild, tempestuous, exciting to be with. She was a reactor—she reacted to everything. Running away was her favorite form of reacting. She'd inveigle me into going with her—I had a piggy bank. It was always very dramatic when we were caught. And that was the point. What she really wanted was to play a scene."

Lucy once conned Cleo into accompanying her to Fredonia, about twenty-five miles from Jamestown, to surprise an adored male teacher who had been transferred to a school there. "He played it very cool, putting us up for the night in a boardinghouse and telephoning Aunt

DeDe to tell her where we were. On his advice, when we got home Aunt DeDe acted like we'd never been away. That devastated Lucille, no reaction, nothing," Cleo recounted.

From the age of ten, Lucy held part-time jobs to help out at home. For fifty cents a week, she led a blind street vendor around town, helping him sell bars of soap and making sure that no one short-changed him. During the summer at Celoron Park, she sold ice cream from a little gazebo or hawked hot dogs on the boardwalk. She had a brief career as a soda jerk at Walgreen's drugstore, but got fired for usually forgetting to put the banana on the banana split.

When Lucy entered her teens, she seemed a typical product of the Roaring Twenties, that euphoric era between World War I and the Great Depression. She was the first girl in the neighborhood to bob her hair, to own a raccoon coat, and to copy the fad for wearing unbuckled galoshes (the true mark of a "flapper" because of the flapping noise given off as one walked). Conservative townsfolk tended to whisper behind her back and labeled her the "Jamestown Hussy."

Lucy certainly looked and acted the part. By fifteen, she was about as tall as she ever would be (five feet six) and could easily pass for much older. Men treated her cautiously, not sure if she was a child or a woman. Her habit of running away from home every few months added fuel to rumors that she was "fast and loose," a popular euphemism of the time.

Gossipmongers suspected that Lucy's $125 raccoon coat was a gift from a sugar daddy, but it actually came from her mother as a bribe against dropping out of school. "Lucille never did seem to care much about getting an education. She could have been a very good student. But aside from gym and acting in the dramatic society, there was something about the routine that irked her. She was so anxious to get out and do things," classmate Pauline Lopus said.

At fifteen, Lucy wanted to quit school because of an article she'd read in *Vogue* magazine about a theatrical academy in New York City that was all the rage with Junior League debutantes. She believed that the John Murray Anderson–Robert Milton School of the Theater and Dance could be the stepping-stone to a career on Broadway or in vaudeville.

The raccoon coat failed to change Lucy's determination, so DeDe finally agreed to send her to the city on a trial basis. Although the school's tuition amounted to a hefty $350 per semester, half was due on admission and the balance after a six-week probationary period. DeDe doubted that Lucy would get any further than that, but thought she should be given a chance to prove what she could do. Arrangements were made for Lucy to stay with a family that DeDe knew in Washington Heights, on the Upper West Side of Manhattan.

In 1926, New York was at its zenith as the capital of "live" show business, with myriad schools, colleges, workshops, and studios offering instruction in everything from the traditional performing arts to juggling and sword-swallowing. Some were in business only to fleece star-struck rubes, but the Anderson-Milton School was one of the most reputable. John Murray Anderson ranked second to Florenz Ziegfeld as a producer of spectacular Broadway shows like the *Greenwich Village Follies* and *Music Box Revue*. His partner, Robert Milton, was a top stage director. Their faculty included such talents as Christopher Morley, Channing Pollock, Robert Edmond Jones, and future queen of modern dance Martha Graham.

Unhappily for Lucy but luckily for DeDe's bank account, she never got past the probation. "I was in and out of there in a quick six weeks," Lucy recalled. "They sent my mother a letter *literally* saying that she was wasting her money! The dopes—that's what I thought of them then—couldn't see what I had to offer. I wasn't discouraged —delayed, yes, but not discouraged. I was struck by the lightning of show business."

Robert Milton gave Lucy a difficult time, or so she claimed: "He had a *method* to his teaching, and ridicule was an important part of it. After he put me down two or three times in front of the whole class for mispronouncing 'water' and 'horses,' I shut up like a clam. I couldn't talk at all. I couldn't think. And the other classes! I don't even remember what they were except for eccentric dancing. I had two left feet and still do."

The school's star pupil at the time was an eighteen-year-old New Englander named Ruth Elizabeth Davis, known as Bette to her classmates. "I never met Bette, but she knocked me out with her performance in one of the school plays," Lucy recalled. "I used to stand in the hallways and wait for her to pass. I'd follow her down the streets for blocks—lost in complete admiration—trying to study her."

Bette Davis would move on to the prestigious Provincetown Players Company in Greenwich Village, but for Lucille Ball it was back to Jamestown High School and part-time jobs to reimburse DeDe for the non-refundable $175 advanced toward her tuition. "New York was a city full of strangers. I was shy, terrified, and so homesick that I would have been physically ill if I'd stayed," she said later.

Lucy quickly got over her disappointment. She was a member of the school cheerleading squad except during the basketball season, when she played center on the girls' team. She hung out at Harvey and Carey's drugstore, dated boys, though not very seriously, and kept up her interest in show business by attending every movie shown in Jamestown.

"We had three theaters in town at the time, and they each changed their programs twice a week," said Lucy's frequent champion Marion Strong. "That meant seeing six movies a week. And Lord help us if the picture was *good*. That meant Lucille would want to see it again!"

But in the summer of 1927, Lucy's life was changed again when a tragedy occurred that haunted the Ball and Hunt families forever after. Lucy's brother, Fred, had been given a .22 rifle that previous Christmas, on the condition that he couldn't fire it before his twelfth birthday, which just happened to be the eve of July 4. When that day came, Grandpa Hunt held a big party and permitted Fred, Lucy, and some of their friends to engage in target practice in the backyard.

Pandemonium broke out when an eight-year-old neighbor, Warner Erickson, darted across the line of fire and got hit in the back by a bullet. Paralyzed from the neck down, Erickson never recovered from the injury and died five years later. In the investigation that immediately followed the accident, police established that the bullet was fired by twelve-year-old Joanna Ottinger, who had never held a gun in her hand prior to that moment.

For negligent conduct bordering on lunacy, Grandpa Hunt had to pay a severe penalty. The embittered parents of Warner went to court and charged Hunt with attempted murder by making a "human target" of their son. While awaiting trial, Hunt was locked up in the county jail to prevent him from skipping town.

Although the shooting was ruled to be an accident, the judge ordered Grandpa Hunt to pay Warner Erickson's medical bills, as well as the legal fees connected with the trial. With only a few hundred dollars in savings, Hunt was forced to sell his house and possessions, which brought a total of $2,602 at public auction. "It broke his heart and his spirit," Lucy recalled.

New living arrangements were required. DeDe and Ed Peterson, together with Lola Mandicos, rented a bungalow to keep the family unit together. With seven people under one roof, including Grandpa, Lucy, Fred, and Cleo, nobody had room to turn around.

Now sixteen, Lucy saw an opportunity to be on her way. She wanted to return to New York to make another stab at breaking into show business. "Much as I loved Jamestown, there was no future for me there," she recalled. "Jamestown is only a place to be *from*. To be from *only*."

Over the next six years, Lucy became a regular commuter between Jamestown and New York, sometimes making the long trip by train or bus but usually hitchhiking to save the fare. Her frequent comings and goings, often in the cabs of Mack trucks or on the backs of motorcycles, only intensified her hometown reputation as a "bad girl" running wild in the Big City.

Maybe she was and maybe she wasn't. Rumors of a sordid past as a prostitute would follow Lucille Ball all her life because of a shortage of verifiable information about her activities circa 1927–33. One thing is certain. She never worked in show business, as she was always the first to admit. "I had no training, no personality, no talent," she said.

Over the years, Lucy told many tales of her unsuccessful assault on the entertainment world, some of which were probably products of her vivid imagination. It's hard to believe, for example, that Earl Carroll, one of the great glorifiers of female pulchritude, would have selected the gawky and skinny teenager to be a show girl in one of his spectacular *Vanities* revues. Lucy claimed she lost the job when she refused to pose nude—tastefully wrapped in cellophane—as part of a "living curtain" tableau.

Lucy also boasted of *nearly* landing a job in the chorus of one of the many traveling road companies of Florenz Ziegfeld's phenomenally successful *Rio Rita*. According to Lucy, she rehearsed night and day for a month without pay (a standard procedure in those days) and was then fired when Ziegfeld brought back the show's original choreographer, Albertina Rasch, to restage one of the big production numbers.

"I didn't know what an Albertina Rasch *was*. I thought it was a disease. I swear, I had never heard the name before. But I was told to go to her office and she asked me if I could do ballet. Hell, I couldn't even *turn around*, so I was out on the street at midnight," Lucy recalled.

Deciding that a glamorous name might impress producers, Lucy changed hers to Diane Belmont, "Diane" for a racehorse that once proved lucky for her and "Belmont" for the famous Long Island track. The new moniker only caused Lucy more problems, and she soon dropped it. Casting directors kept mistaking her for a member of the wealthy Belmont family and instead gave the jobs to applicants who seemed to really need the work.

Back to using her real name again, Lucy tried another gambit to attract attention. Many of the successful show girls had nicknames like "Bubbles," "Tallahassee," "Stormy," "Cupcake," "Louisiana," "Peaches," "Frenchie," and "Angel."

Lucy encouraged everybody to call her "Montana." In her resume, she listed Butte, Montana, as her birthplace, believing that a pistol-packing frontier background had more publicity value than dullsville Jamestown, New York. (Lucy kept up the ruse for so many years that some reference books *still* cite Butte as her birthplace. The confusion comes from the fact that she *did* live there in infancy while her father installed telephone lines for the Anaconda Copper Company.)

No matter what she called herself, Lucille Ball could get no further than auditions. "I had to compete with the established Shubert and Ziegfeld dollies, and believe me, they were a mean, closed corporation," she once said. "I also had a grab on respectability. My grandparents had raised me to have a conscience. I turned down a lot of so-called opportunities because they were only maneuvers. My ambition wasn't high. I just wanted to work."

Lucy supported herself with part-time jobs like selling theatrical cosmetics at Gray's drugstore and clerking at Woolworth's. She briefly considered becoming a beautician. She had a natural flair for hairstyling and makeup, but she lacked the funds to take the course required to get a license. She often bartered her talent, however, by doing her friends' hair in exchange for small favors.

During this time, Lucy lived in Washington Heights with the family that took care of her while she attended the Anderson-Milton School, but she soon gravitated to the inexpensive hotels and boardinghouses on the Upper West Side that catered to show business troupers.

"I once lived in a dump on Riverside Drive where I had to share a hall bathroom with another girl—a girl I never met but who always left her mushy soap behind. My room had a bed, a dresser and a chair. It was so small that after you opened the door, you had to squeeze against the wall to close it. And cold? That terrible wind off the Hudson! I'll never forget how I froze," she recalled.

When she could afford it, Lucy stayed at the comparatively posh Hotel Kimberley at Broadway and 74th Street, where a bullet once ricocheted through the window while she was taking a bath. "Some gangsters were shooting it out in the building next door. Luckily, I wasn't hit. But the bullet punctured the tub and all the water drained out, flooding the room below," Lucy said.

For all its comical aspects, it was a dismal existence. "Sometimes I didn't have a dime to my name. I used to stand around crowded lunch counters watching for some guy to get up and slap down a tip. I'd do a fast slide onto the empty stool, yell for a cup of coffee and pay for it with the change that he left. Sometimes I could save ordering a doughnut if he left one on his plate. People often did that because the sinkers were only two for a nickel in those days," Lucy said.

Lucy often made tomato soup out of catsup and cadged food when a beau took her to dinner. "I had a big handbag which I lined with wax paper to keep it from leaking," she recalled. "With the bag in my lap, I would pop in rolls, leftovers and whatever else I could grab without being conspicuous."

Small wonder that she often went rushing back to Jamestown. "I'd get terribly homesick. It's a horrible illness," she recalled. "You don't eat, you don't sleep, you cry a lot, and you phone your folks for money to come home again. Finally, after going back and forth I don't know how many times, my mother said, 'I worry enough about you as it is. But having to worry about you starving to death is ridiculous. Why don't you just stay home and forget about show business?' " For once, her daughter agreed.

Lucy resumed her studies at Jamestown High School and also joined a theater group called the "Players." Claiming to be an experienced Broadway actress, she brazened her way into the leading role in a production of Bayard Veiller's *Within the Law,* a hit melodrama from 1912 that starred the great Jane Cowl. Lucy portrayed an ex-shop girl taking revenge on a rich family that railroaded her into prison for a crime she didn't commit.

The heroine had a tough, hoydenish side that didn't match up with Lucy's mousy chestnut hair, so her friend Marion Strong urged her to dye it red for the duration of the week-long run. If they'd only known!

"Red hair had become synonymous with that kind of woman, which Clara Bow usually played in the movies," Strong recalled. "We tried shampooing Lucille's hair with Golden Glint, which was a popular rinse at the time. That didn't work too well, so we redid it with real Egyptian henna. Lucille looked sensational, but she had to let it grow back to her natural shade when the play closed. It gave her too wild an appearance."

The critic for the *Jamestown Post* raved about Lucy's work in *Within the Law* and compared it to the best of Jeanne Eagels, perhaps the greatest dramatic actress of that era. Lucy had never seen any of Eagels's legendary stage performances, which included Sadie Thompson in *Rain,* so the comparison meant little to her.

No Broadway or Hollywood talent scouts were in the audience to offer Lucy a contract, but the enthusiastic response sent her tearing back to New York for another try at fame and fortune. This time it was a bit more complicated, because she'd fallen madly in love for the first time in her life.

Teenaged Lucy's romance with twenty-five-year-old Johnny DeVita gave Jamestowners plenty to gossip about. Italians, along with all Roman Catholics, Jews, and blacks, were minorities in that WASPish community. Also, some Jamestown residents claim DeVita had connections with unsavory characters and ran the numbers game for the Jamestown area. His father headed a gang that smuggled whiskey into the Prohibition "dry" United States from nearby Canada.

Friends say that Johnny DeVita's tough manner rubbed off on Lucy, that she began to smoke, drink, and use foul language. "She grew up fast during the time she spent with Johnny. She was smitten with him and loved being fawned over," a high school colleague recalled.

DeVita frequently traveled to New York, so the love affair continued when Lucy returned there. Rumor had it that DeVita set her up in a Manhattan apartment and bankrolled her entry into show business. Neither is true, but the two did keep company for several years.

Still unable to get a job in either the theater or vaudeville, Lucy finally stumbled into a career as a model when a girlfriend took her to a cocktail party in a millionaire's penthouse on Park Avenue. "I'd never been to one of those really swank affairs, so I was dying of curiosity," Lucy remembered. "I met a man there who asked me if I was a model. I thought he was just handing me a line, so I said, 'Oh, no, I don't have the figure for it.' And he said, 'Well, you're wrong. I'm in the fur business. Our models have to be on the slender side or the coats look like stuffed cabbages.'

"So that was the beginning of it. I went to work for that man in his wholesale showroom on Fourteenth Street. From there I graduated to modeling dresses and hats in the garment district. I also did fashion shows at Stern's department store on 42nd Street, opposite the Fifth Avenue public library."

It was all per diem work, which earned Lucy about twenty-five dollars a week if she was lucky. To make extra money, she posed for some of the many commercial artists who had studios in the vicinity of Columbus Circle and Central Park South.

"The artists had a colony there and you could go from building to building applying to model. They did print ads and painted for billboards. I made five dollars an hour posing for ads for things like Iron

Clad stockings, Tourrain coffee and Yardley English Lavender soap," she said.

Roger Furse, a commercial and portrait artist who later became a celebrated movie production designer, took a fancy to Lucy and helped her get her first important job. Furse prevailed on a friend, designer Hattie Carnegie, to hire Lucy as a model in her salon on East 49th Street off Fifth Avenue.

Tiny and tempestuous Hattie Carnegie (who filched one of America's most revered names and was originally Henrietta Kanengeiser) could neither sew nor cut a pattern, but she had a style sense that made her the top dress designer in the United States for a generation. The child of poor Austrian immigrants and a onetime messenger girl at Macy's, Carnegie probably recognized something of herself in Lucille Ball and decided that the young woman could use some help up the ladder.

"That was a ritzy salon and I knew nothing about high fashion. I used to buy my clothes in bargain basements," Lucy recalled. "The experienced models snubbed me. I had such an inferiority complex that just that *alone* could have paralyzed me. But I overcame it. I always wanted to know how to do something well. I wanted to know my craft, so I asked questions and I watched and learned it myself. Miss Carnegie and her associate, Rose Roth, were very kind and they taught me a lot too."

Lucy started off by modeling hats (Hattie Carnegie's original specialty) and moved on to dresses and evening gowns, none of which retailed for under $500. Obviously, Carnegie customers were mainly the rich and the famous. Many of the regulars spent upwards of $25,000 a year.

Each model had clients who were selected for her on the basis of physical resemblance and/or similar measurements. "I modeled things for Constance Bennett and Joan Bennett. Miss Carnegie would snap her fingers and say, 'The Bennett sisters are here! Get the clothes!' And they'd put them on me. And others did things for Kay Francis or Ina Claire or Lilyan Tashman. Miss Carnegie had the chicest clientele in New York," Lucy said.

Because both Bennetts were blondes at the time, Lucy changed her hair color to platinum to make the resemblance even more striking. "It was *very* light blonde, not the white that later became Jean Harlow's trademark. I parted my hair in the same way as Joan Bennett did and tried looking as much like her as I could. Joan worked on the Broadway stage then, so I really modeled more for her than for Constance, who came in from California several times a year to replenish her wardrobe," Lucy remembered.

While working for Hattie Carnegie, Lucy had a devastating experience of which the full truth may never be known, since she told so many different versions of it over the years. According to the earliest versions, Lucy either fractured her spine or broke her back in an auto accident in Central Park. "The doctors told me I'd never walk again," she said in a 1943 interview. "My most vivid recollection of the experience was the dread I had of being pushed through Grand Central Station in a wheelchair when I was taken home to Jamestown. I didn't want people to pity me."

Later versions also start with an auto accident in Central Park, but this time Lucy was thrown from the car and spent the night half buried in a snowbank until someone found her the next morning. Several months later, after a bout with pneumonia that left her in a very weakened condition, she supposedly came down with rheumatoid arthritis right in the line of duty.

"I was modeling an elegant ensemble and I sidestepped to do a turn, where I would drag the coat and slouch like a cat," she said in 1966. "Then I panicked. In a split second, knives seemed to pierce my insides. Writhing in pain, I rolled on the floor. Was I dying?"

According to Lucy, Hattie Carnegie's personal physician sent her by ambulance to a clinic on 113th Street, where she was treated with a serum made from the urine of a pregnant horse. As farfetched as that might seem, such injections were once used to relieve symptoms and to create an improved sense of well-being in the critically ill, although they were regarded as quackery by the medical establishment.

"I became a guinea pig for ten days," Lucy recalled. "My legs were terribly contorted. One was pulled up beside me sideways, the other was drawn up behind me in back. They told me it was one of the worst cases of rheumatic arthritis they'd ever seen."

"They" was apparently a certain "Professor Schuster" or "Schulman." Lucy cited both surnames at one time or another, but no doctor or health professional can be found under those names in the telephone books or medical directories of that period.

Lucy claimed to have spent three years recuperating in an upstairs bedroom of the family's rented house in Jamestown. "Whenever I was alone, I'd get out of my wheelchair, try to walk, and fall flat on my face. They'd hear the crash downstairs, come and pick me up, and warn me against trying to walk too soon. I eventually graduated to crutches, then two canes with twenty-pound weights on my feet, then one cane, and finally I walked! I recovered in three years less than the six that the doctors said it would take."

One can admire Lucy's courage or marvel at her talent for spinning tall tales. Her illness and long convalescence may also have been the result of a botched abortion paid for by gangster sweetheart Johnny DeVita. Whatever the truth, there are big unexplained gaps in Lucy's life between 1927 and 1933. If she was incapacitated by illness for three of those years, what did she do to occupy herself in the other three?

Hattie Carnegie, who died in 1956, left no business records that would prove the duration of Lucy's employment there. Bernard Newman, another celebrated designer and a close friend of Carnegie's, once said that Lucy worked there only briefly and was "mainly Seventh Avenue."

Lifelong friend Marion Strong remembers Lucy working as an elevator operator at Lerner's apparel store in Jamestown at the outbreak of the Depression. In 1931, they both found themselves unemployed.

"Lucille wanted to go back to New York, but only with a friend this time," Strong said. "She helped me get a job as a secretary in an antique shop at twenty dollars a week. Lucille was doing free-lance modeling at a little more money. We shared a room at the Hotel Kimberley for eighteen dollars a week, which was expensive at the time. But Lucille had a lot of friends who kept inviting us to dinner, so we saved money that way."

When Marion returned to Jamestown because of homesickness, Lucy persuaded another friend, beautician Gertrude Foote, to room with her. "I got to know Lucille by way of doing her hair," Foote recalled. "In those days, she stood out like a diamond in a plain setting. She had a kind of long stride, and she wore clothes well. She had sparkling eyes and a daring manner for a girl from a small town. We were direct opposites in temperament—I was extremely shy—but we got along beautifully."

Gertrude also found the Big City overwhelming and soon went back to Jamestown. "Lucille's pace was too fast for me to keep up with. She was *so* ambitious and full of energy. Every night there'd be a party somewhere and she'd insist on taking me along. You could never have a dull moment with Lucille. She'd walk into a room and just light up the place," Foote said.

Manhattanites who knew Lucy then remembered her as a happy-go-lucky person, but hard-boiled and foulmouthed. "Lucille wasn't

No Broadway or Hollywood talent scouts were in the audience to offer Lucy a contract, but the enthusiastic response sent her tearing back to New York for another try at fame and fortune. This time it was a bit more complicated, because she'd fallen madly in love for the first time in her life.

Teenaged Lucy's romance with twenty-five-year-old Johnny DeVita gave Jamestowners plenty to gossip about. Italians, along with all Roman Catholics, Jews, and blacks, were minorities in that WASPish community. Also, some Jamestown residents claim DeVita had connections with unsavory characters and ran the numbers game for the Jamestown area. His father headed a gang that smuggled whiskey into the Prohibition "dry" United States from nearby Canada.

Friends say that Johnny DeVita's tough manner rubbed off on Lucy, that she began to smoke, drink, and use foul language. "She grew up fast during the time she spent with Johnny. She was smitten with him and loved being fawned over," a high school colleague recalled.

DeVita frequently traveled to New York, so the love affair continued when Lucy returned there. Rumor had it that DeVita set her up in a Manhattan apartment and bankrolled her entry into show business. Neither is true, but the two did keep company for several years.

Still unable to get a job in either the theater or vaudeville, Lucy finally stumbled into a career as a model when a girlfriend took her to a cocktail party in a millionaire's penthouse on Park Avenue. "I'd never been to one of those really swank affairs, so I was dying of curiosity," Lucy remembered. "I met a man there who asked me if I was a model. I thought he was just handing me a line, so I said, 'Oh, no, I don't have the figure for it.' And he said, 'Well, you're wrong. I'm in the fur business. Our models have to be on the slender side or the coats look like stuffed cabbages.'

"So that was the beginning of it. I went to work for that man in his wholesale showroom on Fourteenth Street. From there I graduated to modeling dresses and hats in the garment district. I also did fashion shows at Stern's department store on 42nd Street, opposite the Fifth Avenue public library."

It was all per diem work, which earned Lucy about twenty-five dollars a week if she was lucky. To make extra money, she posed for some of the many commercial artists who had studios in the vicinity of Columbus Circle and Central Park South.

"The artists had a colony there and you could go from building to building applying to model. They did print ads and painted for billboards. I made five dollars an hour posing for ads for things like Iron

Clad stockings, Tourrain coffee and Yardley English Lavender soap," she said.

Roger Furse, a commercial and portrait artist who later became a celebrated movie production designer, took a fancy to Lucy and helped her get her first important job. Furse prevailed on a friend, designer Hattie Carnegie, to hire Lucy as a model in her salon on East 49th Street off Fifth Avenue.

Tiny and tempestuous Hattie Carnegie (who filched one of America's most revered names and was originally Henrietta Kanengeiser) could neither sew nor cut a pattern, but she had a style sense that made her the top dress designer in the United States for a generation. The child of poor Austrian immigrants and a onetime messenger girl at Macy's, Carnegie probably recognized something of herself in Lucille Ball and decided that the young woman could use some help up the ladder.

"That was a ritzy salon and I knew nothing about high fashion. I used to buy my clothes in bargain basements," Lucy recalled. "The experienced models snubbed me. I had such an inferiority complex that just that *alone* could have paralyzed me. But I overcame it. I always wanted to know how to do something well. I wanted to know my craft, so I asked questions and I watched and learned it myself. Miss Carnegie and her associate, Rose Roth, were very kind and they taught me a lot too."

Lucy started off by modeling hats (Hattie Carnegie's original specialty) and moved on to dresses and evening gowns, none of which retailed for under $500. Obviously, Carnegie customers were mainly the rich and the famous. Many of the regulars spent upwards of $25,000 a year.

Each model had clients who were selected for her on the basis of physical resemblance and/or similar measurements. "I modeled things for Constance Bennett and Joan Bennett. Miss Carnegie would snap her fingers and say, 'The Bennett sisters are here! Get the clothes!' And they'd put them on me. And others did things for Kay Francis or Ina Claire or Lilyan Tashman. Miss Carnegie had the chicest clientele in New York," Lucy said.

Because both Bennetts were blondes at the time, Lucy changed her hair color to platinum to make the resemblance even more striking. "It was *very* light blonde, not the white that later became Jean Harlow's trademark. I parted my hair in the same way as Joan Bennett did and tried looking as much like her as I could. Joan worked on the Broadway stage then, so I really modeled more for her than for Con-

3

Prince of Santiago

DESI Arnaz was born on March 2, 1917, in Santiago, Cuba, a major seaport on the Caribbean island's southeastern coast. In accordance with the age-old Spanish tradition that honors both parents of a child, he was christened in the Roman Catholic faith as Desiderio Alberto Arnaz y de Acha III.

The adult Desi's blatant earthiness and mangled English gave the impression that he had come straight from the barrio, but he actually had a blue-blooded pedigree. His father, Desiderio II, belonged to a rich landowning family and also served in the government. Desi's mother, the former Dolores de Acha, was a belle of high society, the daughter of one of the founders of the company that made world-famous Bacardi rum.

During Desi's youth, his father was the mayor of Santiago, Cuba's original capital when the island was settled by Spanish conquistadors in the sixteenth century. Although Havana had replaced it as capital, Santiago ranked just behind as Cuba's second most important metropolis. To young Desi, the quaint medieval city seemed like a self-contained empire in which his parents were the king and queen and he was the crown prince.

An only child, Desi couldn't escape being spoiled rotten in such an environment. Waited on hand and foot by the family's staff of black servants, he had the run of the mayoral mansion as well as the Arnazes' own properties, which included a cattle ranch, two dairy farms, and a villa on a tiny island in Santiago Bay. On Desi's tenth birthday, his parents gave him a prized Tennessee walking horse. He owned a car and speedboat long before he reached the legal age to drive them.

"The world was my oyster," Desi recalled. "What I wanted I only needed to ask for. Ambition, incentive, opportunity, self-reliance, appreciation of what I had meant little to me. I had a fast-swelling case of what, in a language I couldn't speak at all then, is called a fat head."

Whatever humility and discipline that Desi possessed came from the strict Jesuit schools that he attended. Although he would have preferred to spend every day swimming and fishing, he had no choice but to comply with the arrangements that had been made for his future.

As soon as he graduated from high school, Desi was supposed to attend the University of Notre Dame in the United States to prepare for a career in law and politics. In retrospect, the notion of bongo-bashing Desi Arnaz as a practicing attorney may seem ridiculous, but it wasn't an unrealistic goal at the time. Both his father and grandfather were college educated. Grandfather Arnaz, or Don Desiderio as everybody called him, was a revered physician who served U.S. Colonel Theodore Roosevelt and his Rough Riders during the 1898 war that won Cuba its independence from Spain.

At an early age, Desi learned about sex and the popular Latin penchant for *la casa chica*. Don Desiderio had just such a "little house" in the country, where he spent a lot of time with his mistress and their nine children. He also had seven legitimate children by his wife, Rosita, who lived in Santiago.

Desiderio II also had a *casa chica*, but he needed to be more discreet because of his political career. Desi never found out about it until after his father's death many years later, when it was too late to ascertain whether he had any illegitimate siblings.

Desi had his sexual initiation at the age of twelve. Not surprisingly, his first sweetheart was a black girl of the same age, a daughter of the family cook. Much of the Cuban population, perhaps even Desi himself, had blood ties to the African slaves brought there by Spanish settlers in the sixteenth century. There were few color barriers, especially when it came to romance and intermarriage.

The interlude took place in the boathouse at the end of a seventy-five-foot-long pier that jutted out into Santiago Bay from the Arnazes' island villa. Though overcome by passion, neither Desi nor the girl had the slightest idea of how to connect their two bodies.

"We had tried a number of ridiculous experiments and were working on a new one when there was a loud knock at the door. It was her mother, asking her to come out. I didn't have any trouble putting on my trunks in a hurry. The small proof of my excitement had disappeared. I wish I could have done the same," Desi recalled.

Frantic, Desi climbed through a window onto the ledge and then did a swan dive thirty feet into the bay. A crack underwater swimmer, he could go about fifty yards without coming up for air. He went twice that distance before he decided it was safe to go home.

Unhappily for Desi, the girl confessed to her mother, who told Señora Arnaz. After dinner that night, Desi's father took him into the study for a stern lecture.

"Have you ever seen me insult your mother? Have you ever seen me embarrass her or make her ashamed of me?"

"No, Dad."

"Then why did you do what you did this afternoon? I know what you were trying to do. You are a boy. But why were you so damned stupid? You could have picked a better spot than our own boathouse. Now you listen to me and listen good. Don't you ever insult your mother that way again or embarrass her as you did. Now get the hell out of here!"

Given such advice at that impressionable age, it's easy to understand why Desi behaved that way throughout his life. Discretion, if not fidelity, was always one of his strong points when it came to romantic relationships.

At fifteen, the "dangerous age" before a boy supposedly becomes a man, Desi was taken to Casa Marina, Santiago's most fastidious brothel, to learn whatever he still didn't know about the mechanics of sex. His father the mayor couldn't risk escorting Desi to such an establishment, so Uncle Salvador, the family layabout, was delegated.

"The ladies of that house were all young and clean and treated me kindly, tenderly, and very expertly," Desi recalled. He returned to Casa Marina many times on his own after discovering that he had unlimited credit as the mayor's son. There was, after all, no danger of the place being raided while he was on the premises. Another of his uncles happened to be chief of police.

Desi grew up during one of the most corrupt political regimes in Cuba's history, that of Gerardo Machado, who would be remembered as "the President of a thousand murders" because of the wholesale slaughtering of his opponents. A puppet of the U.S. government and American business interests, Machado swept into office in 1925 and kept extending his power through control of both the legislature and the military.

During Machado's reign, Cuba, and especially Havana, became a paradise not only for American investors but also for tourists, who flocked there for cheap vacations, gambling, and naughty diversions similar to those in Paris. The island also became a haven for the thirsty millions who were subject to Prohibition on the United States mainland, which was only 112 nautical miles across the Florida Strait.

However, in 1930, the Wall Street crash and the onset of the Depression sent Cuba into an economic and political crisis. Sales of the island's main exports, sugar and rum, decreased by 90 percent, causing bankruptcies, unemployment, and great misery among the largely working-class population. Meanwhile, Machado dined off gold plates in the presidential palace, traveled everywhere in a $40,000 armored car, and had a legion of bodyguards equipped with machine guns and hand grenades.

In 1932, Mayor Arnaz decided to run for election to the House of Representatives as congressman for Oriente province. If victorious, he intended to move the family to Havana, where Desi would finish his last year of high school before going on to the University of Notre Dame in Indiana.

But on June 1, nature gave a forewarning of future dangers when Santiago suffered a major earthquake at one in the morning. Thirty people were killed, but the total might have been much higher, since a movie theater and several other public buildings, all unoccupied at the time, were completely destroyed.

Desi leaped out of bed at the first rumble and ran to his parents' bedroom for shelter and comfort. Later, when he returned to his own room, he found the bed buried under bricks. An entire wall had collapsed on top of it, but the rest of the house had slight damage.

Mayor Arnaz's efforts to rebuild Santiago and to equip the ancient city with modern roads and sanitation helped to win him the election in November. In January 1933, he went to Havana to be sworn in as a congressman, and he began preparations for the family move that summer. He bought a house in El Vedado, Havana's poshest neighborhood.

Meanwhile, the deepening economic crisis in Cuba had worsened the public's misery, leading to widespread rioting and looting by members of Machado's main adversaries, the ABC and Communist parties. Since Cuba had been a protectorate of the United States since the end of the Spanish-American War, President Franklin Roosevelt dispatched Ambassador Sumner Welles to Havana in May 1933 to restore political stability and to protect American business interests.

Sumner Welles's mediation efforts culminated in a general strike and caused the Army to withdraw its support of Machado, who resigned and fled to Miami, Florida, on August 12. The inexperienced provisional President Carlos de Céspedes was soon overthrown in a military coup led by army sergeant Fulgencio Batista, who would become the new chief of state.

Hell broke loose over Machado's escape to Florida. All the members of his government still in Cuba, Desi's father included, were arrested and put into prison to await criminal trial.

Mobs of agitators and looters descended on the homes and property of everybody associated with the Machado regime. Luckily, Desi and his mother received advance warning and went into hiding, but their house in Santiago was wrecked and all their possessions either stolen or burned. Their Essex sedan was turned upside down, the windows smashed, the tires slashed.

"My mother held up pretty well, considering everything that happened. The news of the following day, however, was more than either of us could take. She became hysterical when we learned that they had done the same thing to our farms and to the beach house. They also sank the speedboat and a little fishing boat. Worst of all, they massacred most of the animals—cows, chickens, pigs, horses, goats. It wasn't because they were hungry. They just left them there to rot," Desi remembered.

Dolores Arnaz, or Lolita as everybody called her, managed to stash some savings, equivalent to about $300, inside her girdle. With help from a black servant named Bombale, she and Desi made their way to Havana to stay with relatives while Desiderio II's fate was being decided.

In the capital, Desi witnessed even worse atrocities than in Santiago. "There was one sight I will never forget," he recalled. "A man's head stuck on a long pole and hung in front of his house. Two doors away, the rest of the body was hung outside the house of the man's father."

Desiderio II remained in La Cabana prison for six months. Lolita's uncle, an attorney named Bravo Correoso, finally succeeded in getting him released on a writ of habeas corpus. No definite charges had yet been filed against him, so the court ruled that he could no longer be held. A point in his favor was that he had opted to stay in Cuba rather than fleeing with Machado and his cohorts.

But Colonel Batista decided that Desiderio II would have to leave the country anyway. Until some semblance of law and order was restored to Cuba, the dictator couldn't risk having any associates of Machado around. It was as much for Desiderio's protection as the government's, as he could still be the target of an assassin from the ABC or Communist factions.

Whatever property that Arnaz had left was worthless in its ravaged condition. Borrowing $500 from relatives, he took off for Florida and promised to send for Lolita and Desi as soon as he found a job. At age forty, he would be starting from scratch, but he had no choice. He was lucky to be free.

Three months later, in June 1934, seventeen-year-old Desi stepped off the ferry at Key West and into his father's arms. "When they let me through immigration, I gave Dad the longest, biggest, and tightest *abrazo* ever. He said, *'Bienvenido a Los Estados Unidos de Norte America,* and those will be the last Spanish words I will speak to you until you learn English,' " Desi recalled.

Although he'd studied English in Cuba, Desi had never spoken or read it outside the classroom. "To please Dad, I tried to answer him in English, but nothing too good came out. My ears eventually got used to it pretty well, but my tongue has been fighting a losing battle ever since," he said decades later.

The ex-mayor of Santiago was staying at a boardinghouse on the outskirts of Miami while he and two other refugees started up an import business that supplied ceramic tiling to the building trade. Unable to get credit and with sparse capital of their own, they could only purchase a few hundred dollars' worth of stock at a time, which meant it all had to be sold before they could buy any more.

Desi's mother, accustomed to living like a queen, elected to stay with relatives in Santiago until her husband could support the three of them. She sent Desi on ahead to continue his education. While it now seemed impossible for him to attend Notre Dame, he could at least finish high school in America and get on with his new life.

Desi plainly needed all the guidance he could get. In 1934, Miami only had a small Hispanic population; on his first solo visit to a restaurant, Desi couldn't read the menu or understand the waitress. In embarrassment, he just pointed to four items and ended up with four different bowls of soup. He consumed them as nonchalantly as possible to give the impression that he dined that way all the time.

Through the benevolence of Machado, who reportedly left Cuba with $10 million in gold bullion, Desi's father arranged for him to spend the summer learning English at St. Leo's Catholic School near

Tampa. Still unable to understand most of what was said to him, Desi usually answered "Yeah" or "O.K." to everything. One day he unintentionally volunteered for a boxing match and received such a beating that he couldn't eat solid food for two weeks.

In the autumn of 1934, Desi entered St. Patrick's High School in Miami Beach. As an economy measure, he and his father moved out of their five-dollar-a-week boardinghouse and into the warehouse of Arnaz's import company. They shifted the ceramic tiles to one half of the forty-by-forty-foot area and equipped the other half with two beds, several chairs, a wardrobe, and a two-burner stove. For plumbing, they had to rely on the toilet and sink in the office next door. Rats were a constant menace. They kept baseball bats beside their beds to ward them off.

After school hours, Desi worked for his father's company. At one point, Pan American Importing and Exporting tried to diversify with bananas. The fruit could be purchased in Puerto Rico at three for a nickel and resold in Miami at five cents each. It seemed like a quick way to get rich, but then Desi went to the docks to pick up the latest shipment. The bananas had been too long at sea and had turned rotten.

Arnaz's two partners left the bankrupted company, but he tried to carry on alone selling tiles that he imported from Mexico. Stuck with too many broken and unmatched pieces, he had the smart idea of cementing them together to create artistic effects around doorways and fireplaces. Builders of Miami apartment houses were quick to scoop them up when told it was the latest decorating craze in Latin America.

Arnaz discovered that he could get more money for the fragments than he could for whole tiles. It became his son's job to "manufacture" them. As soon as they received a new order, Desi would load the required number of tiles on the back of the delivery truck and drive through bumpy back streets until all were broken.

Desi and his father now earned enough to eat better, but they still couldn't afford to move from the warehouse or send for Mrs. Arnaz. To build up savings, Desi took a part-time job for a man who raised canaries and sold them on consignment in drugstores scattered around the Miami area. Depending on the bird's pedigree, shoppers could buy a package deal including cage, instruction book, and a month's supply of feed for $4.99 up to $24.99. For a salary of fifteen dollars a week, Desi traveled from store to store every day to feed the canaries, clean the cages, and replace depleted stock.

At St. Patrick's High School, Desi fell in with a crowd of rich kids who seemed to accept him as an equal. His best friend was Alphonse Capone Jr., son of the underworld kingpin, whose father was then serving an eleven-year sentence in Alcatraz for income tax evasion. Young Capone and his mother lived in great luxury in an island enclave off Miami Beach, and frequently invited Desi to be their guest. Little did anyone know that Desi was also soaking up atmosphere for a future television series he would produce, *The Untouchables*.

Desi no longer had the carte blanche of a mayor's son in bordellos, but with his sleek handsomeness and big brown eyes he had no difficulty attracting women. The nearest thing he had to a steady sweetheart was Gabriella Barreras, granddaughter of a Machado official who had the foresight to transfer his considerable fortune to an American bank *before* fleeing Cuba.

Alberto Barreras sympathized with the Arnazes' financial plight and frequently invited father and son to dinner at his mansion in Biscayne Bay. Taking a shine to Desi, Barreras remembered him when a musician friend asked if he knew any young Cubans who might be interested in a job with the resident band at the Roney Plaza Hotel.

Up to then, Desi had never considered a career in show business. Like most Cuban boys, he learned to perform serenades on the guitar at an early age, but mainly as an adjunct to romancing the opposite sex. His guitar had been destroyed in the pillage of the family's hacienda, but he'd managed to buy one secondhand for five dollars in a Miami pawnshop.

Since Desi earned only fifteen dollars a week cleaning birdcages, he leaped at the chance to bring home thirty-nine dollars a week for entertaining, which he happily would have done for free. He passed the Roney Plaza audition easily, but had trouble gaining his father's consent. Desiderio II still had hopes of Desi becoming a lawyer; performing in dimly lighted nightspots seemed just a notch above gangsterism or pimping. But he couldn't quibble with the thirty-nine dollars a week, which would improve their standard of living considerably.

Though Desi was still in his senior year in high school, the working schedule presented no conflict. The Siboney Septet played seven nights a week at the Roney Plaza, plus a Sunday afternoon tea dance.

Since the Roney Plaza ranked as the top hotel in Miami Beach at the time, it was a lucky break for Desi. The Siboney Septet, which consisted of a singer-guitarist (counted as two people!), pianist, maraca shaker, bassist, and two bongo players, was a relief group that performed between sets of the stellar name band on the bill. During that winter of 1936, the headline attraction was the orchestra of Charles "Buddy" Rogers, the wavy-haired actor-singer-bandleader who had just become engaged to silent-movie queen Mary Pickford.

The Siboney Septet specialized in the rumba, one of the most graceful of all ballroom dances. Women loved the rumba because it showed off their whirling skirts and ankles to good effect, but men shied away because it seemed too hard to master. The dance floor would be packed when Buddy Rogers's band played their repertoire of swing tunes and foxtrots, but diners usually returned to their tables while the Siboney Septet performed.

Fearing that he'd soon lose his new job if the crowd didn't get up and dance, Desi persuaded Buddy Rogers to end his sets with "The Peanut Vendor," a novelty hit that could be played in a variety of tempos. As the Siboney Septet replaced Rogers's musicians on the bandstand, they began playing the same song, but as a rumba.

"It worked, because all of a sudden people realized they were dancing to a rumba and then decided it was not so difficult after all. They kept dancing, and that was what we were being paid to make them do," Desi recalled.

But in the midst of success, a sudden visit from a United States Immigration officer nearly ended in the deportation of Desi and his father. Although the Arnazes had been in Miami for over two years, they had not filed for residency papers and were not permitted to work without them. Reviewing the case and realizing how much the family had lost in the 1933 revolution, the agency gave them the option of getting the required permits within ninety days or being sent back to Cuba.

It was easier said than done. The Arnazes could only obtain permanent residency by filing at an American consulate *outside* the United States. Fearful that he might land back in prison if he returned to Cuba, Desidiero II took a cheap steamer to Puerto Rico and applied there.

When his father's mission was successfully completed two weeks later, Desi boarded the ferry to Havana to get his own papers. While back in the homeland, he persuaded his mother to file for U.S. residency as well. She followed him to Miami several weeks later.

A gang of Desi's schoolmates decided to surprise him when he ended his enforced leave of absence and rejoined the Siboney Septet during one of the Roney Plaza's Sunday afternoon tea dances. Nearly packing the room, the teenagers pretended to be bored by Buddy

Rogers's orchestra but became wildly attentive when Desi's group started playing. They all jumped up from their tables and danced, pausing to cheer and applaud whenever Desi sang.

The ovation had the desired effect on Desi's ego, but it also attracted the attention of Xavier Cugat, who was on a busman's holiday during an afternoon off from an engagement at the ultrachic Brook Club. Until a waiter pointed Cugat out, Desi didn't recognize the balding, mustachioed man, who was that era's "king" of Latin dance music.

Desi's swollen ego told him that Cugat wanted to congratulate him on his performance. He strolled by the maestro's table several times, even stopped right in front of him and lighted a cigarette to attract his attention, but he got no reaction. Just as he was packing up his guitar to leave, he heard Cugat call, "Hey, Chico! Come over here, please."

The following afternoon, Desi found himself auditioning for Cugat at the Brook Club. The bandleader asked him if he knew "In Spain They Say Si Si." Desi did, although he'd never actually performed it with the Siboney Septet. Cugat told Desi to attempt it anyway.

Desi was petrified, but when the band set down a torrid beat the likes of which he hadn't heard since leaving Santiago, he felt like he was home again. "My Cuban blood was flowing," Desi recollected. "My hips were revolving, my feet were kicking, my arms were waving. By comparison, Elvis Presley would have looked as if he were standing still. I sang the shit out of that song."

When Desi finished, the musicians applauded. Not one to waste words, Cugat offered him a job, only to be rejected. Desi knew that his parents would never let him accept until he graduated from high school in June. Even then it would be a tough battle convincing them.

"Well, if you're still interested, write to me at the Waldorf-Astoria in New York," Cugat said.

When graduation finally came around, Desi did contact Cugat, but without informing his parents. He figured that the bandleader would have forgotten him by that time, but he got a surprise. Cugat offered him a two-week trial at twenty-five dollars per week, plus one-way bus fare to New York.

Desiderio II thought his son was crazy for even considering a job that paid half what he earned at the Roney Plaza, which was close to home. Desi argued that apprenticing with Xavier Cugat was equivalent to a college scholarship and worth any sacrifice. Lolita Arnaz sided with Desi, so needless to say, he was soon bound for New York.

Desi boarded the Greyhound bus to New York with fifteen dollars in his pocket and most of his entire wardrobe packed into one small valise. When he arrived at the Manhattan depot, a Spanish-speaking porter directed him to a hotel on West 43rd Street where he booked a room for one dollar a night.

Xavier Cugat and his orchestra were performing at the poshest and most expensive nightspot in town, the Starlight Roof, atop a wing of the forty-seven-story Waldorf-Astoria on Park Avenue (then the world's largest hotel, with 2,200 rooms in a magnificent Art Deco framework). Desi had instructions to report there that evening, so he showered, shaved, and donned the sharpest outfit he could select from his meager wardrobe. He had no idea how to reach the Waldorf-Astoria, but he started walking, stopping to ask directions at every corner until he arrived.

Stepping off the elevator at the Starlight Roof, Desi encountered a maitre d' in white tie and tails. He felt like turning back and running down all eighteen flights of stairs, but he finally worked up enough courage to introduce himself and be taken to Xavier Cugat's table. Cugat happened to be conducting at the time, but his ravishing wife, Carmen Castillo, sat watching the show. Desi mistook her for Dolores Del Rio, which was not surprising, since she'd once worked as the Mexican movie queen's stand-in in Hollywood.

"Being led to the table of the great Cugat in front of that magnificently dressed crowd was almost too much for this boy from Santiago. Mrs. Cugat recognized that and tried to make me feel at home, which wasn't very easy while my mouth was wide open and my eyes were popping out of their sockets. Cugie later came over, bought me dinner, and calmed me down with a glass of wine," Desi remembered.

Cugat had no intention of launching his raw protégé on a chic New York audience. Desi became a backstage observer for the balance of the engagement and began rehearsing with several other young male and female recruits for places in the orchestra's forthcoming tour.

Desi made his Cugat debut under rather intimidating circumstances —in a 10,000-seat outdoor amphitheater in Cleveland, Ohio, in Billy Rose's *Aquacade*, which was water show, vaudeville, and musical combined into one colossal spectacle with a cast of 500. Olympic champions Eleanor Holm and Buster Crabbe were the swimming stars, flanked by a hundred AquaBelles and Beaux.

Cugat's orchestra performed on an elevated stage at one end of an artificial lake. While singing "In Spain They Say Si Si" for the first time, Desi nearly skidded off the platform into the water, but one of the dancers grabbed him by the scruff of the neck in time.

Desi passed the two-week trial period and found his salary raised to thirty dollars a week, still less than he'd been earning with the Siboney Septet. After *Aquacade,* the Cugat contingent moved on to the Arrowhead Inn in Saratoga, New York, then in the height of its annual thoroughbred racing season, which attracted sportsmen and celebrities from all over the country.

Bing Crosby, America's number-one crooner and horse fancier, came to see the show one night and enjoyed Desi's singing so much that he invited him for a drink afterwards. Crosby happened to ask Desi how much Cugat paid him. When told, he said, "Why that cheap crook!"

Crosby sent for Cugat and read him the riot act. The bandleader replied, "But he's just starting out, Bingo."

"Never mind the Bingo stuff, you stingy Spaniard," Crosby said. "Give him a raise. One of these days you're going to be asking *him* for a job!"

Cugat finally conceded when Crosby agreed to sing with the orchestra. Crosby loved Latin music, so he obliged with several numbers and dueted with Desi on "Quiereme Mucho."

"Bing sang it in Spanish, which he knew pretty good, and then I did it in my version of English, which was pretty bad. But the Bacardi rum we'd been drinking helped a lot," Desi remembered.

Xavier Cugat kept his part of the bargain by raising Desi's salary to thirty-five dollars a week. For the extra five dollars, Desi also had to walk Cugat's dogs—two Mexican Chihuahuas and a German shepherd—three times a day.

Not surprisingly, Xavier Cugat had become Desi's role model. Born in Tirona, Spain, in 1900, Cugat was only two when his family moved to Havana, where he grew up and studied to be a professional violinist. After a short and discouraging concert career in Europe and the United States, his exceptional talent as a caricaturist won him a job sketching celebrities for the *Los Angeles Times.* In 1920, he became friendly with Rudolph Valentino, who asked him to put together a Spanish-Latin orchestra to play for him on the set of *Four Horsemen of the Apocalypse* (a standard practice during the silent era to put actors in the mood).

Valentino was so impressed by the orchestra, of which Cugat was leader and violin soloist, that he secured a booking for them at the Cocoanut Grove, Hollywood's premier nightspot. Every night, Valentino brought parties of pals like Pola Negri, Tom Mix, Mabel Normand, and Charlie Chaplin to the Grove to dance, soon establishing the Cugat orchestra as one of America's top bands and number one with a Latin repertoire.

Desi was quick to emulate Xavier Cugat's sartorial elegance and impeccable grooming. On stage, Cugat was famed for wearing huge sombreros, with a vividly colored serape draped over his tuxedo and a Chihuahua cradled in his arms. Unlike Cugat, twenty-year-old Desi had no problem with premature baldness, but a few strands of his black hair had turned gray, perhaps due to the trauma of the family's flight from Cuba. Cugat recommended that he start tinting it, which Desi did until well into middle age, when he gradually stopped and let his hair go natural again.

From Cugat, Desi also learned the importance of putting on a show rather than a performance. The Cugat orchestra became popular not only for its music but for production numbers with gorgeously costumed singers, dancers, and musicians. Realizing that many in the audience might not know the samba or the rumba or the tango, Cugat always had choristers doing the steps on stage so that people on the dance floor could learn by watching them.

After six months, Desi realized that he'd advanced about as far as he could with Xavier Cugat. The undisputed drawing card of the unit, Cugat had been getting a bit touchy about the ovations that Desi received in his next-to-closing spot. Also, Cugat refused to raise Desi's salary even one cent above thirty-five dollars a week. In those days, Cugat could get away with low wages because lesser instrumentalists, singers, and dancers weren't protected by the musicians' union. That was the main reason why he could maintain such a large group.

When the orchestra returned to pricey New York for a month's engagement at the Waldorf-Astoria, Desi discovered that he could barely survive on thirty-five dollars a week. "Having to go through the Waldorf kitchen to get to the bandstand helped," he recalled. "I lifted all the food I could and stashed it into my rumba shirt every time we passed through for our ten-minute break. Those wide, full sleeves with all the big ruffles were very useful."

While leaving work at 2:30 A.M. one night, Desi asked Cugat if they could stop at the coffee shop for breakfast and a chat. As soon as they'd ordered, Desi announced that he intended to return to Miami to form a small group similar to the Siboney Septet. "I know just as much as that guy who was the leader—a lot more, really, thanks to you—but I just can't make enough money with you," he told Cugat.

Cugat sensed another maneuver for a pay raise and didn't bite. "You won't have a chance," he said. "There's not many people who know and like Latin music in this country yet. You'll have a tough time. You'll go hungry."

"Well, dammit, Cugie, I'm hungry now," Desi replied. "Besides, my mother and father are there. Maybe I'll fall on my ass, but I've got to try it."

The skinflint bandleader astounded Desi with a sudden burst of generosity. "Okay, I'll do what I can to help you get started. You can bill yourself as Desi Arnaz and his Xavier Cugat Orchestra direct from the Waldorf-Astoria Hotel in New York City. How's that?"

"That's great! Marvelous! Thank you!" Desi said. To show his appreciation, he offered to pay Cugat a royalty for the use of his name, which is probably what the maestro had in mind anyway.

Cugat leaned forward and anxiously rubbed his hands. "How much?"

"The same as you paid me when I started, twenty-five dollars a week. And like you told me then, if we do good, we'll renegotiate," Desi replied.

Cugat knew when he'd been aced. Laughing, he said, "All right, you goddam Cuban, let's see what you can do."

4

Out of the Chorus

BY December 1937, while Desi Arnaz prepared to form his first orchestra, twenty-six-year-old Lucille Ball had made a minor name for herself as a Hollywood actress. Her ascent to full-fledged stardom was one of the slowest in the record books. From the time she arrived in Los Angeles in the summer of 1933, it took three years and twenty-three movies before she even moved out of the bit player ranks and into a *supporting* role of any consequence.

En route to California in their own private railroad coach, Lucy and the other newly chosen Goldwyn Girls had visited the Chicago World's Fair just long enough to appear in a movie short with Ben Bernie, that revered radio star and bandleader known as "The Old Maestro." The film footage is apparently lost to history, but fanatic collectors of Lucille Ball memorabilia have offered thousands of dollars for prints of what was her very first appearance on theater screens.

It might also have been her last. Samuel Goldwyn wasn't exactly bowled over when he met Lucy initially. "We had to line up for Mr. Goldwyn when we got to the studio," she recalled. "You had to have on the inevitable bathing suit. Mr. Goldwyn and forty other men would walk by and stare at you. We were all self-conscious, but those who had already worked as show girls were very well stacked. They were less nervous. They had *it*, you see. I didn't have *it*."

For lack of a more distinctive figure, Lucy decided instead to poke fun at herself. "I put toilet paper and gloves and socks and anything I could find in the bust of my bathing suit. Some of the toilet paper was still trailing out of the top when Mr. Goldwyn came by. If nothing else, he certainly noticed me," she said.

Lucy's stunt won her a screen test, but Goldwyn wasn't impressed and wanted to give her a train ticket back to New York. Luckily for Lucy, Goldwyn first asked the opinion of director Busby Berkeley, who disagreed with him.

"I liked Lucille's test and said so. The next day, I asked Sam's secretary if he had hired that girl I liked and she said he had," Berkeley remembered. "That's how Lucille Ball got her first break in films— because Sam respected my judgment. If I hadn't spoken up, he would have let his personal likes and dislikes rule her out."

Trained in the Broadway theater, Berkeley had been brought to Hollywood by Goldwyn in 1929 to choreograph the first Eddie Cantor talkies and had since moved on to Warner Brothers to stage the astonishing production numbers of *42nd Street, Gold Diggers of 1933,* and *Footlight Parade.* Lucy couldn't have made her movie debut under a more brilliant filmmaker, even if his genius tended toward the sexually perverse. Who could ever forget the scene in *Roman Scandals* in which Lucy is one of a score of "naked" slaves chained to a massive pylon during a public auction of girls, girls, and more girls? (The women actually all wore flesh-colored body stockings and long wigs that hid the seams in their outfits.)

Roman Scandals was an adult, slightly lewd variation on *The Wizard of Oz,* with country bumpkin Eddie Cantor knocked unconscious and dreaming his way back through the centuries from West Rome, Oklahoma, to Imperial Rome, where he becomes the food-tasting slave to the wicked emperor. Suitably underdressed, Lucy appeared in most of the production numbers and crowd scenes, but had no dialogue to speak.

"I didn't know what the hell I was doing," she recalled. "I just did what they wanted me to do. I think the one virtue that helped me was I didn't mind doing anything. *Anything.* There was a big bath scene where they wanted me to wear a mudpack. A lot of the girls advised me not to do it. They said, 'Nobody will recognize you under all that muck.' I told them 'Nobody knows who I am anyway!' and I did the scene. Nothing was beneath me. I'd scream, I'd yell, I'd run through the set. To me it was an education, getting my foot in the door."

Because of some major legal problems (Goldwyn was suing Busby Berkeley for breach of contract and George S. Kaufman and Robert

Sherwood filed for an injunction against Eddie Cantor's constant re-writing of their script), *Roman Scandals* took four months instead of six weeks to complete. During the many production lulls, the penny-pinching Goldwyn wasn't about to pay Lucy fifty dollars a week for just sitting around, so he arranged for her to do bits in some of the other movies shooting on the United Artists lot. Goldwyn himself made only two or three pictures a year, but he owned a piece of UA, a cooperative of independent producers founded in 1919 by Charlie Chaplin, Mary Pickford, Douglas Fairbanks, and D. W. Griffith.

Although *Roman Scandals* is officially the first feature movie made by Lucille Ball, two productions that she worked in for Darryl Zanuck and Joseph Schenck's fledgling 20th Century Pictures reached theater screens in November 1933, a full month before the release of the Goldwyn epic. Lucy and another Hollywood newcomer named Ann Sothern were a pair of bathing beauties in *Broadway Thru a Keyhole*, a Walter Winchell exposé of New York nightlife. In the underworld thriller *Blood Money*, Lucy turned up as a bank robber's moll in a racetrack scene.

Roman Scandals proved such a box-office bonanza that Goldwyn could afford to keep Lucy and the other Goldwyn Girls on the payroll. In the first half of 1934, she appeared in the chorus or had walk-ons in seven more films, including Goldwyn's disastrous adaptation of Emile Zola's *Nana* (which failed to establish its star, Russian-born Anna Sten, as another Garbo or Dietrich) and 20th Century's *The Affairs of Cellini* (in which Lucy played lady-in-waiting to Constance Bennett, her one-time client at Hattie Carnegie's).

Lucy was grateful for any opportunities that came her way. "We were taken in charge and trained. We had dancing and singing lessons. We were taught how to dress, how to fix our hair, our makeup. I was very appreciative of it because I had no talent. What could I do? I couldn't dance. I couldn't sing. I could *talk*. I could barely walk. I had no flair. I wasn't a beauty, that's for sure. I had it all to learn, and a lot of it I never did learn and somehow made it through without it," she recalled.

Convinced that she had little going for her except ambition and enthusiasm, Lucy took to behaving like the studio clown to attract attention. "Lucille's funny faces, pratfalls, and wisecracks had every-one in stitches. She was like the campus cutup at college," actress Gloria Stuart remembered.

Nobody of any importance thought enough of Lucy's clowning to give her a speaking part. But she tried her damnedest to get Samuel

Goldwyn to notice her. One of her favorite tactics was during his morning script conferences. She'd drive up outside Goldwyn's office in her little Ford coupe, slam on the brakes, and toot the horn repeatedly. When the enraged Goldwyn stormed out onto his second-floor balcony, Lucy would call up to him with wide-eyed innocence, "Can the writers come out and play with me now?"

Lucy may have made more of an impression than it seemed. According to her friend Kay Vaughan, Goldwyn once turned up at Lucy's apartment door bearing a huge bouquet of roses and expecting to spend the night. Lucy graciously accepted the flowers and then apologized to Goldwyn by pretending to be in the midst of her period. Would he please be a darling and come back some other night?

Lucy apparently had mixed feelings about the so-called casting-couch approach to getting ahead in show business. "I never knew Lucille to be the sort of girl who would throw herself at men, but if someone propositioned her and she was genuinely attracted to him, he had a good chance of getting somewhere. She wouldn't have let a man like Sam Goldwyn, who was bald, fat, and old enough to be her father, get near her," Kay Vaughan said.

Lucy did have a brief fling with twenty-nine-year-old Fred Kohlmar, one of Goldwyn's chief aides and the head of casting. The affair ended abruptly when a role that Lucy coveted in the Eddie Cantor–Ethel Merman caper *Kid Millions* went to her friend, the much more musically talented Ann Sothern. Lucy landed back in the chorus again, and she never forgave Kohlmar until many years later, when he came to her rescue at a difficult time in her career.

As a Goldwyn Girl and former Hattie Carnegie model, Lucy had no shortage of admirers, but her first blazing romance was with sleekly debonair George Raft, then a new star in orbit following his electrifying performance as a coin-flipping gangster in *Scarface*. Lucy met Raft, then thirty-nine years old, while he was working at United Artists in *The Bowery*. Himself a product of New York's mean streets, he liked his women tough and rowdy, and Lucille Ball fitted that mold in those days.

Raft was Lucy's introduction to the glitzy and raffish Hollywood lifestyle that she knew only from fan magazines. After living in furnished rooms all those years, she was overwhelmed by Raft's penthouse atop the swank El Royale Apartments on Rossmore Avenue. One of the most generous of the big spenders, Raft bought her flashy clothes and took her out to nightclubs and the prize fights in his chauffeured custom-built Cadillac. Rare for those times, he employed a full-time bodyguard who packed a revolver, brass knuckles, and a switchblade knife just in case of trouble.

Lucy reportedly never got over her infatuation for George Raft, but the affair was short-lived because of his hyperactive libido. He had to have sex at least three times a day, preferably with different partners. Lucy discovered that he had a floating harem around town, and she didn't want to be part of it.

Lucy also made the unintentional mistake of introducing Raft to one of her starlet friends, Virginia Pine. Raft fell madly in love with the gorgeous blonde, eventually installing her in a $250,000 mansion in Coldwater Canyon. It was the nearest thing to marriage that the couple could arrange, since Raft already had a wife back in New York who wouldn't divorce him.

Always a good sport, Lucy remained on cozy terms with Raft and Pine. Amusingly, they became a social foursome when Lucy started keeping company with Raft's bodyguard, Mack Grey.

A onetime boxers' manager who changed his name from Max Greenberg, Grey had known Raft during the latter's membership in the murderous Owney Madden gang in New York in the 1920s. They spoke the same language, and Grey knew how to curb Raft's violent temper, which often erupted into fisticuffs when they were out in public. Not many people were aware of it, but Raft knew the gangster's trick of reading lips to gain information. If he spotted another man saying something uncomplimentary about him, he'd race over and punch him in the mouth.

Lucy didn't seem to be bothered by Mack Grey's notorious reputation around town as "Killer Grey." Everybody assumed that he was one because of his connection with George Raft, but the moniker was actually pinned on Grey by prankster pal Carole Lombard after he had an operation for a double hernia (*killa* being the Yiddish word for hernia).

Although Lucy probably didn't realize it at the time, her association with George Raft and Mack Grey may have been one of the reasons for her slow climb to fame. It certainly explains why she never was accepted into the dignified Hollywood society of the time. While tolerated for his box-office magnetism, Raft and his entourage were not welcome in the homes of the image-conscious moguls and the power establishment. Many blamed him for the influx of organized crime into Hollywood, which reached its zenith during the bloody reign of Benjamin "Bugsy" Siegel, Raft's best friend since childhood.

When Lucy finished her chorister chores in *Kid Millions,* Goldwyn terminated her employment. She'd shown no potential, either as an actress or a doxy, and it was time to replenish the Goldwyn Girls with fresh faces.

Thanks to George Raft, Lucy landed a seventy-five-dollar-a-week contract with Columbia Pictures, a onetime "Poverty Row" studio that still specialized in inexpensive bread-and-butter movies but had started to come up with occasional box-office smashes like *It Happened One Night*. It seems that Harry Cohn, president of Columbia and Hollywood's most fanatic horse bettor, owed George Raft a favor for saving him from being bumped off by a bookie to whom he owed $125,000.

Cohn ran Columbia on a one-a-week basis, turning out fifty-two features a year, plus an equal number of one- and two-reel comedies. As a member of the studio's resident stock company, Lucy played foil to the Three Stooges, Andy Clyde, Leon Errol, and Harry Langdon in shorts and acted bit parts in whatever features were thrown her way. She portrayed a telephone operator in Frank Capra's *Broadway Bill,* a beautician in *The Fugitive Lady,* a secretary in *Men of the Night,* and a fight spectator in *Jealousy.*

In February 1935, Lucille Ball saw her name on a movie screen for the first time when Columbia released *Carnival,* the fifteenth feature that she'd appeared in since arriving in Hollywood in the summer of 1933. For her tiny role as a hospital nurse, Lucy was listed sixteenth in a cast headed by Lee Tracy, Sally Eilers, and Jimmy Durante, but it was at least a start toward public recognition.

By this time, Lucy had been separated from her family for almost two years and she missed them terribly. To ease her homesickness, George Raft paid for a train ticket for DeDe Ball, who had recently been divorced from Ed Peterson, to come visit.

"I was flat broke, but George peeled a hundred-dollar bill from his wallet and insisted that I take it," Lucy recalled. "On the day of my mother's arrival, he loaned me his car and chauffeur so I could pick her up at the Pasadena station. When she saw this block-long limousine, she was overwhelmed. The driver took us to the Brown Derby and we had a terrific dinner as George's guests. The night was one of the most marvelous evenings of our lives."

As soon as she could save enough money, Lucy also brought brother Fred, Grandpa Hunt, and cousin Cleo Mandicos to Hollywood, where the family shared a rented bungalow on Ogden Drive, just above Sunset Boulevard. "I had been alone in California, in the sense that I didn't belong to anyone. I was unhappy. I figured out that

I wasn't doing my part in the world, and as Columbia had given me a contract, I decided to share my good fortune," she remembered.

While working at Columbia, Lucy fell under the spell of Carole Lombard, who was in the midst of making *Twentieth Century* with John Barrymore. Lucy used to hang around the set watching Lombard's every move and began copying her, right down to the obscene vocabulary that was a legend in its own time. Three years older than Lucy and not yet the glamour queen she became later, Lombard was flattered by the attention and a close friendship developed.

"Carole just sort of picked me out one day and said, 'Hey, you could do things here. Just hang around and watch.' I was very much in awe of her and I didn't talk much around her, but I didn't miss a thing. She had a lot of great feminine qualities that I admire very much and emulated to the best of my ability—the way she looked and dressed, her graciousness and friendliness. I've always regarded her as my guardian angel, my mentor," Lucy recalled.

Carole Lombard also played matchmaker by introducing Lucy to tall, blonde, and blue-eyed Ralph Forbes, a British leading man who was a close friend of her ex-husband, William Powell. A debonair raconteur, Forbes was the handsomest, most sophisticated man that Lucy had ever been involved with. He literally swept her off her feet, but the affair ended quickly and abruptly when it turned out that the thirty-two-year-old actor was only using Lucy to make another woman jealous.

Lucy soon got another jolt when Columbia Pictures disbanded its roster of secondary actors as an economy measure. Although the motion picture industry was one of the last businesses in America to suffer during the Great Depression, by the summer of 1934 Lucy was lucky to be working at all. The future looked exceedingly grim, because she now had her family as well as herself to support.

Through a friend, Lucy learned that RKO Radio Pictures had a call out for mannequins for *Roberta,* a Jerome Kern musical about a Paris fashion house. Lucy raced to the studio and, as an ex–Hattie Carnegie model, easily landed one of the openings. The short-term job in the Irene Dunne–Fred Astaire–Ginger Rogers starrer paid only fifty dollars per week, twenty-five dollars less than she earned at Columbia, but it was preferable to waitressing at Schwab's drugstore or clerking at a Piggly Wiggly supermarket, the fate of many a movie hopeful in those hard times.

Maxine Jennings, who coached Lucy and the other models in *Roberta,* was both fascinated and repelled by the new recruit. "Lucille had real flair for modeling and could keep time to music, but I'd never met anyone that tough or foulmouthed before. Her standard outfit was a trench coat, with a beret pulled down over one eye and a cigarette dangling from her lips. She gave the impression that she would have killed to make it," Jennings recalled.

Swathed in a gown of ostrich feathers, Lucy was one of twelve models who promenaded through a spectacular fashion show in *Roberta* while Irene Dunne sang Kern's lilting "Lovely to Look At." It was another glorified bit part, but Lucy photographed so exquisitely that she was among five women that RKO decided to retain under option, though still at fifty dollars per week.

In effect, Lucy had reverted to the status of a Goldwyn Girl, although RKO had no special label for its chorines. When she wasn't working in a film, the studio publicity department used her in cheesecake photographs or sent her out to drumbeat the latest RKO releases. One of her first assignments in the latter category was to San Francisco, where Lucy and several other contractees were supposed to appear in a promotional film for the Matson passenger ship line.

Virginia Carroll, a member of the contingent, remembers: "The advertising man in charge took one look at Lucille's very obviously bleached hair and said, 'Who the hell is that blonde? She doesn't look like the type who'd be going on a world cruise.' Lucille wasn't a bit hurt. They paid her anyway and she went back to Los Angeles. A few days later she sent us a telegram that said 'I hope you poor slobs are working your hearts out. I'm cruising the Pacific.' It turned out that Lucille had taken off on somebody's yacht to Catalina Island."

Thanks to the successes of *King Kong, Little Women,* and the Astaire-Rogers musicals, RKO had resolved some of its financial difficulties, so Lucy had lots of work handed her. In her first year with the studio, she had bits or minor roles in six movies, including two more with Fred and Ginger, *Top Hat* and *Follow the Fleet.*

Four of those six films were produced by twenty-nine-year-old Pandro S. Berman, a pudgy boy wonder who was RKO's equivalent of Irving Thalberg and David O. Selznick. After Lucy worked for Berman in *Roberta,* he started taking a personal interest in her career. Realizing that she'd probably never get very far on talent alone, Lucy did nothing to discourage his attentions, and an affair developed.

Under Berman's guidance, Lucy went through a physical transformation. Nine of her crooked front teeth were straightened with tiny pieces of porcelain at a cost of $1,300, a small fortune in those times. Her hairline was raised by means of electrolysis to give her a more prominent forehead. Because RKO had a plethora of blondes under contract, including Ginger Rogers, Ann Sothern, and the still-teenaged Betty Grable, Lucy's hair coloring reverted to its natural chestnut for a time but gradually went rusty when someone pointed out that Hollywood hadn't had a major redheaded star since Clara Bow.

Nothing could be done about Lucy's voice, however, which would limit her to "other woman" and "career girl" parts. "I have a deep *blcch* voice that has no softness or romanticism to it. It's aggressive. I've always had it, no matter how hard I try to dolly it up," she said decades later.

Pandro Berman also made sure that Lucy got preferential treatment from Lela Rogers, who ran the RKO talent school and was one of Hollywood's most awesome stage mothers. Since the newcomer posed no real threat to her daughter Ginger, Mrs. Rogers happily took Lucy under her wing and gave her all the coaching that she so obviously needed.

As part of its training program, RKO had a theater on the backlot where it put on a different play or musical every week for five nightly performances. In between film assignments, Lucy appeared in stage productions of *Love Is Laughing, Fly Away Home,* and *Breakfast with Vanora,* in which she had the title role. She received no extra compensation for the work, but the experience and exposure were well worth it.

Lela Rogers also tried to spruce up Lucy's image as a Hollywood glamour girl. Though for different reasons, both Mrs. Rogers and Pandro Berman disapproved of Lucy's relationship with George Raft's bodyguard, "Killer" Grey. The couple made quite a splash at the costume ball thrown at the Hotel Knickerbocker on the occasion of former child star Jackie Coogan's twenty-first birthday. Lucy and four of her friends went dressed in baby clothes as the Dionne Quintuplets. Garbed as male nurses, Mack Grey and the other girls' swains pushed them down Hollywood Boulevard in the biggest strollers they could find.

Since Pandro Berman was not only married but about to become a father for the first time, his relationship with Lucy had to be kept secret. As a replacement for Mack Grey, Mrs. Rogers encouraged Lucy to date fellow contractee Alan Curtis, a well-bred Robert Taylor lookalike who belonged to the wealthy Neberroth family.

"Lucille's coarseness scared Alan half to death," Maxine Jennings recalled. "He told me, 'I'd love to do what Lela says, but I can't get involved with *her*. My father would disinherit me!' "

In September 1936, Pandro Berman decided that Lucy was ready for bigger roles and cast her as the second female lead in his production of *That Girl from Paris,* a musical concoction starring opera diva Lily Pons, Gene Raymond, and Jack Oakie. Lucy played a trouble-making dancer who gets her comeuppance when a prankster greases the soles of her shoes. Her hilarious pratfalls, done with a deadpan expression on her face, won critical acclaim and marked Lucille Ball as a comic "find" when the movie premiered at New York's Radio City Music Hall.

In the meantime, Lucy came near to realizing her dream of becoming a star on Broadway when Lela Rogers arranged for her to appear in *Hey Diddle Diddle,* a play being produced by Anne Nichols of *Abie's Irish Rose* fame. Pandro Berman gave his blessing to the project. If it proved a hit, he would have justification for acquiring the screen rights and starring Lucy in the movie version.

Unfortunately, *Hey Diddle Diddle* turned out to be even less substantial than the nursery rhyme on which it was *not* based. Barnet Cormack's comedy about the residents of a Hollywood apartment house was yet another spoof of the movie business, the stage world's favorite and most effective way of sniping at its principal competitor. But the producer's insistence on casting the main roles with real screen actors—Conway Tearle, Martha Sleeper, and Alice White, in addition to Lucy—further contributed to the play being snubbed by critics who considered movies an illegitimate art form.

Hey Diddle Diddle never reached Broadway, closing after three weeks of discouraging tryouts in Princeton, New Jersey, Philadelphia, and Washington, D.C. About all that Lucy gained from it apart from the psychological scars was the satisfaction of a favorable review in *Variety,* which said that "as extra girl Julie Tucker, Lucille Ball fattens a fat part and almost walks off with play. She outlines a consistent character and continuously gives it logical substance. Has a sense of timing and, with a few exceptions, keeps her comedy under control."

After Lucy returned to California, her disappointment quickly faded when Pandro Berman consoled her with a plum role in his production of *Stage Door,* a comedy-drama by George S. Kaufman and Edna Ferber that had a moderate success on Broadway with Margaret Sullavan in the lead. For a change, the movie turned out to be an improvement over the play, thanks to extensive revisions to accommodate the talents of Katharine Hepburn and Ginger Rogers, RKO's top female stars at the time.

Lucy's role, of course, was considerably smaller than either Hepburn's or Rogers's. As an aspiring actress living in a theatrical board-inghouse called the Footlight Club, Lucy was billed eighth in the cast and, along with Eve Arden, portrayed one of two resident wiseacres. It was the beginning of a long but friendly rivalry between Lucy and Arden, who up to then had been working mainly on the stage under her real name of Eunice Quedens.

"Eve and I competed for years, but it all started with *Stage Door,* where we both flounced around tossing out acid remarks," Lucy recalled. "Later on, we'd be cast as a lady executive or the proverbial 'other woman.' They were the same roles, actually. You'd walk through a room, drop a smart remark, and exit. They called us 'the drop-gag girls.' I didn't dig it at all, for in such parts you lose your femininity."

Like it or not, Lucy got typed in those parts for the balance of her tenure at RKO. Starting with her next movie, *Joy of Living,* she also became the studio's replacement for Ann Sothern, another drop-gag girl, who'd been promoted to romantic leading roles.

"Ann balked at playing Irene Dunne's kid sister, so I got the part. After that, whenever Ann turned down a script or didn't have time to do something, they gave me the job. But I didn't care. I didn't mind being second choice. I got a whole career out of Ann Sothern's rejects," Lucy remembered.

As a reward for favorable reactions to her performances in *That Girl from Paris* and *Stage Door,* Lucy's salary was upped to $125 per week. She also got her first leading role, but it was nothing to brag about. She portrayed the wife of goofy comedian Joe Penner, originator of the catchphrase "Wanna buy a duck?" in a low-budget howler entitled *Go Chase Yourself.*

In 1938, RKO used Lucy in seven movies, five so-called B programmers and two major As. Both of the latter, *Having a Wonderful Time* (with Ginger Rogers and Douglas Fairbanks Jr.) and *Room Service* (with the Marx Brothers), were produced by Pandro Berman. According to many of Lucy's friends of the time, she and Berman were sharing a love nest in an apartment building on Delongpre Avenue, within walking distance of the bungalow where she ostensibly lived with her family.

Through Berman's influence, Lucy also found jobs for her relatives at RKO. Grandpa Hunt, still a rabid campaigner for Socialist and Communist causes, worked as a carpenter in the props department. Fred Ball served as a messenger and parking lot attendant. Cousin Cleo was an extra in several of Lucy's movies.

Although Lucy's affair with Berman had many benefits, it also prevented RKO's press agents from delving too deeply into her private life when they tried to get publicity for her in the fan magazines and gossip columns. To overcome that problem, Lela Rogers had the bright idea of matching up Lucy and her daughter Ginger with two of the most eligible bachelors in town, who just happened to be RKO contractees as well.

The double-dating arrangement would also benefit the public images of Henry Fonda and James Stewart, who shared a house in Brentwood and were being bracketed with Cary Grant and *his* roommate, Randolph Scott, as possible homosexuals.

As it turned out, Ginger Rogers and Jimmy Stewart became involved in a torrid romance, but Lucille Ball and Henry Fonda never got beyond their first date. As Lucy remembered: "Ginger and I spent hours getting ready, using every trick the studio makeup department taught us—eye shadow, mascara, pancake, deep red lipstick, rouge, the works. Then we drove over to the boys' house in our long organdy dresses, looking just as summery and smooth as we could. Hank cooked dinner, and after we ate, Ginger and the boys turned on the radio in the living room and she tried to teach them the carioca. I was left doing the dishes. When I finished, we went out dancing at the Cocoanut Grove.

"The date stretched into daybreak. We'd had a hilarious, wonderful evening that came to an end at Barney's Beanery on Santa Monica Boulevard. It was still dark when we got there, but daylight when we came out. Hank and Jimmy took one look at us and said, 'What happened?' We said, 'What do you mean, what happened?' And Jimmy said 'Well, your makeup is on awful heavy for this time of the morning!' And Hank said, 'Yuk!' And that's the way it ended for Miss Ball and Mr. Fonda, though I can't speak for Ginger and Jimmy."

Another studio-arranged romance that never blossomed was between Lucy and Milton Berle, a radio and vaudeville comedian being groomed for movie stardom by RKO in musical revues like *New Faces* and *Radio City Revels*. Neither could have known that they would eventually become king and queen of an entertainment medium that barely existed at the time.

Although Lucy and Berle were strongly attracted to each other, no woman stood a chance of landing him, because of the influence of Mrs. Sarah Berlinger, the monster stage mother of them all. "There was no way that Milton and I could be together. Mama was around *all* the time," Lucy recalled.

Lucy had better luck with Broderick Crawford, whom she met through *his* mother, character star Helen Broderick, a drop-gag specialist herself, dating back to the very first *Ziegfeld Follies* in 1907. Crawford (named for his mother and father, vaudevillian Lester Crawford) had just landed in Hollywood to start a film career after triumphing on Broadway as the feeble-brained Lennie in John Steinbeck's *Of Mice and Men.*

A Harvard dropout and an ex-longshoreman on the New York docks, Broderick Crawford already had a reputation as a hard-drinking brawler by the time his parents persuaded him to become an actor. At twenty-seven, the same age as Lucy, he greatly overshadowed her, standing six feet two and weighing 210. His tough-guy appearance would limit him to gangster and character parts, but it was obviously his main appeal to Lucy. He belonged very much in the George Raft–Mack Grey school, but the latter seemed midgets by comparison.

With Brod Crawford, who was single, Lucy could have the kind of open romance that she couldn't have with Pandro Berman, whom she continued to see secretly. Crawford free-lanced, working mainly at United Artists, Warner Brothers, and Columbia, but RKO's publicists were glad to include him in anything that could get Lucy's name and photograph in the newspapers and magazines.

In the autumn of 1938, Lucy and Crawford announced that they were engaged to be married. Whether it was true love or just a publicity stunt can only be guessed at, but the couple never got to the altar.

"Helen Broderick found out about Lucille and Pan Berman from a friend who owned the apartment building where they had their love nest," Maxine Jennings said. "Helen told Brod, and he dropped Lucille immediately. They were both convinced that she'd only been using him to cover up the affair with Pan."

Lucy received a beating and a black eye when she refused to return Crawford's engagement ring, according to another friend. Berman had to grant her two weeks off while she recuperated.

Helen Broderick also squealed to Viola Berman, who must have been a most forgiving wife. At any rate, the Berman marriage stayed intact, and the affair subsided. Lucy and Berman kept meeting occasionally, but the flame burned out when they both became involved in other relationships.

While treating her mother to lunch at the Brown Derby one day, Lucy happened to catch the eye of director Alexander Hall, who stopped by the table to get her telephone number. After a few dates,

Lucy and Hall were living together, dividing their time between a Hollywood apartment and the seventy-five-acre ranch in the San Fernando Valley where he ran a highly successful turkey farm.

Seventeen years older than Lucy, Alexander Hall was divorced from sultry Lola Lane, the first of three singing Lane sisters to become movie stars (followed by Rosemary and Priscilla). Hall had been a child performer in vaudeville, served in the Submarine Service during World War I, and acted in silent movie serials. Turning to film editing, he eventually became a director.

Hall became Lucy's lover-mentor, although he wielded less executive power than Pandro Berman did. Under the studio system, directors were very much under the thumb of producers. Hall had no influence over Lucy's career—he had just joined Columbia after a long stint at Paramount—but he could teach her everything he knew about moviemaking, which was considerable. If Hall could turn a tot named Shirley Temple into a star in *Little Miss Marker,* there wasn't any reason why he couldn't help Lucille Ball become a first-rate comedian.

"I first got to know Lucy when she came to see Al Hall while we were making *There's Always a Woman* and its sequel, *There's That Woman Again,*" actress Joan Blondell remembered. "Lucy's interest and enthusiasm in learning her craft was almost childlike. Everything was a great burst of joy to her and it was contagious."

Under Alexander Hall's influence, Lucy began to blossom at RKO, beginning with *The Affairs of Annabel,* in which she portrayed a scatterbrained movie star trying to revive her career through outrageous publicity stunts. With Jack Oakie co-starring as the press agent, the low-budget comedy did so well at the box office that RKO intended to turn it into a series. But only *Annabel Takes a Tour* followed after Oakie got a swollen head and began demanding $50,000 per picture, which was about a third of the entire budget.

Although Lucy remained on friendly terms with Pandro Berman, he could no longer give her roles for fear of retribution from his wife. After *Room Service,* Lucy never worked for Berman at RKO again, nor did any of the other prestigious A producers seem interested in using her. Instead, she became the so-called queen of the studio's inexpensive B product. What she missed in quality, she certainly made up in quantity.

From September 1938, through the end of 1939, Lucy played the romantic lead in eight B programmers, equally divided between comedies like *Beauty for the Asking* and *That's Right—You're Wrong* and melodramas such as *Panama Lady* and *Five Came Back.* Although RKO had such top leading men as Cary Grant, James Stewart, David

Niven, and Henry Fonda under contract at the time, Lucy always ended up working with the second-stringers and has-beens, including James Ellison, Patric Knowles, Dennis O'Keefe, Richard Dix, and Chester Morris.

Amusingly, despite her lowly status at RKO, Lucy was among the hundreds of actresses who auditioned for the role of Scarlett O'Hara in *Gone With the Wind*. But she never became one of the lucky three dozen (Jean Arthur, Paulette Goddard, Joan Bennett, and Lana Turner among them) who were actually given screen tests prior to the last-minute selection of Vivien Leigh.

Lucy spent a month learning her audition lines and practicing a Southern drawl. When finally summoned before producer David O. Selznick, she got so carried away that she fell down on both knees, reciting the dialogue almost as if she were Al Jolson belting "Mammy." Selznick was too astounded to say anything but "Thanks for coming" before helping her to her feet and rushing her out the door.

Thanks to Carole Lombard, Lucy *almost* got the lead in *The Smiler with the Knife,* a detective thriller intended to be the movie debut of Orson Welles, the so-called Boy Genius of Broadway's esteemed Mercury Players. Lombard considered herself too important to risk working with someone who'd never directed a film before, so she recommended Lucy as her replacement.

As it turned out, Welles detested Hollywood's dependence on big-name stars and would have happily accepted Lucy, but the RKO management wouldn't take the risk. Welles went on to make *Citizen Kane* for the studio instead.

In February 1940, RKO purchased the screen rights to the Broadway musical *Too Many Girls* for $100,000, outbidding MGM and Warner Brothers. A record price for a Broadway show at the time, RKO considered it a bargain because the studio could make it cheaply, with most of the original New York cast working for peanuts. RKO also stood to gain options on long-term contracts with a gallery of fresh new faces who might be developed into stars.

The likelihood of twenty-nine-year-old Lucille Ball, neither a singer nor a dancer, winding up in a musical as a virginal college freshman seemed even more remote than her portraying Scarlett O'Hara. But in Hollywood, fate often works in mysterious ways, and she had to meet Desi Arnaz somehow. So far she knew him only from some conga records she'd heard on the radio. Likable, but nothing she'd buy herself, since her musical tastes ran more to Woody Herman, Artie Shaw, and Benny Goodman.

5

Conga Fever

COMPARED to Lucille Ball, Desi Arnaz achieved celebrity status fairly quickly, but he was hardly an overnight sensation. The first orchestra under his own name debuted on December 30, 1937, at a 250-seat club attached to the Park Central Restaurant in Miami Beach. The nightspot was so new that it didn't have a name yet. And after Desi's debut there, it seemed like the place wouldn't be around long enough to need one.

After quitting Xavier Cugat, Desi teamed up with Cugat's under-paid and disgruntled secretary, Louis Nicoletti, who resigned to become manager of the proposed Arnaz band. With forty dollars between them, they drove to Miami in Nicoletti's decrepit Plymouth and moved in with Desi's parents. By that time, Arnaz Senior earned enough in his tiling and construction business to afford to rent a four-room bungalow, a definite improvement over makeshift living quarters in the company warehouse.

Miami impresarios weren't exactly eager to hire an unknown Latin-American band, so Desi and Nicoletti had to use their considerable talents as con artists to secure a booking. Learning of a new club opening in a side room of the Park Central, they barged into the restaurant pretending to be vacationing big-time spenders, ordering Piper Heidsieck champagne and lavishly tipping the cigarette girl a whole dollar when they bought a pack of premium-priced Herbert Tareytons.

Delighted by their patronage, owner Bob Kelly strolled over to the table to say hello. Desi introduced himself as the singing star of Xavier Cugat's orchestra and Nicoletti as Cugat's manager. He claimed that Cugat had given them a two-week holiday to rest up before starting what was sure to be another record-breaking engagement at the Waldorf-Astoria.

Wildly impressed, Kelly confessed to be having a problem finding a name act to open his new club. Would Desi be interested in filling in until he had to get back to New York?

Nicoletti shook his head. "I don't think so. Even if I could get Cugie's permission, your little place couldn't afford Desi," he told Kelly.

Kelly took offense at being considered a penny-ante operator and said that he could afford to pay as much as the big established nightclubs. Nicoletti was about to quote a price when Desi kicked him in the shins under the table to warn him to slow down before he made a deal they might regret later.

Promising to get back to Kelly as soon as possible, Desi and Nicoletti left and phoned Cugat. Desi wanted to make sure that his ex-boss not only kept his promise of endorsement but also supplied him with musicians for the group. He knew that all the local talent already had commitments for the peak winter season, which officially started in Miami Beach on New Year's Eve.

Cugat promised to help on both counts, so Nicoletti resumed negotiations with Kelly. The upshot was that Kelly could have the Arnaz band if he agreed to credit the Xavier Cugat orchestra in the billing and also ran full-page ads in the Miami newspapers on opening night. Furthermore, the fee for Desi and a five-piece group would be $650 a week for twelve weeks guaranteed. Out of the goodness of his heart, Cugat had given his protégé a leave of absence so that he could become a star in his own right, Nicoletti fibbed.

Desi and his partner figured that they could hire the five musicians at the union scale of seventy dollars per week, plus the train fare from New York. That would leave $300 for all their other expenses, including music, arrangements, wardrobe, transportation, et cetera. They would each draw fifty dollars per week for themselves until they knew how they were doing.

Desi rented a station wagon to pick up the musicians at Union Station, but he had a shock when he met them. Because of a Yuletide manpower shortage, Cugat's contributions to the Latin-American band turned out to be a Spanish drummer who could play only bull-

fight marches, two Italians for violin and bass, and two Jewish Brook-
lynites for piano and saxophone!

During rehearsal, the group sounded even worse than Desi feared.
The players knew only two Latin songs, the hackneyed "Peanut Vendor" and "Mama Inez." By the time they went on stage that night,
they had "mastered" only eight numbers, including a *paso doble* to
pacify the Spaniard.

At least the band looked great. Desi wore a white tuxedo jacket
with satin lapels, black trousers, a ruffled shirt, and a red bow tie with
matching pocket handkerchief. His mother had spent the past week
sewing rumba shirts for the musicians to give them a typical Cubano
appearance.

After the band's first performance, Bob Kelly fired the lot. "That
was the worst thing I ever heard in my life," he screamed at Desi.
"Whether I like it or not, the union says I have to keep you for two
weeks minimum, but after that you're finished! I'd have been better
off hiring a band from the Salvation Army!"

During the next set, radio star Ted Husing came into the club to
case the band for a possible remote broadcast on his nightly music-
and-chat program. Husing took one listen and cringed, but he was
impressed enough by Desi's vocal and guitar work to invite him on
the show as a soloist. "Don't you dare let that cockamamie group of
yours play one note," Husing said.

By the last set of the evening, Desi realized that he'd have to come
up with something completely different by the following night, New
Year's Eve, when the crowd expected a top-notch show for the advanced prices. He tried a rumba, but the band sounded pitiful. Desi's
last hope was the conga, a primitive, easy-to-learn beat that invited
audience participation. During carnival season in Santiago, he'd witnessed thousands of people linking up into a conga line and dancing
nonstop to the irresistible rhythm for several days and nights before
they dropped from exhaustion.

Except to those of Afro-Cuban heritage, the conga was virtually
unknown in the segregated United States of 1937. The quickest way
for Desi to teach it to his musicians was to first get them pleasantly
soused. Calling a break, he ordered a bottle of Bacardi rum to relax
their inhibitions. Then he went into the club's kitchen and borrowed
a big frying pan and two spoons for the violinist to play instead of his
customary instrument.

The patrons out front didn't know what was going on, but somehow it all came together. While the band played and Desi wiggled his

hips to the beat, Nicoletti went out on the dance floor and literally dragged people from their tables to start a conga line.

"In a few minutes several couples got behind Nick," Desi remembered. "Then I jumped from the stage to the top of the bar. It was a long bar, about thirty feet, and I went from one end to the other, back and forth, dancing and beating my drum. From there I jumped onto the dance floor and pretty soon we had the whole goddam club in the conga line."

Word quickly got around Miami Beach about the sizzling new dance being featured at the Park Central. Within a week, the place was packed every night. The audience demanded at least one conga in every set. The dance line often snaked out through the side exit door, around the corner and into the main restaurant, through the dining room and back into the club again.

The owner was ecstatic and rescinded Desi's two-week notice. To prove how wrong he'd been, Bob Kelly wanted to name the club "Desi's Place." The proposed namesake modestly declined, suggesting "La Conga" instead. The sign went up the next day.

Celebrities began dropping by, a sure indication that La Conga was developing into an "in" place. Sophie Tucker, Harry Richman, Eddie Cantor, Helen Morgan, and the Ritz Brothers were among Desi's first boosters.

Joe E. Lewis, the sardonic comedian revered as "The King of Clubs," came in so often that Desi reciprocated one night by leading a long conga line down the street to the Continental Club, where Lewis was in the midst of his midnight performance. Desi and followers completely encircled Lewis, who grabbed on to the end of the line as it returned to La Conga. When Desi realized what had happened, he led the line back to the Continental again so that Lewis could finish his act.

A quick romance developed when Olympic champion Sonja Henie, the radiant "Queen of Ice," pranced into La Conga without her skates. In town to publicize her latest movie, the twenty-five-year-old Norwegian blonde was instantly attracted to Desi. She tried to teach him to ice skate at the indoor rink at the Roney Plaza, but with little success. Desi had better luck instructing her; Henie became the first entertainer to conga on skates when she introduced it in the next edition of her traveling *Hollywood Ice Revue*.

Louis Nicoletti had also fallen in love—with an heiress from one of the Detroit automotive dynasties. As soon as the booking at La Conga ended, the couple eloped on a world cruise, leaving Desi without a manager. For lack of further dates, his musicians returned to New York to get work elsewhere, and he found himself without a band as well.

Xavier Cugat, unhappy over losing the twenty-five dollars per week royalty that Desi paid him, tried to take advantage of the situation by offering him a new contract with the Cugat orchestra. The deal as featured soloist would pay $200 a week, fifty-two weeks a year, five years guaranteed. It was a real temptation for Desi, who'd been lucky to clear fifty dollars a week after paying his band expenses.

Fortunately, he had the sense to show the contract to a lawyer friend, who told him, "According to this, the only thing that Cugat *can't* do is fuck you, and even that's debatable, because I haven't read all the fine print yet." Under the agreement, Cugat would take total control over Desi's career for five years. If Desi signed to do a movie for $500 a week, for example, he would still get only $200, with Cugat pocketing the difference.

Desi rejected Cugat's offer and decided to try to make it on his own. At age twenty-one, he found himself unemployed. The Florida tourist season had ended, so he returned to New York. While hanging out at the headquarters of the musicians' union, he ran into his former bassist, Caesar De Franco, who offered him room and board at his apartment in Brooklyn for five dollars per week.

It turned out to be a bargain, because Mrs. De Franco also did Desi's laundry and treated him like a son. He began dating the manicurist from the local barbershop, who groomed his nails for free and got him a discount on haircuts.

To save the nickel subway fare, Desi often walked into Manhattan over the Brooklyn Bridge. Jobs were hard to find for a Cuban guitarist who couldn't read music or play non-Latin tunes, so he finally had to lie about his credentials to get hired for a band that performed on weekends in a German beer hall in the Yorkville district.

Desi thought he could fake his way through the job by playing as softly as possible. When the leader told him to increase the volume by playing with a pick instead of his fingers, Desi quickly broke all the strings. To make up for the debacle, he offered to sing a few Latin songs, but the band knew only one, the inevitable "Peanut Vendor."

The novelty of a Latin singer with a German band made enough of an impression for Desi to be invited back for four successive weekends. On his second visit, he taught the band to play a conga. The predominantly Prussian clientele, many of whom staunchly supported Adolf Hitler and Nazism in those days, were congaing around the block by night's end.

By this time, the owners of Fan & Bill's Roadhouse near Lake George, New York, who had caught Desi's band in Miami Beach, traced him through the musicians' union with an offer of a booking for the summer months. Desi reassembled the original five musicians, added an accordionist and trumpet player, and increased the group's fee to $1,100 per week. Surprisingly, he got it, thanks to a talent agent who made a tidy bundle by handling both sides of the deal. The agent received 10 percent from Desi and another 10 percent from Fan & Bill's, in a practice that was widespread then but illegal today.

The booking at Fan & Bill's marked the first time that the Desi Arnaz orchestra received billing on its own, without crediting ties to Xavier Cugat. In the fall, the group returned to La Conga in Miami Beach for a run that stretched into the spring of 1939 due to smash business.

With huge crowds expected for the $150 million New York World's Fair, a Mafia syndicate fronted by Mario Torsatti decided to open a Manhattan version of La Conga. Located at Broadway and 51st Street on the site of the defunct Harlem Uproar House, the nitery was lavishly decorated to resemble a tropical garden, complete with exotic flowering plants, palm trees, and midnight-blue lighting effects. Since the Desi Arnaz orchestra had developed a big following among the tourists who wintered in Miami Beach, Torsatti hired the band to launch the New York La Conga.

The Desi Arnaz orchestra quickly made Broadway conga-crazy, but without much help from World's Fair crowds. Most visitors had no money or time to spend after a full day at the 1,216-acre exposition, which had umpteen restaurants, nightclubs, and entertainments of its own. La Conga had to depend on support from the smart set and the demimonde, which, fortunately, turned out in profitable numbers.

Brenda Frazier, the eighteen-year-old heiress debutante whose translucent complexion, ruby lips, and raven hair made for one of the most famous faces in America, became Desi's biggest fan. Wherever Brenda went, reporters and photographers were sure to follow. Especially when she suddenly abandoned her usual haunts of the Stork Club and El Morocco for La Conga, which was definitely on the *wrong* side of Fifth Avenue, the Social Register's dividing line. La Conga's press agents tried to create a romance between Desi Arnaz and Brenda Frazier, but there's no evidence that one ever took place.

Just as helpful to Desi's career as the association with Brenda Frazier was his friendship with a thirty-nine-year-old Russian-Jewish immigrant named Pearl Yanow, better known as Polly Adler, America's most famous procuress. Because of a glitzy clientele of showbiz celebrities, politicians, bankers, corporate leaders, and press lords, Adler probably wielded more power behind the scenes than any woman in the United States except Eleanor Roosevelt.

Polly Adler boasted of having the most beautiful as well as the cleanest "girls" in New York, but she'd been raided so many times that she no longer ran a "house" in the traditional sense. No women actually resided in her lavish six-bedroom apartment on the West Side. Clients phoned ahead, and Adler arranged for someone of their specifications to meet them there for a drink and whatever. In the lingo of the trade, she was a "call house madam" as opposed to the "cathouse" variety.

Desi met Polly Adler when she started dropping into La Conga nearly every night with three or four beautiful women in tow and occupying a prime table. Desi didn't realize it at first, but that was Adler's favorite way of showcasing her wares to the big-time spenders who frequented such places.

One night, Desi spotted one of the most voluptuous redheads he'd ever seen in Adler's group. Noticing Desi's gaping, the club's manager took him over to Adler's table for an introduction. Adler, who had a voice raspier than Wallace Beery's, sized up Desi immediately and asked if he'd like to join them for breakfast after the last show.

Desi had thought Adler to be the mother or aunt of the younger women, so he got a shock when they all arrived at her apartment, which reminded him of a deluxe version of the Casa Marina in Santiago. After a breakfast of caviar, scrambled eggs, and champagne, Desi started to get nervous. "By now, I had realized that I was in a very classy whorehouse, and I was sure that even once-over-lightly would cost at least a hundred dollars," he recalled. "I thanked Mrs. Adler for being such a gracious hostess, but I told her that the place was way beyond my means."

Adler laughed: "That's all right, Sonny, this one's on me." She insisted that he take the redhead he'd been ogling all night, though it was now six in the morning. Desi said he had a two o'clock rehearsal, so Adler promised to wake him at noon.

"I've had my share of delicious sex in my life," Desi remembered, "but that redhead was something else. If there was anything I had not learned already, she taught it to me then. She was insatiable."

Polly Adler knew, of course, that a contented customer always came back. In Desi's case, he returned so many times on a paying basis that she reciprocated by instructing her hostesses to ask their "dates" to take them to La Conga whenever possible. On many nights, the audience seemed equally divided between Polly Adler's referrals and Brenda Frazier's crowd.

During the summer of 1939, Desi discovered that he had a secret admirer in song lyricist Lorenz Hart, who'd seen him performing at La Conga in Miami Beach and had never quite forgotten him. Hart and composer-partner Richard Rodgers arrived at the New York club one evening to offer Desi a role in their next project, *Too Many Girls*. The collegiate musical comedy required a dynamic Latino for a featured part as a football-playing exchange student from South America.

Desi had never heard of Rodgers and Hart or even seen a Broadway show. When they left him a script to study, he didn't know what that was either, but he promised to show up for an audition at the Imperial Theater the following week.

The director, George Abbott, always insisted on *no* preparation prior to auditions, and he threw a fit when he discovered that Lorenz Hart and his constant shadow, dentist "Doc" Bender, had coached Desi in the part for three days.

"You taught him, didn't you?" Abbott raged at Hart after Desi lapsed into reciting the lines, a dead giveaway that he wasn't reading them cold for the first time. Desi had been acting like John Barrymore, waving his arms and emoting all over the place.

Assuming that he'd lost the job, Desi started to leave the stage. "Come back here, Dizzy, or whatever your name is," Abbott shouted. "There aren't many spic actors around who fit this part. You seem to be the only one, so if you don't mind working your ass off, we'll give it a try."

Before Desi could sign the $300-per-week contract, he had to work out a deal with La Conga. The management wouldn't release their star attraction, but they were willing to compromise. Desi could take a leave of absence during the out-of-town tryouts of *Too Many Girls,* but he'd have to continue working at La Conga during the New York rehearsals and after the show opened. The practice of doubling up was fairly common then, but such opportunities rarely arise today, owing to the shrinkage in the live entertainment field.

Although Desi had never even dreamed of a career as a singing-and-dancing actor, it now seemed a distinct possibility. As luck would have it, George Abbott loved ballroom dancing, so he spent a lot more time with Desi than he might have with other apprentices. Abbott became addicted to La Conga, where he frequently led the line and got the brainstorm to build a big production number around the dance in *Too Many Girls*. Abbott also became smitten with Desi's co-worker at the nightclub, the sultry hip-shaker Diosa Costello, and hired her for the show as well.

Too Many Girls would be Rodgers and Hart's tenth collaboration, and their first since the smash *Boys from Syracuse*. Like George Abbott, they preferred to work with talented newcomers rather than deal with the egos of established names. There would be no stars in *Too Many Girls,* although some of the cast achieved that rank later on in their careers.

In George Marion Jr.'s libretto, Desi had the role of Manuelito, one of four fullbacks hired to protect a millionaire's daughter when she enrolls at Pottawatomie College in Stop Gap, New Mexico. It's a wacky sort of campus where football games are played on Fridays and the female students must wear yellow beanies on their heads if they're still virgins. Richard Kollmar, Eddie Bracken, and Hal LeRoy portrayed Desi's footballer colleagues, with a chorus boy named Van Johnson serving as standby for all four roles. Marcy Wescott played the heiress (coincidentally modeled after Brenda Frazier), with Mary Jane Walsh, Diosa Costello, and Lila Ernst as other lead coeds.

To get a collegiate reaction, *Too Many Girls* started its tryout tour in New Haven, Connecticut, home of Yale University. In the finale of the first act, Desi did a conga version of the rallying song, "Look Out," that stopped the show. As the curtain rang down, there was such deafening applause that the stage manager ordered an encore, something traditionally withheld until the very end of a play. During the intermission, George Abbott poked his head into Desi's dressing room and shouted, "Hey, kid, for an amateur you're doing great. Keep it up."

Too Many Girls opened at New York's 1,450-seat Imperial Theatre on October 18, 1939. In a glamorous theatrical custom that was eventually dropped for patriotic reasons when the United States entered World War II and never resumed, most of the first-night audience, including *everyone* seated on the orchestra floor, wore formal evening clothes.

The combination of Rodgers and Hart and George Abbott had everyone expecting a smash hit. Few were disappointed, but the musical score, including such gems as "Give It Back to the Indians," "I Like to Recognize the Tune," and "Love Never Went to College," brought forth only one enduring standard, "I Didn't Know What Time It Was."

Although tradition called for the cast to go to Sardi's restaurant to await the reviews in the first editions of the next day's newspapers,

Desi's workday was only half finished. He still had three shows to perform at La Conga. The following night, he would start doing a fourth show, *prior* to the eight-thirty curtain of *Too Many Girls*. The club supplied a limousine to take him back and forth.

By the time of Desi's final show on opening night, all his friends and colleagues from *Too Many Girls* had drifted over to La Conga from Sardi's to show him the raves of such critics and columnists as Brooks Atkinson, Walter Winchell, Danton Walker, Ed Sullivan, Burns Mantle, and George Jean Nathan. A seemingly chinless brunette named Dorothy Kilgallen, who just happened to be the sweetheart of cast member Richard Kollmar, delivered her review in person by planting a sloppy kiss on Desi's forehead.

Polly Adler took Desi aside and said, "Cuban, you are the biggest fucking hit in town. We're going to celebrate, so if you have any plans for later on, cancel them. Polly's place will be closed to everybody else until tomorrow night. My staff will feed and divert you until you drop. Then you'll know what it's really like to have *too many girls!*"

By the following evening, Desi felt so drained that he practically crawled back to work. After the first act of *Too Many Girls,* George Abbott came backstage and bawled him out for a lackluster performance: "Last night you tore this theater apart, but tonight you looked like you were half dead. Make sure you get plenty of rest. Doubling here and at La Conga isn't going to be easy for you. Don't fuck around!"

Several nights later, Desi had a surprise visit from Irving Pincus, a 20th Century–Fox talent executive, who wanted to sign him as leading man to Alice Faye in a Technicolor musical entitled *Down Argentine Way*. The salary would be $1,500 per week, with an option for a seven-year contract starting at $1,750. The only hitch was that Desi would have to quit both Broadway jobs as soon as the movie was ready to roll in Hollywood.

"The offer was fantastic, but I turned it down," Desi recalled. "I really couldn't figure out what the hell I was doing in a Broadway show to begin with. If it hadn't been for George Abbott, I wouldn't even know how to walk across the stage. I had almost no understanding of American humor, which often plays on words and is very different from Spanish humor. George had to explain all the jokes to me and then demonstrate how to tell them or react to them. If I had any chance of succeeding as an actor, I knew I needed someone like George to teach me. I'd had some incredible luck in two years. The rest would have to wait until I thought I could handle it."

One invitation that Desi did accept was from the National Broadcasting Company to make a guest appearance in a brand-new medium called television. After several years of experimentation, NBC had started a regular program service in conjunction with the New York World's Fair. About 120 TV sets were in use at the time, mainly in the homes of executives of RCA (NBC's parent company) and public gathering places like Macy's exhibition hall and the downstairs lounge at Radio City Music Hall.

Partnered with Diosa Costello, Desi demonstrated the conga on a variety show broadcast on November 12, 1939. He received no compensation except the publicity, and nearly passed out under the intense lighting. He wasn't terribly impressed when a technician showed him the receiver required to pick up the program. Over four feet high, the huge cabinet had a vertically mounted tube called a kinescope. To see the picture, Desi had to look into a mirror in the lid, which picked up the reflection of the fuzzy image.

"Do you really believe that people are going to buy this thing?" Desi asked when told that it sold for $660, nearly the price of an automobile in those days. "I wish you lots of luck, but I think people are gonna stick with their radios."

Desi did see a future for himself as a jukebox star and signed a recording deal with the Columbia label for two singles, which in that era, of course, were issued only in the format of fragile ten-inch, 78-rpm shellac discs. Featuring percussive Latin hits composed by Quintero, Parraza, Curiel, and Valdespi, the four sides sold moderately well to hepcats who considered the conga a Cuban cousin to American swing.

Between his various performing commitments, Desi earned about $850 per week and was doing well. He could afford to dress better and to live better. For his nightclub shows, he now wore custom-tailored white tie and tails. The silk ties were purchased by the gross because he often tore them off and threw them to women in the audience when he got carried away while pounding on the conga drums.

He had come a long way from that rat-infested warehouse in Miami. His Manhattan digs were a penthouse apartment overlooking Central Park, which he sublet furnished from boxing champion Barney Ross. Lorenz Hart resided in the same building, causing rumors in the gay community that he and Desi were lovers, which seems highly unlikely. The forty-four-year-old Hart, considered by many experts to be the most brilliant lyricist in American popular music, was then well advanced into the alcoholism and debauchery that eventually caused his death in 1943.

With Desi's newfound celebrity, it seemed about time that he should have his first serious romance. Columnist Walter Winchell quipped that the conga line at a certain nightclub should be called "The Desi Chain" because of all the feminine hearts he'd broken. One night, thanks to an introduction from Brenda Frazier and her playboy companion Peter Arno, he met a woman who immediately reminded him of Larry Hart's immortal lyrics, "I took one look at you, that's all I meant to do, and then my heart stood still."

Her name was Renée DeMarco, known to her pals as "Freckles." Four years older than Desi, the one-time chorus girl was half of a world-famous dance team with her husband, Tony DeMarco. The Dancing DeMarcos were revered for their inventiveness, whirlwind movements, and amusing habit of talking between themselves and to members of the audience while dancing.

The DeMarcos went through a marital separation in 1938 but continued to work together to honor long-term contracts. Renée described Tony, her senior by thirteen years, as a sadistic tyrant who frequently beat her. Obviously, the team could not continue on much longer. Their dancing became mainly individual solos; they barely touched each other during a performance.

It's easy to understand why the uncultured Desi Arnaz would be attracted to a witty, sophisticated woman of the world like Freckles. Weighing in at 110 pounds, she was a delicate beauty who ranked as one of the best-dressed stars in show business. Her luxurious gowns, which she designed herself and cost thousands of dollars apiece, usually had five or six layers of chiffon or were encrusted with semiprecious jewels.

"She was the most astonishing woman I had ever met," Desi recalled. "Her love, her tenderness, her disposition were unbelievable. She had the understanding and the patience to put up with me, which I'm sure wasn't an easy to job at times. She never nagged, never argued."

For someone born and raised in ultraconservative Burlington, Vermont (as Marguerite Nerney), DeMarco had a remarkably tolerant attitude about sex, which was similar to Desi's. If he had a one-night stand with another woman and Freckles found out, she played dumb and didn't take it as a threat to their own relationship. To her, it was nothing more than a twenty-two-year-old stud sowing his wild oats.

The affair had to be played out secretly until DeMarco got her long-pending divorce. Desi wanted to marry her as soon as that happened, but in the meantime they used DeMarco's apartment in the Pierre Hotel for their trysts.

Due to an unexpected development in his family situation, Desi couldn't very well bring Freckles back to his rented penthouse, which he now shared with his forty-three-year-old mother. Strange though it may seem, Lolita Arnaz had divorced Desiderio II so he could marry a younger woman. She loved her husband so much that she would not stand in the way of his happiness, even though it meant going through a legal process that was forbidden in their Roman Catholic faith. She never remarried and wore her wedding ring for the rest of her life.

Desi hadn't counted on his mother becoming his housekeeper and cook, but that was exactly what she insisted on when she moved in with him. Shocked and disillusioned by what he discovered about his father, Desi became estranged from him for many years. It seems that Desi Senior had been involved with the second Mrs. Arnaz since fleeing Cuba; he continued meeting her secretly even after his son and wife joined him in Miami.

But while Desi may have condemned his father's deceitfulness, it didn't seem to make any difference in his own romantic relationships. While keeping company with Renée DeMarco, he fell hook, line, and sinker for a blue-eyed peroxide blonde who worked at the theater adjacent to his, twenty-three-year-old Betty Grable.

After a long and discouraging movie career similar to Lucille Ball's, Grable had just become the rage of Broadway in a supporting role with Ethel Merman and Bert Lahr in Cole Porter's *DuBarry Was a Lady. Life,* the top magazine in America at the time, ran a cover story on the vivacious singer-dancer that predicted she'd be one of the biggest stars of the upcoming 1940s.

Desi first met Grable while table-hopping at Dinty Moore's restaurant, a favorite hangout for show casts on their dinner breaks between matinee and evening performances. He suddenly found himself sitting next to Grable and didn't want to leave.

"It was impossible to be next to Betty and not want to know her a little better," Desi recalled. "She was gorgeous. What a figure and what legs! Her skin was magnificent, so smooth she looked like a peach."

As two hot young Broadway personalities, Desi Arnaz and Betty Grable were a press agent's dream come true. Grable loved to dance, so she often joined Desi at La Conga after working in *DuBarry* and stayed on until he was ready to take her out to one of Manhattan's all-night bowling alleys or roller skating rinks. At dawn, they'd return to Grable's suite at the Essex House until it was time to get ready for work again.

Desi had met his match in Grable, who could play the field as well as he could, perhaps even better. In between dates with Desi, she also was spending time with bandleader-clarinetist Artie Shaw, a heart-breaker of the time, and Lex Thompson, a millionaire playboy who made the rounds in an antique-filled motor home complete with chauffeur, butler, and cook.

Desi's affair with Grable didn't so much end as go into hibernation. It eventually resumed in Hollywood after *Too Many Girls* completed its run of 294 performances and Desi accepted an offer to repeat his role in the movie version. By that time, Grable had already left *Du-Barry Was a Lady* to replace the ailing Alice Faye in *Down Argentine Way*. It was, ironically, the same movie that Desi turned down when 20th Century–Fox tried to sign him to a contract.

6

Long Distance Love Affair

LUCY and Desi's first scene together in *Too Many Girls* required him to take one glance at her gorgeous physiognomy and swoon dead away in ecstasy. It didn't take much acting skill; by then they were already lovers in real life.

"They were absolutely together night and day," co-worker Ann Miller remembered. "They were enraptured of each other, which is putting it mildly."

Following several purely social evenings that ended at the front door to Lucille's apartment, the affair began after a fiery encounter at a Sunday afternoon beach party at Eddie Bracken's rented house in Malibu. Lucille came alone, expecting to link up with Desi. To her dismay, he brought Renée DeMarco, who'd just arrived in town after finding New York too lonely without him.

Lucille was wearing a pink one-piece bathing suit and matching sandals. She was as close to nude as Desi had ever seen her, and he couldn't take his eyes off her. If she felt a similar excitement about him in his black bathing trunks, she didn't let on. She looked so displeased about Freckles that Desi didn't dare introduce the two women.

Feeling that he owed Lucille an explanation, Desi parked Renée with Van Johnson and wandered off. He found Lucille sitting alone on the beach. She gave him a frosty greeting.

"What's Irene Castle doing here?" she asked, referring to a dancing legend old enough to be Renée DeMarco's grandmother. Desi had previously confessed to the affair, but had given Lucille the impression that it was over.

"Zanuck brought her out for a screen test," Desi lied. He couldn't very well admit that he'd spent most of the past two days—and nights —with Renée.

Lucille patted the patch of sand next to her. "Sit down. I think we'd better have a chat."

They talked and argued until the setting sun seemed to disappear into the Pacific Ocean. There was no doubt anymore that they wanted each other; their jealous natures were the only stumbling block. Desi could not tolerate Lucille's relationship with Alexander Hall any more than she could stand his with Freckles.

Passion finally prevailed. When Lucy went back into the house to change out of her bathing suit, Desi followed her into the bedroom and started to make love to her. Hearing voices approaching, they hid in the closet until the coast was clear. Then they drove to Lucille's apartment and spent a blissful night together.

From that time on, Desi chose to address his beloved as Lucy instead of Lucille. "I never liked 'Lucille.' That name had been used by other men. 'Lucy' was mine alone," he recalled.

Desi never went back to Renée DeMarco. When he phoned to apologize for leaving her in the lurch, she was as understanding as she'd been when he left her previously for Betty Grable. Desi didn't know it, but Freckles had already found a new lover in a man who took her home from the beach party. Perhaps that explained why she so sweetly wished him good luck with Lucy.

As for Alexander Hall, Lucy told him to remove whatever belongings he had in her apartment. When he drove over from his turkey ranch for the pickup, he brought Lucy a freshly killed bird to remember him by. They had a good laugh and remained great friends for the rest of their lives.

Desi virtually moved in with Lucy. For the sake of appearances, he rented a furnished apartment of his own and brought his mother out from New York to take care of it.

Neither could guess how long the affair would last or where it was headed. *Too Many Girls* had a seven-week shooting schedule. Afterward, Lucy would start another movie immediately. Desi had no further Hollywood commitments, but expected to rejoin the stage production of *Too Many Girls* when it opened a limited run in Chicago in September.

In the meantime, the lovers decided to enjoy themselves. They went nightclubbing, often to two or three clubs in the same evening. Lucy had finally learned the full book of Latin dances, more by osmosis than from actual lessons. Hanging out nightly with the dance maniacs at places like the Palladium, Trocadero, Casa Mañana, Florentine Gardens, Cocoanut Grove, and El Zerape, even someone with two left feet would end up mamboing in their sleep.

An exhibitionist in the extreme, Desi loved to perform, whether he was being paid for it or not. When the couple went to Ciro's, for example, he would get up to sing with Emil Coleman's band or sit in on the drums. No one else would dare lead the conga line with Desi on the premises. Lucy was always right behind him, holding on for dear life.

The filming of *Too Many Girls* put no crimp in their social life. On the contrary, it became even more hectic. RKO's press chief, Perry Lieber, saw the coupling as an ideal way of gaining publicity for the movie and for Lucille Ball.

"Except for fashion layouts and leg art in the fan magazines, we'd always had a problem getting publicity for Lucy," Lieber said. "Let's face it, most of her movies were B programmers, and there were no Tyrone Powers or Robert Taylors in her private life that the gossip columnists could write about. Then along comes Desi, who's not a big star, but very promising, very handsome, and very sexy. So they're not exactly Gable and Lombard, but you can still get a helluva lot of coverage."

When Lucy and Desi went out on a date, an RKO still photographer usually trailed after them. He'd snap a roll of candids and then leave. The evening would cost the couple nothing; RKO always arranged for the nightclub or restaurant to pick up the tab in exchange for the free publicity.

For Lucy's twenty-ninth birthday on August 6, Desi had the extravagant idea of surprising her with a party wherever they went that day. A party for each year seemed a bit much, so he settled for five, one at the studio, another at her family's house, at Lucey's restaurant, at Grace Hayes's lodge, and at Slapsie Maxie's nightclub. Needless to say, all the arrangements—including five birthday cakes, an equal number of floral bouquets, and fifty invites to members of the press— were taken care of and paid for by RKO publicity.

Desi's only expense was a diamond-encrusted heart-shaped lapel watch. The first gift that he never gave Lucy, it eventually served as the model for the logo used in the opening titles of *I Love Lucy*.

When *Too Many Girls* wrapped, Lucy and Desi no longer had a practical reason for being together. But they were so madly in love that he decided to stay in Los Angeles for as long as he could while she worked on *A Girl, a Guy, and a Gob*. The screwball farce co-starring Edmond O'Brien and George Murphy promised to be a notch or two above Lucy's usual fare. The producer, Harold Lloyd, was considered a comedic genius in a class with Chaplin and Keaton.

Lucy didn't fancy Desi gallivanting around town without her, but while occupied at the studio there wasn't much she could do but fret. Her worst fears were realized when she began to hear rumors about Desi and ex-flame Betty Grable. Some of Lucy's friends reported seeing Desi and Grable at the Santa Anita racetrack, as well as sipping zombie cocktails at Don the Beachcomber's.

Desi insisted that nothing was going on between them, but Lucy didn't believe him. To stop things from going any further, she phoned her ex-lover George Raft and pleaded with him to intervene.

"Lucy knew that George was nuts about Betty Grable. He'd recently started dating Betty himself, so he wasn't going to stand for her running around with Desi any more than Lucy was," said Grable's friend Betty Ritz. "George threatened Desi with a visit from Bugsy Siegel. George had so many pals in Murder, Inc., that you could never tell if he was kidding or not. But Desi sure wasn't going to hang around to find out."

Lucy would eventually have to learn to tolerate Desi's constant philandering. For all his carousing, they were still very much in love. Just before he left for Chicago to rejoin the stage production of *Too Many Girls*, they spent a passionate night together before parting, tenderly but resignedly, in the morning.

The separation lasted two weeks. As soon as Lucy finished *A Girl, a Guy, and a Gob*, RKO sent her on tour to publicize the release of *Dance, Girl, Dance*. She made certain that the tour ended in Chicago, which gave her a few days of trysting time with Desi at the studio's expense.

Back in Hollywood again, Lucy wasn't too pleased when Harold Lloyd decided to reshoot part of *A Girl, a Guy, and a Gob* after the RKO brass expressed dissatisfaction with the rushes. Missing Desi desperately, she had to force herself to concentrate on her work. She kept running to her dressing room to phone Desi or to take his calls. Their telephone bills were enormous, running upwards of $200 a week apiece.

"We could have bought half of AT&T," Desi recalled.

The conversations weren't always pleasant. Absence may make the heart grow fonder, but it can also kindle jealousy. If Lucy had difficulty reaching Desi, she'd conclude that he was out with another woman, and vice versa. The screaming, the accusations, and the blaspheming that went on between them kept the long-distance wires sizzling night and day.

When *Too Many Girls* ended its Chicago run, Desi returned to New York to resume his bandleading career. With a hit show and a soon-to-be-released movie to his credit, he now seemed ready for the big time. His agent had booked him into the Versailles, the swank East Side supper club. After that, Desi would head a stage bill at the Roxy, the largest theater in the nation with a policy of name entertainers plus first-run movies.

Three thousand miles away in Los Angeles, Lucy viewed those developments with mixed feelings. She was thrilled for Desi's success, but it also became another obstacle to their being together. Her despair drove her into an affair with another man.

Lucy had met middle-aged Gene Markey while he was married to Joan Bennett, her friend since Hattie Carnegie days. But the writer-producer had never shown any romantic interest in Lucy until that summer, when his latest wife, Hedy Lamarr, left him after only sixteen months. A charter member of that irreverent group of New York literati known as the Algonquin Round Table, Markey was famous for his pungent phrases and sparkling dialogue, and Lucy found him a delightful companion and a wonderful lover.

No doubt she also saw Markey as someone who could help her floundering career. He was a staff producer at Paramount Pictures, as well as a close friend of Darryl F. Zanuck, head of 20th Century–Fox. Since Lucy seemed to be going nowhere at RKO, Markey would be a good friend to have in case she needed to move to another studio.

But in the end, Markey became no more than a pawn in the ongoing Lucy-Desi romance, which had progressed too far for what losing Desi would have done to Lucy's pride. She was going on thirty, practically over the hill for a Hollywood leading lady. She had to have Desi, if only to prove that she was just as capable of landing a gorgeous hunk as any of the more celebrated Jezebels of Babylon on the Pacific. She also just happened to love Desi.

Whether Desi felt the same way about Lucy is another matter. "Desi didn't know the difference between love and sex," said a musician friend. "To put it bluntly, love was a good fuck. Desi could get that anywhere. He didn't need Lucy, but she, for whatever reason, needed him.

"Desi didn't really want to settle down with Lucy, or with any other woman for that matter. But Lucy put up such a campaign that he wound up believing that he did."

Lucy's best weapon was jealousy. To keep Desi hopping, she fed the gossip columnists a steady stream of tidbits about her affair with Gene Markey. Of course, the newspapers of that time would never dare use that word, but "steady dating" was near enough to get the message across.

Unfortunately, Lucy carried things a bit too far when she told Louella Parsons that Markey had taken her to Flato's, an ultraexpensive jewelry shop on Sunset Boulevard, to look at engagement rings. Markey took offense at Lucy's out-and-out lie and promptly dumped her for Ann Sheridan.

Meanwhile, *Dance, Girl, Dance* had been demolished by the critics and was proving a box-office flop. Lucy, however, received some fine reviews for her vivid portrayal of the wisecracking burlesque queen, so RKO tried to hype business by sending her on yet another publicity tour.

Lucy's schedule was such that she had to cancel plans to fly to New York to attend Desi's opening night at the Versailles. He was miffed that she couldn't be there to cheer him on, but he scored a big hit anyway; *Variety* called him "the hottest vaude and nitery bet since Carmen Miranda hit these shores."

To keep the flame burning in her absence, Lucy bombarded Desi with telephone calls and mushy follow-up telegrams like "Darling, it was wonderful talking to you tonight, but awful when I hung up and was left alone." She often called him in the middle of the night just to moan sweet nothings in his ear.

Her tactics seemed to be effective. Hearst columnist Louis Sobol reported bumping into Desi at the Versailles as he was dashing to a phone booth to take a long-distance call from Lucy. Afterwards, Desi told Sobol, "Twenty-two minutes, and she pays for all this herself. I guess we get married."

Lucy promised to get to New York by the time of Desi's opening at the Roxy, but again she disappointed him. RKO dispatched her to Milwaukee to attend a charity preview of *Too Many Girls*. It was supposed to be a two-day trip, but it extended into six, including the Thanksgiving holiday.

When Desi saw a wire photo in the *Daily News* of Lucy with Milwaukee's handsome young mayor, he suspected that they were having an affair. Many heated phone calls followed, but Lucy failed to convince Desi that the delay was due to an avalanche of requests for interviews and personal appearances. Her revelation that she'd accepted an invitation for turkey dinner at the mayor's mansion didn't help matters.

After Desi berated her nonstop for forty-five minutes, she realized that her little game may have backfired. She asked the RKO publicist who was traveling with her to get her on the next plane to New York. There were no more commercial flights out of Milwaukee until the next day, but he managed to book her on a single-engine cargo plane.

"I think it was the milk run," Lucy recalled. "I was the only passenger. We took off at four in the morning, and I was scared to death!"

Lucy finally landed in New York at noon on November 29. RKO had reserved a suite for her at the Pierre Hotel. When she checked in, she discovered that the studio had hurriedly arranged a series of press interviews that promised to keep her busy well into the evening.

Thirteen blocks away at the Roxy Theatre, Desi had finished the first of five stage performances that he would give that day between screenings of *Tin Pan Alley* (ironically, starring his ex-lover Betty Grable). He had a ninety-minute break between shows, so he took a cab to the Pierre to visit Lucy. She was in the midst of an interview with Rose Pelswick of the *Journal-American* and couldn't be disturbed. Desi raced back to the Roxy in a murderous mood.

In every interview that Lucy gave, reporters wanted to know the status of her relationship with Desi. The couple had been an item now for five months. In those puritanical times, the next step had to be marriage. There was no way that they could just live together openly without a scandal that would probably ruin them professionally.

Lucy fielded the marriage question as best she could. "Desi has yet to ask me," she told syndicated writer Eleanor Harris. "Besides, it could never work. Since we've known each other, the longest we've been in the same city was when we made *Too Many Girls*. I wouldn't want to end up one of those neglected musicians' wives who sit home doing needlepoint while their husbands are barnstorming around the country."

Little did Lucy know that Desi already had an elopement plan worked out. He was going a bit crazy as he kept returning to the Pierre and finding her tied up with the press. Finally, after he'd finished his next-to-last show of the night at the Roxy, he went back to her suite and threw out a reporter and a publicist who were still there. Since Lucy and Desi hadn't been together in months, conversation was the last thing on their minds.

As he was leaving, Desi said "I have everything arranged to marry you tomorrow. That is, if you would like to marry me."

Lucy was dumbfounded. "Where?" she stammered.

"In Cunneteecut." Desi explained that he'd received an exemption from the neighboring state's usual five-day waiting period. He would have to play truant from the Roxy in the morning, but he expected that they could be back in New York in time for his second show.

"Do you mean we're going to spend the honeymoon in your dressing room? I knew when I met you things weren't going to be normal," Lucy said.

"You love me, don't you?" Desi asked.

"I love you very much."

"Well, I love you very much too. So what the hell else is there?" he said.

Later, when Desi had finished at the Roxy for the night, he returned to the Pierre and found Lucy in a social visit with George Schaefer, the New York–based president of RKO Radio Pictures. She hadn't told Schaefer of the marriage plans for fear that he might spill the beans to the management of the Roxy.

As Desi entered the room, Schaefer furtively tried to attract his attention. Desi couldn't figure out what all the gesturing meant until Lucy finally noticed it and said, "Darling, Mr. Schaefer is trying to tell you that your fly is open." Desi looked down and realized that in the rush to change from his stage clothes, he'd not only forgotten to zip up his slacks but also to put on underwear.

Lucy calmly turned to Schaefer and said, "Desi believes in advertising."

After Schaefer left, Lucy and Desi ate a quick supper from room service and went straight back to bed. At six the next morning, they had to drive to Greenwich, Connecticut, to get married.

"Eloping with Desi was the most daring thing I ever did in my life," Lucy recalled. "I never fell in love with anyone quite so fast. He was very handsome and romantic. But he also frightened me, he was so wild. I knew I shouldn't have married him, but that was one of the biggest attractions."

7

A Ranch Named Desilu

I Love Lucy fanatics will remember that Lucille McGillicuddy and Ricky Ricardo were married at the Byram River Beagle Club near Greenwich, Connecticut, on November 30, 1940. Does it come as any surprise that Lucille Ball and Desi Arnaz were married there as well?

Lucy and Desi could never have known that their personal experiences would one day prove fodder for a TV sitcom. In fact, television was a dream of the future, still in the experimental stage. The nearest thing to *I Love Lucy* then was the extremely popular *radio* series *Fibber McGee and Molly*.

Desi's devotee Lorenz Hart had promised to be the best man. But Hart went on a drinking spree the night before and couldn't be roused from bed. Doc Bender, the lyricist's closest friend, and now working as Desi's theatrical agent as well, replaced Hart. When Lucy couldn't come up with a bridesmaid on such short notice, Desi's business manager, Deke Magaziner, offered to fill in.

It had been snowing lightly when the group left New York by car, so the bride and groom were dressed accordingly. Lucy wore a light-gray woolen suit, topped by a silver fox coat and a matching hat with a huge fur pompom at the front. A navy-blue cashmere overcoat and red silk scarf concealed Desi's double-breasted blue serge suit, white shirt, and printed tie.

They made such a stunning couple that Justice of the Peace John P. O'Brien decided that he couldn't marry them in his drab courthouse chambers. He picked up the phone and made arrangements to conduct the ceremony at the Byram River Beagle Club, a hunting lodge in woodsy river country outside Greenwich.

In the meantime, a crisis developed when Desi suddenly realized that he'd forgotten to buy a wedding ring. Furthermore, although he'd obtained a waiver from Connecticut's five-day waiting period, the clerk neglected to tell him that the couple still needed to take the Wassermann blood test for syphilis.

While Lucy and Desi went to be tested, Doc Bender and Deke Magaziner were dispatched to buy a wedding ring. Greenwich stores closed early on Saturdays, so the only place still open turned out to be a Woolworth's five-and-ten. The two men picked the most tasteful ring they could find, which wasn't easy considering the gaudy selection.

Desi exploded when he saw the ring, but Lucy adored it. "It turned my finger green from the first time I wore it, but it signified so much to me that I never wanted to take it off," she recalled. "Several years later, Desi insisted on having the ring plated in gold, but it still made my skin green."

Just before the ceremony, Desi phoned the Roxy. Since the Thanksgiving weekend was one of the busiest periods of the year, the theater's manager blew his stack over Desi's absence from the first show. But he calmed down considerably when he realized the publicity value in Desi's promise to turn up for the second show with his new bride in tow.

The wedding itself went off without a hitch. Oddly enough, Lucy discovered that she'd been to the Byram River Beagle Club before.

"As a starving model in New York, I once accepted an invitation to a fox hunt there, just for the sake of the big steak breakfast that went with it," she remembered. "But I'd forgotten the loveliness of the room in which we were married. It had a beamed ceiling, two huge fireplaces and lots and lots of windows. Snow covered the ground outside, and the leafless trees were silhouetted against the sky. The view was like something an artist does for a Christmas card."

Lucy and Desi never forgot Justice O'Brien for his kindness in taking them there. Besides providing an abundance of fresh flowers and vintage champagne, he also arranged for a police motorcycle escort to insure that the newlyweds arrived at the Roxy on schedule.

By the time the wedding party drove up to the stage entrance, the Roxy's publicity staff had alerted the newspapers and radio stations. Lucy and Desi had to fight their way through a mob of fans, reporters, and photographers.

"Lucy went upstairs with me and, of course, as soon as we got to my dressing room, I had to do it. The first threshold I carried her over was the one at its door," Desi said later.

Desi received the greatest ovation of his life when he walked onto the stage. The 5,836-seat auditorium was packed beyond capacity; the fire inspector had permitted hundreds of patrons from the first show to remain in the aisles until Desi and Lucy made their appearance.

Probably the most opulent palace of amusement ever built in the United States, the Roxy blended Renaissance, Gothic, and Moorish elements into a gold and bronze fantasy that once inspired a classic *New Yorker* cartoon in which a boggle-eyed child asked her mother, "Does God live here?" Nearly half the seats were in the mezzanine and balcony. Climbing to the topmost rows could cause a nosebleed.

When Desi introduced Lucy, the audience's approval became visible as well as audible. "I'd like you to meet my very lovely bride of just an hour," he said. The Roxy interior suddenly looked as if the roof had been opened to let in the snow. Thousands upon thousands of grains of rice hailed down on the stage, a seeming blizzard in the blaze of the spotlights.

Lucy and Desi embraced, wiped tears from their eyes, and blew kisses to the crowd. They discovered later that the Roxy manager had sent to a wedding caterer for small packets of rice, which were distributed to every patron by the sixty-man ushering squad. An extra service of the house, included in the admission charge of seventy-five cents (twenty-five for children).

Later that evening, Desi threw a wedding party at El Morocco, the East Side celebrity hangout famous for its exotic decor of white palm trees and zebra-striped banquettes. The dress code was strictly formal; the guest list of the couple's New York friends and business associates included Brenda Frazier and Peter Arno, a partially revived Lorenz Hart with Richard Rodgers, George Abbott, Dick Kollmar and columnist-wife Dorothy Kilgallen, and RKO president George Schaefer. Desi wisely skipped extending invitations to Polly Adler and associates.

When Lucy and Desi walked in, the band broke into "The Wedding March," and the couple danced to "I Love You Truly." The party music also included the complete score from *Too Many Girls,* plus songs from Desi's act and Lucy's movies.

It was a delightful but exhausting occasion. Lucy and Desi didn't get back to her suite at the Pierre until six in the morning, fully twenty-four hours from the time they left for Greenwich. They'd consumed so much champagne that they went straight to bed after an argument that would be repeated all their married life. Lucy liked fresh air, Desi didn't. She'd open a window, he'd close it.

This time Lucy prevailed. Desi just wanted to get to sleep. It might be Sunday, but he still had four shows to do at the Roxy, starting at one o'clock that afternoon.

In the middle of their slumbers, Desi awoke with a terrible thirst. He slapped Lucy on the behind and asked her to fetch him some water. Half asleep, she groped her way into the bathroom, filled a glass with water, and brought it back to Desi.

"Here you are, sweetheart," she said, and fell right back to sleep.

Another hour passed and Lucy suddenly woke up, literally as well as figuratively. Shaking Desi, she shouted, "Hey, hey! Listen you. The next time you want a glass of water, get up and get it yourself. I just realized what you made me do."

While wiping the sleep from his eyes, Desi said, "I'm sorry, honey. I'll tell you what. From now on, just make sure there's a pitcher of water on my night table before I go to bed, because I get awful thirsty. And as long as we're awake, I might as well tell you to keep the goddam window closed. I just about froze to death when I had to get up to go to the can."

That little scene from Lucy and Desi's first day of married life eventually got recycled for an episode of *I Love Lucy*.

With RKO still footing the bill, Lucy stayed in New York for the balance of Desi's booking at the Roxy. While he was working, she kept busy promoting *Too Many Girls,* the studio's Thanksgiving holiday release. In Manhattan, Desi wound up competing with himself when the movie opened at nearby Loew's Criterion.

But it wasn't much of a contest. The Criterion was the typical grind house without a stage presentation. For the movie version of a hit Broadway musical to open there instead of at the Roxy or another of the big show palaces like Radio City Music Hall, the Paramount, Capitol, or Strand, indicated that RKO had a clinker on its hands.

Lukewarm press notices and disappointing grosses confirmed that. No one really hated the movie of *Too Many Girls,* but practically every critic compared it unfavorably to the stage production. George Abbott took most of the drubbing. The director's lack of experience behind the camera resulted in an eighty-five minute endurance test for those who admired the zip and inventiveness of his work on the stage.

Bosley Crowther, a most influential movie critic by dint of his byline in the *New York Times,* caused some distress when he praised Lucy's performance but panned Desi's. In what could be interpreted as an expression of Crowther's personal bias, he called Desi "a noisy, black-haired Latin whose face unfortunately lacks expression and whose performance is devoid of grace."

Desi wanted to punch Crowther in the nose, but he had the last laugh when RKO came up with a three-picture contract. While testing audience reactions to *Too Many Girls*, the studio found that most people picked Desi as their favorite in the cast, even though few seemed to know him by name. Comment cards variously described him as "the Mexican boy," "the Spanish actor," "the little Argentine fellow," "the Cuban guy," and "Dise Arnst."

The war raging in Europe and the Far East had caused Hollywood to lose about 40 percent of its foreign business. To gain access to the increasingly important Latin American market, RKO desperately needed to come up with some stars with native-born appeal. At the moment it had only one, scandal-pocked Lupe Velez, who dated back to the silent era and had been reduced to portraying the "Mexican Spitfire" in a series of B comedies.

Desi's contract for $10,000 per picture wouldn't make him rich, but it did seem to guarantee marital togetherness. Lucy was delighted that he'd be spending far less time on the road than they originally anticipated.

Rumors began circulating that Lucy had engineered the deal for exactly that reason, but that seems unlikely. "After Pandro Berman left the studio for MGM, the turnover of production executives was so rapid at RKO that Lucy never even had a chance to shake hands with most of them. Her movies were not box-office hits, so she had no clout in that way either. In fact, she was lucky to have a contract," publicist Perry Lieber recalled.

Lucy and Desi's honeymoon amounted to the cross-country rail trip back to Los Angeles. It took five days to get there via two luxurious trains: the Twentieth Century Limited from New York to Chicago and the Santa Fe Super Chief the rest of the way. On each, the couple booked two adjacent bedrooms and opened the center partition to form a compartment. Every morning, at Desi's order, Lucy received a fresh bouquet of red and white carnations, her favorite flowers.

"For the entire trip we made love, we ate marvelous food, we rested, we had a wonderful time," Desi recalled. "I had my guitar with me, and for the first day and into the night, I kept strumming it and mumbling to myself. Lucy later told me that she got worried and thought I'd already tired of her. But I was just writing a song for her."

The song, entitled "My New World with You," plus the red and white carnations, became an annual ritual when Lucy and Desi reached their wedding anniversary.

Back in Hollywood, crystal gazers like columnist Sheilah Graham and radio commentator Jimmy Fidler were predicting that the marriage would last a month at the most. Desi's reputation as a playboy, plus the six-year age difference between bride and groom, seemed insurmountable obstacles.

Lucy and Desi tried to prove the gossipmongers wrong. In the rush to get married, there'd been small consideration of life *after* the ceremony, so finding a home became a matter of utmost concern.

Lucy, who often looked to her friend Carole Lombard Gable for inspiration, decided that something similar to the Gables' ranch in the San Fernando Valley would do very nicely. Having spent the happiest years of his youth on the family's country estates in Cuba, Desi couldn't have agreed more.

Unfortunately, the Arnazes were a long way from the upper income bracket of the Gables. While they shopped around for a bargain, they set up housekeeping in Lucy's Hollywood apartment, which immediately caused havoc with the neighbors. Desi loved to throw parties and surround himself with other musicians. The building rocked all night as everybody from Carmen Miranda and Ish Kabibble to Gene Krupa and Constantin Bakaleinikoff came to join the jam sessions.

Lucy and Desi followed up dozens of leads from real estate agents and newspaper ads, but nothing excited them until Jack Oakie advised them to check out a new development near his home in Chatsworth. The little community stood practically at the L.A. city limits, about ten miles from the House of the Two Gables in Encino, but it still qualified as part of the far-flung San Fernando Valley.

When builder William Sesnon took them on a guided tour, the couple knew instantly that they'd found their Shangri-la. Sesnon had created a batch of five-acre estates, each with a rambling ranch house in Colonial style, swimming pool, and an orange grove of several hundred trees. Although the development was all flatland, the views of the surrounding mountains and countryside were breathtaking because the area was so sparsely developed. Lucy and Desi couldn't believe their luck when Sesnon accepted their offer of a $1,500 down payment. He arranged a ten-year mortgage to pay off the $13,000 balance.

Before they could strike a deal, the couple still had to consult their business managers. Andy Hickox and Deke Magaziner said that Lucy and Desi could probably manage it if they put themselves on strict allowances to make sure that they were able to meet the mortgage payments.

"Okay, okay," they joyfully promised.

As soon as the legal papers were signed, the couple decided that they needed to put a name to their little patch of heaven. The goal, of course, was an equivalent of "Pickfair," the palatial Beverly Hills estate of Mary Pickford and Douglas Fairbanks, who were the acknowledged royals of Hollywood during the silent era.

With pad and pencil in hand, Lucy and Desi experimented with various combinations like "Arnaball," "Ballarnaz," "Lucydes," "Desicille," and "Ludesi." Nothing fully satisfied them until "Desilu." Without realizing it, they'd named not only a home but a future corporate empire as well.

8

War and Marriage

THE year 1941 was hardly the best time for Lucy and Desi to be starting married life. Day after day the war news grew more ominous. Staggering Axis victories in Europe, North Africa, and the Far East brought the conflict closer and closer to American shores. Although the United States had kept a neutral stance for two years, participation seemed not only inevitable but overdue.

Despite the gravity of the times, Lucy and Desi weren't quite ready to build a bomb shelter into their new home; they could barely keep up with the moving-in expenses. With considerable help from her mother and Lolita Arnaz, Lucy made all the curtains and drapes. Friends threw a shower and contributed kitchenware, silver, and linens. Milton Berle sent a case of toilet paper.

For bric-a-brac, Lucy started collecting china plates and old-fashioned oil lamps in thrift shops. She saved all sorts of glass bottles and hand-painted them to decorate the screened-in porch. Whenever she had money to spare, she bought secondhand equipment for a home beauty parlor. On weekends, she loved to give permanents, egg shampoos, facials, and manicures to her relatives and friends.

Lucy had never been much of a cook, but Desi taught her all his favorite Cuban dishes like *arroz con pollo* and black beans with *picadillo*. They started a vegetable garden and purchased a large incubator with a hundred fertilized eggs. Desi built a coop, and they soon had their first batch of baby chickens to fill it.

Alexander Hall gave them a pair of Holstein calves from his ranch, and Grandpa Hunt built a shed to house them. Lucy and Desi both loved animals. Before they knew it, they had six dogs and twenty-two cats running about the place.

Even the livestock had pet names. Lucy became so attached to them that whenever Desi wanted to kill any for food, she called him a murderous monster. He once bought a pig which he intended to fatten up and roast for Christmas in the Cuban tradition. But by holiday time, the pig was known as "Little Sancho" and they had the usual American store-bought turkey instead.

The Arnazes were now sufficiently celebrated as a couple for RKO to consider teaming them in a movie. While the story department tried to find a suitable co-starring vehicle, Lucy made *Look Who's Laughing,* and Desi did *Father Takes a Wife.*

Look Who's Laughing proved to be RKO's highest grossing release of the year next to Alfred Hitchcock's *Suspicion,* but Lucy's presence in the cast wasn't the reason. The movie brought together five immensely popular radio personalities: ventriloquist Edgar Bergen and monocled dummy Charlie McCarthy, Jim and Marian Jordan of *Fibber McGee and Molly* fame and Harold Peary of *The Great Gildersleeve.* In that pre-TV era, the public turned out in droves to see the celluloid embodiments of their favorite voices.

Desi never lived down *Father Takes a Wife,* an unintentionally distasteful bedroom farce teaming Gloria Swanson and Adolphe Menjou, relics of silent movies, as expectant parents. In a supporting role as an operatic tenor named Carlos Bardez, Desi was supposed to sing "Perfidia," but his voice proved unsuited to the classical orchestration and had to be dubbed. For years after, he received letters from fans in Spanish-speaking countries asking why he suddenly lapsed into singing with an Italian accent.

It became clear that Desi's thick Cuban accent and lack of acting experience were going to limit his progress as a movie star. The studio enrolled him in elocution classes, and Lucy started coaching him at home, but it was hopeless.

In his next movie, a B musical entitled *Four Jacks and a Jill,* Desi played an immigrant taxicab driver masquerading as a South American king in exile. Critics said his only believable moments were when he performed "The Boogie Woogie Conga."

Lucy, meanwhile, encountered career problems of her own when the latest RKO management commissioned George Gallup's American Institute of Public Opinion to poll the popularity of the studio's stars. Lucy scored badly: 40 percent of the people polled said that they'd never seen a Lucille Ball movie, only 33 percent could recognize her when shown a photograph.

"It is apparent that so far as the great majority of theatergoers are concerned, Lucille Ball is still a more or less unknown quantity," Gallup said in his report. "My personal opinion is that she is going to be grievously handicapped by her age. She is already older than 65 percent of the theatergoing public (exclusive of children under twelve). Our findings have shown that, as a general rule, theatergoers prefer actresses of their own age."

If Lucy really was over the hill at age thirty, she put up a hard fight when RKO tried to cut a third of her $1,500-a-week salary. The financially strapped studio finally backed down after Lucy's agent, Arthur Lyons, claimed breach of contract and threatened to sue for a million dollars. Still, it appeared certain that Lucy's days at RKO were numbered.

Just for spite, production head Harry Edington assigned Lucy to *Valley of the Sun*, RKO's most expensive western (at $650,000) since its 1931 Oscar winner *Cimarron*. Her role as a frontier cafe owner not only wasted Lucy's talent but also subjected her to six weeks of punishing location work near Taos, New Mexico, in 110-degree heat.

Since RKO seemed to be taking its time choosing Desi's next movie, he tagged along to keep Lucy company, or so he claimed. The real reason was to make sure that she didn't get too chummy with leading man James Craig, a rugged six-footer whose stock in trade was his resemblance to Clark Gable. Desi made such a nuisance of himself that director George Marshall banned him from the set. To keep busy, Desi gave free conga lessons to several hundred full-blooded Indians who were working as extras.

Just as *Valley of the Sun* neared completion, an atypical and unexpected rainstorm turned the desert terrain to sludge and caused a week's delay while the production unit moved to a new site near Santa Fe. Lucy started feeling unwell and called for a doctor, who discovered that she was pregnant.

The Arnazes were ecstatic as they headed back to Los Angeles, but Lucy suffered a miscarriage several weeks later. Distraught, she concluded that she'd never be able to have a child.

Desi reacted similarly. "You've got to remember that Desi was the last man in his family. It was up to him to carry on the Arnaz name, so this was a bitter disappointment, but not the end of the world. He and Lucy promised each other to keep on trying. What else could they do?" said a close friend.

Gloom set in at Desilu, intensified by Desi's stalemated movie career. RKO kept interest alive by announcing plans to cast him in a musical with Ginger Rogers and in a Caribbean swashbuckler with Maureen O'Hara, but nothing materialized.

It was a touchy situation, but one often faced by Hollywood couples. Although Lucy wasn't in the major league, she still had star status and Desi didn't. Raised to believe in male dominance, he couldn't cope with being less successful than his wife. Thankfully, Lucy wasn't the type to lord it over him, or the marriage would have been finished.

But a crisis developed one night when the Arnazes donned their fanciest formal clothes to attend a premiere at the Pantages Theatre, that monument to Art Deco at the famous intersection of Hollywood and Vine. Desi spent the entire afternoon waxing and polishing his Buick convertible so that they'd make a terrific impression when they drove up to the festive klieg-lighted affair.

And indeed they did, except that when the Arnazes were getting ready to leave, Desi overheard an usher putting in a call for "Lucille Ball's car, please!" For the Buick's true owner, it was the final indignity. Desi managed to contain his rage until they'd driven less than a block. Then he screamed at Lucy, "That does it. I'm leaving this goddam town and getting a job!"

Nothing that Lucy said could dissuade him, least of all recalling gossip queen Louella Parsons's recent prediction that he'd be the greatest Latin matinee idol since Rudolph Valentino. Desi knew it was all bullshit, planted by the RKO publicity department.

The next morning, Desi instructed his agent to find work for a reorganized band. Since the musicians were all in New York and Desi also had a track record there that he didn't have in Los Angeles, the first bookings would have to be away from home. Lucy had various work commitments that prevented her from accompanying Desi, so it would be the first big test of the marriage.

As soon as Desi left town, the soothsayers who'd been predicting divorce started to crow. Maybe the couple had lasted more than a month, but they had yet to celebrate their first wedding anniversary. Lucy and Desi thought they knew better and tried to ignore the rumors.

To keep up the mortgage payments, Lucy was earning extra money by making guest appearances on various radio shows at seventy-five or a hundred dollars a shot. Listeners often heard her trading quips with crooner Rudy Vallee, comedian Phil Baker, or Edgar Bergen and Charlie McCarthy on *The Chase and Sanborn Hour*. She also played

dramatic parts on *Lux Radio Theatre* and *Screen Guild Playhouse,*
which specialized in condensed versions of recent or vintage movies.

At RKO, Lucy was anxiously waiting for production to begin on
The Big Street, a Damon Runyon fable of Broadway tinhorns that
would mark the humorist's debut as a movie producer. Runyon originally wanted Carole Lombard for his leading lady, but after Lombard
read the script she said that the role of a nasty gold-digging nightclub
singer was better suited to Lucille Ball. Lucy took her idol's recommendation as a great compliment, but it also may have been a dig at
her tough persona.

The leading male character was Little Pinks, a restaurant busboy
who secretly adores the singer. RKO had acquired the property as a
vehicle for its great character star Charles Laughton. But when Laughton began to have doubts that he could play such a meek and mild
character, RKO arranged to "loan" him to 20th Century–Fox in
exchange for Henry Fonda.

Because of all those machinations, *The Big Street* seemed to be
taking forever to begin shooting, but Lucy was determined to be in
the movie. She thought the role was the best that RKO had yet offered
her, the one that could finally mean a breakthrough into the big
league.

Meanwhile, Desi and his band had opened at the Rumba Casino,
yet another new Manhattan nightclub designed to capitalize on the
craze for Latin music. At the end of the run, he accepted an invitation
from the State Department to join a delegation of movie stars and
entertainers being sent to Mexico City to promote President Roosevelt's Good Neighbor Policy. Funded by the Rockefeller Foundation,
the project had a dual purpose: to foster goodwill so that the Latin
American countries stayed allied with the United States in case it
went to war against the Axis powers, and to increase trade for American companies that had lost so much of their business in Europe and
Asia.

Lucy was furious over not being invited to accompany Desi on the
three-day junket. But she simply didn't belong in the same category as
the big stars who went—Clark Gable, Robert Taylor, Norma Shearer,
Lana Turner, James Cagney, Hedy Lamarr, and Bing Crosby, to name
just a few—whereas Desi could at least speak the language and report
back to the State Department on Mexican reactions to the visit.

How much information Desi picked up for the State Department is
unknown, but when he wasn't making personal appearances at six or
seven theaters a day, he kept busy with the women. "Desi and Mickey

Rooney seemed to be in a contest to see who could score the most," columnist Earl Wilson recalled. "Mickey went after the big names, including Norma Shearer, who was old enough to be his mother. Desi seemed to prefer the local talent, especially if they were blondes."

By the time Lucy got wind of Desi's philandering, he was back in New York headlining the vaudeville bill at Loew's State. The long-distance telephone lines sizzled as Lucy phoned her husband three or four times a day just to berate him and then hang up before he had a chance to reply. Desi would ring Lucy back, scream at her, and also hang up.

Since those verbal battles were juicier than any radio programs of the time, the switchboard operators at Desi's hotel usually listened in. One night, the fighting was so vicious that Lucy, who usually called Desi back within minutes, gave up in disgust and went to bed.

The hotel operator on duty at the time was so accustomed to the frequency of the couple's calls that the silence alarmed her and she took it upon herself to phone Lucy.

"Why haven't you called Desi back?" the operator asked. "He's in his room feeling miserable. He didn't mean any of the things he said, and I'm sure you didn't either, so why don't you call him back and make it up with him? He's just a baby."

Lucy broke up laughing and couldn't get back to Desi fast enough to tell him what the operator said. Harmony was restored, at least temporarily.

The Arnazes didn't know how long their work would separate them. But a sudden opportunity to be together occurred when RKO suspended Lucy without pay for refusing to be loaned to 20th Century—Fox for *Footlight Serenade*.

Lucy's refusal to make the musical was understandable. Pride and jealousy prevented her from playing a supporting role to longtime rival Betty Grable, who was not only well on her way to becoming Hollywood's top box-office star, but also Desi's ex-girlfriend. Furthermore, working in *Footlight Serenade* would almost certainly cost Lucy that coveted role in *The Big Street*, which now seemed likely to be shooting at the same time.

While on RKO's suspended list, Lucy flew to New York to be with Desi and to make sure that he wasn't misbehaving. By this time, he was starring in *Havana Fiesta*, a revue produced for the so-called subway circuit of vaudeville theaters in Brooklyn, the Bronx, and Queens. Performances ran continuously from noon to midnight; admission was twenty cents until 1 P.M., sixty cents thereafter.

While it might have seemed that Desi's career had reached rock bottom, it was more indicative of a problem that most entertainers faced if they wanted steady employment in the live entertainment field. After you'd played a major club such as Rumba Casino and a Broadway theater like Loew's State, there had to be a cooling-off period before the bookers would want you back again. Even then you were expected to come in with fresh material or even a whole new act so that the customers who'd seen you the last time wouldn't feel cheated.

While Lucy and Desi were dining at Sardi's one night, they ran into Sidney Piermont, the head booking agent for the Loew's circuit. Piermont had a sudden brainstorm and asked them if they'd be interested in teaming up. He offered them a definite date at Loew's State on Broadway, plus a tour of Loew's theaters in other cities.

Lucy and Desi stayed up all night considering Piermont's proposal. Working on stage was radically different from appearing in a movie, where all sorts of technical trickery could hide Lucy's deficiencies as a song-and-dance performer. What could she do in front of a live audience besides just stand there and look gorgeous?

Still, the idea had merit. Neither saw themselves becoming a permanent team like George Burns and Gracie Allen or Blossom Seeley and Benny Fields. Lucy had no more desire to stop making movies than Desi did entertaining, but if they teamed up occasionally it could mean extra income and fewer separations. The latter was a big inducement to Lucy in her determination to keep Desi from straying.

Whatever the outcome, it was a professional challenge that the couple couldn't afford to pass up. They immediately started planning an act which, fortunately for inexperienced Lucy, did not require a marathon effort. Sharing the bill with four other acts, the Arnazes would be on stage for maybe fifteen minutes of an hour show presented between screenings of a feature movie.

To save on hotel bills, Lucy and Desi had arranged to stay in the penthouse apartment of some wealthy friends who were vacationing in Palm Beach. The couple had lots of space to rehearse their vaudeville act, but for the better part of December 7, 1941, they stayed glued to the radio as news dribbled in about a Japanese attack on American ships near Honolulu, Hawaii.

By the next day, "Pearl Harbor" was a name that would live in infamy; the United States had finally entered a war that was already 827 days old and threatening disaster for the Allied side. Lucy and Desi reacted no differently than many other Americans. They panicked. In the Arnazes' case, fear included their home and relatives back in Los Angeles. Rumors were rampant that the Japanese would soon attempt a sneak attack somewhere along the West Coast.

Although they had a contract to open at Loew's State on January 1, nothing could stop Lucy and Desi from making a quick trip west by plane to batten down the hatches. On their first night back at Desilu, Chatsworth had an air-raid drill. The area was so rustic that wardens patrolled on horseback rather than by foot.

The couple hired an elderly handyman as resident caretaker, since Lucy would need someone about the place once Desi got drafted into military service. At twenty-four and in perfect health, that seemed inevitable. The only question was whether he would serve for Cuba or the United States. He'd already applied for U.S. citizenship but had yet to receive his final papers.

Christmas became a sad occasion that year. As the war news grew worse, Lucy and Desi wondered if it might be the last they would ever celebrate. The Japanese had taken Hong Kong and Wake Island. Nazi bombers continued to raid London and other British cities.

Back in New York, *Smilin' Through* happened to be the title of the Jeanette MacDonald–Brian Aherne movie playing at Loew's State when Lucy and Desi unveiled their vaudeville act. Those two words pretty well summed up the positive, upbeat attitude that people needed to have in wartime, and the couple tried their best to encourage it with their music and funmaking.

Desi cleverly chose the routines so that Lucy's croaky vocalizing was kept to a minimum. Wearing a tuxedo throughout, he opened the act with "Spic and Spanish" (from *Too Many Girls*) and Carmen Miranda's famous "South American Way." Lucy then made a grand entrance in a white evening gown, and the couple sang and danced to "You and I."

While Lucy scooted off for a costume change, Desi pounded his conga drums and sang "Babalu," which over the years became his trademark and most requested number. Lucy returned in a garish satin dress to join him for a duet of "Cuban Pete." Special rhymed lyrics soon revealed her to be "Sally Sweet, the Queen of Delancey Street." The couple always left the audience howling for more when Lucy mimicked Desi's swivel-hipped "Chick, chicky boom" and did an outrageous bump that knocked the straw hat off his head.

Although Loew's State was much smaller than the Roxy or Radio City Music Hall, its 3,450 seats still held a lot of people, and Lucy often suffered stage fright during the week-long engagement. During one show, she had such a bad experience that she thought her vaudeville career would be one of the shortest on record.

In the midst of the "You and I" duet, she fell out of step with Desi and became so nervous that she forgot the words to the song. Overcome by embarrassment, she ran off the stage into the wings. The moment she got there, she realized that unless she went straight back on, she'd be licked forever.

To the amazement of Desi, the orchestra, and everybody in the audience, Lucy walked to the front of the stage and announced, "Ladies and gentlemen, this has never happened before, and it will never happen again. With your permission, I won't leave this stage until I do this song and dance right."

And without waiting for an answer, she proceeded to do it on the next try. "People were so amused that there was an avalanche of applause when I got through," Lucy recalled. "But believe me, it taught me the importance of preparation and rehearsals. I never wanted to be caught short like that again."

For the week of Lucy and Desi's run, Loew's State grossed $27,129 (at ninety-five cents a seat tops), which *Variety* described as "good but not great" business for the New Year's holiday period. That probably wasn't Lucy and Desi's fault. The screen attraction, *Smilin' Through,* was a so-called moveover that had already played two weeks on its own at the Capitol Theatre.

Because of the world situation and sudden movie commitments, Lucy and Desi had to put their act in mothballs. RKO had finally set a starting date for *The Big Street* to speed Henry Fonda's intended enlistment in the Navy. The studio also had plans to put Desi into uniform, but only for a supporting role in a patriotic flag-waver entitled *The Navy Comes Through.*

In the short time that the Arnazes were away, fantasy-prone Hollywood had awakened to the realities of war. Security was beefed up at every studio to protect against sabotage. Japanese employees were dismissed, portions of soundstages were being converted to bomb shelters. RKO suddenly became the safest place to work. "They haven't had a hit in fifteen years," Bob Hope quipped.

Everybody was rushing to do something for the war effort. Lucy accepted Rosalind Russell's call to join the Women's Emergency Corps. Desi entertained at benefits for the Red Cross and British War Relief. Both pledged their services to the Hollywood Victory Committee, which coordinated talent for bond rallies, camp shows, and hospital tours.

On January 16, 1942, Lucy had one of the worst shocks of her life when she learned that Carole Lombard had been killed in a plane crash while returning from a tour in which she sold over $2 million in war bonds. Lucy tried reaching Clark Gable to offer condolences, but he'd already left for the accident site at Table Rock Mountain, near Las Vegas, Nevada.

According to Lucy, it was hardly the end to the friendship between the two women. Over the years, she claimed that Lombard often visited her in dreams and advised her on important matters.

Since Lombard had been instrumental in getting her the role in *The Big Street,* Lucy became determined to honor her friend's memory with the best performance she could muster. But the part of Gloria Lyons, a paranoiac shrew who's known as "Her Highness" and spends most of the film as a hopeless cripple in a wheelchair, seemed more suited to Bette Davis or Barbara Stanwyck than it did to Lucille Ball.

Lucy was so worried about the part that she might have given up if she hadn't sought help from Charles Laughton. Although he himself had quit the movie for a similar reason, he loved Leonard Spigelgass's script and had enough confidence in Lucy to believe that she could do justice to the part.

"My advice to you is to play it as written," Laughton told her. "This woman is the bitchiest bitch that ever was. Don't soften it. Play it truthfully."

Carole Lombard would have been proud of Lucy's riveting performance in *The Big Street.* At the movie's release, *Time* magazine's James Agee wrote that "Pretty Lucille Ball, who was born for the parts Ginger Rogers sweats over, tackles her 'emotional' role as if it were sirloin and she didn't care who was looking." *Life* said, "The girl can really act," while *Variety* called it "a superb performance." Louella Parsons predicted an Academy Award nomination (which never happened).

But Lucy hated making the movie. She received small help from the young director, Irving Reis, newly upgraded from the B programmer division. She had even less personal rapport with Henry Fonda than she did when they dated; he seemed to be taking himself even more seriously since winning an Oscar nomination for *The Grapes of Wrath.*

Desi also made a constant nuisance of himself by hanging around the set to make sure that Lucy and Fonda weren't having an affair. The closest he came to catching them at anything was Fonda showing some snapshots of his wife, Frances, and their two young children, Jane and Peter.

Lucy seldom visited Desi on the set of his movie. She had complete trust in her friend Jane Wyatt, who was the only woman in *The Navy Comes Through*. Lucy didn't see any romantic competition in Pat O'Brien, George Murphy, Jackie Cooper, ex-heavyweight boxing champ Max Baer, or any of the remaining forty-seven men in the cast, even if some of them were gay.

For the first time in his life, Desi was enacting a non-musical role, that of a Cuban sailor in the U.S. Merchant Marine. Based on a story by Borden Chase, the rabble-rousing fantasy was typical of wartime: the crew of a decrepit freighter turn it into an invincible supership that blasts Nazi bombers to smithereens and dispatches U-boats to the bottom of the Atlantic.

The Navy Comes Through was the last movie in Desi's three-picture contract with RKO. The studio decided to not exercise its option to extend the contract. In other words, he was fired.

"I knew I would be going into the service soon anyway, so it didn't bother me too much," Desi recalled. "Acting in movies was not as important to me as my music. For *Too Many Girls* plus the other three movies, I earned a total of $38,000. I could do much better than that playing nightclubs and theaters."

Desi's dismissal was part of a studio economy drive that threatened to affect Lucy as well. RKO faced receivership once again, this time due to the box-office failures of Orson Welles's *Citizen Kane* and *The Magnificent Ambersons,* plus the abandonment of two other costly projects that had been in preparation by Welles and documentarian Pare Lorentz. And though the company had prestigious distribution deals with Walt Disney and Samuel Goldwyn, the contracts were so favorable to the producers that RKO actually lost money releasing hits like *Dumbo* and *The Pride of the Yankees*.

Charles Koerner, previously head of RKO's theater division, took over as production chief. Koerner had a good understanding of what moviegoers wanted and knew that a star like Lucille Ball was expendable. She'd never been a box-office draw, and RKO had no roles for her that couldn't just as easily be played by actresses who got a fraction of her $1,500-a-week salary.

Direct from *The Big Street*, Lucy landed in *Seven Days' Leave*, a musical trifle for moviegoers seeking relief from wartime worries. The plot, which gave bachelor soldier Victor Mature only seven days to get married in order to qualify for a $100,000 inheritance, was merely an excuse for guest turns by the orchestras of Freddy Martin and Les Brown, singer Ginny Simms, Mexican bombshell Mapy Cortes, and personalities from the hit radio programs *The Great Gildersleeve, Truth or Consequences,* and *The Court of Missing Heirs.*

Unfortunately, *The Big Street* proved a box-office failure, so *Seven Days' Leave* became Lucy's swan song at RKO. Her contract would not be renewed. In the nearly eight years that she'd been with the studio, she'd appeared in no less than thirty-two movies!

"Charlie Koerner wished me luck elsewhere, but I didn't want to leave. They almost had to carry me out. They could have put me in D pictures and I wouldn't have cared, so long as I kept on working," Lucy said later.

With both halves of Desilu suddenly unemployed, steps had to be taken immediately if they didn't want to be evicted for failing to keep up the mortgage payments. The future seemed uncertain indeed.

9

Technicolor Jessie

LUCY sent Desi into a jealous rage when she signed a long-term contract with Metro-Goldwyn-Mayer on August 6, 1942, which just happened to be her thirty-first birthday. Desi's indignation wasn't over the deal itself, which aligned Lucy with Hollywood's leading studio, but over the way that she engineered it—with help from her ex-lover Pandro Berman.

Since joining MGM from RKO in 1940, Berman had produced hits like *Ziegfeld Girl* and *Honky Tonk* and become a trusted confidant of Louis B. Mayer, the movie world's acknowledged "Mogul of Moguls." Exactly how Lucy persuaded Berman to get MGM to hire her can only be guessed at, but it was probably not through a renewal of their affair.

"Lucy was so much in love with Desi that it would have been impossible for her to be unfaithful," a friend said. "But Pan Berman had a wife and two kids. A divorce suit could ruin him financially. Lucy may have threatened to reveal some secrets she knew about his relationship with another actress he brought with him from RKO."

Since MGM was renowned for a roster of "more stars than there are in heaven," gossipmongers wondered why the studio needed to add Lucille Ball to its female list when it already had so many bigger names, like Lana Turner, Judy Garland, Hedy Lamarr, Myrna Loy, Katharine Hepburn, and Joan Crawford.

An even bigger mystery was why MGM would choose Lucy to star in Cole Porter's *DuBarry Was a Lady,* which had been a huge hit on the stage for Ethel Merman. Certainly Lucille Ball lacked the talent to even understudy Ethel Merman, the undisputed queen of Broadway musicals.

Producer Arthur Freed credited the casting to Lucy's fine performance in a similar role as a nightclub singer in *The Big Street.* Freed didn't seem bothered by the fact that Lucy's vocalizing had been dubbed by Martha Mears, who wound up subbing for her again in *DuBarry Was a Lady.*

Incredibly, although Lucy had made forty-seven movies to date, *DuBarry* would be her first photographed in color. As part of MGM's publicity campaign to create "a new look for her new studio," hairstylist Sidney Guilaroff dictated that her tresses should be dyed "strawberry pink" because it matched "the fire of her soul."

"That explanation was ridiculous," Lucy recalled. "That particular shade of red was a happy color. It was good with my eyes and it gave me the right finishing touch before the cameras. It proved lucky for me, things finally began to happen in my career. Maybe I looked kinda strange in person, but I wasn't worried about that."

When Lucy checked into MGM, Louis B. Mayer assigned her the dressing room once occupied by Norma Shearer, the studio's First Lady during her marriage to production head Irving Thalberg. Mayer's gesture, while typical of the paternal interest that the fifty-seven-year-old mogul took in his studio "family," may also have been sexually motivated.

"L.B. knew how Lucy advanced herself at RKO via Pandro Berman," said a onetime aide. "It's very possible that he thought he could score points by pampering Lucy with that royal treatment that MGM was so famous for. L.B. tried it with many other actresses, so why not Lucy?"

Besides fanning Desi's jealous nature, Lucy's move to MGM came at a sensitive time in their marriage. Desi's self-esteem was at an all-time low because of the constant needling he took about his civilian status. Why wasn't he in uniform? Was he a draft dodger or a limp-wristed pansy?

Actually, while trying to enlist in the Navy, Desi discovered a legal technicality that prevented any branch of the armed forces from accepting him before he became a full-fledged U.S. citizen. He was eligible to be drafted, however, so his fate became a case of which document the post office delivered first—his citizenship papers or the proverbial "Greetings" from Uncle Sam.

In the meanwhile, Desi devoted most of his time to entertaining for the Hollywood Victory Committee. Lucy spent many sleepless nights worrying about her husband's activities while he traveled around the country in private trains loaded down with gorgeous stars and starlets. She longed to join Desi on those tours, but MGM wouldn't give her time off.

While working in behalf of the victory crusade, Desi had to pass up many professional offers. But in September 1942, he happily put in a week at Hollywood's El Capitan Theatre in *Ken Murray's Blackouts,* a slightly risqué variety show that always played to SRO crowds of furloughing GI's. In his guest-star slot, Desi performed several songs and then gave conga lessons to busty Marie Wilson, the revue's resident dumb blonde, and the chorus line of high-kicking grandmothers known as "The Hollywood Elderlovelies."

Without informing Desi, Lucy had started badgering Louis B. Mayer about signing her husband to a contract. Whether it was just to get Lucy off his back or to make her feel indebted to him, Mayer finally attended one of Desi's performances in *Blackouts* and was impressed enough to summon him to his office the next day.

During the meeting, Mayer praised Desi's talent and compared him to Busher, the pride of the mogul's stable of thoroughbred racehorses. "Busher looks very common when he's around the barn, but when they put a saddle on him, and he goes out on the track, you know he's a champion. The same thing happens to you when you hang that drum around your shoulder. Up to that point you're just another Mexican," Mayer said.

"Not Mexican, sir, Cuban."

"Well, one of those Latin fellows," Mayer continued. "I want to see what we can do with you around here." He pressed the intercom button and asked for Lana Turner to be sent in.

While Mayer directed the action, Desi had to sweep Lana Turner into his arms and kiss her passionately. After she left, Mayer made him repeat the scene with Judy Garland.

"What a sweet job. My bird really wanted to fly!" Desi recalled.

Mayer was sufficiently interested to offer Desi a contract starting at $500 a week. Since that happened to be $1,000 a week less than what Lucy received at MGM, Desi's pride was hurt, and he demanded more. Mayer, who felt he'd been overly generous to begin with, admired Desi's chutzpah and they settled for $650.

If keeping Desi close to home was Lucy's motive for getting him the MGM contract, then she must have been disappointed. The studio had no immediate assignment for her husband, so he took off with sneezy funnyman Billy Gilbert on a USO tour of American military bases in the Caribbean. The trip nearly cost Desi his life when he made a flying visit to his relatives in Santiago, Cuba, and the Navy plane got lost in thick fog. His childhood memories of the area ultimately saved the pilot from crashing into the sea.

During Desi's absence, Lucy tried to suppress her loneliness by concentrating on work, of which she suddenly had plenty. Before she'd even finished *DuBarry Was a Lady,* Arthur Freed picked her to replace the recently married, suddenly pregnant Lana Turner in *Best Foot Forward.* Lucy also was required to make a guest appearance in *Thousands Cheer,* MGM's first entry in Hollywood's wartime craze for glorified vaudeville revues with "all-star" casts. Her unexpected emergence as a musical comedy star caused *Life* magazine to christen her "Technicolor Tessie."

In light of the wartime shortage of color film, Lucy was extremely lucky to work in three consecutive Technicolor productions. She never looked more beautiful than in *DuBarry Was a Lady,* garbed in both streamlined contemporary fashions and the sumptuous eighteenth-century balloon skirts of Madame DuBarry. Her red hair was covered by a huge wig, champagne-colored and studded with jewels, for a forty-minute dream sequence in which she cavorted with Red Skelton as Louis XV and Gene Kelly as a revolutionary known as the "Black Arrow."

Lucy portrayed a publicity-seeking movie star similar to her erstwhile Annabel Allison in *Best Foot Forward,* a prep school musical similar to *Too Many Girls* (and also directed on Broadway by George Abbott). Arthur Freed selected a new singing double for Lucy in Gloria Grafton, but the voice still didn't seem to match the face in her only number, "You're Lucky." Most of Hugh Martin and Ralph Blane's songs, including the rousing "Buckle Down Winsocki," were given to June Allyson and/or Nancy Walker, MGM's new contractees from the New York stage.

In *Thousands Cheer,* Lucy joined Ann Sothern, Marsha Hunt, and Connie Gilchrist as candidate WAVEs awaiting medical examination by Frank Morgan, a lecherous barber posing as a Navy physician. The smutty five-minute sketch seemed out of place in the rousing military recruitment booster, which featured seventeen stars, including Judy Garland, Mickey Rooney, Eleanor Powell, Red Skelton, Lena Horne, Margaret O'Brien, Kathryn Grayson, Gene Kelly, and June Allyson.

Desi Arnaz would have fitted perfectly into the variety format of

Thousands Cheer, but Louis B. Mayer opted to use him in a dramatic role in *Bataan,* a tribute to the thousands of fighting men recently killed or taken prisoner in the worst defeat in U.S. military history.

In MGM's executive office, the mourning seemed to be mainly for the film's star, Robert Taylor, who was about to enlist in the Navy (more to escape domineering wife Barbara Stanwyck than out of patriotism, according to gossip). Taylor was MGM's top leading man after Clark Gable, who'd joined the Air Force following the death of Carole Lombard.

A close copy of John Ford's classic *The Lost Patrol, Bataan* was a stark tragedy in which thirteen men are picked off one by one by Japanese snipers, aircraft fire, or malaria. The characters covered a spectrum of American types, including Robert Walker as a scared kid from the Midwest, Lloyd Nolan as a wisecracking corporal, Barry Nelson as a son of Polish immigrants, the very Irish Thomas Mitchell as a Jew named Jake Feingold, and black baritone Kenneth Spencer as a grave-digging private with a hymn for each victim he buries.

Desi played the movie's token Hispanic, a jitterbugging Chicano named Felix Ramirez. As one of the last men to be killed, he had a longer role than most of the other actors and he played his deathbed scene to the hilt.

"I died slowly of malaria, shaking like hell," Desi remembered. "When we rehearsed the scene, I was inside a mosquito net while Robert Taylor was on the outside. There was no way I could make any impression in that setup, so I asked our director, Tay Garnett, if he could remove the net and let me improvise my dying speech instead of following the script. Bob Taylor said it was O.K. with him, so as I was about to die, I kind of went back to my childhood and recited the *Mea Culpa,* not in Spanish or English, but in Latin as I did it in Jesuit school."

Desi's death scene may not have been the noblest in the movie—commanding officer Robert Taylor digs his own grave and then uses it as a machine-gun nest while vainly blasting away at the enemy—but the performance won him his first acting award, a "Best of the Month" citation from *Photoplay* magazine.

Bataan was a box-office blockbuster, seemingly achieving its goal of fostering hope that the United States would eventually turn that bitter defeat into victory. "If it fails to work your Yankee doodle dander into a lather, then you're no true American," said columnist Walter Winchell.

A solid performance in a hit movie should have been Desi's breakthrough into movie stardom, but unfortunately World War II intervened. In May 1943, a month before the release of *Bataan,* he finally received his draft notice, which meant, as it did for all eligible men, dropping everything for at least two years of military service.

Lucy and Desi had been expecting it for so long that the only shock waves were over separation. "Lucy didn't seem too worried about Desi getting killed or wounded. There was a good chance that he'd be assigned to an entertainment unit rather than to combat duty. And while Lucy hated being parted from Desi, she thought that the service would keep him out of mischief and put a damper on his womanizing," a friend said.

Meanwhile, on the home front, which in this case wasn't far away, Lucy had problems of her own to contend with. The career of Technicolor Tessie suffered a definite setback when MGM assigned her to the black-and-white *Meet the People,* a patriotic variety show that smacked of the B's she made at RKO.

In it, Lucy portrayed yet another version of Annabel Allison, this time a snooty Broadway star who tries to prove she's a regular gal by working as a welder in a Delaware shipyard. The flimsy script, which used only the title of a topical stage revue of the time, showcased the musical and comedic talents of Dick Powell, Bert Lahr, June Allyson, Rags Ragland, Virginia O'Brien, the King Sisters, the Vaughn Monroe orchestra, and Spike Jones and His City Slickers.

After *Meet the People,* MGM seemed to lose interest in Lucy as a major performer. It would be more than six months before she got another assignment, and that would only be a token appearance in the mammoth $3.5 million *Ziegfeld Follies* project. It was rumored that Lucy's sudden fall from favor at MGM may also have been punishment for rebuffing the advances of either Louis B. Mayer or producer Arthur Freed.

While Lucy waited for another assignment, the studio kept her busy by constantly lending her to network radio programs in exchange for plugs for its latest movies. She acted or appeared as a guest on programs such as *Philip Morris Playhouse, Lady Esther Presents Orson Welles, Blue Ribbon Town, Burns and Allen,* and Bing Crosby's *Kraft Music Hall.*

With MGM's blessing, Lucy also pitched into the war effort as never before. She led scrap metal drives, raised funds for "Bundles for Bluejackets," promoted the "Knit a Sweater for the Boys in Service" campaign, and endorsed V-mail stationery. For a fan magazine photo layout that urged women to apply for essential civilian jobs, Lucy posed as a toll booth collector, cab driver, and gas station attendant.

But Lucy's greatest, if most unusual, contribution to World War II happened quite by accident. While driving home from the dentist after having several teeth filled, she suddenly heard noises coming from her mouth that sounded like Morse code.

As soon as she got back to Desilu, Lucy reported the incident to the police, who referred her to the FBI. An agent said that her new dental fillings might have acted as a receiver. Could she please take him to the exact location where she heard the noises?

The FBI started an immediate search of the area surrounding the spot that Lucy pointed to in Coldwater Canyon. Several hours later, investigators found a transmitter hidden in a tool shed. It turned out to belong to a Japanese gardener who was part of a spy ring operating up and down the Pacific Coast.

By this time, Desi had injured a knee during basic training and been classified for limited service, with a job at a special Army training camp for illiterates. Bizarre as it might seem, Desi taught reading and writing to young draftees who'd proved deficient in those skills in their entrance examinations. Before long, the commander asked him to organize some entertainment for the youths, most of whom felt lonely and isolated, having never been away from home before.

For once, being Mr. Lucille Ball had its compensations. "Thanks to Lucy, we put on the biggest shows anyplace around," Desi remembered. "Lucy just phoned people and told them they had to come. We had Ann Sheridan, June Allyson, Lana Turner, Tommy Dorsey and his orchestra, Mickey Rooney, Lena Horne, Martha Raye, and many more."

As word got around the Army circuit that such star-studded shows were being staged at an out-of-the-way camp for illiterates, the top brass decided that Desi's organizing ability could be used more effectively elsewhere. He was transferred to Birmingham Hospital, a major receiving center for casualties arriving from the South Pacific.

Lucy couldn't have been happier. Her husband's new base was located in the San Fernando Valley community of Van Nuys, only a few miles from Desilu. Unfortunately, proximity proved more of a problem than an advantage as time went on. Although 1944 would bring definite assurances of Allied victory in World War II, the year proved nearly disastrous for Lucy and Desi's marriage. For Lucy personally, it started on a sad note with the death of her beloved grandfather, Fred Hunt, on January 9.

A social crusader to the very end, Hunt spent many an evening on Sunset Boulevard lecturing streetwalkers about the evils of their profession and offering them five dollars to take the night off. For a while he even served as neighborhood air-raid warden, but the trouble was that Grandpa had a hernia. By the time he'd donned his double truss and gotten dressed, the all-clear had already sounded.

As they had once promised him, Lucy and her mother took Grandpa Hunt's remains back to Jamestown for burial. The funeral service was more like a merry wake as relatives and friends kept trying to top each other's stories about Fred Hunt's eccentricities, and everybody ended up laughing instead of crying.

Back in Hollywood again, Lucy had no job waiting, which depressed her to no end, because MGM increased production to an all-time high in 1944 in celebration of its twentieth anniversary. Esther Williams had *Bathing Beauty,* Lana Turner *Marriage Is a Private Affair,* Greer Garson *Mrs. Parkington,* Judy Garland *Meet Me in St. Louis,* Irene Dunne *The White Cliffs of Dover.* Lucy coveted playing a seductive harem dancer opposite Ronald Colman in *Kismet,* but the role went to Marlene Dietrich, a free-lancer not even under contract to the studio.

In April, Lucy finally had a morsel of work thrown at her when Arthur Freed and director Vincente Minnelli started filming *Ziegfeld Follies of 1944,* a spinoff of *The Great Ziegfeld,* MGM's classic 1936 biography. Since the legendary showman (played by William Powell) died in the first film, MGM brought him back as a heavenly angel to introduce a *Follies* more colossal than any he could have produced on a theater stage.

MGM's Technicolored *Follies* would be a fairly accurate reflection of the plotless annual revues of 1907–31, which mixed comedy sketches and solo turns by star performers with awe-inspiring production numbers featuring veritable legions of glorious Ziegfeld Girls. In the huge cast of MGM contractees like Fred Astaire, Judy Garland, Gene Kelly, Esther Williams, Lena Horne, Red Skelton, and Kathryn Grayson, the only authentic *Ziegfeld Follies* star was the original "funny girl," Fanny Brice.

Ironically, though Lucy was never considered good enough for a Ziegfeld show during her New York modeling days, she finally made it in 1944 as lead mannequin in Fred Astaire's opening song-and-dance number, "Bring on the Beautiful Girls." While the scene amounted to only four minutes of screen time, it took thirteen days to shoot, cost $130,000, and featured a revolving carousel with a dozen real horses and chorus girl riders.

Making her grand entrance seated sidesaddle on a white stallion (Silver of *Lone Ranger* fame), Lucy wore a long-sleeved silk and brocade gown, shocking pink in color and encrusted with glittering gems, with a matching headdress of 1,200 ostrich feathers. She proceeded to uncage an octet of ballerinas costumed as panthers in black sequins, lashing them into action with several cracks of her jewel-studded whip.

Lucy neither spoke nor sang, and it was a sheer waste of her talent, but she made a tremendous visual impact, to say the least. Unfortunately, the movie as a whole encountered so many production problems that the public did not see her in it for another two years, with the title suitably changed to "Ziegfeld Follies of 1946."

With so little work coming her way, it wasn't an easy time for Lucy as she tried to cope with feelings of resentment and rejection. Luckily, she had the security of a long-term contract that required MGM to pay her $2,500 a week for forty weeks a year (a studio calendar year), whether it had assignments for her or not.

With time on her hands, Lucy continued to help Desi in his job at Birmingham Hospital, where he'd now advanced to the rank of staff sergeant in the psychiatric division. He worked with so-called basket cases, combat veterans who were usually mentally disturbed as well as seriously wounded. Desi had to make sure that the patients had something to divert them from the moment they arrived from the Pacific war zone.

Birmingham Hospital was short on recreational facilities, so Lucy helped to raise funds that eventually paid for a swimming pool, bowling alley, and plush upholstered seats to replace the auditorium's backless benches. She persuaded Billy Wilkerson, publisher of the *Hollywood Reporter,* to print a similarly styled patients' newspaper, the *Birmingham Reporter,* with Desi as honorary editor in chief.

Lucy also unintentionally gave herself grounds for a divorce action by regularly providing Desi with scores of beautiful young starlets that she rounded up from MGM and other studios. The women doled out refreshments to the patients, assisted in bingo games, and served as dance partners at parties.

"When the boys were being loaded off a ship and you asked them if you could get them anything, the first thing they usually wanted was a glass of cold milk," Desi recalled. "We had trucks loaded with milk, and these gorgeous girls to pour it as the guys disembarked. Some would drink four quarts, one after another, before leaving for the hospital."

For fear of being court-martialed if he got caught, Desi had been avoiding getting too involved with the hospital nurses, but the constantly changing array of starlets became an irresistible temptation. Happily for him but not for Lucy, he also had considerable freedom of movement. With Desilu only fifteen minutes away, he had the commander's permission to go home on weekends as well as after work if he wasn't scheduled for night duty.

But "home" for Desi could just as easily be a hotel room or another woman's apartment. To make matters worse, he wasn't very discreet about his affairs. Gossip columnists often knew about them before Lucy did. She felt humiliated and ashamed.

To get back at Desi, Lucy started going out on public dates with other men, usually with younger actors from MGM like Peter Lawford and Scott McKay. According to her friend Ann Miller, Lucy also had a brief fling with a struggling free-lancer named Robert Mitchum. They met while Mitchum was working at MGM in a small part in *Thirty Seconds Over Tokyo*.

But Lucy's behavior apparently did not have the desired result of making Desi jealous and more attentive. In September 1944, two months before the couple were to celebrate their fourth wedding anniversary, she filed for divorce.

Lucy's official complaint charged "extreme mental cruelty," which was about as explicit as Hollywood stars could get about their marital problems in those circumspect times. Years later, however, she attributed the divorce to Desi's affairs with all those bingo helpers and milk girls.

"The worst thing about it was that it was *me* who supplied them to him," Lucy said.

10

Period of Adjustment

NOBODY timed it exactly, but Lucy and Desi's divorce couldn't have lasted more than half a day. "It was the shortest-lived interlocutory in the history of the California courts," Lucy recalled.

Friends believed that neither Lucy nor Desi wanted the divorce, that it was just another instance of their playing games with each other. "Lucy was putting Desi to the test. She believed that if he really loved her, he wouldn't let her go through with it," said Kay Vaughan, a close friend since their Goldwyn Girl days.

"Desi couldn't stomach the idea of a divorce," said Ken Morgan, a lifelong friend. "For all his philandering, Desi was a very devout Roman Catholic. This was a time when the Church forbade divorce under pain of excommunication."

Lucy put up a front of grim determination, refusing to talk to Desi except through lawyers. He had a legal advantage over her. While serving in the Army during wartime, he could ask for a postponement of the case until he received his discharge. To get Desi to agree to a speedy hearing, Lucy surrendered her right to collect alimony.

To demonstrate her seriousness, Lucy moved out of Desilu and rented a furnished apartment in Beverly Hills. On October 14, the day before she was scheduled to appear in court, Desi phoned to invite her to dinner that same night. Although he wasn't contesting the divorce, he wanted to talk to her about it without lawyers present. Lucy reluctantly agreed.

Obtaining a twenty-four-hour military pass, Desi put on his best dress uniform and took Lucy to Mocambo, the Sunset Strip nightclub famous for its surrealistic decor and dazzling aviary of live birds. "When Lucy and Desi walked in, everybody did a double take because their split-up had been in all the papers," said owner Charlie Morrison. "From the way they did the rumba together, you'd have thought they were newlyweds."

Afterward, the couple went back to Lucy's apartment for what turned out to be more than a nightcap. The next morning, "Lucy got up and started to get dressed," Desi recalled. "I asked her where she was going and she said 'I'm divorcing you this morning.' I thought she was crazy to be going through with it now, but she had her mind made up. She'd bought a new suit and a new hat and she didn't want to disappoint all the reporters who would be down there at the courthouse."

Before she left, Lucy kissed Desi on the cheek. "I won't say too many nasty things about you. I'll be back as soon as I can," she promised.

"Lucy had to have her day in court, if only to justify the $2,000 she'd spent on legal fees," said an MGM press agent who accompanied her. "I don't think it really bothered her that she'd come out of it looking like a complete idiot. This was the biggest shot she'd ever had at making the front pages."

During the fifteen-minute hearing, Lucy testified that Desi "spent too much money. When we argued about it, he became angry and went away. I never saw him for a week. That was a habit of his—going away whenever we had an argument. He always ran out on me rather than stay and talk the matter out. It left me a nervous wreck. I got no rest at night at all."

Once the divorce was granted, Lucy went straight back to Desi, who'd been keeping the bed warm for her. That immediately voided the interlocutory decree, which had a one-year waiting period before it became final. According to California law, if a couple reconciled within that time, the divorce was automatically canceled.

Life resumed as usual for the Arnazes. "Desi and I wanted a baby," Lucy recalled. "I believed in the notion that if you wished hard enough for something, it would happen, so I used to cut pictures of babies out of magazines and paste them in dimestore albums. Under each picture I'd scribble something like 'Hey, when are you going to have me around the house?' I wound up with a pile of scrapbooks but no baby."

The nearest thing to an addition to the family was the Duchess of Devonshire, the sole survivor of the pair of Holstein calves given to them when they moved into Desilu. The black-and-white cow, which now weighed 2,200 pounds, had fallen in love with Desi and often came mooing for him at the bedroom window in the middle of the night. She was probably the only one of Desi's many girlfriends that Lucy could find reason to laugh about.

Because of the wartime manpower shortage, the Arnazes couldn't find anyone to milk the Duchess on a regular basis. "She used to yell and scream all the time," Lucy recalled. "At five one morning, she jumped right through the barn window. We took her to a dairy farm and boarded her there. Before we knew it, the bill had run up to $1,500, so we gave her to them with our blessings."

Although Lucy and Desi had once hoped to put the ranch on a paying basis by selling eggs, it was threatening to put them in the poorhouse. With several hundred chickens to care for, production costs were averaging $4.50 per egg!

The patriotic couple also had an enormous victory garden, profuse with corn, artichokes, potatoes, carrots, and radishes. Dressed in a wide-brimmed sunhat and cotton coveralls, Lucy spent many hours tending it, but she would have preferred to be working in a movie.

With the help of her friend Katharine Hepburn, Lucy finally wangled a part that she thought suited her, even though it fell into the supporting category. The role was that of a wisecracking real estate agent in *Without Love*, written for Hepburn by Philip Barry following their tremendous success with *The Philadelphia Story*. Only a moderate hit on Broadway with Elliott Nugent in the male lead, the romantic comedy had been purchased by MGM at Hepburn's request for her third co-starring vehicle with Spencer Tracy. The two stars were fast becoming one of Hollywood's legendary couples, both on and off the screen.

Working in company with two such overpowering personalities as Hepburn and Tracy, Lucy was bound to get lost in the shuffle. But she delivered her sassy dialogue about the wartime housing shortage with gusto and received some of the best reviews of her career. Long-time admirer James Agee wrote in *The Nation*, "It is good to see Lucille Ball doing so well with the kind of role new to her." Newspaper critic Alton Cook said, "Every time Lucille Ball strolls in to drench the place with acid wit, it's a pleasure."

After *Without Love*, Lucy went jobless for several months, until MGM finally plunked her into a cameo in *Bud Abbott & Lou Cos-*

tello in Hollywood. The slapstick fat-and-skinny duo were America's number one box-office attraction, which was the reason they could demand their full names in the title.

At age thirty-four, Lucy seemed to have reached rock bottom in her career. Portraying none other than Lucille Ball herself, she exchanged a few wisecracks with Abbott & Costello as they created pandemonium throughout a movie factory that looked exactly like MGM (renamed "Marathon Studios" to protect its dignified image).

Lucy later calculated that during the years 1944–45, MGM actively employed her for a total of eleven weeks. For the rest of the time, she just collected her paychecks and wandered around the studio, which was large enough to get lost in. Covering 172 acres in Culver City, it had thirty soundstages, 147 ancillary buildings, a fully stocked zoo, woods and gardens, a large lake, and 4,000 regular employees.

Lucy loved to drop in on the many pals she had around the lot. She advised Judy Garland on her forthcoming wedding to Vincente Minnelli, consoled Lana Turner over the breakup of her short-lived marriage to Steve Crane, and played hopscotch with child actresses Margaret O'Brien and Elizabeth Taylor.

Lucy had a special place in her heart for Lionel Barrymore, eldest of the legendary acting siblings and long a widower confined to a wheelchair by crippling arthritis. When she knew Desi would be getting a weekend leave, she often brought Barrymore to stay with them at the ranch. One night he fell asleep while smoking and set the guest cottage ablaze. While Lucy manned the garden hose, Desi dashed in and rescued Barrymore, but several cats that were in the house with him got roasted alive.

At MGM, Lucy also became fast friends with two other seeming failures who would be major influences on her talent—comedian Buster Keaton and director Edward Sedgwick. One of the wealthiest and most revered stars during Hollywood's silent era, Keaton had fallen on hard times and now worked for MGM as a consultant at $100 a week, dreaming up visual gags for Red Skelton and Abbott and Costello. Sedgwick, a onetime vaudevillian who'd directed seven of Keaton's classic comedies, had a similar job.

"Buster and Eddie Sedgwick were the first people to really sit me down and teach me all about slapstick comedy and the importance of props," Lucy recalled. "They were masters at it, both were headliners on the stage when they were only tiny kids, believe it or not. Attention to detail, that's what it's all about. If I had to work with grapes, a loaf of bread, a cup of coffee, whatever, I had to test them first to know what I was eating or drinking, how hot or cold it was, how it got there, how it would ride on the tray."

Sedgwick had been aware of Lucy's potential for years, having first noticed her around the Samuel Goldwyn studio when both were working there in 1933. "I'd see her telling a story to a friend and watch her facial expressions change. She'd illustrate it with everything she had. Add to that the sheer glamour of her posturing in front of the camera and I knew she had it," he remembered.

On the MGM backlot, Keaton and Sedgwick shared a small office where they spent most of their time building fantastic machines similar to those drawn by Rube Goldberg, the legendary newspaper cartoonist. Keaton's "whole logical continuities of mad activity" were so brilliant that engineers came to study them, and magazines like *Scientific American* and *Popular Mechanics* ran articles about them.

Lucy landed on Louis B. Mayer's blacklist by helping Keaton and Sedgwick erect the "Venetian Blind Raiser." The sound of chimes introduced a one-minute explosion of events in which the window blinds flew up, a .32-caliber pistol fired a blank cartridge, an Edison phonograph played John Philip Sousa's "Hail to the Chief," and a large portrait of Louis B. Mayer shot up from behind the sofa on wires.

Needless to say, Mayer was deeply offended by the irreverence of it and ordered everything dismantled. Since Keaton and Sedgwick were already treated like outcasts, Lucy bore the brunt of Mayer's wrath, receiving no assignments for several months and then only through the intervention of another close friend on the lot.

In this case, Van Johnson truly owed Lucy a favor, since she and Desi had been instrumental in MGM signing him to a contract after he finished his chorus job in *Too Many Girls*. Shrewdly promoted as the typical "boy next door," freckle-faced Johnson hit a responsive chord with wartime audiences and now trailed only Bing Crosby as America's favorite male star.

At that stage in her tenure at MGM, Lucy had even less chance of becoming Van Johnson's leading lady than Lassie did. She had to settle for playing second banana to Esther Williams, the studio's current box-office queen.

The Technicolored *Easy to Wed* was a musical remake of 1936's *Libeled Lady*, with Johnson and Williams taking roles originally played by William Powell and Myrna Loy, and Lucy teamed with Keenan Wynn as replacements for Jean Harlow and Spencer Tracy. Apart from her skill as a champion swimmer ("Wet she's a star, dry she ain't," said Fanny Brice), Esther Williams had even less musical ability than Lucy. Between them, they kept the voice dubbers and dance coaches working overtime.

Since Lucy had always adored Jean Harlow, it was an opportunity to pay homage to her idol as well as to prove that a "dumb broad" could be played just as authoritatively by a hennaed redhead as by a peroxide blonde. Critics were unanimous in claiming that Lucy stole the movie in two hilarious scenes, one in which she learns how to imitate a duck's response to a drake's mating call, and the other in which she throws a temper tantrum worthy of Sarah Bernhardt.

While *Easy to Wed* was being filmed in the spring of 1945, a finish to World War II suddenly seemed possible as Nazi Germany surrendered to the Allied forces and Japan continued to suffer devastating losses. Lucy and Desi celebrated V-E (Victory in Europe) Day at the Hollywood Canteen, leading a conga line of military personnel and volunteer workers that snaked right out to the sidewalk and down the block on Cahuenga Boulevard.

On August 6, the American B-29 *Enola Gay* dropped the first atomic bomb on Hiroshima, leveling 90 percent of the city. Three days later, another nuclear blast devastated a third of Nagasaki. Never one to miss a golden opportunity, Louis B. Mayer announced plans for the first movie about the A-bomb, *The Beginning or the End*.

V-J (Victory over Japan) Day arrived on August 14 and World War II finally ended after nearly six years and 45 million deaths, most of them civilian. Lucy and Desi had real reason to be euphoric. The war caused them few sacrifices, and Desi's military service never took him more than fifty miles from home.

The war years barely altered the face of American show business, which had enjoyed a financial boom that showed every sign of continuing. Movies, radio, and the various forms of live entertainment were still the dominant factors, but changes were brewing. The U.S. Department of Justice had ordered all the major movie companies to dispose of their theater holdings and end their monopolistic practices. And with the lifting of wartime restrictions on the production of television receivers, manufacturers were predicting that 5 million sets would be in use by the end of the decade.

While millions of returning GIs and their families would be hard pressed for jobs and housing, the Arnazes had no such postwar adjustments to make. They were mainly concerned about the date of Desi's discharge from the Army, which was holding up some important career decisions for both of them.

Although he'd been off the payroll while in the service, Desi still had a contract with MGM. Thanks to several automatic increases, his salary rate had gone from $650 to $1,000 a week. Since he'd received fine reviews for his performance in *Bataan,* he had great hopes of finally achieving his dream of movie stardom.

Having become great friends with Esther Williams, Lucy believed she'd fixed it so that Desi could play the male lead in the bathing beauty's next movie, a Mexican extravaganza entitled *Fiesta.* Wacky as it might seem, Desi's role would be as Esther's twin brother; both are trained to become bullfighters like their famous father, but Desi's character prefers to be a composer-musician.

As soon as he received a definite date for his discharge from the Army, Desi visited MGM to meet with Jack Cummings, who, besides being the producer of *Fiesta,* just happened to be Louis B. Mayer's favorite nephew. Cummings had some bad news for Desi. He'd decided to cast the role with Ricardo Montalban, a promising Mexican actor whom MGM had just signed to a long-term contract. Cummings didn't specify that the deal was made as a favor to Montalban's sister-in-law, Loretta Young, but Desi found out anyway and got very upset.

"It was quite a heartbreaker for me," he said later. "I was sure I was a cinch to star in that film. I also worried about how many parts were going to come up for that type of lead. If MGM was that sold on Montalban, I was going to be there playing second fiddle and doing whatever parts they didn't want him to do. I guess it was out of sight, out of mind. I had been gone two and a half years and they had forgotten what they had hired me for—musical comedies."

Desi's experience was the proverbial last straw where MGM and both Arnazes were concerned. Lucy had become increasingly unhappy at the studio and decided to pack it in when her next assignment was *Two Smart People,* in which she and John Hodiak, MGM's second-string Gable, played rival sharpies in the art forgery racket. Made by MGM's B programmer unit, the comedy-drama was directed by the apprenticing Jules Dassin (who later went on to better movies like *Never on Sunday* and *Topkapi*).

Lucy encountered no resistance in severing her relationship with MGM. Her contract was due for review anyway, and the studio had no reason to renew it. She'd made nine movies during her three-year association, but after a good start with *DuBarry Was a Lady* and *Best Foot Forward,* she really became one star too many to fit into the production schedule. For the roles she was getting now, MGM could just as easily make do with actresses who earned a fraction of her $3,000 a week.

With no other studios rushing to sign her, Lucy had no choice but to become a free-lance, a status that lacked the security of a long-term contract but that promised to earn her bigger bucks. For example, making three independent pictures a year at $65,000 each (not an unreasonable goal or fee for 1945–46) was considerably more lucrative than appearing in the same number of movies at MGM for a yearly stipend of $120,000.

Desi found it less easy to leave MGM. He owed $30,000 to the Internal Revenue Service for back taxes, a debt that he had planned on settling from the $40,000 he stood to earn at MGM during the year that still remained on his contract. Furthermore, while in the Army, he'd borrowed $1,500 from MGM, which he promised to pay back at the rate of $100 per week when he resumed filmmaking.

Convinced that his future now rested in personal appearances and recordings rather than movies, Desi approached Milton Krasny, one of the head agents at General Artists Corporation, about forming a new orchestra with a different sound from other Latin American groups. "It would combine the pulsating Afro-Cuban beat of Machito with the lushness of Andre Kostelanetz," Desi said.

During the war years, the band business had seen phenomenal growth and success. GAC had no hesitation in advancing Desi $8,000 toward putting together a new aggregation. From that sum, he took $1,500 in cash and personally handed it to Benjamin Thau, MGM's business head, in settlement of his contract. He'd paid off his debt to the studio, but also lost $40,000 in guaranteed earnings. The IRS would just have to wait a bit longer.

The first warless year of the decade, 1946, loomed as a dangerous one for the Arnaz marriage. With Desi back on the personal appearance circuit, the couple had no chance of avoiding the separations and jealousies that had caused so many problems in the past.

In the space of two weeks, Desi assembled a twenty-two-piece orchestra that included trumpets, trombones, saxophones, clarinet, flute, violins, guitar, piano, bass, drums, bongos, maracas, and congas. Much to his jealous wife's displeasure, there were two vocalists besides Desi himself: jazz singer Amanda Lane and a Latino dynamo known as Dulcina.

In an audition, Desi's new group so impressed Herman Hover, the owner of Ciro's, that he booked the band in preference to Charlie Spivak's, one of the top crowd-pullers of the time. To glamorize the opening, Desi persuaded Hover to restore Ciro's first-night entry requirement of formal dress, which had been dropped during the war years.

Lucy pitched in to make the opening a success by personally phoning every star she knew and urging them to attend. Among those turning out were Errol Flynn, Lana Turner, Tyrone Power, Marlene Dietrich, Rita Hayworth, Orson Welles, Hedy Lamarr, Ann Sheridan, Alan Ladd, Judy Garland, Robert Taylor, and Barbara Stanwyck. Humphrey Bogart, who came with new wife, Lauren Bacall, surveyed the gorgeously groomed crowd and told Desi, "No wonder they all fuck each other."

Ciro's patrons always got their money's worth for the $9.95 deluxe dinner tab. Desi and the band played for an hour of dancing, then put on an hour show that ended with him and the entire contingent of musicians and singers in an explosive production number built around "Babalu."

The Desi Arnaz orchestra received rave reviews in the Hollywood trade papers and enjoyed a solid twelve-week run at Ciro's. Desi did two shows a night, six days a week, and Lucy was there practically all the time.

"Lucy didn't trust Desi out of her sight," said Ciro's owner Herman Hover. "She always sat ringside, practically on the stage. Desi pitched his songs straight to her. He couldn't avoid it."

One night, Lucy came in wearing a low-cut dress, which sent Desi into a jealous panic when he noticed the way men were ogling her. When he bawled her out later for showing too much cleavage, she told him "Just because you own the tree doesn't mean some other guy can't enjoy looking at the apples."

By this time, Lucy always wore a gold slave bracelet that her husband gave her with the following inscription inside: "My name is Lucille Ball Arnaz. If lost, return me to my master—Desi." Her attempts at control were less successful. After five years of marriage, Desi finally agreed to wear a wedding ring, but only out of sight on a gold chain around his neck.

Desi's success at Ciro's earned him an RCA Victor recording contract, a film offer from Universal Pictures, and an extensive road tour starting with the Copacabana in New York.

Produced in twelve days while Desi worked nights at Ciro's, the movie *Cuban Pete* took its title from one of the most popular songs in his repertoire. The black-and-white musical ran only sixty-one minutes, featuring Desi in four songs and the King Sisters and swing organist Ethel Smith in four additional numbers. The scant plot concerned a perfume company's efforts to sign Desi as star of its weekly radio program.

The advertising campaign for *Cuban Pete* promised that "He'll have you in a whirl with his torrid samba swirl." Desi received extravagant billing as "The Rhumba-Rhythm King!"

Although it was only a B programmer, *Cuban Pete* re-established Desi with the public after a long absence and also boosted sales of his first RCA record, a doublesider featuring "Babalu" and "Brazil." From the $10,000 that Universal paid him for the movie, $5,000 went straight to the Internal Revenue Service. He'd made a deal to pay them 50 percent of his income until his $30,000 debt was settled.

While everything seemed to be coming up roses for Desi, Lucy was headed for a nervous breakdown. "After Desi got out of the Army and started touring, I was living by myself at the ranch and feeling miserable. Lonely, no kids, just animals. Desi's life was another story. There were no idle moments for Desi. He didn't miss a trick," she recalled.

Part of Lucy's unhappiness stemmed from envy over Desi's career, which had started to look like it might eclipse hers. At age thirty-five and after thirteen years in movies, it seemed unlikely that Lucille Ball would ever be one of Hollywood's legendary names. At best she had a few more years of starring roles to look forward to before casting directors started considering her only for character parts.

In her new independent status, Lucy could no longer rely on a studio like MGM or RKO to regularly supply her with jobs. For her first free-lance assignment, she pulled another skeleton out of her closet and secured the female lead in *The Dark Corner,* a 20th Century–Fox release produced by Fred Kohlmar. The former executive assistant to Samuel Goldwyn had briefly been Lucy's lover when she worked as a Goldwyn Girl.

Fox intended *The Dark Corner* as a showcase for its new contractee, fifty-five-year-old Clifton Webb, the onetime Broadway revue star who created a sensation in his first major film role as the decadent Waldo Lydecker in *Laura.* Webb had a similarly villainous role here, with Lucy playing the acid-tongued secretary to private detective Mark Stevens.

The murder mystery marked Lucy's first appearance in a so-called *film noir.* It was far from her usual comedic romps, and she received harsh treatment from the director, Henry Hathaway, an ornery veteran of westerns and action-adventures.

"He was not a nice man," Lucy remembered. "I happened to be doing this romantic dramatic moment, when I was thrown completely off. Never in my life had I had trouble remembering lines, but I suddenly got stuck. I got a case of the nerves and I began to stutter.

"Hathaway started swearing at me in front of everyone, 'Are you drunk or something? What the hell kind of actress are you? Go back to your fucking dressing room until you know your lines.' That was the worst thing he could have done to me. I was trembling all over."

Lucy had to be taken home and put to bed. "I somehow managed to finish the movie, but after that I didn't leave the house for months, literally. I couldn't speak without stuttering. I was totally panicked, under a doctor's care. Desi was away, I was terribly lonely. It was not an easy time by anyone's standards," she said.

Happily, an agent named Kurt Frings came to Lucy's rescue. "Edward G. Robinson, a client of mine and a close friend of Lucy's, said she was having problems and asked me to pay her a call. She didn't have an agent at the time. Eddie thought that going back to work would be the best cure for what ailed her," Frings recalled.

Frings happened to be wearing a white suit on the day he drove over to Desilu. When he rang the doorbell, Lucy looked through a peephole and refused to admit him.

"In her confused state of mind, she must have thought I'd been sent to take her away to a sanatorium," Frings said. "I had to recite the names of all my clients and their phone numbers before she relaxed. She finally let me in when I mentioned Olivia de Havilland. It turned out that Lucy admired Olivia very much for the battles she'd fought with Jack Warner over actors' contractual rights."

A dynamic Prussian Jew who'd been lightweight boxing champion of Europe before fleeing the Nazi regime in 1935, Frings quickly won Lucy's confidence. Without too much additional persuading, he got another of his clients, director William Seiter, to hire her for a Universal comedy entitled *Lover Come Back* (unrelated to the later Doris Day–Rock Hudson movie).

Lucy had worked for Seiter previously, first in a walk-on in her very first RKO film, *Roberta,* and then with the Marx Brothers in *Room Service.* Oddly enough, he didn't remember her. "All these years later, he asked, 'Who is she?' He took me on only as a favor to Kurt Frings," she said.

As Lucy recollected: "I told Seiter about the stutter. Hell, he could tell himself. 'Wha-wha-wha-what do you want me to do, Mr. Seiter?' I asked him. He said he needed a week with me, hour after hour, day after day. He took me under his wing. He told me to just talk to him, to talk and talk. So every day I went to talk and talk. He saved me, and so did George Brent, who was my leading man."

A dashing lady-killer who'd been lusted after by practically every actress he'd starred with, including Bette Davis, Olivia de Havilland, and Ann Sheridan (to whom he was briefly married), Brent may have had an ulterior motive in befriending Lucy, but she was oblivious to it. Many years later, she met him at a party and thanked him for his aid and comfort.

"I said, 'George, I don't know if you realize how kind you were when I was broken down.' And he said, 'What are you talking about?' So I said *Lover Come Back*. And he said, 'Oh, yeah, I remember. You were beautiful. I just wanted to help out.' We never talked about it again," Lucy said.

Released in the summer of 1946, *Lover Come Back* may have restored Lucy's confidence in herself, but it did nothing to bolster her sagging career. The black-and-white bedroom farce, in which she and former ballerina Vera Zorina competed for George Brent's affections, played the bottom half of double bills, the fate of most Universal product of that time. At some theaters it even ended up in support of *Cuban Pete,* which did not improve the harmony in the Arnaz household.

The couple's relationship had again become largely dependent on the telephone cables. When Desi opened at the Copacabana, Lucy flew to New York for the opening and stayed two weeks, but such visits were rare and impractical.

Desi scored such a success that he was held over at the Copacabana, the top nightclub in America at the time (operated by showman Monte Proser but actually owned by a Mafia syndicate headed by Frank Costello and Lucky Luciano). With Peter Lind Hayes as the featured comedian, Desi packed them in for three shows a night at 8:30 P.M., midnight, and 2:30 A.M. The schedule was typical of Manhattan nightlife then, but as extinct today as the countless show spots themselves.

A highlight of every show were eight shapely legged Copa Girls, reputed to be "the most beautiful in the world." Needless to say, Desi got to know most of them intimately, and the Copa's publicity staff made certain that all the gossip columnists knew about it.

"Even though I was married, the press agents decided to keep building me up as a playboy and a ladies' man, which they considered would be good for business. I must confess that I did not discourage them," Desi recalled.

"Desi flirted with everybody he met," said comedian friend Joey Adams. "Spying a pretty woman, an absolute stranger, on the street, he'd sashay up and whisper, 'How'd you like to go on the road with me?' "

Desi's womanizing became so well known that it backfired on him one night while he was in the midst of singing his much requested version of "Tabu." A drunken patron, who'd been heckling him all evening, shouted "How many Copa Girls have you fucked so far?"

Desi pretended not to be bothered and continued with the song. But Monte Proser and the house bodyguards went after the man, and Proser broke his hand in the ensuing fracas. The offender, who turned out to be a Canadian multimillionaire, was beaten to a pulp, taken out to the street, and hurled head-first onto the floor of his waiting limousine.

When Lucy learned of the incident, she phoned Desi and demanded to know if he'd told the man how many Copa Girls he'd slept with. Desi berated her for accusing him of misbehavior based on remarks made by a drunk. "Hah!" she snapped and hung up.

Out of respect for Lucy's feelings, friends urged Desi to at least be more circumspect, but discretion and fidelity were not part of his nature. "I was an old-fashioned Latin, raised observing and believing in the classic double standard. Your wife is your wife and you want to know that you can trust her and be secure in that knowledge. Your fooling around can in no way affect your love for her. That relationship is sacred and a few peccadilloes mean nothing," he once said.

After closing at the Copa, Desi and the band started a national vaudeville tour at the 3,800-seat Chicago Theatre, the Windy City's foremost showplace. To keep peace in the family, Desi had hired Lucy's younger brother, Fred Ball, as road manager. Fred had orders from Lucy to keep the ladies away from Desi, but the best he could do was to divert a few into his own bed instead.

Before the war, Desi had worked in theaters on a salary basis, but now he had a fifty-fifty split with the management. He provided the stage show and they took care of the movie and the house operation. With his twenty-two piece unit, Desi had a "nut" of $5,000 a week, which meant that he could win or lose, depending on business. Although he wasn't sure if Middle America was ready for "Babalu," Desi was delighted when the first week's gross in Chicago was $65,000, out of which he personally pocketed $27,500.

"We had an even bigger gross the second week," he said. "We went on to break Tommy Dorsey's record at the Riverside Theatre in Milwaukee and tied it at the Orpheum in Omaha."

Of course there weren't enough big presentation houses around for Desi to play them fifty-two weeks a year, but between theaters, nightclubs, and recordings, he earned about $200,000 in 1946. Giving up that $40,000 MGM contract had been a wise choice after all.

In October 1946, Lucy engineered a deal that brought Desi back to Hollywood for a prolonged stay. While making a guest appearance on Bob Hope's weekly NBC radio program, she discovered that the Stan Kenton orchestra was going back on the road and relinquishing its spot as the show's resident band. Bombarding Hope with copies of Desi's rave reviews and *Variety*'s reports of his box-office successes, Lucy didn't let up until she got her husband the job. Although it meant Desi had to cancel or postpone some lucrative bookings, the national radio exposure, plus the opportunity for marital togetherness, seemed well worth the sacrifice.

In his rush to get to Los Angeles from Omaha to start the job, Desi nearly made Lucy a widow. The DC-3 airplane that he chartered for himself and the band turned out to be a decrepit cargo carrier for fruits and vegetables. After an hour in the air, one of the two engines failed, but the pilot managed to return to Omaha for emergency repairs.

Back in the air again, everything seemed normal until the pilot called Desi into the cockpit and confessed that he'd never flown farther west than Wyoming. While he thought he was headed in the right direction, he didn't know where he was supposed to land once he reached the vicinity of Los Angeles!

After saying a quick prayer, Desi took the vacant co-pilot's seat, donned the other pair of earphones, and helped the pilot make radio contact with the air traffic controllers at L.A. Airport, who finally brought the plane in safely.

By this time, Lucy hadn't worked in a movie for six months, but friends like Hope, Bing Crosby, Eddie Cantor, and Jack Carson often used her on their radio programs. Kurt Frings kept trying to get Lucy a studio deal similar to the ones she'd had at RKO and MGM, but there were no takers.

"Hollywood had a bad case of postwar jitters," Frings recalled. "The labor unions, which were subject to wage freezes during the war, were now demanding huge increases that would double the cost of production. That caused the studios to cut back, and B program movies were the first to feel the crunch. Lucy, unfortunately, had an identification with that sort of product, so it was rough finding jobs for her."

In November 1946, Frings managed to get two back-to-back assignments for Lucy through clients of his who also fled Europe during the Nazi era, director Douglas Sirk and the sibling producers Raymond and Robert Hakim.

The black-and-white United Artists whodunit entitled *Lured* was Lucy's first project outside the usual Hollywood glamour factories. Produced on a tight budget at a small rental lot, General Services Studios, the movie still managed to look expensive, thanks to a cast including George Sanders, Charles Coburn, Cedric Hardwicke, and Boris Karloff, plus Douglas Sirk's great visual style (which reached full bloom in the 1950s with Technicolor tearjerkers starring the likes of Rock Hudson, Jane Wyman, and Lana Turner).

For the umpteenth time, Lucy played a singing show girl (dubbed by Annette Warren), an American stranded in Victorian London when her play closes. After her roommate is murdered by a serial killer who meets his victims through ads in the lonely hearts columns, Lucy volunteers to be the bait in Scotland Yard's manhunt. Though the plot of *Lured* may seem timely today, 1947 audiences couldn't have cared less. Lucy had another flop to add to her list.

Her Husband's Affairs, produced by the Hakim brothers for Columbia Pictures release, promised to be more beneficial to Lucy's career. The spoof of the advertising business was written by Ben Hecht and Charles MacArthur, authors of the classic newspaper satire *The Front Page.* Lucy's co-star, Franchot Tone, was a suave and sophisticated farceur of the first rank. The young directing prodigy, S. Sylvan Simon, had been responsible for a slew of hit comedies starring Red Skelton and Abbott & Costello.

Incredibly, *Her Husband's Affairs* happened to be Lucy's sixtieth movie since arriving in Hollywood in 1933. No celebration of that fact was made at the time, because it would have made her seem like an old workhorse ready for the glue factory. The movie in itself was evidence of that.

Lucy and Franchot Tone portrayed a husband-wife team responsible for the marketing of a revolutionary shaving cream that removes men's beards without need of a razor. At least that's the claim of the inventor, who extracted the magical cream from embalming fluid. Actually it works in reverse, growing hair on bald heads and even Santa Claus whiskers on Lucy's lovely chin.

Hilarious though the idea might have seemed in concept, the unbridled slapstick seemed labored on the screen and pleased neither critics nor fans of screwball comedy. Columbia sneaked the movie into theaters at the bottom of the bill with *The Swordsman,* an equally brain-less swashbuckler with Larry Parks, star of *The Jolson Story,* as a Scottish Robin Hood in kilts.

Now based in Los Angeles for Bob Hope's radio program, Desi spent more time on the set of *Her Husband's Affairs* than any of Lucy's previous films. He didn't trust her around Franchot Tone, an ex-husband of Joan Crawford and a notorious womanizer who could have given Desi a few pointers.

"I doubt if anything of a passionate nature really took place be-tween Lucy and Franchot, but they sure put on a good show whenever Desi came around," said associate producer Raphael Hakim. "Know-ing Lucy, she probably put Franchot up to it to provoke Desi. It was her way of getting back at him for all the tomcatting he did."

Desi's job with Bob Hope had given Lucy another cause for con-cern. As the show's musical director, Desi had responsibility for au-ditioning candidates for the featured spot of female singer, which had been changing weekly since the departure of Hope's longtime associ-ate Frances Langford.

"I have no proof that Desi used his position of power like the proverbial casting couch, but a girl did stand a much better chance of getting on the show if she was gorgeous and stacked than if she had buck teeth and weighed 300 pounds," said an NBC executive.

Desi's association with Bob Hope gave him an education that even-tually proved invaluable in his career as a television mogul. He saw how Hope got involved in every aspect of the program, from casting to direction. Every show was a collaborative effort between Hope and a dozen writers who each wrote a full script. Hope would then take bits and pieces from the twelve scripts and paste them into a final version that ran thirty minutes, less commercials.

Although Desi later claimed that he learned the basics of comedy from watching Bob Hope perform, it must have taken years to sink in. Hope considered Desi so deficient as a funnyman that he made him stick to singing and leading the band.

"Every time Desi went to the mike, it was like an enchilada fell out of his mouth. He couldn't get a laugh," Hope recalled.

Desi's weekly radio broadcasts were stimulating sales of his record-ings, so RCA Victor released a batch of them in his first album, *Ba-balu.* In that pre-LP era, the collection of eight songs required four ten-inch shellac discs, which were breakable and packed for protec-tion in individual manila sleeves in a hardcover binder.

With his career going so well, Desi had his heart set on making another movie, but the closest he could get was one of Universal's two-reel *Name Band Musicals,* which theaters ran as fillers to boost attendance from the teenage set. In the fifteen-minute *Jitterumba,* Desi and the band performed three numbers on Universal's stock nightclub set. The finale found him dressed as a college professor in cap and gown, giving a rhythmic geography lesson to the tune of "Managua, Nicaragua," a novelty hit of the time.

Desi's working close to home really didn't improve marital harmony. Between radio commitments, recording sessions, and club dates at Ciro's and the Hollywood Palladium, he had little time to spend with Lucy. She worked during the day, while his jobs usually were at night.

"Most of the time, we would meet at the top of Coldwater Canyon about five-thirty in the morning as I was driving to the studio and Desi was returning to the ranch from one of his nightclub engagements. The same thing would happen in reverse about seven o'clock at night. That's married life?" Lucy wondered.

"If we were in a hurry," Desi recalled, "we just waved and honked our horns as we passed. If we had a few moments to spare, we'd park and sit in Lucy's car, talking and stealing a few kisses before we went on our separate ways again." When Lucy and Desi *were* together, their jealous and temperamental natures invariably led to battles over suspected infidelities and their conflicting careers.

"For all the arguing, fighting, and accusations, I'm convinced that we lasted through it because we had something extra-special going for us," Desi recalled. "We were very much in love, and when we had the time to be together, our sexual relationship was heavenly. Also, we had a good sense of humor. We were able to laugh at ourselves and at our sometimes absurd and stupid arguments."

Whenever hostilities became too overheated, Desi would stuff a few changes of clothes into a suitcase and move into a hotel room until peace could be restored. The hotel and laundry bills got to be astronomical, so the guest cottage in the backyard of Desilu was converted into the errant spouse's doghouse. Desi kept some of his clothes there to save having to pack a bag when Lucy kicked him out.

In June 1947, after a full season with Bob Hope, Desi resigned in order to resume touring with the band. The radio stint had served its purpose as a career booster, and he stood to earn much bigger money from personal appearances.

Lucy also decided to take to the road, not with Desi but on her own, and in a suprisingly different venture for her. With no movie work in sight, she signed a contract with theatrical producer Jules J. Leventhal to make a six-month national tour in Elmer Rice's *Dream Girl,* which had been a critically acclaimed smash on Broadway during the 1945–1946 season.

Lucy's salary was $2,000 a week, which for half a year's work amounted to far less than the $75,000 fee she could get for a movie that usually took about a month to six weeks to shoot. But Lucy thought it would be worth the monetary sacrifice if she could establish herself in the theater, if only to get Hollywood casting directors to take her more seriously and offer her better parts.

And at age thirty-six, it could be the equivalent of discovering the Fountain of Youth. Free from the merciless magnifying lens of the movie camera, a stage actress could figure on playing romantic leads well into her fifties if she kept trim and healthy.

Lucy had taken on an arduous assignment in *Dream Girl,* which was written by Elmer Rice as a showcase for his talented actress wife, Betty Field. The role of bookstore owner Georgina Allerton, who spends most of her time in romantic daydreams, was one of the most exacting parts in the modern theater, second only to Elizabeth Barrett in *The Barretts of Wimpole Street.* Critic Lewis Nichol said, "It pales Hamlet into polite insignificance."

While working in movies, Lucy had become accustomed to memorizing and shooting a page or two of dialogue a day, so the discipline required for the stage did not come easily. "They handed me 113 pages of lines and gave me ten days to learn them," she recalled. "I discovered that I had one minute per act off stage, and that was for costume changes. I asked myself, What if I have to go to the bathroom?

"I would have given up if I hadn't caught the flu. I had a high temperature while I was learning the lines and I think it helped. In my delirium, having to give a performance six nights a week, plus two matinees, no longer seemed impossible."

Paramount Pictures had purchased the screen rights to *Dream Girl* as a vehicle for the pyrotechnic Betty Hutton. Lucy's tour would be the public's last chance to see the play before the movie came out. Evenly divided between week-long engagements in big cities and one-nighters in smaller ones, the itinerary started on the East Coast in Princeton, New Jersey, and ended back home in Los Angeles.

Lucy and Desi's traveling schedules occasionally gave them a chance to be together. After finishing an engagement in Madison, Wisconsin, he flew to visit her in Detroit while the band drove on in their chartered bus to the next booking in Akron, Ohio. Desi intended to stay overnight with Lucy and then fly to Akron the next morning.

The Arnazes were enjoying their time together when a telephone call jolted them out of bed with some horrifying news. The driver of the band bus had fallen asleep at the wheel and collided with a truck outside Rolling Prairie, Indiana. There were no fatalities, but ten of the musicians were hospitalized with critical injuries. Concertmaster Charlie Harris, who'd been sitting in Desi's usual place, lost an eye and also suffered a broken arm and leg.

"If Lucy hadn't been in Detroit and I hadn't wanted to go and see her, I would have been in that seat. *Que sera, sera,*" Desi said later.

Chartering a plane, Desi rushed to the accident scene and found conditions to be even worse than he'd been told. The bus had ignited in flames after the collision; the occupants might have been burned to death if the driver of the truck hadn't rushed to their rescue. The bus's only exit door was jammed, so he took an axe and hacked a hole big enough for everybody to escape.

In the age-old tradition of "the show must go on," it certainly did for the Desi Arnaz orchestra in Akron, Ohio. All the musicians who hadn't landed in the hospital insisted on performing despite their bandages and plaster casts. And for the missing, General Artists Corporation sent temporary replacements loaned by the leaders of the Duke Ellington, Tommy Dorsey, and Xavier Cugat bands.

After Detroit and for the next couple of years, Lucy and Desi spent more time apart than together, which enriched the telephone company but not their relationship. "When we did meet, we always had a tempestuous time. We'd either make love like mad or fight like hell," Desi remembered.

Lucy was extremely jealous of Desi's two female vocalists. The Latin singer Dulcina had been with him from the beginning, but he kept replacing her American counterpart. Lucy believed it was because Dulcina satisfied Desi's sexual needs while the others proved less cooperative.

Desi and the band were booked into most of the big show palaces in the country, from the Paramount in New York's Times Square to the Orpheum in Seattle's Times Square. In between, they played nightclubs, dance halls, and state fairs.

Lucy, meanwhile, stuck it out with *Dream Girl,* mainly for the sake of the all-important booking at the Biltmore Theatre in Los Angeles, when she hoped to knock Hollywood out with her performance. For a time, it looked like she'd never make it.

"We were in Oregon and it was the Christmas season," Lucy recalled. "There was this terrible flu going around called 'Virus X.' Half the cast caught it and ended up in the hospital. Our producer ran out of money and wanted to cancel the rest of the tour. So I paid the hospital bills and some of the salaries out of my own pocket.

"I told everybody I'd get them to the Biltmore. 'All you have to do is cooperate. If I hear of anybody not getting enough rest or not taking care of themselves, I'll punch you.' Well, they all got well, and we opened at the Biltmore, and I got sick!"

Luckily, that happened several days after the opening night, so Lucy at least got the rave reviews she'd been gambling on. Edwin Schallert of the *Los Angeles Times* wrote that "Miss Ball is a striking presence in the footlight world. She has efficiency as a comedienne. She can tinge a scene delicately with pathos. She has special facility in dealing with sharp-edged repartee. She apparently never overdoes the sentimental side of a role."

During her first matinee at the Biltmore, Lucy started to feel the effects of Virus X herself. "I was delirious during the whole performance. I finally collapsed. I thought I would die and was wishing I would. I spent several days in the hospital without even knowing it," she said.

Lucy's understudy took over in *Dream Girl,* but by the time the star returned, permanent box-office damage had been done. "The publicity over my illness killed advance ticket sales. There was nothing in the till, so we had to close shortly after I went back," she said.

It would be many years before Lucy gave any more thought to a theatrical career, but she felt good about the experience. "You haven't really been in show business until you've been on the stage," she said at the time. "I know what it is now to do one-night stands, and to act before audiences that aren't show-wise, as well as those who are. I know what it is to experience poor houses in remote areas and big audiences in major centers. And I've learned how you have to modify and key everything that you do to the public you're playing for."

To celebrate her liberation from the grueling six-month tour, Lucy flew to New York for a brief reunion with Desi while he played the Zanzibar, a Broadway nightclub that competed with the Latin Quarter and Diamond Horseshoe for the out-of-town tourist trade.

Besides the usual hugs, kisses, and screaming matches, the visit resulted in Lucy making her first television appearance. More out of curiosity than anything else, she agreed to be a guest panelist on Dumont's *Charade Quiz,* hosted by Bill Slater. One of television's first game shows, the half-hour program featured celebrities acting out charades sent in by viewers (mainly from New York, Pittsburgh, and Washington, D.C., which was the extent of the Dumont Network at the time).

Lucy's appearance on *Charade Quiz* was something of a coup for the program's producers, because Hollywood guest stars were hard to get. All those under contract to the major studios were forbidden to appear on the infant medium, which the moguls were treating like an enemy until proven otherwise. As a free-lancer, Lucy didn't have to worry about such restrictions.

Nothing earth-shattering came from Lucy's TV debut, but it did make an impression on a certain CBS programming executive who happened to be watching. "Lucy was very spontaneous, very natural. She had the studio audience in hysterics," Harry Ackerman recalled. "I thought that CBS could do something with her, but I really had nothing specific in mind at the time."

Ironically, when Ackerman finally did come up with a project to offer Lucy, it was for radio rather than television.

11

TV Is the Thing

IN the annals of show business, 1948 will be remembered as the beginning of the television era (at least in the United States, which had a head start on the rest of the still war-scarred world). About 750,000 TV sets were installed in homes that year, almost quadrupling the 200,000 already in use and bringing the national total to nearly a million.

While those figures might seem meager for a country with a population of 130 million, most of the sets were concentrated in big cities, where it was easy to spot their potential for keeping people at home and emptying everything from theaters and nightclubs to sports arenas and bowling alleys. Once the technology reached the hinterlands, the fall-out effect on competing forms of entertainment promised to be catastrophic.

Besides the tremendous increase in TV sets, 1948 also brought scores of new stations, daytime as well as nighttime broadcasting, and the first major news and entertainment programs. If they didn't yet own sets themselves, millions flocked to their neighbors' homes, corner saloons, or store demonstrations to watch the presidential nominating conventions (Truman—Dewey), the World Series (Cleveland Indians—Boston Braves) and especially the medium's first big stars—kinetic Milton Berle, stonefaced Ed Sullivan, and homespun Arthur Godfrey.

How Lucille Ball and Desi Arnaz would fit into all this was uncertain, but it didn't take too much brainwork for them to realize that sooner or later there'd be a place for them in a medium that had an insatiable need for actors and entertainers. With that in mind, they formed Desilu Productions, to coordinate all their activities in movies, radio, television, personal appearances, and recordings.

Lest it seem that the Arnazes and their business advisers had uncanny foresight, such companies were actually becoming a necessity among free-lance performers for money-saving reasons. The word "Productions" was simply a Hollywood requisite that looked impressive on a letterhead but did not necessarily mean that the company would ever actually produce anything beyond a tax shelter.

Nineteen forty-eight was also the year that the Hollywood studios first began to feel the impact of television on theater box offices. Although weekly attendance figures had held steady at an all-time high of 90 million people since the end of World War II, they would drop to 70 million within the year and to 60 million by the end of the decade.

When Lucy finished touring with *Dream Girl,* she found an industry dramatically changed from the one she left six months before. Financially troubled for years, RKO had been taken over by eccentric tycoon Howard Hughes. MGM was seeking a new production head to replace moldering Louis B. Mayer. The death of innovative director David Wark Griffith in abject poverty seemed to signify an official end to the great Hollywood epoch that started in 1916 with his colossal production of *Intolerance.*

Lucy hadn't made a movie in more than a year. The last one, *Her Husband's Affairs,* had been a flop, so agent Kurt Frings was encountering great resistance to her $75,000 fee. Finally, Lucy herself begged another favor from Bob Hope, asking him to request her for his leading lady in his next Paramount project, *Sorrowful Jones.* Hope and occasional teammate Bing Crosby were the leading male box-office stars of the time. Paramount wanted to keep him happy, so Lucy got the part, which had been intended for Rhonda Fleming, the studio's own redheaded contractee.

Sorrowful Jones marked Lucy's return to Damon Runyonland, but this time her role as a nightclub singer had more humor and tenderness than her role in *The Big Street. Sorrowful Jones* was a remake of *Little Miss Marker,* the 1934 Runyon fable that turned six-year-old Shirley Temple into the box-office darling of the Depression era. Mary Jane Saunders had the role this time, with Hope and Lucy (Adolphe Menjou and Dorothy Dell originally) as the racetrack bookie and lady friend who find themselves stuck with the child when her father leaves her as an IOU for a gambling debt.

Although Hope and Ball never received the acclaim of Tracy and Hepburn or even Hope and Crosby, *Sorrowful Jones* would hardly be their last teaming. Melville Shavelson, one of the film's scriptwriters, thought the two stars were perfectly matched and brought out the best in each other.

"Bob had such an effortless style that Lucy realized she'd have to pull out every stop to grab the audience's attention. He was very aware of what she was trying to do, so they were constantly testing each other. Both had split-second timing and their rapid-fire exchanges were a joy to watch and to listen to," Shavelson said.

During the filming of *Sorrowful Jones*, Lucy received a proposal from the Columbia Broadcasting System to star in a weekly radio series entitled *Our Miss Brooks*. When she read the pilot outline, she thought that the title role of a sarcastic, worldly-wise high school teacher was much better suited to her friend Eve Arden. The network promptly took Lucy's advice and hired Arden instead, but programming executive Harry Ackerman soon offered Lucy another project that proved more to her liking.

While it might seem strange that CBS would be commissioning new radio programs at a time when the medium seemed about to be swallowed up by television, there was a method to the madness.

"Bill Paley, the head of CBS, saw it as a quick and inexpensive way to create television programming," said Harry Ackerman. "It was similar to a pre-Broadway tryout. If a show was successful on the radio, we could easily transfer it to television. If it flopped, we wouldn't lose much. One of the beauties of radio was that you didn't have to spend money on sets, costumes, or scenery changes. The listener supplied all that in his imagination."

From the beginnings of big-time radio in 1925, the really top comedy stars had almost always been men. Following Milton Berle's lead, most of the great radio comedians who were still active moved over to television, starting with Jack Benny, Red Skelton, Edgar Bergen, and Ed Wynn.

William Paley wanted some female comedians on television as well, but they first had to prove themselves on radio. That was another reason why CBS-Radio suddenly started programs like *Our Miss Brooks* and *My Friend Irma* (with Marie Wilson). Until that time, the leading radio comediennes could be counted on one hand: Fanny Brice, Gracie Allen, Joan Davis, Judy Canova, and Cass Daley.

Radio comedy in general evolved directly out of vaudeville, night-clubs, and Broadway revues (and not out of movies, which at that time were silent). Radio's first comedy shows usually had a variety format built around stars like Eddie Cantor, Ed Wynn, Jack Pearl, or Jimmy Durante performing their stand-up routines in front of a microphone.

When listeners began to tire of that approach, dramatized or so-called situation comedy came into vogue, sometimes with stars like Jack Benny and Burns and Allen portraying fictionalized counterparts of themselves, but more often built around invented characters such as Fanny Brice's Baby Snooks. Over the years, the most popular radio sitcoms included *Amos 'n' Andy, The Goldbergs, Lum and Abner, Fibber McGee and Molly, The Adventures of Ozzie and Harriet,* and *The Life of Riley.*

Lucille Ball's contribution to radio's twilight years would be *My Favorite Husband,* adapted from Isabel Scott Rorick's novel *Mr. & Mrs. Cugat.* The lighthearted story of young banker George Cugat and his scatterbrained wife, Liz, had already been the basis for a flop 1942 Paramount movie, *Are Husbands Necessary?* (ironically, with original *Dream Girl* Betty Field in the role now being taken by Lucy).

My Favorite Husband went on the air July 5, 1948, as a sustaining (unsponsored) one-shot filler for *Our Miss Brooks,* which had its premiere delayed a week because of script problems. Both programs fell into the category of summer replacements, which meant that CBS probably wouldn't add them to the regular schedule if they failed to attract a sizable audience.

Suave movie and stage actor Lee Bowman portrayed Lucy's husband on the first program, which went over so well that CBS decided to turn it into a continuing series in another time slot starting two weeks later. Meanwhile, some major changes were needed: Lee Bowman had other commitments, while scriptwriters Frank Fox and William Davenport had an exclusive contract for the Ozzie Nelson–Harriet Hilliard series in the fall.

Richard Denning, a once-promising movie star whose career never recovered from his being miscast as a jungle Tarzan opposite Dorothy Lamour in *Beyond the Blue Horizon,* took over as George Cugat. Two young CBS staff writers named Madelyn Pugh and Bob Carroll Jr. saw an opportunity for themselves and wrote a script on specula-tion that not only won them a permanent assignment on *My Favorite Husband,* but also a lifelong association with Lucille Ball.

When *My Favorite Husband* resumed on July 23, *Variety* called it "the sleeper of the summer season. It's a smart, adult comedy that never plays down to its audience. Lucille Ball's high spirits, good timing and arch delivery, and Richard Denning's slightly helpless foil make them a good team." General Foods decided to sponsor the program for the fall-winter season in behalf of its Jell-O dessert mix.

My Favorite Husband took up only a few hours a week for Lucy, including rehearsals, so she could easily work in movies simultaneously. During the summer of 1948, she returned to RKO for a one-picture assignment in *Easy Living,* a melodrama set in the world of professional football. To celebrate her homecoming after six years, the studio commissary introduced the one-dollar "Lucille Ball Special"—Salisbury steak, fried onions, and mashed potatoes with gravy.

Portraying the proverbial secretary with a heart of gold, Lucy took fourth billing in *Easy Living* to Victor Mature, Lizabeth Scott, and Sonny Tufts, which just about explains why the movie was one of the last projects initiated by Dore Schary before RKO's new owner, Howard Hughes, fired him as head of production. The film also proved the last of thirty-three that Lucy made for RKO during her career.

Between movies and radio, Lucy could not leave the Los Angeles area, which meant even fewer chances to be with her barnstorming husband. "It was awful," she recalled. "You can't conduct a marriage on the phone. You can't have *children* on the phone. We were in our eighth year, and we'd spent something like seven and a half of them apart."

Like everybody else in the nation, Desi could hear his wife on the radio for half an hour every Friday night, which sometimes was preferable to having a screaming match with her on the telephone. At least he got some laughs from the program.

But after two months on the air, *My Favorite Husband* failed to sell enough Jell-O to satisfy General Foods. CBS brought in Jess Oppenheimer, a writer-producer long associated with such stars as Jack Benny, Fanny Brice, and Edgar Bergen, to overhaul the program. Audience research indicated that it might be too sophisticated for listeners in the hinterlands.

Working closely with Madelyn Pugh and Bob Carroll, Oppenheimer quickly turned *My Favorite Husband* into a hit. To end confusion with a certain bandleading rival of Desi Arnaz's, the Cugats became the All-American Coopers, "two people who live together and like it." George was still a banker, but most of the plots focused around

Liz's misadventures in running their two-story white house at 321 Bundy Drive in "the bustling little suburb of Sheridan Falls."

In retrospect, it could be said that *My Favorite Husband* was *I Love Lucy* without the Spanish seasoning. All the main character types were in place, although they had been standard in many radio sitcoms for years. Besides the zany housewife and the harassed husband, there was an accomplice/confidant for each. Gale Gordon portrayed Rudolph Atterbury, George's short-tempered boss. Bea Benaderet played his wife, Iris, Liz's best friend.

My Favorite Husband taught CBS a valuable lesson about Lucille Ball. Like most comedians, she needed the feedback of a live audience to fully activate her talent. "When we first began rehearsing the show, I was appalled at Lucy's lack of energy," said network executive Harry Ackerman. "But on the night we started broadcasting with an audience in the studio, Lucy absolutely bloomed. She got so many laughs I had to cut four minutes out of the show while we were on the air."

Even with a studio audience, producer Jess Oppenheimer still found fault with Lucy's work. "She stuck behind the script. She didn't fully trust her instincts as a clown. I tried to encourage her to ham it up more, to allow a pause for the laughs I was sure she could get," he said.

Oppenheimer told Lucy that he was going to send her to school. "I got her a pass to one of Jack Benny's Sunday broadcasts. Jack was the master of the silent reaction, which he would hold sometimes for twenty seconds on *radio*. Lucy came back and said, 'I never realized what you can do with just a script and a microphone.' From then on, she became much more free, much more daring," Oppenheimer said.

The success of *My Favorite Husband* boosted Lucy's salary for the program to $3,500 a week and also caused the movie moguls to consider her in a new light. The star of a hit radio show had a built-in following of millions waiting to be tapped.

Lucy and agent Kurt Frings decided to gamble on an offer from Columbia Pictures of a three-picture contract at $85,000 apiece. "I might have gotten more money elsewhere, but it was a non-exclusive deal, which meant we had the freedom to accept other offers when they came along. Also, Columbia had a reputation for making pictures quickly and economically, so $85,000 for three or four weeks' work was not to be sneezed at," Frings recalled.

Lucy's friend S. Sylvan Simon had his own production unit within Columbia, which was another reason why she signed with the studio.

Recently frustrated in attempts to buy Red Skelton's contract from MGM, Simon envisioned starring Lucy in a series of slapstick comedies similar to the highly successful *The Fuller Brush Man*, which Skelton made for Simon at Columbia on a loan-out deal.

Lucy also hoped that Simon would be a buffer between her and studio chief Harry Cohn. Next to Louis B. Mayer, Cohn had the dubious distinction of being the most despised executive in Hollywood. Lucy had never forgiven him for firing her during those early starlet days when she desperately needed work. She could have the last laugh now, but she needed to stay on Cohn's good side, if only for her husband's sake.

"Lucy had been hocking me about getting Desi back into movies," Kurt Frings recalled. "While I was negotiating the Columbia deal, I told Harry Cohn that it would make Lucy very happy if he gave Desi a job. Harry choked on his cigar and told me where Lucy could stuff that suggestion.

"But Harry changed his mind after discussing the idea with Jonie Taps, the head of the music department. Jonie admired Desi very much and thought the studio had nothing to lose by hiring him for an inexpensive musical similar to *Cuban Pete*. Harry may have been an S.O.B. to work for, but he could recognize a good deal when one got dumped in his lap."

In February 1949, Lucy and Desi returned to full-time marriage when he suspended touring to accept Columbia's movie offer. Although it was only a short assignment, Desi hoped there would be more films to follow. He also dreamed of opening his own nightclub on the Sunset Strip, which would eliminate the need to spend so much time on the road.

There were days when the Arnazes could actually drive back and forth to work together, which hadn't been the case for six years. Production of their Columbia projects overlapped, but the two movies had little in common beyond the torch-bearing Lady Columbia trademark that would appear in the opening credits. Where Lucy and Desi were concerned, the biggest difference was in their compensation, $85,000 for her and $15,000 for him, which didn't sit too well with the latter.

Two years had passed since Lucy last worked for S. Sylvan Simon in *Her Husband's Affairs*. To make up for that fiasco, the producer gave Lucy a tailor-made script entitled *Miss Grant Takes Richmond*, in which she played a scatterbrained character similar to the one she did on radio, and had William Holden as leading man. Holden had not yet reached superstar status, but he was the nearest thing to a hot romantic idol that Lucy had been teamed with since before World War II.

Though the title suggested a Civil War epic, the contemporary comedy concerned secretary Ellen Grant's mad passion for boss Dick Richmond, a real estate agent whose office is a front for an illegal gambling operation. In her attempts to restore Holden to respectability, Lucy grapples with every slapstick device from exploding typewriters to runaway bulldozers.

Lucy happened to be seven years older than Holden in real life, but director Lloyd Bacon kept the close-up shots to a minimum, and the age difference was hardly noticeable. Holden tended to be a bit stolid in some of his performances, but he loosened up in Lucy's company and they made a delightful team.

Columbia's production philosophy stressed quantity over quality. Harry Cohn believed in releasing a new movie every week of the year. Out of the fifty-two, he was bound to have a few hits and the rest could turn a profit if their budgets were kept low enough. Made for $325,000, *Miss Grant Takes Richmond* was one of twelve A pictures on the studio's schedule in 1949.

The remaining forty were cheap bread-and-butter projects: westerns with Gene Autry, Randolph Scott, and Charles Starrett; additions to series like *Blondie, Boston Blackie,* and *The Lone Wolf;* and exploitation items such as *Air Hostess* and *Make Believe Ballroom* (based on the popular radio program).

Desi's movie, *Holiday in Havana,* which had a ten-day shooting schedule, belonged in the latter category. His $15,000 fee was the biggest single item in the $60,000 budget. The borrowed sets, costumes, and location footage already had been charged off to *We Were Strangers,* John Huston's recently completed John Garfield–Jennifer Jones melodrama about Cuban revolutionaries.

Holiday in Havana had an almost nonexistent plot about a music festival, with Desi as a bandleader named Carlos Estrada and starlet Mary Hatcher as his dancer sweetheart, Lolita Valdez. Desi wrote the title song and also performed five other numbers in the seventy-three-minute movie, including "Rumba Rumbero," "The Straw Hat Song," and "Made for Each Other." The director, Jean Yarbrough, had been hired away from Monogram's *Bowery Boy* series, so it's not surprising that the finished product marked an end to Desi's movie career for some years to come.

With no other studio offers in sight, Desi took his band back on the road again, though he tried to stay within commuting distance for the sake of marital harmony. Shuttling back and forth between month-long engagements at Ciro's in Los Angeles and the Palace Hotel in San Francisco, he earned top money and also managed to keep his wife very contented.

"Desi was starting to have a guilty conscience about spending so much time away from home," a friend said. "He was taking a lot of flak from marriage experts like Hedda Hopper and Louella Parsons, who both adored Lucy and thought she was being shamefully neglected."

Desi's parents also were pressuring him to give them some grand-children. Strict Roman Catholics (which nonetheless didn't stop them from getting divorced), they interpreted their son's barren marriage as God's punishment for getting wed in a civil ceremony outside the sanctity of the Church. In the eyes of the devoutly religious, Lucy and Desi had been living in sin all this time.

Exactly why the couple still were childless is a mystery, but it wasn't for lack of trying. Both claimed to have undergone medical tests that proved them capable of having children. Lucy had suffered at least two miscarriages so far. Could the difficulty be due to her alleged abortion as a teenager, or was it just bad luck?

In the spring of 1949, Desi literally got down on one knee and begged Lucy to remarry him in an official Catholic ceremony. "I thought that perhaps, after all the troubles we had in the past, this might prove to her that I really loved her very much, and that I wanted to anchor our marriage down in all ways," he recalled.

Overwhelmed by Desi's unexpected proposition, Lucy accepted on the spot. To prove her own determination to make the marriage work, she started taking religious instruction at a local church. She also promised Desi that any children they had would be raised in the Catholic faith.

The wedding took place at Our lady of the Valley Church in Chatsworth on June 19, 1949, nine years almost to the day from the couple's first meeting during the filming of *Too Many Girls*. Only relatives and close friends attended. Director Eddie Sedgwick, the Buster Keaton sidekick who'd become like a father to Lucy since their MGM days, gave the bride away. Ken Morgan, a press agent married to Lucy's cousin Cleo, was best man. Desi's mother served as matron of honor.

Father Michael Hurley performed the ceremony. Denied the traditional virgin-white finery, Lucy still looked a vision in a halo-like hat and an ankle-length cocktail dress with a spray of fresh flower buds and lilies-of-the-valley pinned to the waist. Desi wore a cream-colored suit with a white shirt and black tie.

"When I saw Lucy coming down the aisle, I got as much of a thrill as the first time we got married, perhaps even more," Desi remembered. "The church and all made it seem so much more real. Lucy looked lovely, with those big blue eyes looking straight at me."

Groucho Marx sent the couple a telegram: "What's new?" Not enough to warrant taking a honeymoon, although neither Lucy nor Desi had time for one anyway. They went right back to work the next day.

On both the marital and professional fronts, Lucy had plenty to smile about for a change. Despite the growing popularity of television, radio still had an enormous audience, and *My Favorite Husband* continued to register top ratings. And *Sorrowful Jones* did such big business—almost as much as Bob Hope's teaming with Jane Russell in *The Paleface*—that Paramount hired Lucy for another go with the ski-jump-nosed comedian.

The Technicolored *Fancy Pants* was based loosely on Leo McCarey's classic *Ruggles of Red Gap,* which starred Charles Laughton as a British butler working for a rich family in an American hick town and fluttery ZaSu Pitts as his spinster sweetheart. To suit the talents of Bob Hope and Lucille Ball, the characters became an unemployed actor impersonating a butler and a brazen heiress who consorts with outlaws. The slapstick western's hokey plot scarcely resembled the charming 1935 original, but provided enough laughs to keep Hope and Ball fans satisfied.

During the filming of *Fancy Pants,* Lucy discovered that she was pregnant again. Desi felt sure that God had rewarded them for getting remarried in the sanctity of the Church. They were devastated when Lucy had another miscarriage three months later. Doctors told them not to give up hope. But by this time, Lucy had turned thirty-eight. If she wanted to have a successful pregnancy, it would have made sense to take life easy for a while, but her career was going too well to even consider that.

In anticipation of moving *My Favorite Husband* to television, CBS began testing Lucy's potential in the medium by booking her as a guest star on some of its variety programs. On December 8, 1949, she made her debut on network TV in a comedy sketch on *Inside USA with Chevrolet,* a half-hour revue hosted by comedian Peter Lind Hayes and his wife, Mary Healy.

The Hayeses were close friends of the Arnazes, and Lucy envied their professional success as a couple. For her next TV guest shot, she insisted that Desi appear with her, hoping it might lead to CBS considering them for a program of their own.

Ed Wynn, the bespectacled and babyfaced comedian long revered as "The Perfect Fool," agreed to put them on his CBS show, which was the budding TV industry's first weekly variety hour to originate in Los Angeles rather than New York.

The first joint television appearance of Lucille Ball and Desi Arnaz took place on Ed Wynn's broadcast of December 24, 1949 (seen later on the East Coast via kinescope). The couple took bows together, but performed separately. Lucy portrayed vampish Theda Bara in Wynn's spoof of silent movie acting. Desi did his trademark "Cuban Cabby" song-and-dance routine where he tosses his straw hat in the air, catches it with one hand and then plunks it back down on his forehead.

As luck would have it, not too many people saw the program because of the Christmas holiday. It put an end to the couple's team aspirations temporarily, but not for long.

12

Not Without My Husband

BY the time the twentieth century reached midpoint in 1950, it was obvious that television would play as dominant a role in mass entertainment during the second half of the century as movies had during the first fifty years. TV's growth was even more spectacular in its rapidity. By the end of 1949, there were almost 4 million receivers in use and ninety-eight stations on the air nationally (in contrast to 1.2 million sets and forty-nine stations at the close of 1948). Manufacturers were predicting sales of at least 5 million sets in 1950.

Despite those developments, Hollywood was still basically a motion picture town. Out of loyalty to the 19,000 theaters that dotted the nation, all the major studios—MGM, Paramount, Warner Brothers, 20th Century–Fox, RKO, Columbia, Universal-International, and United Artists—regarded television as the enemy and refused to supply movies or to produce original programming for the rival medium. The TV industry had started in New York, drawing its talent from radio, the stage, and the other performing arts, and promised to remain based there for as long as Hollywood maintained its belligerent attitude.

Nineteen fifty would mark Lucille Ball's seventeenth year in movies. Despite the industry's grim financial prospects, the year looked like it might be her best yet. For the second film in Lucy's three-picture deal with Columbia, S. Sylvan Simon wanted her to star in *Born Yesterday*, a hit play by Garson Kanin that Harry Cohn purchased as a vehicle for Rita Hayworth before she fled to Europe to start married life as Princess Aly Khan.

Lucy seemed well suited for the role of scatterbrained Billie Dawn, certainly more so than Rita Hayworth, but Simon met with unyielding resistance from director George Cukor, who insisted on hiring Judy Holliday. Though an unknown quantity to movie audiences, Holliday had triumphed in the part on Broadway after Jean Arthur, the play's original star, quit during the tryout tour.

Instead of *Born Yesterday* (which eventually won Holliday an Oscar for her performance), Lucy had to settle for another of Simon's projects, *The Fuller Brush Girl*. It wasn't much of a consolation prize, but the role of a house-to-house peddler at least made full use of Lucy's talent for slapstick.

A spinoff of Red Skelton's *The Fuller Brush Man*, the movie had him re-creating the part in a brief cameo appearance. The male lead was Eddie Albert, quite a comedown from William Holden and a tipoff that Lucy had returned to B movieland (if indeed she ever left).

For the sake of her hilarious escapades, which ranged from being trapped in a rolling barrel to masquerading as a burlesque stripper, Lucy suffered more injuries than she did in all her previous movies combined. She sprained both wrists, displaced six vertebrae, pulled a leg muscle, caught a cold that developed into pneumonia, and was temporarily blinded.

"I was operating a telephone switchboard, and one of the gags was a wind machine hooked up to the board which squirted talcum powder out of the holes. One blast got me right in the eye. I didn't work until every speck was out, four days later," Lucy recalled.

In the midst of the filming, Lucy got into serious trouble with Harry Cohn when she disappeared for a week. *The Fuller Brush Girl* had such a tight schedule that director Lloyd Bacon could only shoot around Lucy for a couple of days. Harry Cohn was livid, since he still had to pay everyone while they sat around waiting for the star to return.

Although Columbia's publicity department managed to keep it out of the gossip columns at the time, Lucy had flown to San Francisco to break up an affair that her husband was having with a new singer in his band.

"Desi was appearing at the Palace Hotel," agent Kurt Frings recalled. "One of the musicians whom Lucy relied on for information told her about Desi and the girl, so she raced up there determined to catch them in the act. I don't think she did, but she and Desi had a terrible row that went on for several days before peace was restored."

When Lucy finally returned to work on *The Fuller Brush Girl,* publicist Herb Sterne couldn't resist asking her, "How was the weather in San Francisco?"

"Just great!" she smiled.

For nearly all ten years of the Arnaz marriage, they had yet to resolve the crucial problems of their disparate careers. There seemed no way of avoiding the troublesome separations except through consolidation. They thought that if they worked together as a team, perhaps they could settle down into a more "normal" life together as husband and wife. For that reason, it was hardly surprising that when CBS approached Lucy about transferring *My Favorite Husband* to television, she demanded that Desi be cast opposite her.

"Some of the executives back in New York thought Lucy had lost her marbles," Jess Oppenheimer recalled. "One of them said, 'Who would believe her married to a wop?' Of course he'd picked on the wrong nationality, but it didn't excuse his prejudice. Such discrimination was rampant not only in broadcasting but throughout show business at the time."

When told of the home-office reaction, Lucy said, "What do you mean nobody'll believe it? We *are* married!"

In anticipation of Lucy eventually coming to her senses, CBS assigned Madelyn Pugh and Bob Carroll to writing a half-hour pilot script. For the TV version of *My Favorite Husband,* the network intended to retain Richard Denning as Lucy's co-star. He had movie experience and was only three years younger than Lucy, an age difference that shouldn't be noticeable on the standard ten-inch screen of the time.

William Paley, who hoped to put *My Favorite Husband* on CBS's fall schedule, tried to talk Lucy out of Desi as leading man. "He's a bandleader, Lucille. He can't act. What'll we do with him?"

"Bill, I'm sorry," Lucy said. "I'm not going to go on the air unless it's with Desi. If I can't do a television show with him, I'm going to travel with him."

Lucy had to eat her words when Paley refused to give in. The Arnazes decided to revive their old vaudeville act to prove that the American public would accept them as a team. Their last booking had been at Loew's State in New York in January 1942, so some hard preparation was needed before they could hit the road again.

Friends pitched in to help. Madelyn Pugh and Bob Carroll contributed jokes and connecting patter. Buster Keaton and director Eddie Sedgwick advised on the slapstick routines. Pepito, a famous Spanish clown who had worked with Desi in nightclubs and with Lucy years ago in *Annabel Takes a Tour,* taught them two of his specialties involving trick props.

Taking about twenty minutes to perform, the act started with Desi singing several numbers and ended with the "Cuban Pete–Sally Sweet" duet they first did in 1942. The meat of the new material came in the midst of Desi's opening solo. Dressed in a shabby swallowtailed tuxedo and crushed fedora, Lucy came running down the theater aisle carrying a cello and demanding an audition with "Dizzy Arnazy."

When Desi brought her up on stage, Lucy created pandemonium in the band by displacing all the musicians while setting up her cello. Designed by Pepito, the instrument had a secret compartment from which Lucy proceeded to take a stool, a trumpet, a plumber's plunger, gloves, fake flowers, and, of course, a cello bow.

After the cello, Lucy played a xylophone-horns contraption like a trained seal in the circus. Barking hoarsely and flipping the overlong tails and sleeves of her tuxedo, she waddled on her stomach across the stage. For an encore, she did a belly slide worthy of a baseballer stealing home plate.

Desi's booking agent, General Artists Corporation, arranged the tour so that a true cross section of America could see the couple perform. Despite the competition from television, many of the big theaters presenting movies with stage shows were still operating, but deeply in the red in most cases.

First stop was June 2, 1950, at the Chicago Theatre, where the Arnazes shared the bill with *Love That Brute,* a Paul Douglas–Jean Peters comedy directed by Lucy's ex-lover Alexander Hall.

For the showbiz record, Lucy and Desi were reviewed in *Variety*'s "New Acts" department, where the critic raved about their "funny quips and terrific burlesque situations. They have the makings of one of the top vaude comedy teams. If the redheaded gal wants to slide on her tummy for five or six shows a day past this initial five-week tour, GAC should have no trouble lining up dates."

According to *Variety,* the Chicago Theater grossed $50,600 for the week's engagement, described as "sturdy" business for the 3,800-seat theater, which hadn't been doing well since the advent of television. The Arnazes apparently were the main crowd puller, since the movie *Love That Brute* was proving a box-office flop in solo bookings elsewhere around the nation.

From the Chicago Theatre, Lucy and Desi moved on to a two-week engagement at the much larger New York Roxy, where the screen attraction was a Richard Widmark–Gene Tierney melodrama entitled *Night and the City.*

Amazingly, despite plummeting attendance figures, New York still had five theaters *besides* the Roxy running stage shows with a feature movie. Lucy and Desi had live competition from Charlie Spivak's orchestra and singer Rose Murphy at the Capitol, a Cab Calloway revue at the Strand, comedian Jan Murray and singing film stars John Payne and Patricia Morison at the Paramount, nine acts of traditional vaudeville at the RKO Palace, and a pop-classical extravaganza at Radio City Music Hall.

Again because of the dud movie on the bill, Lucy and Desi received most of the credit for the Roxy grossing $69,000 the first week and $60,000 the second. *Variety* rated it "okay" business, noting that it was only half what Radio City Music Hall grossed in the same two weeks with the Spencer Tracy–Elizabeth Taylor comedy *Father of the Bride* heading the bill.

The Roxy, of course, had a sentimental attachment for the Arnazes. Practically ten years had passed since Desi brought Lucy on stage on their wedding day and the audience showered them with rice. This time the couple had another experience to remember. Lucy once again proved pregnant.

Curiously enough, Lucy and Desi first heard about it on the radio. While relaxing in their dressing room between shows on a Sunday night, they tuned in to columnist Walter Winchell's fifteen-minute newscast to catch up on the latest gossip.

Famous for his staccato delivery, Winchell opened with the expected "Good evening, Mr. and Mrs. North America and all the ships at sea" and surged into his first exclusive: "Flash! After ten years, Lucille Ball and Desi Arnaz are expecting a bundle from heaven!"

Desi shook his head in disbelief, but Lucy was overjoyed. "It's true! It's true!" she screamed. "If Winchell says so, it must be true!"

What happened once again demonstrated that Walter Winchell had the best spy network in the gossip trade. On the previous Friday, after feeling nauseated and run-down for several days, Lucy consulted a doctor. He couldn't find anything wrong but suspected that she might be pregnant. Lucy took a rabbit test which was sent to a medical laboratory for return on Monday morning. In the meantime, someone at the lab blabbed the positive result to a Winchell assistant who kept in daily contact with such places in hopes of scooping the competition.

The next day, Lucy confirmed Winchell's report to the *Daily News*'s Florabel Muir. "You can tell the world about it, but don't say child. We're hoping for twins—a boy for Desi and a girl for me," Lucy said.

To protect Lucy's health, Desi canceled plans to extend the vaudeville tour, but they still had to fulfill their remaining dates in Buffalo and Milwaukee to avoid being sued for breach of contract. The only change in the act was a minor cutback in Lucy's gymnastics.

When the five-week tour ended, Lucy and Desi were discouraged by the outcome. Audiences were highly enthusiastic, but the press gave scant attention to vaudeville presentations. The *Variety* rave was really all that they had to show CBS to prove that the public would accept them as a couple. Box-office grosses were above average, but hardly the record-shattering kind needed to convince CBS.

At best, the Arnazes had succeeded in establishing themselves as a team in the theater and nightclub field, a depressed industry threatening to become extinct. Although it still was Desi's bread and butter, the grueling work and travel had no appeal for Lucy, especially now that her dream of raising a family seemed possible.

During the flight back to Los Angeles from Milwaukee, Lucy became sick and went to bed as soon as the couple got home. Two days later, Desi rushed her to Cedars of Lebanon Hospital and the conclusion was the same as before. Another miscarriage.

This time, a despondent Lucy received little sympathy from the doctors, who read her the riot act for continuing the arduous vaudeville tour when she knew she was pregnant. She promised to take better care of herself in the future. What else could she do?

In an interview with Louella Parsons, Lucy said, "I'm going to concentrate on my radio program and avoid any movie projects that call for physical strain. I'll stick to quiet comedies or somber dramas. Nothing that will make me stand on my head or hang by my eyebrows from a chandelier."

Lucy didn't always practice what she preached. Although she did return to *My Favorite Husband* in September, agent Kurt Frings was also negotiating with Cecil B. DeMille for her to appear in *The Greatest Show on Earth*. DeMille wanted Lucy for the role of a circus performer whose specialty is sticking her head face-up under the raised hoof of a trained elephant!

"I thought she was nuts to even consider the offer. DeMille wouldn't permit doubles to be used, and she could be killed or seriously injured if anything went wrong," Kurt Frings said.

But Lucy couldn't be talked out of it. DeMille's *Samson and Delilah* had recently grossed $9 million, making it one of the biggest hits in movie history up to that time. His new epic, featuring an all-star cast *plus* the entire Ringling Brothers, Barnum & Bailey Circus, promised to be even more successful. Lucy had never been involved with such a prestigious movie in her entire career.

Meanwhile, she traveled back and forth to Palm Springs, where Desi and the band were in temporary residence at the newly opened Chi Chi Club, the desert resort's first big nightspot. CBS had seemingly given up on moving *My Favorite Husband* to television, so the couple had assigned TV agent Don Sharpe to find some other joint project for them in the medium. The Arnazes met with several writers to develop an idea for a series, but nothing jelled beyond what seemed a ripoff of a popular new CBS-TV series starring George Burns and Gracie Allen.

"The pilot script was about a successful orchestra leader, Desi Arnaz, and his movie star wife, Lucille Ball, and how a reporter and a photographer from *Life* magazine loused up their plans for a quiet wedding anniversary celebration. It was a very funny script, but not honest. I felt the television audience would not identify with this kind of couple," Desi recalled.

Agent Don Sharpe, meanwhile, finally aroused some interest in the Arnazes at NBC, mainly because of that network's bitter rivalry with CBS. During TV's formative years, the two dominated the airwaves, with the ABC, Dumont, and Mutual networks barely in the running.

William Paley had stolen some of NBC's biggest radio stars and programs, including Jack Benny, Edgar Bergen and *Amos 'n' Andy*, and put them on television, so NBC welcomed any chance to retaliate. Lucy had a major CBS radio program and obviously could succeed on television. As for Desi, his records were selling well for RCA, NBC's parent company, so why not give him a chance as well?

The possibility of losing Lucy to NBC forced Paley to reconsider his position. He asked West Coast programming head Harry Ackerman what could be done to keep Lucy at CBS short of teaming her with Desi, which Paley still adamantly opposed.

In Ackerman's opinion, the crux of this issue wasn't so much Lucy and Desi teaming up as it was their having work that would not separate them. "She wants him home every night. She wants a normal married life. She doesn't want him chasing around the country where he can get into trouble," Ackerman said.

Ackerman suggested hiring Desi for a weekly radio program. It would make Lucy happy by keeping Desi on the homefront, and it might also lessen her resistance to doing a TV show on her own when she saw that CBS had her best interests at heart. Paley agreed.

Whether or not Desi realized that CBS was just using him as a pawn to keep Lucy at the network, he rejected its offer of a musical quiz show entitled *Your Tropical Trip*. Desi would host the program and also perform with his band while contestants competed for a jackpot of a two-week vacation in some Latin American paradise.

A "sustaining" show of the type that networks put on to fill unsold commercial time, the low-budget program would be broadcast weekly on Sunday afternoons. "The money was much less than what I could earn playing theaters and clubs," Desi recalled. "By the time I paid for the band, the arrangements, and the copyists, I wouldn't have much left for myself."

In November, Lucy turned out to be pregnant again. With the couple's tenth wedding anniversary approaching, the news was the best present anyone could have given them.

Realizing it might well be her last chance to have a baby, Lucy swore to follow doctors' orders not to take any unnecessary risks. To help out in every way that he could, Desi decided to accept CBS's radio offer after all because it would keep him in Los Angeles. It would also finally give him time to supervise the building of a long-planned addition to their house, which included a nursery.

Unfortunately, Lucy's pregnancy meant that she would have to resign her dangerous role in *The Greatest Show on Earth*, which Cecil B. DeMille intended to start filming in January at Ringling Brothers' winter headquarters in Florida. But for the time being, she kept her condition secret. She still had hopes of making the remaining movie in her three-picture deal with Columbia Pictures before her pregnancy became too advanced.

Lucy's producer friend S. Sylvan Simon had suffered a nervous breakdown (he eventually committed suicide in May 1951), so she no longer had a champion at Columbia. "Now that Harry Cohn had Judy Holliday under contract, he thought he didn't need two comediennes on the lot," said agent Kurt Frings. 'The gentlemanly thing to do would have been to buy out Lucy's contract and to send her packing, but that wasn't Harry's style. He kept ignoring her, hoping to make her feel so miserable and unwanted that she'd wind up paying *him* $85,000 just to get the hell out of there."

Although she'd decided to not take the DeMille assignment, Lucy pretended to Cohn that she would. In asking Cohn to approve the deal, she was counting on him trying to block it by coming up with a project himself. Although Columbia had first call on Lucy's services, Cohn could only withhold permission for outside work if it conflicted with the studio's own plans for her.

Realizing that Lucy had him over a barrel, Cohn tried to outsmart her. "He sent me a script about the size of a small pamphlet called *The Magic Carpet*. As I read it, I became hysterical with laughter. It was what we called 'a lease breaker.' If the studio wanted you out of your contract, they sent you the worst piece of junk, expecting you to reject it. If you did, that automatically freed them from the commitment. In my case, I would have been out $85,000," Lucy recalled.

Produced by Sam Katzman, a specialist in serials and exploitation quickies, *The Magic Carpet* was quite a tradeoff for DeMille's $5 million *Greatest Show on Earth*. Though nominally the star, Lucy served only as femme fatale in an Arabian Nights tale about a mysterious vigilante known as "The Scarlet Falcon."

Advertised as offering "1,001 thrills and 1,001 delights," the movie marked Columbia's first use of Super Cinecolor, a cheap alternative to Technicolor that tended to make everyone but the camels in the cast look like they had jaundice. John Agar, the first but already ex-husband of Shirley Temple, and Patricia Medina, Harry Cohn's protégée of the moment, played the romantic leads, with future TV star Raymond Burr as the villain.

In her role as the bare-midriffed Princess Narah, Lucy spent most of the time posing seductively on a divan while harem slaves fed her grapes. "I quickly found that pregnancy made me expand like a balloon, but, of course, I couldn't tell anybody, not even the wardrobe girl who was trying to tuck me into my diaphanous trousers and jeweled breastplates," she remembered.

"I walked around all day trying not to breathe, and every night the wardrobe girl said, 'I simply don't know what's happening, Miss Ball. I let your things out last night myself.' And I said carelessly, 'Apparently you didn't let them out far enough. You're going to have to let them out some more.' "

As soon as she finished working in *The Magic Carpet*, Lucy couldn't get to a telephone fast enough to call Harry Cohn.

"Harry? This is Lucille Ball."

"What the hell do you want?"

"I just want you to be the first to know that Desi and I are going to have a baby."

"Why you bitch," Cohn replied. "You screwed me, didn't you? Why didn't you tell me before the picture?"

Needless to say, Lucy never worked for Harry Cohn again, but his reaction was mild compared to that of Cecil B. DeMille when she broke the news to him.

Since Cecil Blount DeMille was tantamount to God in Hollywood, Lucy decided to confront him personally in his office at Paramount Pictures. Taking Desi along for support, she hoped to put on a performance that would cause DeMille to remember her when it came to casting whatever movies he made after *The Greatest Show on Earth*.

As Lucy remembered it: "I went to see Mr. DeMille with tears streaming down my face. 'Why are you crying?' he asked, and I said, 'I've always wanted to work with you, and this may be the only opportunity I'll ever have, but I can't do your picture. I'm pregnant.' It was very sad. Even Mr. DeMille had tears in his eyes."

DeMille's mood changed after Lucy told him the story of how she had concealed her pregnancy from Harry Cohn so that she could collect her $85,000 and wind up her Columbia contract. Sensing that she might be one of those actresses who would make any sacrifice for the sake of her career, DeMille suggested that she undergo an abortion.

"Why don't you do something about it? You can always have another baby, but roles like this come along only once in a lifetime," DeMille said.

Had it been anyone other than Cecil B. DeMille, Desi would have pounced on him and beaten him to a pulp. But the couple just sat there in shocked disbelief until Lucy finally said, "You don't understand, Mr. DeMille. Desi and I have been praying for this for ten years. There will be other opportunities to work together, at least I hope so, but the baby is more important."

When Lucy went off to powder her nose before leaving, DeMille said to Desi, "Congratulations, Mr. Arnaz, you're the only man in history who screwed Lucille Ball, Columbia Pictures, Paramount Pictures, Harry Cohn, and C. B. DeMille all at the same time."

13

Meet the Ricardos

AFTER ten years of marriage, Lucy and Desi had some serious decisions to make about the future. On the domestic side, things never seemed rosier. They were expecting their first child. Desi's new radio job promised to keep him close to home so that they could lead as normal a family life as possible for people in the cockeyed world of show business.

Careerwise, the couple had cause for concern, especially Lucy. *The Magic Carpet* seemed an ominous preview of coming attractions if she intended to resume moviemaking after the baby arrived. Nearly forty, she'd been a Hollywood fixture for going on three decades, which made her a dinosaur in the eyes of studio casting directors. With production being cut to the bone as the result of ever declining theater attendance (down 35 percent since 1948), she had slight chance of getting anything but the junk rejected by bigger stars who were in the same boat.

Lucy was still luckier than many of her contemporaries because she had her radio series to fall back on. *My Favorite Husband* earned her $136,500 a year, but not for much longer unless she changed her mind about doing the television version. Though it seemed like financial suicide, she was still holding out for a TV show with Desi or nothing.

Since Desi did not depend on movies for a livelihood, his situation differed from Lucy's but was also imperiled. His radio program didn't pay enough for him to want to continue much longer. If *Your Tropical Trip* didn't lead to something in television, he'd have to return to touring with the band. With the closings of many theaters and night-clubs, the competition for bookings at the remaining ones had become cutthroat, so he faced less work and/or lowering his asking price.

By December 1950, agent Don Sharpe still hadn't been able to make a TV deal for Lucy and Desi, but NBC had promised to come up with a definite offer before the end of the year. Not one to sit around waiting, Sharpe covered all his options by warning CBS that it had only a few weeks left to make a counter proposal, guessing that they would. The network was being trounced in the audience ratings by NBC and could hardly risk losing a potential winner to its rival.

In the latest A. C. Nielsen research, NBC had eight of the Top Ten programs, including the first six: *Texaco Star Theater* (Milton Berle), *Fireside Theater* (half-hour plays), *Your Show of Shows* (Sid Caesar and Imogene Coca), *Philco Television Playhouse* (hour plays), *The Colgate Comedy Hour* (rotating stars like Eddie Cantor and Martin and Lewis), and *Gillette Cavalcade of Sports* (Friday-night boxing). CBS held seventh and eighth places with *Talent Scouts* (Arthur Godfrey) and *Mama* (family sitcom), while NBC took ninth and tenth with *Robert Montgomery Presents* (hour plays) and *Martin Kane, Private Eye* (a series moved over from radio).

Harry Ackerman, the CBS programming executive responsible for Lucy's role in *My Favorite Husband,* didn't want to lose her if he could help it. He told Don Sharpe that the network would make an audition film with the Arnazes if they could come up with an acceptable format within sixty days. Then, if the pilot succeeded in attracting a sponsor, the show would be scheduled for the 1951–52 season that started in September.

Once he had Ackerman's offer, Sharpe went back to NBC, which sensed a squeeze play and decided that the Arnazes weren't worth a bidding war. "That was just fine with me," Sharpe said later. "Lucy had been with CBS for over two years and I had hopes that they would keep her with the same creative team she'd worked with so successfully on *My Favorite Husband.* At NBC, she would have been starting from scratch with people who didn't know her."

Ackerman concurred, and immediately assigned Jess Oppenheimer, Madelyn Pugh, and Bob Carroll to what became known, at least tentatively, as *The Lucille Ball–Desi Arnaz Show.* To get started, Oppenheimer read the material that had been written for the Arnazes earlier, which set them up as glamorized versions of themselves.

By the time she was three and a half, her family had nicknamed her "Lucyball."

Desiderio Alberto Arnaz y de Acha on the day he graduated from grammar school.

(*Left*) Newly arrived in Hollywood, starlet Lucille Ball poses for one of her first publicity photographs.

(*Below, right*) Lucy, left, wore a long blond wig and little else in her movie debut as a slave girl in *Roman Scandals,* starring blackfaced comedian Eddie Cantor.

(*Bottom, left*) Talent executive Lela Rogers and famous daughter Ginger were friends and mentors to Lucy at RKO Radio Pictures.

(*Bottom, right*) A happier moment in Lucy's stormy matrimonial engagement to fledgling actor and future Oscar winner Broderick Crawford.

[*Top*] Lucy and close friend Ann Miller clowned
with the Marx Brothers in the 1938 film version
of Broadway's farcical *Room Service.*
[*Above*] Xavier Cugat, the Spanish-born
bandleader who popularized Latin American
music throughout the world, hired Desi as a
singer. He became Desi's mentor and role model.
[*Right*] Broadway went conga crazy when Desi
started pounding the drums in Rodgers & Hart's
Too Many Girls.

[*Right*] Newly acquainted while filming *Too Many Girls*, Lucy and Desi take a stroll around the studio that later became part of their television empire.

[*Below, left*] The newlyweds observe tradition, in this case across the threshold of Desi's dressing room at New York's Roxy Theatre.

[*Below, right*] Starring opposite Henry Fonda, Lucy gave her best and bitchiest dramatic performance as the crippled nightclub singer in Damon Runyon's *The Big Street* (1942).

[*Above*] Lucy tends the garden at the San Fernando Valley homestead known as Desilu.
[*Left*] Nearly blending in with the wallpaper, Lucy and mama DeDe Ball put the finishing touches on the living room drapes.
[*Below*] The furloughing staff sergeant and his wife enjoy a night out at Ciro's, where they usually ended up leading the conga line.

[*Above, left*] On CBS-Radio's zany *My Favorite Husband,* Lucy and Richard Denning portrayed Liz & George Cooper, All-American antecedents of Lucy & Ricky Ricardo.

[*Above*] Nine years after their secular wedding, Lucy and Desi decided that re-marriage in the Roman Catholic faith might save the troubled match. Desi's mother, Lolita Arnaz, left, beams approval.

[*Left*] Due to subsequent format and character revisions, the pilot episode of *I Love Lucy* was shown only to potential sponsors and never broadcast as part of the series.

[*Right*] The Arnazes were the official stars of *I Love Lucy,* but William Frawley and Vivian Vance contributed equally to the merriment in the supporting roles of friendly landlords Fred & Ethel Mertz.

[*Below*] Lucy and Desi huddle with the creative forces behind *I Love Lucy,* scriptwriter Madelyn Pugh, her bearded partner Bob Carroll, and head writer and producer Jess Oppenheimer.

[*Bottom*] Before each filming session, Desi stepped out of character to warm up the studio audience, which invariably included Lucy's mother, DeDe Ball, among its loudest laughers.

[*Top*] Lucy Ricardo got drunk while demonstrating the alcohol-laced tonic, but Lucille Ball didn't. The bottles were actually filled with apple pectin.

[*Above*] Unable to keep up with the flow, and with their mouths already stuffed, the candy wrappers wonder where next to hide the goodies as the supervisor calls for a speed-up of the assembly line.

[*Right*] Stomping barefooted on grapes was like stepping on eyeballs, Lucy said after filming this scene with Teresa Tirelli, an actual employee of the California winery that supplied the vat and its contents.

[*Above*] While stalking William Holden's autograph at the Hollywood Brown Derby, Lucy Ricardo accidentally dumps a pie on his head. Later, after Lucy dons a disguise, Holden sets her putty nose on fire as he goes to light her cigarette.
[*Right*] Betty Grable, Lucy's longtime friend and Desi's ex-sweetheart, also married a bandleader — trumpeter Harry James. The two couples found plenty to talk about while working together in the 1958 special, "Lucy Wins a Racehorse."

[*Above*] Robert Stack, second from right, portrayed G-Man Eliot Ness in Desilu's *The Untouchables,* the anti-crime series that caused the Mafia to issue a contract on Desi's life.

[*Left*] A family trip to Europe in 1959 failed to restore marital harmony.

[*Below*] Guest star Ernie Kovacs wasn't the only one with a mustache in the very last Ricardo caper, filmed on March 2, 1960, the day before Lucy sued Desi for divorce.

[*Above*] Audiences loved Lucy in *Wildcat* (shown here with Paula Stewart), but the Cy Coleman-Carolyn Leigh musical became one of the costliest flops in Broadway history.
[*Below*] Lucy and Gary Morton were married by her friend and spiritual advisor, Norman Vincent Peale, at the minister's Marble Collegiate Church in New York City.

[*Top*] After the divorce, Lucy and Desi's only public appearances together were at the annual meetings of Desilu stockholders.

[*Above*] Desilu's *Star Trek* debuted to low ratings in 1966 but developed into one of the most successful TV and movie properties of all time.

[*Left*] *The Mothers-in-Law,* starring Eve Arden and Kaye Ballard (NBC, 1967–69), was Desi's only success as an independent producer.

[*Above*] Gale Gordon, known as king of the slow burn, had the longest run of all Lucy's sidekicks in the assorted series that followed *I Love Lucy*.
[*Left*] Ann Sothern, a close friend since their early Hollywood days and once the star of her own Desilu series, often guested on Lucy's later programs.

(*Above*) Lucie Arnaz found happiness and had three children with her second husband, actor-writer Laurence Luckinbill.
(*Left*) Desi Junior and Liza Minnelli became star-crossed lovers right after his breakup with Patty Duke.
(*Below*) At age 64, Desi portrayed a corrupt politician in what proved to be his last movie, *The Escape Artist*, produced by Francis Ford Coppola's Zoetrope Studios.

[*Above*] Desi and his second wife, Edie, on a rare night out in Hollywood. The twenty-two-year marriage ended with her death from cancer in 1983. Desi's followed three years later.

[*Below*] Lucy and family at the 1984 banquet held by Variety Clubs International to honor her many years of fundraising efforts for children's charities.

(*Left*) Playing a homeless bag lady in *The Stone Pillow,* Lucy looked all of her nearly 74 years. Filming the TV movie in a Manhattan heat wave seriously damaged her health.

(*Below*) Lucy and Bob Hope, often a team in movies, radio, and TV over the years, won a standing ovation at the 61st annual Academy Awards ceremony on March 29, 1989. Lucy died three weeks later.

(*Below, left*) In the days following Lucy's death, thousands of admirers flocked to Hollywood Boulevard to sign a memorial scroll that extended a full block from her designated star on the Walk of Fame.

"I rejected all of it as Lucy and Desi already had," Oppenheimer recalled. "I preferred to stick closer to the flavor of *My Favorite Husband* because it was working so well for Lucy. So, with a few minor adjustments, I hit upon the idea of a middle-class working stiff who works very hard at his job and who likes nothing better than coming home at night and relaxing with his wife, who doesn't like staying home and wants a career of her own. That was the nucleus. In fact, one of the lines in the script had Desi saying, 'I want a wife who's just a wife.' That bit of dialogue pretty much summed up our basic premise. CBS liked it, and best of all, so did Lucy."

Whether Desi liked it or not didn't seem to matter. CBS treated him like "the star's husband," someone they had to tolerate if they wanted Lucille Ball.

Because of Lucy's pregnancy, the pilot had to be filmed with dispatch and with minimal risk to her health. To save time in the scriptwriting, Pugh and Carroll decided to incorporate some of the material that had worked so successfully for the Arnazes during their vaudeville tour of the past summer.

To compensate for Desi's limited acting skills, the format for *The Lucille Ball–Desi Arnaz Show* was built around his actual personage. But instead of a world-famous Latin-American bandleader, he portrayed a struggling go-getter named Larry Lopez. His All-American wife, Lucy Lopez, had the same nickname as Lucille Ball, but bore slight character resemblance. Mrs. Lopez was just an ordinary housewife who dreams of being in show business herself but who lacks any kind of talent.

The pilot script was performed live before an audience at CBS Studio A in Hollywood on March 2, 1951, which just happened to be Desi's thirty-fourth birthday. In that time before videotape, the copy needed to screen for potential sponsors was made by filming the images off a TV monitor during the closed-circuit broadcast. The resulting kinescope left much to be desired in visual quality, but shooting TV programs on film was equivalent to making a movie and prohibitively expensive for the infant industry.

To make sure that the half-hour pilot stayed within its $19,000 budget, CBS assigned the highly experienced Ralph Levy of *The Burns and Allen Show* to direct. There were only two sets—the Lopezes' Manhattan living room and the interior of a nightclub. Besides Lucy and Desi, the cast consisted of Pepito the clown, actor Jerry Hausner as a talent agent, the musicians from Desi's band, and a few extras as nightclub patrons.

The opening eight-minute scene established the basic premise of the series. When Lucy Lopez discovers that her bandleader husband is due to audition for a television show, she tries to persuade him to include her in his act. "George Burns uses his wife in the show," she says.

"I don't want my wife in show business," Larry insists. To prevent Lucy from turning up at the audition, he sends her on a long trip downtown to deliver some important papers to their attorney.

Meanwhile, the clown in Larry's show gets sick and is sent to the Lopez apartment to rest. When Lucy comes home and finds him there, she conspires to take his place at the audition.

In Act Two, the scene shifts to the nightclub, and the action is virtually a replay of the Arnazes' vaudeville routine. After Larry performs "Babalu," Lucy meanders on stage disguised in the clown's tacky tuxedo and proceeds to demonstrate her trick cello and to impersonate a trained seal.

The physical high jinks were scaled down to accommodate Lucy's pregnancy, but she still suffered a slight mishap when she accidentally stuck herself in the stomach with the bow while playing the cello. To save doing the whole scene over, she just went on with it and prayed that no damage had been done.

Although Desi often claimed later that the pilot found a sponsor within forty-eight hours of CBS submitting it to advertising agencies, the record proves otherwise. Don Sharpe shopped the series up and down New York's Madison Avenue for several weeks before Milton H. Biow finally expressed interest in behalf of his client, Philip Morris Cigarettes. At that time, tobacco commercials were still rampant on television.

"I must be candid and say I was not overwhelmed by the Ball-Arnaz pilot, but I thought it had a better than average chance for success," Milton Biow recalled. "At the time, Philip Morris was disenchanted with its first two TV sponsorship ventures, video versions of radio's *Truth or Consequences* and Horace Heidt's show."

On both radio and television then, it was customary for major advertisers like Philip Morris, Coca-Cola, General Motors, Procter & Gamble, et cetera to be involved in the production of the programs they sponsored, rather than to just buy commercial time as most of them do now. Before Biow could recommend his client spending upwards of a million dollars on *The Lucille Ball–Desi Arnaz Show*, he screened the kinescope for some of his friends, including public relations wizard Benjamin Sonnenberg and songwriter Oscar Hammerstein II.

Hammerstein told Biow, "Keep the redhead, but ditch the Cuban."

"But he's her husband. It's a package deal. To get her, we have to take him," Biow replied.

"Well, for God's sake, don't let him sing. No one will understand him," Hammerstein said. "Make it a warm, human story built around a wholesome, lovable, dizzy couple."

While Biow and Philip Morris deliberated, CBS came up with a new title for the program. *The Lucille Ball–Desi Arnaz Show* proved too much of a mouthful, but the couple weren't famous enough as a team to warrant the Burns and Allen treatment with *The Ball and Arnaz Show*. Furthermore, Desi considered himself king of the castle and kept insisting that he should receive top billing in whatever title was finally used.

Who actually suggested the title *I Love Lucy* is unknown, but he or she deserves a medal for solving the problem cleverly and diplomatically. When Lucy first heard it, she had her doubts, but, as she said later, "People would know that the 'I' was Desi. That gave him first billing. And then, how could you go wrong with 'love' in the title? I decided to go with it—after exactly half a second."

In late April, Philip Morris decided to take a chance on *I Love Lucy* as the coming fall season's replacement for bandleader Horace Heidt's *Youth Opportunity Show*. The CBS variety series featuring talented amateurs and fledgling professionals was currently being slaughtered in the Monday-night-at-nine slot by NBC's televersion of *Lights Out*, the classic radio suspense series by Wyllis Cooper and Arch Oboler.

But several mammoth production problems still had to be overcome before *I Love Lucy* could go forward. While CBS had originally intended to broadcast the program every other week like *The Burns and Allen Show*, Philip Morris wanted to run it weekly. Thirty-nine episodes were needed for the initial season (nowadays, most programs make twenty episodes and fill the rest of the season with repeats).

Agent Don Sharpe told the Arnazes that doing a weekly show would mean stopping all their other professional activities. There'd be no time to spare for moviemaking, radio programs, or vaudeville and nightclub bookings.

"We'll gamble everything on this show. The answer is yes," Desi said.

"Everyone warned Desi and me that we were committing career suicide, by giving up highly paid movie and band commitments to go for broke on TV," Lucy remembered. "But it was either working together or good-bye marriage! Ever try being married seven years out of ten by long-distance call and wire?

"Then I dreamed about Carole Lombard. She was wearing a very smart suit—Carole always dressed very beautifully—and she said 'Take a chance, honey. Give it a whirl!' After that, I knew *for certain* that we were doing the right thing."

Lucy later ran into Clark Gable at a party and told him how his long-deceased wife kept turning up in her dreams to offer marvelous advice. "He stared, gulped, and plowed off in a daze," she recalled.

Another crisis developed when Milton Biow telephoned the Arnazes to find out how soon they intended to move to New York to start work on the series. Lucy, who'd gained thirty pounds during seven months of pregnancy, took to bed for fear the shock would cause her to miscarry.

"Everything we had done, trying to work as a team, we had done in order to see if we could at last be together and stay home. And now in particular, when we were anxiously awaiting the arrival of our first child, there was no way we would move to New York," Desi recalled.

Due to the three-hour time differential between East and West coasts, as well as for lack of a cross-country transmission system, most major programs originated in New York because the more densely populated eastern half of the nation provided a larger audience than the half west of Chicago. CBS wanted *I Love Lucy* to be televised live so that eastern viewers would receive a clear picture rather than a blurry kinescope.

The only solution seemed to be to produce the show on film and to make as many prints as were needed to give the whole nation the same top quality picture. Philip Morris accepted the idea immediately, but CBS balked.

"We like Lucy working in front of an audience," Harry Ackerman told Desi. "That's the way she does her radio show and she's a lot better with an audience than without one. If you do it on film, she will not be able to work in front of an audience and we don't want that."

While the answer to that problem was obvious, it also seemed impossible to accomplish. Because of safety regulations, spectators were not permitted on studio soundstages. And the stages in conventional theaters were built to accommodate only one major set at a time, which was fine for a game show but too time consuming for programs with several scenery changes. In studios, the sets were built side by side so that the actors and camera crews could move back and forth between them without interruption.

Rather than admit defeat, Desi said he'd find a way to satisfy CBS, but that it would probably mean increasing their present budget of $19,500 per half-hour episode. "Trying to sound as if I knew what I was talking about, I took a figure out of the air and told them, 'At least $5,000 more, $24,500 for each episode,' " Desi recalled.

Although the figures seem ridiculously cheap today, an increase of $5,000, or $195,000 for the 39-episode series, amounted to a big bundle in 1951 (the federal minimum wage then was seventy-five cents per hour). After much agonizing, Philip Morris and CBS each offered to pay an additional $2,000 per episode if the Arnazes would make up the $1,000 difference.

Up to then, in the deal negotiated by Don Sharpe, Lucy and Desi were supposed to be paid a total of $5,000 per episode and would also own 50 percent of the I Love Lucy series. CBS now wanted to cut the couple's salary by $1,000 per episode as their contribution to the revised budget.

A born gambler, Desi told Sharpe that they'd take the $1,000 cut if CBS gave up its 50 percent stake in I Love Lucy, thus making the Arnazes the sole owners. "We really were not risking too much money," Desi said later. "In our income tax bracket, we might have ended up with about $5,000 of the $39,000 we were losing. So in effect, we were buying the other half of the series for $5,000."

CBS agreed, which wasn't as uninformed as it might seem in retrospect. In those early days of television, nobody gave much thought to residuals or what a library of programs could be worth in the future. Since most shows were broadcast live, they literally disappeared into thin air unless kinescoped, and those copies were so inadequate that the networks usually destroyed them as soon as they'd served their purpose. CBS probably thought it had gotten the better half of the Arnazes by giving up something that was worthless anyway.

Lucy and Desi had finally turned themselves and their Desilu company into full-fledged producers. As sole owner of I Love Lucy, Desilu would be responsible for producing the series from monies received from CBS and Philip Morris. CBS also would supply creative input from its Hollywood office, but the task of getting the show out of development and in front of the cameras fell to Desilu, or rather to Desi alone. Lucy, gigantic and waddling around the house by now, could do little but offer advice while she tried to avoid any strain that might trigger another miscarriage.

By this time, Lucy had made sixty-seven movies over a span of eighteen years, so Desi's dilemma over finding a way to film I Love Lucy in front of an audience didn't faze her. "You better start by getting someone who knows something about photography," she told him. "Why don't you try Papa Freund?"

"Papa" was sixty-one-year-old Karl Freund, a Czech-born cinematographer who moved to Hollywood in 1929 after working for Germany's Ufa Studios on such silent masterpieces as *The Last Laugh, Metropolis,* and *Variety.* Once described as "the Giotto of the screen," he was a master of light and shadow, a virtuoso of camera movement. In America, his credits included *Dracula, The Good Earth* (for which he won an Oscar), and *Key Largo.* He also had a brief fling at directing with the horror classics *The Mummy* and *Mad Love.*

Freund held a special place in Lucy's affections for photographing her so exquisitely in the Technicolored *DuBarry Was a Lady.* That probably meant more to her than the fact that Freund was a major innovator, one of the first to liberate the stationary camera by using dollies and cranes, as well as the inventor of the Norwich light meter and the process shot for special effects.

Freund's inventions had made him rich enough to retire from moviemaking for private research. When Desi contacted him about working on *I Love Lucy,* he wasn't interested, but expressed surprise that Lucy, at age forty, was embarking on a TV career.

"You know, Lucille's no chicken. To make her look good in the close-ups, I would have to use special lighting, put a little gauze on the lens," Freund said.

"I don't know that end of it, Papa. You are the master at that," Desi said. He went on to enumerate all the technical problems he had in the hope that the challenge would prove irresistible to Freund. It did, so much so that Freund agreed to take the job at basic union scale until Desilu could afford to pay him the $1,500 a week he could get at MGM or Paramount.

On the recommendation of CBS's Harry Ackerman, Desi also hired a young production manager named Al Simon, who developed a way to film the TV version of *Truth or Consequences* before an audience.

"Desi invited my wife and me to dinner and to meet Lucy at the ranch in Chatsworth," Simon recalled. "We had a lovely meal that Desi prepared himself and then the two of us retired to a makeshift theater where Desi ran the *Lucy* pilot for me. I loved it, and told him there was no reason why we couldn't successfully come up with a method for filming it with thirty-five-millimeter cameras, because I had already done it for Ralph Edwards. Desi was relieved, and I went right to work."

Meanwhile, the equally important task of writing thirty-nine scripts for the first season of *I Love Lucy* fell on the shoulders of Jess Oppenheimer, Madelyn Pugh, and Bob Carroll. The kinescope pilot obviously couldn't be broadcast as part of the series, so they started from scratch by making some significant changes that reflected their own thinking, plus that of Lucy and Desi themselves.

Desi hated the name Larry Lopez, which reminded him too much of his bandleading rival Vincent Lopez. "We also thought the alliteration was a little too heavy—Lucy and Larry Lopez," Madelyn Pugh remembered. "It had a phony ring to it. Just who thought up the name Ricky Ricardo is hazy after all these years, but, like most of the creative decisions we made, it probably was a joint effort."

Another major change was made by Jess Oppenheimer, who thought that the Ricardos should have another couple as friends and neighbors. "Lucy needed a girlfriend: someone to talk to, confide in, scheme with. A person who could help move the plot along. The same went for Ricky, who needed someone to connive with and to advise him in the battle between the sexes," Oppenheimer said.

Oppenheimer stole two characters from *My Favorite Husband* and cleverly reshaped them for *I Love Lucy*. In the radio program, the foils for Lucy and her husband had been a wealthy couple who usually had the upper hand in what went on.

"We decided to reverse roles for the TV show," Oppenheimer said. "We wanted the Ricardos to have a few more pennies than the neighbors, but not a lot more. We were very careful to make the couples different in some ways, yet very alike in others."

The high-toned Rudolph and Liz Atturbury thus became dumpy Fred and Ethel Mertz, a surname that Madelyn Pugh borrowed from a doctor she'd known in her native Indianapolis, Indiana. As for Fred and Ethel, the names just sounded funnier than other combinations the writers toyed with, including Joe and Mary, Walter and Gloria, and Harry and Bess (then the tenants of the White House).

Lucy wanted her co-actors from *My Favorite Husband* to portray the Mertzes. But CBS had Gale Gordon on hold for the planned TV version of *Our Miss Brooks,* while Bea Benaderet already was appearing on *The Burns and Allen Show* in the role of next-door-neighbor Blanche Morton. On radio, actors expert at different voices often worked in more than one series at a time, as Gale Gordon did on *My Favorite Husband* and *Our Miss Brooks,* but the practice didn't carry over to television, where there was a face to contend with as well.

Before Lucy could come up with any further casting suggestions, she had a much more urgent problem. "The baby was overdue. I expected it in mid-June. By mid-July I was still waiting. My doctor was more fidgety than I, and badly in need of a vacation. He waited and waited. Nothing happened, so he scooted for a weekend," she recalled.

Hours after the doctor left town, Lucy sensed trouble. "Something was wrong—I knew it. Upset, I visited another doctor, who pounded his fist on the desk. 'Now! Your baby has turned.' He phoned my doctor in the desert and insisted on delivery by cesarean section. The baby was over four weeks late," Lucy said.

Lucie Desiree Arnaz was born July 17, 1951, at Cedars of Lebanon Hospital in Los Angeles. She weighed in at seven pounds, six ounces, measured twenty-one inches long, and bore a strong resemblance to her father at the same age. Doctors reckoned that the bump on her nose may have been caused by the cello-bowing mishap that her mother suffered while making the *I Love Lucy* pilot.

Lucy had intended the baby's first name to be Susan, in honor of her valiant actress friend Susan Peters, who'd been performing from a wheelchair since a paralyzing shotgun accident in 1945.

"Desi decided to surprise me and named the baby Lucie while I was still knocked out. He thought the spelling would keep us separate and maybe help the mailman. But the poor kid spent her whole life reminding people to spell it 'I-E' instead of 'Y,' " Lucy said years later.

When Lucy saw the infant for the first time, she tried to speak, but all she could do was cry. "I was weak from surgery, couldn't control my elation, and the doctor refused to let me see her unless I stopped crying," she recalled. "I'll never forget the first time I burped her. Picture me trying to sit up in a hospital bed. Lucie is wrapped in a disinfected cone of a blanket, which is stiff as cardboard. I coo and play with her teeny fingers for a second. Lucie slips down—whoops! —into the cone. I lift her up for a burp, pat her back, and she bounces out of the cone and falls on the pillow behind me on her head!"

Not many babies have songs composed in their honor or have them broadcast on the radio, but Lucie Desiree did. Desi expressed his joy over the new arrival in a song called "There's a Brand New Baby at Our House," which he wrote with composer friend Eddie Maxwell.

The day after Lucie's birth, Desi performed the song for the first time on his CBS radio program *Your Tropical Trip* (which was due to go off the air in September). In his introduction, he told the audience that he intended to make a recording of the number so that when Lucie grew up she would have definite proof that "her old man sang and that there once was a thing called radio."

14

Brand New Baby

"LITTLE Lucie transformed our life. To have a baby at the age of forty and after ten years of marriage seemed almost like a miracle. I believe that whatever success Desi and I had after that we owed to Lucie. She was our lucky charm," Lucy recalled.

But with *I Love Lucy* due to start production in September, the Arnazes were unable to devote as much time to Lucie as they wanted to. Grandmothers and hired nurses looked after her most of the time, since Lucy knew next to nothing about taking care of babies.

"I once changed Lucie eighteen times in four hours. I thought she had to be dry all the time," she recalled.

While Lucy recuperated at home from the cesarean operation, she held bedside meetings with the scriptwriters and spent hours on the phone trying to help Desi with the detail work. Until production arrangements were made, nobody knew what the first episode of *I Love Lucy* would be like.

"We were restricting ourselves to simple plots that could be shot live if necessary—with a minimum of sets and costume changes," said Jess Oppenheimer. "We borrowed many of the basic premises from *My Favorite Husband*. About half the scripts for the first season of *I Love Lucy* were originally radio scripts, rewritten to fit our television format."

Karl Freund and production manager Al Simon devised a three-camera system for filming *I Love Lucy* that revolutionized the television industry. Previously, most TV shows had used only one camera, but Desilu's so-called Multicam allowed the action to be photographed by three 35mm cameras simultaneously. The camera in the center made all the long shots, while the two side cameras filmed the close-ups. Later, an editor spliced the best shots together. A dubbed laugh track became unnecessary, because engineers recorded the audience reaction as part of the sound while production was going on.

The most innovative technique in Multicam was Freund's overhead lighting system hung from the ceiling and top walls. The intensity of the lighting had to be uniform throughout the set, otherwise the shots from the three cameras wouldn't match. The complete absence of floor lamps and cables permitted mounting the cameras on "crab" dollies that could be moved in every direction.

None of that would have been possible if Desi hadn't found a suitable production site at General Service Studios, just south of Santa Monica Boulevard in central Hollywood. Built during the silent era, the outmoded seven-acre plant was on the verge of bankruptcy, so the owners were all too willing to accept Desi's offer to rent Stage 2 for $1,000 per week and to remodel it to include seating for 300 spectators.

CBS advanced Desilu $50,000 toward the renovation and rental. While work went on, the Arnazes stepped up their search for the actors who would portray Fred and Ethel Mertz. Someone suggested Marjorie Main and Percy Kilbride, from the *Ma and Pa Kettle* movie series, but that choice seemed unlikely at best.

For Fred Mertz, Lucy wanted sixty-five-year-old James Gleason, the tough-talking wiseacre who was one of Hollywood's most beloved character actors, but Desilu couldn't afford his $3,500-a-week salary. William Frawley, a year younger than Gleason, turned out to be an ideal—and more affordable—substitute at $350 a week.

Although he was another famous character face, the balding, hawk-nosed Frawley had been reduced to fifty-dollar one-shot assignments on radio soap operas because of his heavy drinking; movie and TV casting directors regarded him as unreliable and difficult to work with. It seemed like a sad finale to a career that spanned five decades.

Born in Burlington, Iowa, on February 26, 1887, Frawley studied to be a secretary, still a predominantly male profession in those days. Possessed of a clear Irish tenor voice, he drifted into show business via amateur theatrics and small-time vaudeville. In 1914, he married redhaired entertainer Louise Broedt. They formed a comic singing-and-dancing act called Frawley and Louise, which enjoyed a solid success in vaudeville until the couple were divorced in 1927.

Frawley never married again. After the divorce, he switched over to the Broadway stage and appeared in such musicals as *Bye, Bye, Bonnie, She's My Baby,* and *Sons o' Guns* (co-starring with the great tap dancer Jack Donahue).

In 1933, Paramount Pictures signed Frawley to a long-term contract on the strength of his hilarious performance as a hardboiled press agent in the Broadway production of the Ben Hecht–Charles MacArthur farce *Twentieth Century.* Paramount refused to loan Frawley to Columbia for the John Barrymore–Carole Lombard movie, but kept him working steadily in four or five pictures annually during the eight years he was under contract. In 1941, he turned to free-lancing. By 1951, Frawley had appeared in a total of 103 movies. Surprisingly, he'd never worked with Lucy in all that time, though they were in separate sequences of *Ziegfeld Follies.*

When Frawley heard that the Arnazes were casting for a new TV series, he phoned them and asked to be considered for a role. "After he hung up, I kept seeing his puss and remembering how good he was at the kind of gruff character he usually played. The more I thought about it, the more I became convinced he was Fred Mertz," Desi recalled.

When Desi suggested Frawley's name to CBS and Philip Morris, they were appalled because of the actor's reputation as an alcoholic. "The more they kept tearing this guy apart, the more I liked the idea," Desi said. "According to my contract as executive producer, I had complete creative control of the show. I made up my mind to hire Frawley regardless of what they said."

Desi decided to put Frawley to the test by meeting him for drinks at Nickodell's Restaurant, a showbiz hangout adjacent to the Paramount and RKO studios. As soon as they sat down, Frawley ordered a double bourbon and instructed the waiter to keep bringing them.

Starting to regret coming, Desi got straight to the point and told Frawley that while he wanted to hire him, CBS and the sponsor considered him a drunk and a thoroughly undependable person.

"Well, those bastards, those sonsabitches," Frawley said. "They're always saying that about me. How the hell do they know, those bastards?"

"I don't give a damn whether you drink or not," Desi replied. "I like to drink myself, and I'll drink you under the table any time you'd like to give it a try, except during working hours. But Lucy and I have everything going on this project. She's given up her motion picture career and I've given up the band business. If we fail, I don't want it to be because some character like you loused us up."

"All right, so what's your problem? William Frawley is now sitting next to you and willing to listen to any proposition you're willing to offer him to make your show a success," the actor said.

Desi took his time answering. "Okay, Bill, I'll tell you what I'll do with you. The first time you are not able to do your job, I'll try to work around you for that day. The second time, I'll try to manage again. But if you do it three times, you are through, and I mean *through*, not only on our show, but you'll never work in this town again as long as you live. Is that fair enough?"

"All right, goddam it, that's fair enough," Frawley said. "Okay, Cuban, we have a deal. We'll show all those bastards how wrong they are."

Lucy and Desi had a more difficult time finding their Ethel Mertz. William Frawley was sixty-four, but an actress in his age bracket would look too grandmotherly to be the type of woman that Lucy Ricardo would choose for a bosom buddy. And from the practical standpoint, an elderly actress just wouldn't be agile enough to participate in Lucy's strenuous monkeyshines.

Lucille Ball was also very much the star of *I Love Lucy,* so she wasn't likely to hire any actress who might steal her thunder. Expert comedians like Lee Patrick, Irene Ryan, Connie Gilchrist, Ellen Corby, and Kathleen Freeman were immediately disqualified.

Peroxide blonde Barbara Pepper, the supporting actress who'd been a close friend of Lucy's since their Goldwyn Girl days, desperately wanted to play Ethel. Though a year younger than Lucy, she was about thirty pounds overweight and could look frumpy enough for the part. But Pepper was also an alcoholic, and the Arnazes couldn't take a chance on having two potential time bombs as their co-stars.

Marc Daniels, who would direct the first season of *I Love Lucy* episodes, tried to solve the casting dilemma by suggesting an actress he knew from his apprenticeship in the Broadway theater. Her name was Vivian Vance, but neither Lucy nor Desi had ever heard of her before.

Vivian Jones was born on July 26, 1912, in Cherryvale, Kansas, but the family soon moved to Albuquerque, New Mexico. She took her professional surname from Vance Randolph, a dramatics teacher who encouraged her to pursue a stage career. Moving to New York in 1932, she passed her very first Broadway audition and won a small role in Jerome Kern—Oscar Hammerstein II's *Music in the Air,* which ran seven months.

To fill the gaps between plays in those Depression years, Vivian performed as a singing comedian in nightclubs. She understudied

Ethel Merman and also played minor roles in two Cole Porter musicals, *Anything Goes* and *Red, Hot and Blue.* She graduated to bigger and better parts with Ed Wynn in *Hooray for What,* with Gertrude Lawrence in *Skylark,* and with Danny Kaye and Eve Arden in Cole Porter's *Let's Face It.*

Vivian Vance might have become a major Broadway personality if it hadn't been for her marriage in 1941 to Philip Ober, who acted with her the previous year in a flop comedy entitled *Out from Under.* Ten years older then Vivian, Ober had played many leads on Broadway, but had never made it into the star ranks. He was extremely jealous of Vivian's professional successes and made sure that she knew who was master.

"My husband liked to dominate and discipline me," Vivian Vance recalled. "I kept trying to please him, but nothing I did was right. There were times when I would literally beat my head against the bedroom wall in frustration."

In 1945, while touring in the national road company of *The Voice of the Turtle,* Vance had a nervous breakdown. "I became perpetually fatigued and felt like I couldn't go on living. One morning I woke up in my hotel room and the walls seemed to be closing in on me. My hands were shaking helplessly. I was in a state of violent nausea, weeping hysterically from causes I didn't know," she said.

For two years, Vance lived like a zombie in her husband's shadow. Psychoanalysis finally saved her. After six months of therapy, she felt alive again, although she had no interest in returning to acting. To further her recovery, the Obers moved to a small ranch near Vance's childhood home in Albuquerque.

In 1949, longtime friend Mel Ferrer coaxed Vance and Ober into taking supporting roles in *The Secret Fury,* a melodrama that he was directing for RKO with Claudette Colbert and Robert Ryan in the leads. Ober went on to work in other movies, but Vance wasn't keen. She didn't make another film until 1951: the Jane Wyman tearjerker *The Blue Veil.*

Vance really wanted to return to the stage, but she got cold feet when Mel Ferrer, one of the directors of the La Jolla Playhouse near San Diego, offered her a week's work at the summer theater. The play was John Van Druten's *The Voice of the Turtle,* in which Vance had been appearing at the time of her nervous breakdown.

"Fate sure is a funny thing," she recalled. "At first I said no. The play had too many bad memories for me. But then I thought, what the heck! It's only for a week."

In its original Broadway production in 1943, the three-character comedy smash had starred Margaret Sullavan, Elliott Nugent, and Audrey Christie. This time around, ex-piano prodigy Diana Lynn and Mel Ferrer had the romantic leads, with Vance again as the caustic "other woman" she portrayed in the 1945 road tour.

Marc Daniels was so certain that the Arnazes would want to hire Vivian Vance for *I Love Lucy* that he insisted on driving them down to La Jolla to catch her Saturday night performance. Lucy, still recuperating from surgery, didn't feel up to the two-hour car ride, so Desi went alone with Daniels and Jess Oppenheimer.

"Vivian was playing this very sarcastic bitch in the play. It was not what you would call typecasting for Ethel Mertz," Desi recalled. "Nevertheless, right after I saw her do the first scene, I knew we had found the woman we needed. She was such a wonderful actress, so honest. Every line, every reaction, every move she made was just perfect. I couldn't wait to get backstage to talk to her."

Unhappily, Desi didn't get the reception he expected when he went to discuss the part with Vance. "I really don't care to have anything to do with it," she said. With her background in the theater, she meant every word. In 1951, television was still a silly new medium that "serious" actors considered just a passing fad.

Marc Daniels was furious with Vance afterward. "You idiot, take the job if they offer it to you! It's going to be a great show. I've already seen six or seven scripts and the pilot. It's going to be terrific," he said.

Still unconvinced, Vance returned to her home in Albuquerque when the play closed. "But Desi kept phoning. Finally, against my real desire and best judgment, I agreed to take the job for thirteen weeks at $350 a week. Desi couldn't promise that the show would continue beyond that," she said later.

To guarantee Ethel Mertz's dowdy image, it was stipulated in Vance's contract that she had to be twenty pounds overweight. That clause caused great resentment, but at least no one ever asked her to get on a scale to prove that she was keeping to the agreement.

CBS and Philip Morris had selected October 15 as the premiere date for *I Love Lucy*. By the time rehearsals for the first episode started on September 1, Lucy and Vance still hadn't met. The latter arrived at the studio early that morning, determined to make a good impression.

"I was scared to death, so I fortified myself by getting all dressed up in my best clothes. I'm the kind of woman who likes to wear blue jeans, slacks, and sloppy shirts. But not this day. I was meeting Lucille

Ball for the first time. She'd always been one of my favorites in all those splashy MGM Technicolor movies," Vance recalled.

"Then suddenly this creature walks in—old sweater, old pair of blue jeans, a thing tied around her head. It was Lucy. She looked me up and down and said, 'Well, you're certainly dressed up!' I breathed a sigh of relief and said, laughing, 'This is the last time you'll see me this way.' "

Renovators still hadn't gotten around to the dressing rooms. "The windows were so grimy you couldn't see through them," Vance said. "We walked in and Lucille handed me a can of Bon Ami cleanser. 'Clean out the john,' she told me. It was hard, but I got a scrub brush and went to work. We didn't even have hot water."

To break in the new production facilities, the first episode filmed was "Lucy Thinks Ricky Is Trying to Murder Her," which had a simple plot requiring a minimum of scenery and camera setups. Gullible Lucy Ricardo, an avid reader of murder mysteries, overhears one of Ricky's telephone conversations and concludes that he intends to kill her. Actually, he was only talking about replacing the singer in his band.

Due to various technical problems, the filming of "Lucy Thinks Ricky Is Trying to Murder Her" had to be delayed a day to Saturday night, September 8. Normally, to give everyone a chance to rest up over a long weekend, Desilu hoped to produce each episode in four days, with script conferences on Tuesday, rehearsals throughout the week and the final shoot at eight o'clock Friday night before an audience.

General Service Studios' Stage 2 had been renamed the Desilu Playhouse, with a spiffy theaterlike entrance at 6633 Romaine Street. A grandstand with five rows of steel benches provided seating for 300 people. Ushers supplied by CBS handed out cushions to anyone who wanted them. Since camera magazines needed reloading every ten minutes, it would take about an hour to film a half-hour episode (which actually ran twenty-four minutes and thirty seconds, less commercials and credits).

Just before the first audience could be admitted, an inspector from the Board of Health threatened to cancel the performance for lack of adequate toilet facilities. Through a construction oversight, Desilu Playhouse had a men's room, but none for women.

Lucy came to the rescue. "Tell the ladies they can be my guests. They can use the john in my dressing room until we can build a separate one," she said. The health inspector approved.

Afraid that the crowd might be in a hostile mood after being held outside on the sidewalk for half an hour, Jess Oppenheimer told Desi to warm them up with some welcoming remarks and a few jokes. Desi grabbed a microphone and headed for center stage without realizing that he'd forgotten to zip the fly of his trousers. As usual, he wasn't wearing underwear.

"I noticed it just in time, but when Desi tried to close it, the zipper got stuck. The more he panicked, the less cooperative the zipper was. He was very nervous, so somebody standing nearby volunteered and got it unstuck for him," stage manager Herb Browar remembered.

In what became standard practice for all future filming nights, Desi strolled out and talked to the audience about the three-camera system and how the script would be performed straight through like a play. After a few corny jokes, he introduced Vivian Vance, William Frawley, and finally "my favorite wife, the mother of my child, the vice-president of Desilu Productions—I am the president—my favorite redhead, the girl who plays Lucy, Lucille Ball!"

While the orchestra played the *I Love Lucy* theme, the star dashed out with her red hair flying. "Lucy was just as good as Hope or Jolson or Chevalier about taking over an audience," Desi said later. "She went over and kissed Bill and Vivian. She then came to me and said, 'How ya doing, you gorgeous Cuban?' and threw kisses to the audience. The whole atmosphere had a happy, carnival type of feeling."

From the moment that director Marc Daniels shouted "Action!" everything went so smoothly that no one was aware of Lucy's extreme nervousness. "I don't remember much about that night except trying to protect my stomach," she said years later. "Lucie was about seven weeks old by then, and I was still wearing a huge bandage from the cesarean operation. I was more concerned about having an accident than anything else. When the laughs started coming in, I was very relieved. I thought, Whew! It's working!"

When *I Love Lucy* had its very first broadcast on October 15, 1951, the episode shown was *not* "Lucy Thinks Ricky Is Trying to Murder Her." Because of some problems with the Multicam system, the program turned out to have some flaws that weren't serious enough for it to be scrapped, but still not up to the high standards of a series premiere. Three more episodes of better technical quality had been filmed in the meantime, so they were shown in the opening weeks and "Murder" did not air until November 5.

By premiere night, *I Love Lucy* was $220,000 over budget. Desi, who hadn't yet hired a financial executive for Desilu, was doing the bookkeeping himself at home after work. Nonrecurring expenses like the rebuilding of the stage floor, a special Movieola for viewing all three Multicam films simultaneously, and an automatic sprinkler system were charged off to whatever episode happened to be shooting at the time, rather than amortized against the whole season's output. Consequently, the first show cost approximately $95,000, the second $85,000, the third $75,000 and the fourth $60,000.

CBS was getting very nervous because the contract required the network to pay the overage whenever the budget exceeded the agreed upon $24,500 per episode. Insiders were betting that CBS would lose more than half a million dollars in the first year of *I Love Lucy*. But as it turned out, nobody had anything to worry about, least of all Lucy and Desi.

15

Expecting Again

HAD it not been for another redhead, a natural one named Arthur Godfrey, *I Love Lucy* might never have achieved the success it did. When the series premiered at nine o'clock on Monday night, October 15, 1951, it came on directly after the freckle-faced humorist's *Talent Scouts,* the number-one show in the Nielsen ratings at the time. When Godfrey signed off that night and for many weeks afterward, he urged viewers to stay tuned for a wonderful new program starring Lucille Ball and Desi Arnaz.

If the homespun Godfrey could cause millions of Americans to buy ukuleles and garish Hawaiian sportshirts, then one can imagine the tremendous hold he had on the public. Viewers stuck to CBS and *I Love Lucy* rather than switching over to NBC's *Lights Out,* which had long dominated the nine o'clock time slot on Monday nights.

Godfrey also raved about the series on his top-rated CBS morning *radio* program. "Arthur never knew how much he helped us," Lucy recalled. "Everybody didn't have a TV set in those days. People used to write to tell me that they first heard about the show from listening to Arthur. They would go to a neighbor who had a set and watch our show there, sometimes even if they were on the outs with the person and it meant making up in order to see it."

Over the years, *I Love Lucy* has gone through so many reruns that the original identification of the series with Philip Morris cigarettes has been forgotten. But from the premiere night onward and for as long as Philip Morris continued to sponsor the series, *I Love Lucy* had an unofficial fourth star in Johnny Roventini, the four-foot midget who wore a bellboy's uniform and introduced each program with his inimitable cry of "Call for Philip Mor-rees." The premiere of *I Love Lucy* started off with Johnny's wailing and the syncopated rhythm of the Philip Morris theme song (Ferde Grofé's "On the Trail"). The opening title credits depicted a cartoon Lucy and Desi romping atop a giant pack of the sponsor's product.

Amusingly, in real life, Lucy had been a chain smoker of a competing brand since her modeling days as a Chesterfield Girl. When the chairman of Philip Morris found out, he was furious and made Desi promise that if Lucy must continue smoking Chesterfields, she should at least carry them inside Philip Morris packages. Desi soon tired of making the changeover every morning, so he refrained one day just to see if Lucy would notice the difference. When she didn't, Desi stopped switching, but Lucy went on believing that she was puffing Chesterfields.

Due to the postponement of "Lucy Thinks Ricky Is Trying to Murder Her," the very first episode of *I Love Lucy* to be broadcast was "The Girls Want to Go to a Nightclub." The plot revolved around Lucy and Ethel's fierce determination to go nightclubbing at the Copacabana, even though Ricky and Fred have tickets to the boxing matches. Neither duo will give in, so the men arrange to take blind dates to the fights. When Lucy and Ethel find out what's going on, they masquerade as hillbillies and try to pass themselves off as the women their husbands are expecting.

While the nation was getting its first dose of Lucy's antics, the Arnazes were so wrapped up in working on a future episode that they nearly forgot to watch the premiere broadcast. When it finally dawned on them, they found that General Service Studios didn't have even one TV set on the premises! It was too late to drive all the way back to the ranch in time to see the program in their own living room, but director Marc Daniels saved the day by inviting everybody to his house in nearby Laurel Canyon. Only William Frawley took a rain check; a longtime resident of the old Hotel Knickerbocker in Hollywood, he was more interested in getting back to his room so he could tune in the fights on the radio.

If the audience reaction in Daniels's living room was any indication, then *I Love Lucy* could have been an overnight disaster. Perhaps because they'd already seen the episode umpteen times in the screening room, Lucy, Desi, Vivian Vance, and Jess Oppenheimer watched grimly, criticizing every scene and nitpicking for technical flaws. The reception that night was fuzzy, because of some transmission problems at the local CBS station.

"The only one who was laughing a lot was Vivian's husband, Phil Ober, who hadn't seen the show before. He had this deep baritone laugh like 'HO HO HO.' But the rest of us just sat there motionless, staring at the set," Marc Daniels recalled.

Contrary to popular belief, *I Love Lucy* wasn't an instant success. In fact, the day after the first telecast, O. Parker McComas, the president of Philip Morris, wanted to cancel its contract. He told Biow advertising executive Terence Clyne that he found the program "Unfunny, silly, and totally boring." Clyne made McComas promise to reserve decision until a few more episodes had been aired.

Adding fuel to McComas's discontent was a partial pan in the *New York Times,* the nation's most influential newspaper. Critic Val Adams called the first half of the show "refreshing," but considered the second part in which Lucy and Ethel carried on like randy hillbillies to be "absurd" and "utterly unbelievable." In Los Angeles, the two morning trade papers were, as usual, on opposite sides of the fence. The *Hollywood Reporter* called the program "situation comedy at its very best," but *Daily Variety* judged the slapstick preposterous and predicted that the series would not survive the season.

By the end of November, after seven weeks on the air, *I Love Lucy* was the sixteenth most popular TV program in the nation, according to the American Research Bureau. By January 1952, it had jumped to fifth place on the ARB list. Nielsen ratings were averaging 43.5 percent per show, which meant a weekly audience of about 21 million people. Needless to say, Philip Morris had second thoughts about canceling its sponsorship.

Why was *I Love Lucy* becoming so popular? First of all, with television still in its infancy, anything new was bound to make an impact. *Lucy* was refreshingly different from any of the other situation comedies on the air at the time. Surprisingly, the three major networks carried only eight other sitcoms during that 1951–52 season; three of them, *Young Mr. Bobbin, Crime with Father,* and *Stud's Place* were short-lived. Of the remaining five, three were transfers of longtime radio programs: *Amos 'n' Andy* (being performed for the first time by black actors), *Burns and Allen,* and *The Aldrich Family.* Created expressly for television were *Mama,* based on the hit play and movie *I Remember Mama,* and *The Stu Erwin Show,* which focused on a bumbling high school principal and his family.

Compared to its competition, *I Love Lucy* most closely resembled *Burns and Allen,* but not by much. George and Gracie were a considerably older and more affluent couple than Ricky and Lucy; the Burnses emphasized jokes and scatterbrained repartee in what was essentially an extension of their legendary stand-up vaudeville act.

So many of the pioneer television programs passed undocumented that it would be foolhardy to call *I Love Lucy* the first slapstick sticom, but it certainly was unique for its premiere season. Although there were lots of slapstick comedians on TV at the time—Milton Berle, Red Skelton, and Jackie Gleason were the most popular—they had variety shows and featured casts of characters that varied from week to week.

To find an equivalent of *I Love Lucy,* one really had to go back to the movie two-reelers and features of the early 1930s in which Stan Laurel and Oliver Hardy got into one fine mess after another with their wives. *I Love Lucy* simply reversed the sexes; Lucy and Ethel were Laurel and Hardy, with Ricky and Fred as the combative spouses.

Moldering away in vaults, the Laurel and Hardy comedies had an unexpected revival when the infant TV industry was desperately in need of programming, but *I Love Lucy* modernized the format and made it more palatable for the majority audience, which wasn't interested in watching reruns of Hollywood's distant past. One of the series' main attractions for 1951 viewers was its fresh look, which combined the technical polish of a theatrical movie with the intimacy of the TV medium.

At the time *I Love Lucy* premiered, Lucille Ball was also a TV rarity —a female comedy star. Gracie Allen was the only other woman with a sitcom, while Imogene Coca and Martha Raye had the field pretty much to themselves in variety shows. Turning up week after week in the same character, Lucy suddenly gave millions of women someone to identify with and root for.

Rather than repelling audiences as CBS had feared, Desi's flamboyant Cuban-ness apparently had the opposite effect of attracting viewers. The big cities that made the majority of TV markets in 1951 had large immigrant populations that could easily identify with Ricky Ricardo. And most non-immigrants had a relative or friend who reminded them of Ricky. Empathy and identification were really the keys to the increasing popularity of *I Love Lucy.*

As the show's popularity grew, crazy things started happening all over the country. For all competing forms of entertainment, *I Love*

Lucy night became known as "Black Monday." In Detroit, an investigation took place when water levels in the reservoirs took a drastic drop on that night between 9:30 and 9:35 P.M. It seemed that everybody put off going to the bathroom until *I Love Lucy* ended. The Marshall Field department store in Chicago changed its evening shopping hours from Monday to Thursday after a huge decline in business. In New York, cabbies packed the bars, making it hard to get a taxi while *I Love Lucy* was being telecast.

The first batch of *Lucy* episodes set the pattern for the entire series to come. Lucy Ricardo was always involved in some wild scheme to foster one of her ambitions: to make Ricky demonstrate his undying love for her; to break into show business; to outdo one of her more affluent friends; to squirm out of a predicament caused by her own bragging, stupidity, or softheartedness; or to prove a point to Ricky and/or the Mertzes.

Six of the biggest laugh-getters were "Pioneer Women" (while emulating her forebears, Lucy bakes a loaf of bread so enormous that it pins her against the wall as it pops from the oven); "Lucy Does a TV Commercial" (and gets drunk on an alcohol-laced health tonic called Vitameatavegamin); "The Moustache" (when Ricky grows one, Lucy dons Santa Claus whiskers in protest and discovers she's used glue that sticks for a lifetime); "The Walk-In Freezer" (accidentally trapped inside, Lucy turns into a human popsicle); "New Neighbors" (to escape being caught as a snooper, Lucy hides under a slipcover and pretends to be an armchair); and "Job Switching," perhaps the crown jewel of all *Lucy* stories.

In the latter, Ricky and Fred try their hands at housekeeping while Lucy and Ethel take jobs in a candy factory. After proving incompetent at chocolate-dipping and boxing, the women end up wrapping individual pieces that pass them on a fast-moving conveyor belt. Unable to keep up, they start stuffing the product into their mouths, under their hats, and into their clothing to avoid being fired.

Director William Asher recalled filming the scene in which Lucy gets into a chocolate-slinging battle with another worker: "We hired a real candy-dipper from See's Chocolates for the part. Since she wasn't a professional actress, she was very timid and had a hard time actually plastering *the* Lucille Ball. Finally, determined, she really nailed Lucy, damn near broke her nose. Lucy was fine, though. She just played it up and ran with it for all it was worth."

Early on, Lucy and her writers invented a form of shorthand that they called "naturalizing," in which certain code words were inserted into the script so she'd know when to go into one of those zany facial expressions that became her trademark. "Puddling up," for example, meant that Lucy's eyes would fill with tears just before she emitted a banshee wail. "Light bulb" signaled the alarming look that crossed her face when she had a brainstorm. The frequent "spider" indicated baring her teeth and making a pinched guttural noise.

Jess Oppenheimer, Madelyn Pugh, and Bob Carroll were undoubtedly the unsung heroes of the series. "I am not funny," Lucy said many years later. "My writers were funny. The situations were funny. What I am is brave. I have never been scared. If they wanted to throw me into a cement mixer, I would try it, and if I came out alive, I would say 'O.K., let's go with it.' You have to believe in your writers. It's a kind of blind faith that you must have."

By the spring of 1952, *I Love Lucy* was not only the number-one program on the air but also the first in the history of American television to be seen in at least 10 million households. The program of April 7 entitled "The Marriage License," in which the Ricardos (like the Arnazes in real life) go through a second wedding ceremony, had a 70.5 percent audience share and reached 10.6 million homes. It was watched by about 30.7 million people, nearly a fifth of the entire population of the United States, according to the American Research Bureau. With the possible exception of Republican presidential candidate Dwight D. Eisenhower and wife, Mamie, Lucille Ball and Desi Arnaz had suddenly become the most publicized couple in America.

Lucy and Desi made the cover of the May 26 issue of *Time*. Fan magazines gave their success story more space than the concurrent romance between Marilyn Monroe and Joe DiMaggio or the marital battles of Frank Sinatra and Ava Gardner. It was a startling turnaround for two people who had never been major newsmakers during their twelve years of marriage.

Hedda Hopper called them "Hollywood's Ideal Couple." Knowing so little about Lucy and Desi's private life, the public accepted them for what they appeared to be on the TV screen. Lucille Ball was a lovable, childlike housewife, and Desi Arnaz a devoted husband who never played around. Their onetime divorce, if anyone remembered it at all, was laughed off as a prank that Lucy Ricardo might pull to teach Ricky a lesson.

Although hardly mirror images of the Ricardos, the Arnazes *were* about as near to wedded bliss as they ever would be or had been in the past. Parenthood and *I Love Lucy* had finally brought the togetherness that they considered the key to marital harmony. Of course, too much togetherness—being in each other's pockets twenty-four hours a day—can also be a problem, but they'd had so little of it that they didn't see it that way.

Now that Lucy and Desi had proved themselves as a professional team, they intended to stick to that exclusively. When filming of *I Love Lucy* shut down for the summer, they would make vaudeville appearances at the Roxy in New York and the Palladium in London. The percentage deal could earn them $250,000 for a total of three weeks' work. Agents were scouting for a property that the couple could make as a theatrical movie during their summer recess of 1953.

Plans were also under way to produce a weekly radio program from the *I Love Lucy* sound tracks. Director Eddie Sedgwick, a longtime friend and the godfather of baby Lucie, had been hired to assemble a ninety-minute feature movie from some of the *I Love Lucy* episodes. The movie would be released theatrically in the many foreign countries that were still lagging behind the United States in the TV revolution.

Apart from their involvement with *I Love Lucy,* the Arnazes were about to expand Desilu Productions by taking on their first outside projects. Eve Arden, star of radio's *Our Miss Brooks,* was so impressed by the Multicam system that she persuaded CBS to assign Desilu to producing the TV version of the series. Feisty baseball manager Leo Durocher and his actress wife Laraine Day wanted Desilu to film their projected series, *Double Play,* in which they would interview sports celebrities.

Despite its shared name, Desilu was pretty much Desi's domain. Lucy had no head for business and left the running of the company to him. Between the demands of *I Love Lucy* and her baby daughter, she had all that she could handle.

Lucy had reached two milestones in her life simultaneously. She was suddenly a major star *plus* a first-time mother, and a bit sensitive about it all happening at the fairly ripe age of forty. "You print my age and I'll break your back," she cheerily threatened an interviewer.

No one was more surprised than Lucy herself when she turned out to be pregnant again in May 1952. The news was kept secret from the press and public for a month. Gossipers later attributed the delay to Lucy giving thought to an abortion. She supposedly feared CBS canceling *I Love Lucy* if her condition prevented her from working.

Since the series was the top program in America at that time, it seemed unlikely that CBS would take such a drastic step. But the network did have a major problem because none of the next season's episodes had been filmed yet. Lucy's delicate health, plus her tendency to blow up like a balloon during pregnancy, would mean eliminating the strenuous slapstick that was her hallmark. It didn't take much brainpower to figure out that the easiest solution to the problem would be to incorporate Lucy's condition into the story line by making Lucy Ricardo pregnant as well.

Television programming today is so explicit that it may be hard to believe that in 1952 the Columbia Broadcasting System immediately rejected the suggestion of Lucy being pregnant as a violation of the network's Standards and Ethics Code. CBS claimed that pregnancy couldn't be depicted or discussed on television except in the context of a news or educational program.

Actually, there was precedent for it in one of the earliest TV sitcoms, *The Mary Kay and Johnny Show,* loosely based on the married life of its stars, Mary Kay and John Stearns. When Mary Kay became pregnant in 1948, her condition was promptly written into the script and her full nine months of progress were shared with the televiewers. Cameras went right into the waiting room of the hospital with Johnny on the night that Mary Kay actually gave birth. Two weeks later, baby Christopher joined the cast as himself.

But television had changed drastically in the four years since *Mary Kay and Johnny.* Now that it reached tens of millions of homes instead of a few thousand, the medium found itself in a situation similar to that of the Hollywood movie industry, which in 1933 adopted its own code of moral and ethical standards to ward off censorship and pressure groups. TV programmers had to be even more careful about content because the public airwaves were involved and under the jurisdiction of the hard-nosed Federal Communications Commission.

Desi had been in the TV business long enough now to realize that it all boiled down to getting the sponsor on his side. Without sponsors to underwrite the cost of production, the networks couldn't exist. Not even CBS, NBC, ABC, DuMont, and Mutual *combined* could afford to produce all the programming that any *one* of those networks used in a week.

With Philip Morris and the Biow advertising agency solidly supporting CBS's no-pregnancy stance, Desi decided to pull rank by writing to the tobacco company's top executive, board chairman Alfred E. Lyons. The letter said, in part, "You are the man who is paying the money for this show and I guess I will have to do whatever you decide. There's only one thing I want to make certain that you understand. We have given you the number-one show in the country and, up till now, the creative decisions have been in our hands. Your people are now telling us we cannot do this, so the only thing I want from you, if you agree with them, is that you must inform them that we will not accept them telling us what not to do unless, in the future, they will also tell us what to do."

In other words, if you no longer trust us running the show, do it all yourself and let's see if you can do it as well or better. Within the week, Lyons sent the following memo to all those concerned at Philip Morris and CBS: "Don't fuck around with the Cuban!"

Frank Stanton, president of CBS, capitulated, but reluctantly, insisting that every episode concerning Lucy Ricardo's pregnancy would have to be carefully monitored from the writing stage onward to make sure that nothing offensive sneaked into America's living rooms. For that purpose, CBS insisted on a mini-version of the National Conference of Christians and Jews to sit in on script conferences, rehearsals, and the final shoot.

By phoning around various congregations in the Los Angeles area, Desi came up with a three-man panel comprising Monsignor Joseph Devlin of St. Vincent's Roman Catholic Church, Reverend Clifton Moore of the Hollywood Presbyterian Church, and Rabbi Alfred Wolfe of the Wilshire Synagogue.

"They were with us four days a week and never objected to anything," Desi recalled. "As a matter of fact, we had the word 'pregnant' in one of the shows and the CBS censor would not let us say it. But the rabbi, minister and priest said, 'Well, what's wrong with "pregnant"? That's what it is.' "

CBS recommended using the French word *enceinte*, which should send most TV viewers rushing to dictionaries if nothing else. The religious advisers suggested "expecting," which seemed perfect for the Arnazes' purposes. Desi/Ricky would have trouble pronouncing it and Lucy could have fun imitating him: "Yeah, like he said, I'm 'specting."

Because of Lucy's history of miscarriages, doctors didn't want her working past the fifth month. Since the delivery would again have to be by cesarean section, they could predict fairly accurately that it would be in mid-January 1953. That meant that with a little bit of luck and some astute program scheduling, Lucille Ball and Lucy Ricardo could probably have their babies on the same night, which would make for some priceless publicity.

For the first time since *I Love Lucy* started, the scriptwriters found themselves locked into a continuing plot format. Previously, each episode was a self-contained story; funny things *happened* to the Ricardos and Mertzes every week, but there were no startling changes in their lives. But once Lucy Ricardo discovered she was pregnant, each plot would have to carry over logically into the next one at least until the baby's birth. After that, unless the baby was killed off or turned into an equivalent of never-aging comic strip characters like Nancy or Little Lulu, the stories would have to follow the infant's growth and development.

The Arnazes canceled their summer vaudeville bookings so that production could begin immediately on the twenty-one programs that would start airing on September 15 and had to be completed before Lucy took maternity leave. To get a head start with scripts that had already been written, Jess Oppenheimer decided to introduce Lucy Ricardo's pregnancy in one of the December episodes.

To break up the monotony of plots dealing with parenting, Madelyn Pugh and Bob Carroll devised a flashback technique that started some episodes with the main characters reminiscing about some memorable moment in the past. While they were all memories for the Ricardos and Mertzes, five of the adventures were new to televiewers and seven were repeats of shenanigans from the previous season.

The biggest problem in writing the pregnancy episodes could only be solved by Lucy and Desi themselves. Should the Ricardo baby be a boy or a girl? Since the birth episode would be filmed several months before Lucy's actual delivery, there was no way of ensuring that fiction and reality would overlap. If they did, it would be an incredible news story and publicity bonanza, but the Arnazes weren't sure that they wanted it to happen that way.

"If the Ricardos had a daughter, we were afraid that little Lucie would get upset. She'd want to know why her baby sister was on the show and she wasn't. If we made it a boy, she would be able to tell the difference between the Ricardos' make-believe family and our own," Lucy recalled.

Desi also hoped it would being him luck in having a boy of their own. "I was the last male in the Arnaz family," he said later. "If I didn't have a son, that would be the end of the Arnaz name. This was our last chance, because Lucy couldn't have any more kids after this one. The doctor said two cesareans were enough at her age. Another one could be extremely dangerous."

To help things along, Lucy gathered up all the photographs that she could find of Desi as a baby and hung them everywhere at home and at the studio. Every time she passed one, she prayed for a boy and hoped the fetus got the message.

On October 3, Desilu filmed the first pregnancy episode, in which Lucy had to break the news to Ricky. Numerous complications prevent her from doing so, and she finally goes to the Tropicana to tell him, even if it means interrupting his performance. The scene is cleverly written so that Ricky wakes up to the news while singing "We're Having a Baby, My Baby and Me," a request that Lucy planted with the headwaiter before she sneaked into the audience.

The script had an emotionally charged ending, with Ricky shouting for joy and dragging his wife up on stage to finish the song with him. But then Desi unexpectedly began to cry, causing Lucy to do the same.

"This strange thing happened," Jess Oppenheimer said. "Suddenly Lucy and Desi remembered their own real emotions when they discovered they were finally going to be parents. Both of them started sobbing and couldn't finish the number. It was one of the most moving things I've ever seen. The studio audience and the production crew cried right along with them. I ordered a retake, but everybody yelled 'No! No! No!' Life couldn't be any realer than that."

The Ricardo baby became the most closely guarded secret since the H-bomb. Everyone connected with the series at Desilu, CBS, and Philip Morris received a five-page memorandum of instructions on how to deal with the news media and the public. No one, not even newly elected President Dwight D. Eisenhower, should know that Lucy Ricardo was *enceinte* until that program actually aired on December 8.

The memo contained a section headed "The Secret Gimmick About the Baby's Sex," which had to be kept confidential until January 19, 1953, when the episode entitled "Lucy Goes to the Hospital" would be shown.

"The Ricardo baby will be a boy regardless of the sex of the actual Arnaz baby," the memo said. "Of course, if the Arnaz baby does happen to be a boy, then all writers and editors can assume that the producers of *I Love Lucy* are clairvoyant and possessed of sheer genius. If it happens to be a girl, the story (and the truth) is that Desi was so set on having a boy that he went ahead and filmed the Ricardo baby as if it were, regardless."

According to the Nielsen tabulations, 67.8 percent of the American households with TV sets were tuned in to *I Love Lucy* on the night that she broke the news to Ricky. The next day, CBS launched a massive publicity campaign to whip the world into suspense over whether the baby turned out to be a boy or a girl. (By this time, the series was also a smash hit in Canada, England, Europe, Australia, Japan, and Latin America.)

With Christmas and the spirit of birth and regeneration very much in the air, newspapers went bananas with editorials, special features, and contests that offered Cadillacs and deep freezers to the readers coming closest to guessing both the sex and the exact time of arrival of the Arnaz baby. Radio and television coverage was equally frenzied. The news departments of NBC and ABC suspended their customary blackouts of CBS happenings because it was a real human interest story, regardless of how much publicity it might be generating for *I Love Lucy*.

The chances of Lucille Ball and Lucy Ricardo having a baby on the same day were about a million to one, but that's exactly how it worked out because of the real Lucy's cesarean operation. Dr. Joseph Harris scheduled it for eight in the morning of January 19, just ten hours before the crucial *I Love Lucy* episode would first hit the airwaves in the Eastern time zone. So many reporters wanted to follow Desi into the maternity waiting room at Cedars of Lebanon Hospital that they had to draw straws to select just one.

Lucy, having gained thirty-seven pounds by this time, was given a spinal anesthetic so that she could remain conscious during the operation. "What is it? What is it? Can't you at least give me a hint?" she kept asking the doctor.

"Relax, honey," Dr. Harris said. "A few more minutes and we'll know."

The Arnazes had selected two names for the baby, Desi Jr., or Victoria Dolores. At 8:15 A.M., Dr. Harris shouted, "It's a boy."

"I'm so glad, Desi will be so happy," Lucy muttered, then promptly fell asleep.

In his excitement, Desi ran into the hallway screaming, "It's a boy! It's a boy!" He told the Associated Press reporter, "That's Lucy for you. Always does her best to cooperate. Now we have everything."

Desi rushed to the telephone to inform Jess Oppenheimer that Lucy had followed his script exactly. "Terrific! That makes me the greatest writer in the world," Oppenheimer said. "Tell Lucy she can take the rest of the day off!"

Within minutes, the news had gone completely around the world. School principals popped into classrooms to inform anxious students and teachers. Western Union offices were jammed with well-wishers trying to send congratulatory telegrams. Since few knew the Arnazes' address, many sent them collect care of CBS-Hollywood. CBS stopped accepting them when the charges threatened to bankrupt the network.

The Arnazes eventually had to hire four secretaries just to handle the congratulatory mail. They received 27,863 letters and cards, 3,154 telegrams, and 638 packages. The gifts were catalogued, and each sender who enclosed a return address got a note of thanks.

Desi's personal gift to Lucy was a Hammond organ, which virtually played itself and was something she'd wanted for years. He also gave her a gold medallion of the Tree of Life to hang around her neck. The inscription on the back read "Lucy and Thumper," the nickname they gave to the rambunctious fetus.

Louella Parsons gushed that Lucille Ball's accomplishment was a miracle second only to the birth of Jesus Christ. To no one's surprise, that night's episode of *I Love Lucy* introducing Ricky Jr. (portrayed that one time only by baby James Ganzer) became the most watched program in the history of television.

According to the A.C. Nielsen Company, 71.7 percent of the potential TV audience tuned in, or roughly 30 million households and 117 million people (the total U.S. population in 1953 was an estimated 156 million). By comparison, the next day's telecast of President Eisenhower's inauguration scored four points *lower* at 67.7!

"How about that?" Desi marveled at the time. "It looks like Lucy's more popular than Ike. I wonder if we could run her for President in fifty-six?"

16

Red Blues

"THERE'S a Brand New Baby at Our House" briefly became the equivalent of the national anthem in early 1953 when Columbia Records released a single performed by Desi Arnaz with the Norman Luboff Choir and Paul Weston's Orchestra. No one seemed bothered by the fact that the song was actually written in honor of Lucie Arnaz eighteen months earlier; it became permanently identified with the new addition to the Arnaz and Ricardo families.

Lucy and Desi would celebrate their thirteenth wedding anniversary in 1953, but it hardly seemed like it would be an unlucky year for the couple. In February, *I Love Lucy* received its first Emmys from the Academy of Television Arts and Sciences, which had been handing out awards since 1949. The series won for "Best Situation Comedy of 1952," while Lucille Ball was named "Best Comedienne."

Two weeks later, the Arnazes signed a new contract with Philip Morris for $8 million, the biggest deal in television history up to that time. Desilu would receive $4 million for producing ninety-eight episodes of *I Love Lucy* through the 1954–55 season, with the balance of the money going to CBS for commercial time.

The respected TV critic Jack Gould of the *New York Times* rushed into print with an analysis of the deal, which he described as "economic confirmation of the obvious. . . . Not since the heyday of the fifteen-minute broadcasts of 'Amos 'n' Andy,' which back in the 1930's brought American home life to a halt every evening, has a program so completely caught the interest and affection of the public. 'I Love Lucy' is probably the most misleading title imaginable. For once all available statistics are in agreement: millions love Lucy."

Lucy and Desi were praised for "always knowing what they are about." Gould said, "Every installment begins with a plausible and logical premise. Casually the groundwork is laid for the essential motivation: Lucy vs. Ricky. Only after a firm foundation of credibility has been established is the element of absurdity introduced. It is in the smooth transition from sense to nonsense that 'I Love Lucy' imparts both a warmth and a reality to the slapstick romp which comes as the climax. The viewer has a sense of being a co-conspirator rather than a spectator in completely unimportant yet amusing high jinks."

Gould also considered Lucy's Emmy to be well-deserved:

She is the unrivaled top TV comedienne of today, a complete personality blessed with a very real and genuine comic artistry. How she was ever wasted as a sexy glamour girl in the motion pictures passes all understanding anywhere except Hollywood.

Miss Ball's gifts are those of the born trouper rather than the dramatic school student. First and foremost is her sense of timing; in this respect she is the distaff equivalent of Jack Benny. Maybe it is a roll of her big eyes. Maybe it is the sublime shrug which housewives the world over will understand. Maybe it is the superb hollow laugh. Maybe it is the masterly double-take that tops the gag line. Whatever it is, it comes at the split-second instant that spells the difference between a guffaw and a smile.

But the most durable and recognizable quality conveyed by Miss Ball —perhaps it is the real heart of "I Love Lucy"—is wifely patience. Whatever the provocation or her exasperation, she is always the regular gal and the wonderful sport. On stage and off, Miss Ball is a person.

In an interview at the time, Desi called his wife "the female Charlie Chaplin," a label that stuck to her for the rest of her life. "There's nobody else that can do what Lucy does with her face, with her walk, with her action," Desi said. "*I Love Lucy* was designed for her, built for her. All the rest of us are just props—Bill, Vivian, and me. Darn good props, but props. In a Lucy script, everything starts with her and works backwards. You think it will be funny if Lucy gets her leg stuck in the barre while taking ballet lessons, so the whole idea is how to land her in that predicament."

Success and adulation were turning Lucy into a control freak on the set. She deferred to no one, not even Desi, in her determination to turn out a perfect show every week. After all her years in the Hollywood studios, she knew every light, every camera angle, every acting and directing trick in the book. After the first season of *I Love Lucy*, the star's dominating ways caused director Marc Daniels to quit. William Asher replaced him, but from then on Lucy pretty much called the shots.

No doubt part of Lucy's perfectionism stemmed from her feeling that the Arnazes didn't deserve all their good fortune. After the birth of her second child, she started to fear that it all would crumble. Quite by accident, she happened to read Norman Vincent Peale's best-seller, *The Power of Positive Thinking,* a copy of which someone left behind at the studio one day. It impressed her so much that she bought more of the New York clergyman's published writings and gradually accepted the fact that she and Desi deserved their success after long years of struggle and heartache.

"After walking around with a numb feeling of foreboding inside you all the time, it takes someone to tell you that if you didn't deserve what you have, you wouldn't have it," Lucy recalled.

The Arnazes had become so popular that in April 1953 they made the cover of *Life* magazine one week and *Look,* its main competitor, the following week. A new pocket-sized magazine of program listings called *TV Guide,* published weekly in ten regional editions that blanketed the nation, featured three-month-old Desiderio Alberto Arnaz y de Acha IV on the cover of its premiere issue.

TV Guide dubbed little Desi "Lucy's $50,000,000 Baby." That was the estimated jackpot of net sales from myriad souvenir items from which Desilu would receive a 5 percent royalty. A life-sized twenty-one-inch vinyl replica of Ricky Jr. sold 125,000 units in its first month at $14.98 each. A carriage cost $12.98; an extra "Sunday suit" of clothes for special occasions was $3.98. For real babies, there were Ricky Jr. robes, bonnets, booties, and potty chairs. Mothers could buy a waterproof diaper bag identical to the one used by Lucy Ricardo on TV. For adults, the Ricardos had their own matching "Mr. & Mrs." lounging pajamas at $6.95 each. Would-be conga kings could buy a copy of Ricky's smoking jacket for $16.98.

Both the baby and his parents turned up in *I Love Lucy* coloring books, paper doll sets, and a King Features comic strip, which ran in 132 newspapers. Publisher Art Moger issued the first-ever fanzine in 3-D, Hollywood's latest attempt to combat TV competition. Using scenes from *I Love Lucy* that were printed in composite in two colors, the comic-format magazine looked like a botched job unless viewed through cardboard glasses with red-and-blue lenses that came with it.

Desi Jr. and Little Ricky became permanently fixed in the public's mind as the same person, although the Arnazes never intended to use their son as an actor in the series. "A child psychiatrist warned us against it," Desi recalled. "We didn't want our daughter watching her brother in the show and wondering why she wasn't in it as well. And to put a baby in such a pressured situation would create enormous problems for him later on. I'd seen child actors who were spoiled monsters by the time they were ten."

Under the California labor law, an infant could only be photographed for thirty seconds at a time. Ricky Jr. was first portrayed by a set of identical twins named Richard and Ronald Simmons, who were four and a half months older than Desi Jr. A doll doubled for the twins during rehearsals; they "worked" only on the filming day at a salary of twenty-five dollars each.

The Ricardos' experiences with the newborn baby became the most popular episodes of *I Love Lucy* so far, with Nielsen ratings just a few points below the 71.9 of hospital night. Until the character was old enough to have a personality of his own, the scriptwriters used Little Ricky mainly as the motivating factor in plots like "No Children Allowed," in which the Ricardos are nearly evicted by the landlord Mertzes, and "Lucy Hires a Maid," with a bossy servant threatening to take over the entire household.

Since *I Love Lucy* had become notorious for emptying theaters and similar places of amusement on Monday nights, it seemed about time that Hollywood tried to capitalize on the Arnazes' popularity by teaming them in a movie. Not surprisingly, Lucy's former lover Pandro S. Berman, still one of the top producers at MGM, had the inside track. Lucy not only owed Berman a favor for his help in the past, but the prospect of the Arnazes returning in triumph to the studio where they were dumped a decade earlier also had its psychological rewards.

By 1953, the movie business seemed on the verge of a resurgence thanks to the development of new innovations such as 3-D with Polaroid glasses; wide-screen processes like Cinerama, CinemaScope, and VistaVision; and stereophonic sound recording.

But up to now, Hollywood had a limited but discouraging experience in its attempts to transfer TV stars onto the big screen. Milton Berle's *Always Leave Them Laughing,* released at the peak of his TV fame in 1949, flopped miserably. Danny Thomas fizzled in a remake of *The Jazz Singer,* as did Alan Young in *Aaron Slick From Punkin Crick.* Neither Bob Hope nor Red Skelton had had a hit movie since they started appearing regularly on television.

MGM owned a property that Berman thought would be an ideal

vehicle for Lucy and Desi, but he had a difficult time convincing *his* boss, Dore Schary. "Metro wanted no part of it," Berman recalled. "They subscribed to the theory that the audience wouldn't pay to see actors they could get at home for free. For that reason, all the big MGM stars like Clark Gable, Esther Williams, Robert Taylor, and Ava Gardner were forbidden to work in television. But I insisted that my project was different from *I Love Lucy* and that the Arnazes could make the picture hilarious. If it was funny enough, I had no worries about people flocking to see it."

MGM originally purchased *The Long, Long Trailer* as a potential collaboration between Berman, director Vincente Minnelli, and scriptwriters Frances Goodrich and Albert Hackett, who'd all worked together on the highly successful *Father of the Bride* and *Father's Little Dividend* (both starring Spencer Tracy, Elizabeth Taylor, and Joan Bennett). The novel by Clinton Twiss was another domestic comedy based on true-life experiences, in this case a newlywed couple taking their honeymoon trip in a house trailer.

Lucy and Desi signed on for *The Long, Long Trailer* at a combined fee of $250,000, reportedly the most that MGM had ever spent on "outside" talent. When the Arnazes left MGM at the end of World War II, Lucy's contract paid $3,000 per week and Desi's $1,000 per week. Seven years and a hit TV series later, the studio was paying them each roughly $21,000 per week for the six-week shoot.

Ironically, Desi negotiated the deal for *The Long, Long Trailer* with Benjamin Thau, the same executive who handled the Arnazes' departure from MGM in 1946. Now Thau interpreted the couple's financial demands as revenge for the way they'd been mistreated by the studio in the past.

To demonstrate that he held no grudge, Desi offered to make a bet with Thau. If *The Long, Long Trailer* failed to equal the grosses of MGM's all-time comedy champion, *Father of the Bride,* the Arnazes would return $25,000 of their quarter-million fee. On the other hand, if the movie outgrossed *Father of the Bride,* MGM would have to pay the Arnazes an additional $50,000. Thau jumped at the opportunity and had the clause written into the contract.

The Arnazes made *The Long, Long Trailer* during their summer break from filming *I Love Lucy.* To avoid any embarrassment on the set, Pandro Berman conveniently took off for England to supervise *Knights of the Round Table,* another of his productions (and MGM's first in the CinemaScope process). Berman knew that Vincente Minnelli, director of such classics as *Meet Me in St. Louis* and *An Ameri-*

can in Paris, would encounter few problems keeping to schedule with two stars accustomed to turning out a TV show every week.

"It was an inexpensive picture to make, and a painless one," Vincente Minnelli said later. "The only problem I recall is that we always had to put a couple of pillows under Desi whenever we showed the two of them driving along in their car. Though Lucy and Desi were about the same height, she looked much taller when they were sitting next to each other."

The sole concession to *I Love Lucy* was that the husband had to be changed to a foreigner to accommodate Desi's accent. In *The Long, Long Trailer,* Lucy and Desi were called "Stacy and Nicholas Collini" ("Tacy and Nicky" for short), which sounded more Italian than Hispanic.

"On television, Lucy and Desi handled manufactured situations and passed them off as real. The slapstick interludes in our movie, however, were based on the author's actual experiences," Minnelli recalled.

"Lucy, for example, gets into the trailer while Desi is driving and promises to have a gourmet dinner ready by the time they reach their evening's destination. It's one misadventure after another, food falling on the floor, Lucy slipping on it, et cetera. At the end of the bumpy ride, Desi opens up the trailer door and Lucy looks like she's been wallowing in a pigpen. Only then is it explained to them that it's illegal to ride in trailers while in motion because of the dangers involved."

The third star of the movie, of course, was the thirty-six-foot mobile home. At the end of filming, the manufacturer presented the Arnazes with an even larger forty-five-foot version, which they transformed into a nursery-playhouse in the yard of their Chatsworth ranch.

Liza Minnelli, the director's seven-year-old daughter by ex-wife Judy Garland, had a bit part in *The Long, Long Trailer,* but the scene landed on the cutting-room floor. Little did anyone know that Liza would eventually have a flaming romance with Desi Jr., who was then barely six months old.

Lucy and Desi had spent so little time with the children in recent months that the entire family took off for their new beach house in Del Mar when *The Long, Long Trailer* wrapped. Established as a playground for celebrities by Bing Crosby and some of his Hollywood cronies, the summer resort near San Diego was famous for its thoroughbred racetrack, which evoked a vanished era of Spanish colonial grandeur. The surrounding landscape of rolling hills and palm trees reminded Desi of his native Cuba; he loved to go there to gamble and to loll on the beach with Lucy and the kids.

The vacation took on nightmarish overtones when Lucy received a summons to Los Angeles for a closed-door meeting with an investigator for the House Un-American Activities Committee. It was the second time within a year that Lucy had been called to answer questions relating to documents that showed that she and other members of her family had been registered members of the Communist party in 1936.

On both occasions, the testimony that eventually became public record seemed to clear Lucy of any suspicions that she was a Communist agent advocating the overthrow of the U.S. government. On September 4, 1953, she told investigator William Wheeler that she, as well as her mother and brother, registered to vote Communist to please Grandfather Fred Hunt, the only father any of them had ever known.

"It sounds a little weak and silly and corny now," Lucy said, "but at the time we knew we weren't going to have Daddy with us very long. If it made him happy it was important at the time. But I was always conscious of the fact I could go just so far to make him happy. I tried not to go any farther. In those days that was not a big, terrible thing to do. It was almost as terrible to be a Republican in those days."

Lucy claimed that she never heard Grandpa Hunt use the word "Communist," that he always talked about "the workingman" and read the *Daily Worker*. "I have never done anything for Communists, to my knowledge, at any time," she said. "I have never contributed money or attended a meeting or even had anything to do with people connected with it, if to my knowledge they were. I am not a Communist now. I never have been. I never wanted to be. Nothing in the world could ever change my mind," she said.

Fred Ball, who now worked as his sister's gofer at Desilu, testified that his Communist registration lost him a job in a defense plant during World War II and also nearly prevented his enlistment in the Army. "Grandpa was not a rabid anarchist. All he cared about was the poor guy next door, 'the workingman.' We used to listen, not because of any interest we had, but rather because of the courtesy we felt we owed him."

That might have been the end of it except that America was in the midst of a Communist witch-hunt led by Senator Joseph McCarthy, and Lucille Ball just happened to be the star of the most popular television program in the land. Two days later, Lucy and Desi were stunned when Walter Winchell dropped an ambiguous bombshell on his Sunday night news program: "The top television comedienne has been confronted with her membership in the Communist party!"

Who fed Winchell the tip is a mystery to this day, but there are plenty of suspects, starting with FBI chief J. Edgar Hoover and Senator McCarthy himself, two of the newshawk's closest friends. Fingers have also been pointed at NBC, ABC, and practically everyone else who had a motive for trying to knock *I Love Lucy* from its number-one perch.

In case anyone had missed it, Winchell's "blind" item turned up again the following morning in his nationally syndicated newspaper column. Two days later, rival Hearst columnist Jack O'Brien wrote—totally without foundation—that "Lucille Ball has announced that she intends to retire in two years. It may be a lot sooner than she thinks."

Lucy became hysterical, convinced that everything that she and Desi had worked so long and hard for would be wiped out in a flash. Neither of the Arnazes knew what to do, so they consulted MGM's publicity chief, Howard Strickling, who had a stake in the matter because of the imminent release of *The Long, Long Trailer*. Long instrumental in keeping the secrets and indiscretions of stars like Clark Gable, Spencer Tracy, Joan Crawford, Ava Gardner, and Elizabeth Taylor *out* of the newspapers, Strickling advised the Arnazes to ignore the backbiting. He was sure it would all blow over if they kept silent and didn't add any fuel to the fire.

Strickling didn't count on the nation's fear of a Soviet-Communist takeover. The 1951 treason convictions of Julius and Ethel Rosenberg confirmed for many the extent of Communist subversion. Senator McCarthy had whipped the public into a frenzy with his unproved accusations of a widespread "Commie-Pinko" conspiracy among government leaders, academics, intellectuals, and entertainers.

Early in the morning of September 11, Lucy and Desi were awakened by the sound of voices outside their bedroom window. Desi ran into the yard in his pajamas and discovered a reporter and photographer from the *Los Angeles Herald-Express*. They demanded an interview with Lucy for that afternoon's edition, which would carry a front-page story about her Communist voting registration!

Desi booted the duo off the premises and phoned their superior, city editor Agnes Underwood. He demanded that she withhold the story, at least until she had a chance to talk to Congressman Donald

Jackson, who was chairman of the House Un-American Activities Committee and could confirm Lucy's innocence. Underwood said it was too major a story to hold, but that she'd try to reach Jackson for a follow-up article.

At noon, the *Herald-Express* hit newsstands with a four-inch banner headline printed in red ink: "LUCILLE BALL A RED!" Most of the front page was taken up with a photostatic copy of Lucy's 1936 registration card. In the best tradition of Hearst-owned newspapers, pioneers in yellow journalism, the picture had been cropped so that the "Cancelled: 12-30-38" stamped on the card didn't show.

The Arnazes' telephones never stopped ringing. Superpatriot Hedda Hopper, who'd been getting the cold shoulder from Lucy all week, insisted on a statement for her next column.

"They found a registration card in the 1936 primaries," Lucy told Hopper. "They asked me about it. They refreshed my memory. I never had anything to cover up or be afraid of. I gave them a sworn statement testifying to that."

When Lucy broke down in tears, Desi took over the conversation. "It's terrible, Hedda, that something the poor kid did in 1936 to please her grandfather can kick back in her face now. She has never in her life done wrong to anybody, has never had any sympathy for those Commies. There's nothing red about Lucy except her hair, and even that's not legitimate!"

Although *I Love Lucy* was off the air at the moment (replaced by *Racket Squad* for the June–September season), Lucy and Desi had a filming that night for the fall-winter lineup. It would be the first episode produced at Motion Picture Center, another studio that Desilu had leased to expand its production space. The company now had $6 million in commitments, including *Our Miss Brooks* and a new Danny Thomas series entitled *Make Room for Daddy,* further reason why the couple were so concerned about the fallout from the latest headlines. It might mean the end of their whole burgeoning empire.

Fearful of riots and being booed off the stage by the audience, Lucy wanted to postpone the evening's filming until the public knew the truth about the rumors and fabrications. Desi persuaded her that it would only make matters worse by canceling. It would be taken as further proof that she really did have something to hide. He started placing some phone calls to see what remedies could be made in the meantime.

Desi didn't know President Eisenhower well enough to call *him,* but he did have a casual acquaintance with J. Edgar Hoover, a racing fanatic whom he often ran into at the Del Mar track. Desi got through immediately to Hoover in Washington by phone and asked if the FBI had any proof of wrongdoing in Lucy's case.

"Absolutely nothing! She's one hundred percent clear as far as we're concerned," Hoover said.

Desi next phoned CBS president Frank Stanton in New York to apprise him of the *Herald-Express* story and his chat with J. Edgar Hoover. Desi said he didn't know yet what Philip Morris's reaction would be, but if the company decided to cancel *I Love Lucy,* the Arnazes wanted to go on network television to tell their side of the story.

Desi asked to purchase *I Love Lucy*'s usual 9 P.M. time slot that Monday, which meant pre-empting *Racket Squad.* He told Stanton, "Whatever it costs, Desilu will pay. Lucy and I will tell the story about Grandpa and all the goddam things Lucy had to go through. We've got to let the American people know what this is all about. She is not going to be crucified by malicious insinuations, distorted facts, and/or false accusations. Besides, Lucy and I telling all the stories about Grandpa could be funnier than some of our shows."

Stanton said that CBS would support the Arnazes in whatever they decided to do, but that the air time would cost them $30,000. (The same half-hour went for $750,000 in 1991.) Desi gulped and said he'd take out a second mortgage on the ranch if necessary. Happily, Philip Morris chairman Alfred Lyons decided to take a neutral stance, for the moment at least.

Lucy still couldn't refrain from breaking down in tears every few minutes. On the recommendation of the CBS publicity department, Desi persuaded Congresssman Jackson and some of his commitee members to hold a six o'clock press conference to exonerate Lucy. It would be impossible for the Arnazes to attend because they'd be starting work at the studio by that time, but Desi asked his friend James Bacon of the Associated Press to phone him with a report as soon as the meeting ended.

The episode to be filmed that night was the sixty-eighth to date, "The Girls Go into Business," in which Lucy and Ethel open a dress shop and wind up their only customers. Desi's traditional warm-up of the audience was delayed until the call from James Bacon came through backstage. Lucy and Desi clutched the phone between them as they heard Bacon say, "They cleared her a hundred percent, no question about it. We all love Lucy kind of stuff."

The couple embraced and whooped for joy. "Red, come out swinging," Desi joked as he headed off toward stage front.

Speaking off the cuff, Desi said, "Ladies and gentlemen, I know that you've read a lot of bad headlines about my wife today. I came from Cuba, but during my years in the United States Army I became an American citizen, and one of the things I admire about this country is that you are considered innocent until you are proven guilty.

"Lucille is no Communist! Lucy has never been a Communist, not now and never will be. I was kicked out of Cuba because of Communism. We both despise the Communists and everything they stand for!

"Up to now, you have only read what people have said about Lucy, but you have not had a chance to read our answer to those accusations. So I will ask you to only do one thing tonight, and that is to reserve judgment until you read the newspapers tomorrow where our story will be. In the meantime, I hope you can enjoy the show under these trying circumstances."

After his usual introduction of Vivian Vance and William Frawley, Desi got carried away with the most strangulated sentence of his lifetime: "And now the girl to whom I've been married for thirteen years and who, I know, is as American as J. Edgar Hoover, President Eisenhower, or Bernie Baruch, my favorite wife, the mother of my children, the vice-president of Desilu Productions, my favorite redhead, the girl who plays Lucy—Lucille Ball!"

With her face made up even heavier than usual to mask the worry lines, she walked out from the wings dressed in a typical Lucy Ricardo blouse and skirt, topper, and hat. A doctor stood by in case she had a nervous collapse. She certainly looked like she might until everybody in the audience jumped to their feet applauding or shouting, "We love you, Lucy!"

She just stood there, sobbing, laughing, and blowing kisses as the band played the *I Love Lucy* theme. She hugged Desi, Vivian Vance, and William Frawley, and then went back to the spectator section to embrace her mother, brother, and other relatives and friends in the crowd. She even kissed some of the reporters and photographers who'd come expecting a public execution.

"How the hell she ever got hold of herself and went on to do one of the finest performances of her life, after that terrible ordeal, only proves what a tremendous actress she was," Desi recalled. Fortunately, that night's script contained no frantic slapstick. In the end, after unloading their unsuccessful dress shop for what they consider a tidy profit of $500, Lucy and Ethel discover that the new owner resold it to a developer for $50,000.

The following afternoon, by which time reporters had a chance to read the full transcript of Lucy's testimony, the Arnazes held a poolside press conference at the ranch. Dressed casually, Lucy wore a white blouse and pink toreador pants, Desi a cabana top and trunks. Cocktails, hot dogs, and hamburgers were doled out as they fielded questions.

"I was pretty numb last night, but I was thrilled by the way the audience acted," Lucy told columnist Harrison Carroll. "It was sensational, more than you could hope for. I'm glad the whole thing has come out. We asked them, begged them to bring it out.

"Do I think it hurt me? I have more faith in the American people than that. I feel that any time you give them the truth, they're with you."

In the midst of the proceedings, the maid told Desi that there was a visitor at the front door. When Desi went to see who it was, he found Larry Parks standing there with a huge bouquet of red roses for Lucy. The thirty-eight-year-old actor, acclaimed for portraying Al Jolson in two hit biopics, was probably the most celebrated victim of the House Un-American Activities Committee. He'd been on every studio's blacklist since testifying in 1951 that he belonged to the Communist party during World War II.

Because the sight of Larry Parks presenting flowers to Lucille Ball might have been misinterpreted by those who considered Parks the greatest traitor since Benedict Arnold, Desi had to tactfully turn him away.

"Larry understood. He had suffered enough from the same kind of bad publicity and was a perfect gentleman about it. I really felt like a shit, but I couldn't take the chance of some sonofabitch accusing him and Lucy of belonging to the same cell," Desi recalled.

At the end of the two-hour press conference, Dan Jenkins of *TV Guide* called for attention and said, "Ladies and gentlemen of the press, I think perhaps you will agree with me that we all owe Lucille Ball an apology." As everybody applauded, Lucy dabbed the tears from her eyes with an embroidered handkerchief.

On Sunday night, it all came full circle when Walter Winchell, who started the whole mess, opened his radio broadcast with "Mr. and Mrs. North America and all the ships at sea: During this past week, Donald Jackson, Chairman of the House Un-American Activities Committee, and all its members cleared Lucille Ball a hundred percent. So did J. Edgar Hoover and the FBI, plus every newspaper in America. And I'm sure that tonight Mr. Lincoln is drying his tears over her ordeal."

Since *I Love Lucy* didn't resume broadcasting for another month, it was impossible to get an immediate reading on how much damage the scandal had caused. Meanwhile, press coverage continued and letters from the public poured in by the thousands, mostly supportive but sometimes scathing and hateful.

Westbrook Pegler, a right-wing columnist almost as feared as Walter Winchell, wrote: "In some published comments on the affair of Lucille Ball, I detected a threat that any loyal American who does not forgive this woman will be punished. I do not react favorably to threats and I would not forgive her anyway, because she did not come clean but had to be tracked down and exposed. The propositions that she was only 24-years-old and that her grandfather was a family tyrant, a Socialist who made her do this, have no value at all with me."

Although Hedda Hopper came out in Lucy's defense, she also printed some hostile letters from readers. Maureen Maloney, a member of Gold Star Mothers, wrote, "My son didn't vote Red to please his grandpa, but he did die in Korea for his Uncle Sam." Thomas Kenley of Oklahoma City said, "So the only thing RED about Miss Ball is her hair, eh? Hedda, how can you be taken in, or are you, too, part of this conspiracy? Certainly convenient to have a dead grandpa, isn't it? They should re-name the show 'I Loved Grandpa.'" Baltimore's George Clark advocated shaving Lucy's head and sending the locks to Moscow for exhibition in Lenin's tomb in Red Square.

Everybody at Desilu, CBS, Philip Morris, and MGM was anxiously awaiting the return of I Love Lucy to the airwaves on October 5 for its third season. Amusingly, some of the next day's newspaper reviews examined the program with a fine-tooth comb for signs of the scandal's effect on Lucy's performance but found none. Small wonder, since the episode shown that night, dealing with Lucy's distress over being virtually ignored in a Life magazine article about Ricky, had been filmed five months before the incident.

Overnight rating services indicated that the Lucy opener reached about 62.7 of the potential audience, which was considerably below the all-time high of 72.9 of Little Ricky's birth night but far ahead of the 41.9 rating of the final show of the previous season. Lucy also slaughtered its main competition, although it wasn't much to begin with: singer-comedian Dennis Day on NBC and a public affairs series called Junior Press Conference on ABC.

"I Love Lucy" remained number one in the weekly ratings, followed by Arthur Godfrey's Talent Scouts, which still preceded it at eight-thirty on CBS's Monday night lineup. Variety predicted that I

Love Lucy would be season champion for the second consecutive year, but expected to find it in a close race with NBC's *Dragnet,* which aired on Thursday nights at nine and had been steadily gaining in popularity since its debut the same season as *Lucy.*

By November, the scandal over the Communists in Lucille Ball's closet seemed not only forgotten but forgiven. Lucy and Desi were invited to perform at the White House at the personal request of Ike and Mamie Eisenhower, who were avid *I Love Lucy* fans.

At a nationally televised dinner party honoring the first anniversary of the President's landslide victory over Adlai Stevenson, the Arnazes, together with Vivian Vance and William Frawley, enacted a short sketch in their *Lucy* characters and received a standing ovation from the VIP guests. Afterward, Lucy and Desi joined the Eisenhowers at the dinner table.

"God bless America," Desi recalled. "I told the President that when Lucy and I first tried to get the show on the air, nobody believed that the public would accept a foreigner with an accent as an average American husband. The President said, 'Out in Kansas they said I'd never be President. You know what we are? A couple of walking miracles!' "

17

America's Happiest Couple

ON November 30, 1953, Desi surprised Lucy with a thirteenth wedding anniversary party at the Mocambo, still the chicest nightspot in town. Lucy expected the couple to be dining with Vincente Minnelli and his intended bride, Georgette Magnani, but it turned out to be a black-tie party for forty relatives, friends, and co-workers in one of the club's private rooms.

Since it just happened to be a Monday night, at five minutes before nine o'clock waiters wheeled in a dozen table model television sets on trolleys so that everybody could watch their favorite show. That evening's episode, which by Pacific Coast time had already been broadcast in most of the nation, was entitled "Too Many Crooks," with both Lucy and Ethel suspected of being an apartment burglar known as "Madame X."

By that time in the history of *I Love Lucy* (seventy-five episodes so far), it was hard to confuse the lives of the Ricardos and the Arnazes, yet the majority of TV viewers seemed to be doing exactly that.

There were no new developments in the story of the Ricardos except that to make Little Ricky a more active participant, the scriptwriters had advanced his age to two, a year older than Desi Jr. Big Ricky still conducted the band at the Tropicana. Lucy continued on her merry way with high jinks such as serving as a live target for a knife-throwing vaudevillian, overloading the apartment with junk to convince Ricky they should move to a larger one, and disrupting one of his performances by flying through the air on a steel wire à la *Peter Pan*. No major crisis comparable to the Communist scandal had threatened the Ricardos or was likely to in their carefree world.

In marked contrast, Lucille Ball and Desi Arnaz were no longer the couple they were before *I Love Lucy*. As stars of the most popular program on television, the industry and the news media treated them like royalty, the first "King and Queen of Hollywood" to achieve that status from outside the movie business. Their predecessors, of which there seemed to be just one couple in each decade, were Douglas Fairbanks and Mary Pickford in the 1920s, Clark Gable and Carole Lombard in the '30s, and Humphrey Bogart and Lauren Bacall in the '40s.

I Love Lucy also brought the Arnazes their long desired togetherness, which in the long run proved more destructive than beneficial. As partners in Desilu, they often disagreed and battled over business matters. And being constantly in each other's way only intensified Desi's need to escape into all-night drunken revels with other women.

As one of the most idolized couples in America, the Arnazes were under tremendous pressure to keep their personal problems secret, to set an excellent example by leading an upright life and by being good parents to their children. Ironically, though Lucy and Desi had wanted a family all their married life, the babies finally came at an inconvenient time when the couple was least able to give them the personal attention they wanted to.

In a sense, Lucy and Desi had two sets of children, the real ones and Desilu Productions, each competing for their time, love, and attention. If Lucie and Desi Jr. got shortchanged, it was not intentional. While they were still toddlers, their parents had to trust in grandmothers and governesses while Mommy and Daddy took care of the bigger and more demanding child themselves.

After a full day at the studio, Lucy rushed home to feed Lucie and Desi their dinner, play with them for an hour or two, and get them ready for bed. All the cooking and housework had already been done for her by servants. If corporate business didn't keep Desi Sr. too late at the office, he usually arrived just in time for the children's goodnight prayers. Otherwise he saw them only in the morning during breakfast.

For Lucy, superstardom and parenthood arrived almost simultaneously. She'd waited years for both of them and had almost given up hope, which probably explains why she became a perfectionist in everything; extremely demanding of herself and others at work, a strict wife and mother at home.

Desi had an extra burden on his shoulders in the running of Desilu. Besides acting in each episode of *I Love Lucy* and supervising all the production details, he had to stay on top of seven other Desilu series, as well as deal with outside producers who used the studio's facilities. Fortunately, he had a photographic memory that came in handy both on the set and in the executive suite.

"We didn't use TelePrompTers in those days," Lucy recalled. "After reading the script once or twice in his office, Desi would come down to the run-throughs and be letter perfect in *everybody's* dialogue, not only his own. He never made a mistake, but he sure let us know whenever the rest of us did. We could have killed him."

Desi's diligence often paid big dividends. One day, the CBS auditors found an alleged million-dollar discrepancy in his books and demanded immediate repayment. Enraged, Desi took six cartons of files home with him, dumped the contents all over the floors and stayed up the whole night to prove that CBS had made a mistake. The next morning, he took the papers back to the studio, spread them out in the corridors of the administrative building, and took his CBS accusers on a document-by-document tour to show them where *they* had gone wrong.

In February 1954, Lucy and Desi added movies to their success story when *The Long, Long Trailer* premiered at New York's 6,000-seat Radio City Music Hall, still the most coveted theatrical booking in the world. Ironically, Russell Markert, one of Lucy's beaux during her Gotham modeling days, produced the accompanying stage revue, "Dancing Around."

The first week grossed a socko $162,000, according to *Variety*. General admission was $1.25 from opening until 1 P.M., $1.80 thereafter, with reserved seats in the first mezzanine going for $2.75. Quite a bargain by today's standards, when just a ninety-minute movie at the local sixplex is likely to cost $7.50.

By 1954, thanks largely to *I Love Lucy* and TV competition generally, the average weekly attendance at U.S. movie theaters had plummeted to 49.2 million from the all-time 1946–48 high of 90 million. The biggest hit of 1954 would be *White Christmas,* which earned $12 million in rentals in the United States and Canada, followed by *The Caine Mutiny,* with $8.7 million, and *The Glenn Miller Story,* with $7 million.

On *Variety*'s list of 1954's box-office winners, *The Long, Long Trailer* ranked seventeenth with rentals of $4 million, considered terrific business for that time when the average admission price was 44.7 cents (as compared to $4.80 in 1990). Of MGM releases that year, only *Seven Brides for Seven Brothers* ($4.75 million) and *Knights of the Round Table* ($4.4 million) did better. The movie also outpulled 1950's *Father of the Bride,* winning Desi $50,000 in his bet with Benjamin Thau that *The Long, Long Trailer* would become MGM's biggest comedy hit.

The success of *The Long, Long Trailer* surprised the movie moguls who believed that the public wouldn't pay to see stars that they could watch for free on home TV. Why people turned out in droves seemed to be a combination of wide screen and color photography (color TV was still very much in the experimental stage, ten-inch black-and-white sets were the norm), excellent critical reviews, and a general affection for a couple who had become more like friends and neighbors than actors.

MGM production head Dore Schary promptly signed Lucy and Desi for two more films, with the proviso that production could not interfere with their work schedules for *I Love Lucy.* This time, the couple would also share in the profits and co-produce the two movies via their Zanra (Arnaz spelled backwards) Productions Company.

While basking in the success of *The Long, Long Trailer,* Lucy and Desi also received reconfirmation of their TV popularity when *I Love Lucy* won an Emmy award for "Best Situation Comedy" for the second consecutive year. Having copped the previous year's Emmy for "Best Comedienne," Lucy lost out this time to Eve Arden (of the Desilu-produced *Our Miss Brooks*), but Vivian Vance won as "Best Supporting Actress."

William Frawley also was nominated for an Emmy that year, but got trounced by Art Carney of *The Honeymooners.* When Vance won and he didn't, Frawley caused a rumpus at the awards banquet by snarling right in front of her, "It goes to prove that the whole vote is rigged."

Since fantasy and reality often overlapped on *I Love Lucy,* many viewers believed that the Arnazes were best pals with Vance and Frawley, but that was hardly the case. Frawley, in fact, was nobody's friend and kept to himself, calling Lucy and Viv "brass-bound bitches" and Desi "that Cuban heel" behind their backs.

"Bill was a holy terror to work with," Vivian Vance recalled. "He was quick to explode in red-cheeked rage and was mad at everybody most of the time. Working was a nuisance to him. It kept him from his hobbies of boozing in saloons and chewing the rag with other baseball fanatics. He never knew what the stories were about. When he got a script, he tore out the pages with his lines and threw the rest away."

Although Vance and other aggrieved co-workers hoped that Frawley's drinking would eventually cause him to be fired, that never happened. The Arnazes tolerated his irascibilty and occasional benders because he suited the part of Fred Mertz so perfectly. The also felt a certain obligation to keep him on the payroll, since he supported two spinster sisters and several other relatives.

Vivian Vance's personal relationship with the Arnazes was of the love-hate variety. They got along famously on the work level, but Vance resented the couple's financial success as well as the tendency of the public and the news media to treat *I Love Lucy* like a one-woman show. Being second banana to Lucille Ball was no easy task.

For her part, Lucy always spoke glowingly of Vance: "My god, what a gal to work with. We had so much fun on the set we didn't want to go home. She was also a great show doctor. She could always tell when a script needed work."

Vance once said that "Lucy and I were just like sisters. We adored each other's company. We had so many laughs together that we could hardly get through filming without cracking up."

According to Vance, rumors began circulating that she and Lucy were lesbian lovers. Apparently it was all in the imagination of Vance's actor husband, Philip Ober, who was extremely jealous of her success and delighted in tormenting his wife.

"My husband told me that people were talking about us. 'You ought to be more careful about the hugging and kissing you do on the show. You behave like a couple of dykes in heat.' That sent me leaping into my car to drive to my psychiatrist. I asked him if there was anything the matter with me that he'd never told me about. He said there wasn't," Vance recalled.

The 1954–55 season would turn out to be the third consecutive year that *I Love Lucy* was the most watched TV program in the nation. Through a lucky fluke, Desilu also gained part ownership in a new series called *December Bride,* which quickly became the second-most popular sitcom on the air.

December Bride had been a CBS radio series about a giddy widow living with her daughter and son-in-law. Although CBS had an option to transfer it to television, network executives wanted a bigger star than sixty-one-year-old Spring Byington, who'd been playing the title role from the start on radio. Writer-creator Parke Levy disagreed. He bought back CBS's 50 percent interest and resold it to Desilu out of admiration for its success with *I Love Lucy,* which, of course, also had roots in radio through Lucy's *My Favorite Husband.*

Desi thought *December Bride* was perfect just the way it was, so most of the first season's episodes were adapted from scripts that had already been used on radio. Since it had a previous identification with CBS, neither NBC nor ABC was interested in taking the series. Desi finally succeeded in getting it back on CBS when he discovered that chairman William Paley had never been consulted about the transfer of rights to Desilu.

December Bride happened to be one of Paley's favorite shows, so he was furious and accused Desi of unscrupulous dealings. To keep the peace, Desi sold 50 percent of his half interest to CBS, which left Desilu and the network equal partners. Desi also insisted that *December Bride* be scheduled for Monday nights at nine-thirty, immediately behind *I Love Lucy,* so it could pick up that audience. Needless to say, the new series was soon in the Top Ten as well.

Desilu had less success with two series which starred revered character actors but never got beyond the pilot stage because of network disinterest: *Mr. Tutt* with Walter Brennan and *Country Doctor* with Charles Coburn. The company had slightly better luck with *Willy,* starring June Havoc (sister of stripper Gypsy Rose Lee), who'd had a disappointing movie career similar to Lucy's. The sitcom about a lady lawyer in a small New England town sold to CBS, but lasted only one season against the perennial NBC favorite, *Your Hit Parade.*

Compensating for those disappointments was Desilu's *Lineup* with Warner Anderson and Tom Tully, one of the first crime series to feature location filming. It premiered on the CBS network in October 1954 and eventually ran for six years. The program later earned a fortune in syndication under the title *San Francisco Beat* and inspired many copycats, most notably *The Streets of San Francisco* in 1972.

In December 1954, the Arnazes received a nasty Christmas surprise when *Confidential,* the most notorious muckraking magazine of the time, came out with a cover story inquiring "Does Desi Really Love Lucy?" The article marked the first time since *I Love Lucy* went on the air that the public had any reason to doubt the wedded bliss of America's second-most favorite couple after Ike and Mamie.

Started in 1952 as a snarling alternative to the sappy fan magazines that covered the celebrity world, *Confidential* by this time had a circulation of 4 million, exceeding that of the revered *Saturday Evening Post* and *Look.* Professing to "telling the facts and naming the names," its research was conducted by an army of private detectives, wiretap experts, and hidden microphone specialists, to say nothing of call girls, hotel clerks, nightclub waiters, office cleaners, and anyone else who might have some dirt to sell.

Besides the Arnazes' alleged marital problems, the January 1955 issue of *Confidential* blew the whistle on black entertainer Eartha Kitt's romance with the Jewish grandson of movie pioneer Adolph Zukor, presidential hopeful Senator Stuart Symington's criminal record as a car thief, champion boxer Rocky Marciano's racket of putting on "fake" exhibition fights, and actress Susan Hayward's bare-bottom spanking for calling husband Jess Barker a "queer." Ironically, the magazine also carried an unconnected story about Desi's longtime friend, the now retired Polly Adler, who'd just organized Prostitutes Anonymous for women trying to quit the profession.

No one was more shocked than Lucy and Desi themselves when they read Brad Shortell's article detailing Desi's escapades with "cuddle-for-cash babes," from recent months to as far back as his Army service during World War II. Among other tidbits, the story claimed that Desi spent the night of August 3, 1953, with a prostitute named Mindy in Bungalow 5 of the Beverly Hills Hotel. An encounter with two call girls identified as Ginger and Babs allegedly took place in Ginger's apartment in North Hollywood during the winter of 1951.

The article also dredged up a skeleton in the closet—the Arnazes' near divorce in 1944, which CBS and Desilu publicists had been trying to keep quiet for fear it would tarnish the couple's happily married image. Ten years earlier, the names of Lucille Ball and Desi Arnaz didn't ring bells with much of the public, but now that they were household commodities it became shocking news to all those admirers who were reading it for the first time.

"The split never took effect because it was granted in California, where the rule says the unhappy couple must live apart for one year before the decree is valid. Lucy and Desi slightly missed this cooling off period by getting together the very first night after her decree," *Confidential* claimed.

"Close friends who watched this pixilated episode asked Lucy just what was her idea of going to such expense and trouble, if she obviously never meant to break it up. She offered an explanation as daffy as though it came from the Lucy on her TV role. It was all an effort to teach Desi a lesson, she said. If that was the objective, it fell far short of its goal, because Desi has been prowling like a bachelor wolf ever since."

Like the majority of *Confidential*'s targets, Lucy and Desi chose to ignore the article rather than file a libel suit that could only result in even more scandalous publicity. But several years later, a Los Angeles County grand jury investigating *Confidential*'s sources of information heard that at least part of the story came from an admitted prostitute named Ronnie Quillan. She testified that the magazine paid her $1,500 for tips about Desi and jazz singer Herb Jeffries (subject of a separate story in another issue).

The *Confidential* exposé seemed to have no detrimental effect on the popularity of *I Love Lucy*. In the first three months of 1955, the series enjoyed an average audience share of a whopping 51 percent per episode, thanks no doubt to the introduction of a continuing story about Ricky's attempts to become a movie star. The scenarios about the Ricardos' and Mertzes' misadventures in Hollywood permitted guest appearances by major box-office draws who had rarely, if ever, worked in television before, including John Wayne, William Holden, and Rock Hudson.

The Holden episode contained one of the funniest moments in the history of *I Love Lucy,* and it all happened by accident. While Lucy Ricardo is heavily disguised to prevent the actor from recognizing her after she unintentionally dumped a tray of desserts on him at the Brown Derby, Holden offers to light her cigarette and sets her false nose on fire. To literally save her skin, the real Lucy extinguished the flaming schnozzola in a handy cup of coffee.

"You think I was taken by surprise? Bill Holden almost fainted," she said later.

Another hilarious movieland story had Lucy trying to fool a star-struck friend by impersonating Clark Gable, Gary Cooper, Jimmy Durante, and Harpo Marx. The latter turns up unexpectedly in the flesh and pretends to be her mirror image in a re-creation of his pantomime solo in the 1932 Marx Brothers classic *Duck Soup*.

In real life, Lucy and Desi were about to "go Hollywood" themselves. After fourteen years of residence at their ranch in the San Fernando Valley, the couple had grown sick of the daily commute to the studio. Desi had the bright idea of buying a helicopter, which could whisk them back and forth to work in ten minutes rather than the forty-five it generally took by car on Los Angeles's increasingly congested freeways and boulevards. The Arnazes certainly would have made an impression—the first airborne royalty of Hollywood—but CBS talked them out of it for safety reasons. The chances of Lucy and/ or Desi being killed or maimed in a crash seemed all too possible.

House hunting suddenly became a top priority after the telephone switchboard operator at Desilu started to receive calls from a self-proclaimed kidnapper who threatened to abduct one of the Arnaz children if their parents didn't pay him $1 million in cash within forty-eight hours. Though it proved to be the prank of a mentally disturbed fan, Lucy and Desi realized how vulnerable they were in their rustic surroundings.

The most logical move would be to Beverly Hills, which had originally been developed as a safe haven for Hollywood celebrities in the rip-roaring 1920s. The independent city within Los Angeles had its own government and the most diligent police force in the nation. Strangers strolling its residential streets were likely to be interrogated and ordered to leave if they didn't have a solid reason for being there.

Desi had his hands full running Desilu Productions, so Lucy started scouting Beverly Hills on her own with the help of real estate agents. One day, a broker took her to a mansion on a corner of Roxbury Drive, north of Sunset Boulevard. Lucy liked it enough, but as they were leaving she spotted a house directly across the street that appealed to her even more. Something about the two-story white brick-and-clapboard Colonial reminded her of the posh residences around Jamestown, New York, that were far beyond her family's means while she was growing up.

She asked if she could see the interior, but the broker had no listing for it and doubted if it was for sale. Lucy couldn't be dissuaded. She marched across the street to 1000 North Roxbury and rang the front door bell.

"An elderly woman named Mrs. Bang finally opened the door. I introduced myself, but the name didn't seem to mean anything to her, and I could have been the Avon Lady for all that mattered," Lucy recalled. "It turned out to be one of the luckiest and yet saddest moments of my life. Just the night before, Mrs. Bang and her husband had been talking about selling the house because it contained too many reminders of their son and only child, who'd recently been killed in an accident while serving in the Army. She broke down in tears as she told me the story and then took me on a tour of the house, which I fell in love with immediately."

Asking permission to use the phone, Lucy called Desi at the studio and told him to drive over immediately. "Honey, I'm in a meeting right now and can't leave. If you like the place that much, buy it. I'm sure I'll love it too," he said.

Mr. Bang had gone out on an errand, so Lucy waited until he returned. Like his wife, he felt that moving would be the best therapy for the couple's depression over their son's death. Lucy made them an offer of $75,000. Mr. Bang demanded $85,000. Since there would be no brokerage fees involved, Lucy agreed and they shook hands on the deal.

Meanwhile, Desi was negotiating to purchase the controlling interest in Motion Picture Center, the Hollywood studio where Desilu leased space for most of its production activities. Desi had an inside tip that Harry Cohn, who'd given Lucy such a hard time during her tenure at Columbia Pictures, intended to buy Motion Picture Center and make it part of the Columbia plant.

"That scared the hell out of me," Desi recalled. "Harry Cohn was a man I admired at times, but I knew he was absolutely ruthless in business. If Desilu became dependent on him for its life, it could be a short one. I was certain that if he at any time needed our stages, we would be out on the street looking for another place."

Luckily, Harry Cohn had so many people who despised him, the owners of Motion Picture Center included, that Desi got first crack at the property. Desilu's tax attorney worked out a deal for a new mortgage that gave Desilu voting control of the studio. Lucy and Desi as individuals became members of the board of directors.

Desi realized that buying into Motion Picture Center would be just a stopgap for Desilu. MPC lacked a back lot for outdoor work as well as most of the technical departments and facilities that major studios like MGM or Universal could offer. To compete on an equal footing with those giants, Desilu would need additional space, plus many more employees to help carry the work load.

Desi was now thirty-eight years old, Lucy nearing forty-five. With two young children to consider, he wondered whether the backbreaking task of running a television empire was really worth it in terms of the couple's health and happiness. If they ended *I Love Lucy* and sold the backlog to CBS, they could realize at least $3 million. Investing that sum conservatively, they could live quite comfortably on the interest of about $150,000 per year, without even touching the capital.

Lucy thought that Desi had lost his senses. She loved being the "Queen" of television, considering it just reward for the twenty years she'd spent slaving away in grade-B movies. Despite her devotion to husband and children, her career still came first and always would.

I Love Lucy continued to be so popular that in April 1955 CBS started Sunday evening reruns of the series in the six to six-thirty time slot. It marked the first time in television history that viewers could watch past episodes of a program while the latest ones were running in prime time. In the three years that *I Love Lucy* had been on the air, about 25 million households had purchased their first TV sets, so many people had never seen the old episodes before.

To avoid confusion, the reruns were entitled *The Lucy Show*. Sponsor Lehn and Fink, manufacturer of products like Hinds hand lotion and Lysol disinfectant, leased the first fifty-two episodes of *I Love Lucy* for $30,000 each. The $1.56 million that Desilu received in the deal more than paid back the $1.24 million spent to produce the shows originally.

The Long, Long Trailer did so well at the box office ($4.5 million in rentals so far) that MGM was eager to start production on the first of the two movies in its new deal with the Arnazes. Studio head Dore Schary suggested a property that had been collecting dust on the shelves since its purchase in the 1940s as a possible team effort for Spencer Tracy and Katharine Hepburn. Lucy and Desi might have seemed illogical replacements for that duo, but MGM thought that the public would flock to see them in anything short of *Romeo and Juliet*.

Helen Deutsch, the versatile scriptwriter of MGM hits like *I'll Cry Tomorrow, Lili,* and *King Solomon's Mines,* received the assignment of transforming Marya Mannes's short story "The Woman Who Was Scared" into a proper vehicle for Lucy and Desi. Entitled *Forever, Darling,* the project unintentionally contributed to the eventual demise of MGM as Hollywood's pre-eminent production center.

Up to then, MGM rarely produced movies outside its own studio complex in Culver City, but Desi persuaded Dore Schary to shoot *Forever, Darling* at Desilu's facilities in Motion Picture Center. Desi claimed that by using methods similar to those employed for Desilu's television films, MGM could shave half a million dollars from the movie's budget. Furthermore, Desilu did not have to contend with the huge operating overhead that MGM did because of the latter's long-standing contracts with the labor unions and with its thousands of employees.

Amusingly, *Forever, Darling* gave Lucy another opportunity to help out a former lover and mentor. As a co-producer of the movie, she insisted on hiring Alexander Hall as director. Active since silent days, Hall hadn't been in much demand recently and was delighted to get the job.

Just before *Forever, Darling* started production, Lucy and Desi made the big move to Beverly Hills from their ranch in the San Fernando Valley. Except for having to give away whatever livestock they had left, pulling up stakes after thirteen years wasn't as traumatic as expected.

To help the children adjust to their new surroundings, Desi added on many of the features of their previous home, starting with an enormous playroom and a backyard swimming pool. Lucy kept most of the Early American ranch furnishings (purchased from the Sears, Roebuck and Montgomery Ward catalogs), but gradually replaced them with authentic antiques of the same period. The Arnazes would never have to worry about price tags again.

Lucy also splurged on new equipment for her home beauty parlor, where she soon had an unexpected visit from royalty. "I'd invited Vivian Vance over and we were sitting with bleach in our hair and muck on our faces," she recalled. "The doorbell rings and it's a man from the chamber of commerce stopping by with the Crown Prince of Thailand and his wife for a surprise visit. Viv and I looked like we sometimes did on *I Love Lucy,* and I guess they figured we always looked like that. So they filed into my living room and posed for pictures with us. Somewhere in Thailand, there are photos of Viv and me looking like hell."

As luck would have it, Lucy and Desi had the Jack Bennys as next-door neighbors at 1002 North Roxbury Drive, while the James Stewarts lived just down the block. Jack Benny loved to play jokes on the Arnazes, often strolling over to serenade them on his violin when they least expected him. He never stopped kidding them about Mr. and Mrs. Ronald Colman being buried in their basement. In the fantasy world of Benny's radio and TV shows, "Ronnie and Benita" supposedly occupied the house now owned by the Arnazes, although the Colmans never did in real life.

Surprisingly, the move to Beverly Hills fostered a close friendship between Lucy and someone she'd feared for years, the ferocious Hedda Hopper, who lived nearby. While walking her dog, the gossip columnist began stopping by to chat with Lucy, who at first suspected her of snooping for dirt about the Arnazes. But as time went on, they began confiding in each other about their problems (Hopper's actor son had just left his wife and children—for a man), and the older woman turned out to be a good ally to have as the Arnazes' marriage continued to deteriorate. Hopper not only leaned on other journalists to protect the couple's happy image, but also used her influence with the police whenever Desi's drinking got him into trouble.

To commemorate their change of address, Lucy and Desi used their new home as a setting in the episode of *I Love Lucy* that they were making at the time. When Lucy Ricardo and Ethel Mertz get off a sightseeing bus in Beverly Hills in "The Tour," the mansion supposedly owned by movie star Richard Widmark actually belonged to the Arnazes.

The moment marked one of the few times in the history of *I Love Lucy* that filming took place outdoors on location. To avoid disrupting the posh neighborhood, the balance of the action, in which Lucy Ricardo tries to steal a grapefruit from a tree in Widmark's backyard as a souvenir, was performed in the studio. Prop men built an exact duplicate of a portion of the wall that surrounded the grounds.

"The Tour" signaled the end of production for the fourth season of *I Love Lucy* programs. Without pausing to rest, Lucy and Desi began working on *Forever, Darling,* which had a seven-week shooting schedule, including ten days of exteriors at Yosemite National Park in northeastern California. The debonair British actor James Mason co-starred with the Arnazes, in a role originally intended for William Powell when MGM was considering the project for Katharine Hepburn and Spencer Tracy.

Forever, Darling would prove a major disappointment for *Lucy* fans expecting another slapstick howler like *The Long, Long Trailer*. This time, Desi had the unlikely role of Lorenzo Vega, a research chemist whose experiments seem more important than his gorgeous wife, Susan. James Mason, as a heavenly guardian angel, comes to Lucy's aid, finally reconciling the couple when they take a camping trip to test Desi's new formula for an insect repellent.

The most memorable thing about *Forever, Darling* was the title tune, composed by Bronislau Kaper with lyrics by Sammy Cahn. The song became a tradition in the Arnaz family, played whenever they had an anniversary or birthday to be celebrated. In later years, Desi would sing "Forever, Darling" at the weddings of both children.

Forever, Darling turned out to be Lucy and Desi's third and last movie together. The management of Radio City Music Hall, which did big business with *The Long, Long Trailer,* rejected the new film as substandard, so it wound up having its world premiere on Broadway at Loew's State, the onetime presentation house where Lucy and Desi performed their first vaudeville act way back in 1942. In general release, the Eastman Color comedy barely returned its production cost of $1.4 million. By mutual agreement, the Arnazes and MGM decided to drop the remaining project in their co-production deal. Nobody wanted to risk the embarrassment of another failure while *I Love Lucy* was still topping the popularity polls.

Although *Lucy* continued to capture about 51 percent of the potential audience in its Monday night time slot, Philip Morris decided to cancel sponsorship of the series in June 1955, the official ending to TV's 1954–55 season. Identified with the program for the full four years of its run, the cigarette manufacturer had watched sales plummet as the result of highly publicized medical studies linking lung cancer to smoking. Spending millions of advertising dollars a year on a show oriented toward young, health-conscious viewers no longer made economic sense.

Sponsors were literally standing in line awaiting just such an opportunity, so CBS quickly made a new deal with General Foods, which had previously hawked Jell-O dessert mixes on Lucy's radio program *My Favorite Husband*. Procter & Gamble also came aboard in behalf of Cheer laundry detergent. Both companies actually made a better fit with *I Love Lucy* then Philip Morris, because the products advertised were more likely to be found in the homes of folks like the Ricardos and Mertzes.

I Love Lucy lost one of its most important components that season when producer and chief writer Jess Oppenheimer quit to join CBS's archrival, the National Broadcasting Company, as head of West Coast programming. Oppenheimer had become fed up with Desi's tendency to take credit for the producer's contributions to the success of *Lucy*, so he was happy to make the break.

Much to Desi's displeasure, he had to give Oppenheimer a piece of the action as a going-away present. As one of the creators of *I Love Lucy*, Oppenheimer was entitled to a royalty from all future episodes, as well as from reruns of the entire series. The arrangement eventually made him a multimillionaire.

Oppenheimer's departure placed an even heavier burden on Desi's shoulders in the running of Desilu. Rather than hiring a replacement for Oppenheimer on *I Love Lucy*, Desi took over the production reins himself, while Madelyn Pugh and Bob Carroll continued to share the writing, assisted by newcomers Bob Schiller and Bob Weiskopf.

By this time, Desilu had four series on the air, plus ten more in development. In the latter category, the most promising seemed an anthology project featuring adaptations of great short stories, with Orson Welles as host and occasional star and director.

After making two acknowledged masterpieces in *Citizen Kane* and *The Magnificent Ambersons*, Welles proved too much an *enfant terrible* for Hollywood to handle and fled to Europe, where he also eventually bottomed out. But Desi was convinced that Welles's genius could raise the cultural level of commercial television, so he advanced Welles money to settle his problems with the Internal Revenue Service, which enabled him to return to the United States. As soon as Welles arrived with his pregnant Italian wife in tow, he didn't want to stay in a hotel, so the Arnazes gave him the use of the guest house while he made a half-hour pilot based on John Collier's "The Fountain of Youth."

"Orson thought we were the Arnaz Hotel," Lucy recalled. "He was like 'The Man Who Came to Dinner,' scaring the kids and terrorizing the servants. The pilot was supposed to be filmed in five days but took six weeks. When he spent $10,000 on the wrap party, Desi kicked him out on his buttkus. Orson had a brilliant mind, but he was so wasteful and irresponsible. He left a huge trail of disasters in his wake as he just sailed through life."

Needless to say, "The Fountain of Youth" never went to series, but it eventually landed on television three years later as an installment of NBC's *Colgate Theater* and wound up winning a coveted Peabody Award for excellence. In the meantime, Welles paid off some of his debt to Desilu by guesting on *I Love Lucy* in an episode in which he demonstrated his skills as a magician by levitating the reluctant red-head on the tip of a broomstick.

With aggravations like Orson Welles adding to the day-to-day pressures of running Desilu, it was small wonder that Desi began to depend more and more on alcohol to get him through.

"Most people start the morning with a cup of coffee, but Desi always had a shot of bourbon as soon as he got out of bed," onetime Desilu vice-president Martin Leeds recalled. "After he arrived at the office and went through the mail, he usually fixed himself a daiquiri around ten-thirty and kept replenishing it until he went home at night. Amazingly, he still functioned very well. It took several years before the steady drinking caught up with him and started to radically affect his behavior."

18

Studio Moguls

WHEN *I Love Lucy* returned to the airwaves after its summer recess of 1955, the stories continued to revolve around the Ricardos' misadventures in Hollywood. MGM cancels plans to star Ricky in a musical version of *Don Juan,* so Lucy tries to pressure the studio into finding another vehicle for her husband by planting a false rumor that Rodgers and Hammerstein want him for a Broadway show. The scheme backfires when MGM, instead of putting Ricky to work, decides to release him from his contract so that he can accept the stage offer. Their Hollywood dreams dashed, the Ricardos and the Mertzes finally head back home to New York by train, where Lucy becomes the dupe of a jewel thief posing as an FBI agent.

The Hollywood episodes of *I Love Lucy* enjoyed such high audience ratings that the scriptwriters weren't about to let go of a good idea. The Ricardos are barely re-established in their apartment when Ricky accepts an offer to take his band on a tour of England and Europe. A full season of stories could be spun from that, with Fred Mertz working as Ricky's band manager and Lucy and Ethel going along for the ride. Little Ricky, still too young to be a major character, could be conveniently written out while left at home with Grandma McGillicuddy.

Unlike the Ricardos, who would travel as far as Italy in their transatlantic journey, the Arnazes rarely strayed beyond the walls of Motion Picture Center to film the episodes. There was no way that Desi could spend five months abroad and run Desilu at the same time. *I Love Lucy* viewers would have to settle for painted backdrops and stock movie footage of the real thing. In that era of small-screen black-and-white receivers, TV producers could get away with such subterfuge more easily than they can now, when color and high-definition pictures have made location filming almost mandatory.

As luck would have it, production of "Bon Voyage," the episode that celebrated the Ricardos' departure on the SS *Constitution*, coincided with Lucy and Desi's fifteenth wedding anniversary. Co-workers surprised the couple with a huge three-tiered cake and king-sized bottles of champagne.

Gossip hen Hedda Hopper sent a congratulatory telegram claiming that the Arnazes had set a new longevity record for a star-crossed Hollywood marriage. Hopper was probably correct if one didn't count George Burns and Gracie Allen, who dated back to the vaudeville era and really belonged in another category of showbiz celebrities. Lucy and Desi's closest competition among contemporaries were Humphrey Bogart and Lauren Bacall, who were married ten years by that time.

Yet there wasn't much correlation between the marriage played out in public and the real one. While the Ricardos seemed like they would never hit the showbiz jackpot, the Arnazes' Desilu empire was grossing about $15 million annually, employing 800 people on its payroll, and using up more raw film every week than Paramount and Universal combined. Besides *Lucy*, the company produced *December Bride, The Sheriff of Cochise, Those Whiting Girls, Lineup,* and *Wire Service,* and provided facilities for fifteen other series.

It was starting to look like Desilu had a hand in everything on television, but it did have competition from other Hollywood independents like Ziv, Four Star, and Filmways. Some of the big movie studios had also joined the "enemy" with companies like Warner Brothers Television and Columbia Pictures' Screen Gems.

Despite an occasional spat, the Ricardos were apparently still passionate for each other, although TV censors never allowed viewers to see them sharing the same bed (they had twin mattresses with a common headboard). But in the decade and a half that the Arnazes had been together, the six-year age gap between them had gradually taken its toll on their intimate relationship.

At forty-four, and especially since her two cesarean operations, Lucy no longer held any sexual allure for Desi. Since moving to Beverly Hills, they had been occupying separate bedrooms. Desi often spent the night elsewhere, playing cards with cronies or cavorting with floozies, but returning by early morning to get ready for work and to breakfast with the children.

According to one of Desi's top aides at the studio, Lucy kept dropping unsubtle hints to him that her husband should be more attentive. The executive finally confronted Desi: "For God's sake, couldn't you at least fuck her once or twice a month? It would make her so happy. Put a bag over her head if she turns you off that much." Desi sorrowfully said he couldn't.

Desi had a penchant for young, big-busted blondes. One of his favorite diversions was driving down to San Diego to pick up strippers and chorines who worked at the legendary Hollywood Burlesque Theater on F Street. "Desi would take five or six girls back to his hotel suite and make them nice and cozy in the parlor before calling them into the bedroom one by one until he'd screwed the lot. If he'd brought a friend with him from L.A., the guy was invited to share the goodies, but not in the same room with Desi. He did have his limits," said onetime Desilu vice-president Martin Leeds.

Another of Desi's great weaknesses was gambling. Although managing Desilu kept him from frequenting the racetracks, he had accounts with all the bookies in town. Friends say that whatever money he lost was his own, that he was scrupulous about never dipping into the Desilu treasury. During football season, he was known to go hogwild, betting $5,000 a game on his favorite teams.

During a golfing weekend in Palm Springs, Desi won $18,000 in an all-night gin rummy game. Since the wealthy loser owned land in the area, instead of cash he offered Desi two adjacent lots that were then worth $9,000 apiece. Desi accepted and eventually spent another $150,000 building a vacation house on the site.

As far as the world knew, the Arnazes were blissfully happy. When *Forever, Darling* was released in February 1956, the movie's title seemed to their fans an accurate prophecy of the couple's future. So what if the film flopped at the box office? Not even Lucy and Desi were infallible.

On television, the couple could still do no wrong; the concurrent episodes of *I Love Lucy* set in Europe were among the funniest ever filmed. Many viewers consider the masterwork of the entire series to be "Lucy's Italian Movie," in which Lucy lands a bit part in a neorealistic melodrama entitled *Bitter Grapes* (*Bitter Rice* having been an international hit for voluptuous Silvana Mangano as a rice picker in the Po Valley paddies). Guessing that the movie will be about indigent winemakers, Lucy disguises herself as a peasant and sneaks off to a town near Rome to see what life in a vineyard is really like.

Lucy gets more than she bargained for when she's mistaken for an employee and ordered into a huge vat to mash grapes with her bare feet. Working in tandem with a hefty Italian woman more than twice her size, Lucy quickly falls into the rhythm of the job, but finally gets into a slugfest with her partner when she tries to stop for a rest.

The episode had a surprise ending in which Ethel Mertz gets the upper hand over Lucy Ricardo for a change. Returning to Rome looking battered and wine-stained, Lucy is forced to relinquish the *Bitter Grapes* role, which turns out to be a dowdy American tourist rather than the busty Italian vixen that she supposed. Director Vittorio Fellipi (a sendup of DeSica and Fellini) ends up hiring Ethel instead.

While the Ricardos and Mertzes continued on their merry way around Europe, the writers of *I Love Lucy* were already sketching plans for the following season's programs. The characters couldn't go on living out of suitcases indefinitely. Eventually they'd have to return to a "normal" existence, if there was such a thing for that zany quartet.

To introduce a fresh element, Little Ricky would become a major character in the series. Raising a rambunctious three-year-old in a cramped Manhattan apartment had lots of comic potential and also provided the motivation for a startling shake-up in the friendship between the Ricardos and the Mertzes. What if Lucy and Ricky suddenly decided to move from the Mertzes' apartment building and buy a house in the country?

Once again, the Arnazes had to consider casting their own son in the role of Little Ricky. Desi Jr. was the spitting image of his father, but the couple still felt the same way as they did at his birth. "We didn't want his sister watching her brother in the show and wondering why she wasn't in it. It would create too many psychological problems for both of them," Desi recalled.

Because of the California law limiting the time that babies and toddlers could spend being photographed, Little Ricky had been portrayed by sets of identical twins, but the character had now reached an age where he could be played by one actor. Finding him proved more difficult than it might have seemed. The boy not only needed to look like a miniature Ricky Ricardo, but also had to be an accomplished drummer like his dad.

While watching bandleader Horace Heidt's *Show Wagon,* an NBC variety program originating from a different American city every week and featuring local talent, Lucy and Desi found the solution to the problem in Keith Thibodeaux, a tiny drum virtuoso from Lafayette, Louisiana. Before the night was over, Desi tracked down Keith's father by telephone and made arrangements for the two of them to fly out from New Orleans for an audition.

Keith turned out to be five years old, but the scriptwriters could easily advance Little Ricky's age a bit without jolting viewers. Bearing a strong physical resemblance to Ricky/Desi, he won the part after proving that he could play the skins at least as well as Desi could.

As a condition of a seven-year contract that started at a salary of $461 per week, the boy took the professional name of Richard Keith (Thibodeaux being deemed too difficult to spell and pronounce). His father quit a job as an insurance agent to work in Desilu's publicity department, where he could always be close at hand if Keith needed him on the set.

Since Keith had no acting experience, Lucy and Desi decided that it would be to everyone's advantage if he came to live in their house during the production season. Treated like one of the family, Keith was more likely to give a natural and relaxed performance than if he saw the Arnazes only when it came to working with them at the studio.

The arrangement enabled the couple to spend as much time with Keith as they did with their own children. Desi taught him to speak Spanish, which would be required in the scripts from time to time. Lucy became Keith's acting coach, supervised his schooling, and even selected the clothes that he wore as Little Ricky.

"It was as if we suddenly had three children instead of two," Desi recalled. "During the weekends and our summer hiatus, Keith would come to Palm Springs or Del Mar with us. I taught Lucie, Desi, and Keith how to swim, ride horses, handle boats, and fish expertly."

Many years later, Keith remembered it a bit differently. "My dad worked at Desilu, so Lucy was his boss. She'd call up and say 'I want Keith to come over and play with Little Desi this weekend.' Sometimes I'd cry because I had something else I'd rather do, but my dad didn't want to risk his job and that was that. One day, while Desi was supposed to be on a diet, we stole a chocolate cake from the kitchen and ate the whole thing between us. Lucy found out and banned me from the house for three months. She could be harsh. You had to walk softly if she was angry or not feeling well. She had a temper. She would slam doors. She also had a big heart and could be a joy to be around. But I was always pretty much in awe or scared of the lady, really."

Richard Keith's first appearance as Little Ricky took place in the series opener of October 1, 1956, which focused on Lucy's efforts to persuade Bob Hope to make a guest appearance at the opening of Rickys's new nightspot, Club Babalu. One can only guess at what went on in the minds of the Arnaz children that night while they were watching the program and saw their best pal, Keith, portraying Mommy and Daddy's little boy.

The experience proved especially traumatic for four-year-old Desi Jr., who would suffer an identity crisis well into adulthood. Because the public tended to confuse Lucille Ball and Desi Arnaz with the characters of Lucy and Ricky Ricardo, many viewers believed that Little Ricky and Desi Jr. were the same person. Playmates of Desi's who did know the difference still expected him to behave like his TV counterpart.

But according to Desi Jr., he and his sister learned early to differentiate between what they saw on I Love Lucy and what happened at home. "On TV, my mother was overplayed and my dad was underplayed," he recalled. "Those were difficult years—so many funny things happening on the tube to people who looked like my parents, then the same people agonizing through some terribly unhappy times at home, and each of them trying to convince Lucie and me separately that the other was in the wrong."

Making Little Ricky a major character in I Love Lucy provided an opportunity for Desilu to produce a spin-off series built around Fred and Ethel Mertz. By using the child as the motivation for the Ricardos to quit crowded Manhattan for a healthier existence in rural Connecticut, the scriptwriters could easily create a new pair of neighbors as comedy foils for the Ricardos.

Meanwhile, the landlord Mertzes would stay behind and have a separate series of their own, perhaps turning their apartment building into a boardinghouse for retired entertainers like themselves. Fortunately for the integrity of I Love Lucy, the project never got off the drawing board because of Vivian Vance's veto.

"I loathed Bill Frawley, and the feeling was mutual," she recalled. "Whenever I received a new script, I raced through it, praying that there wouldn't be a scene where we had to be in bed together. There was no way I could do a series with him on our own, so when Desi asked me, I refused. I still wouldn't budge when he offered me a bonus of $50,000 just to do a pilot. When Bill found out, he was furious, not because he wanted to work with me any more than I did with him, but because he stood to earn a lot more money than he did on Lucy. He never spoke to me again except when work required it."

Following a couple of episodes in which the Mertzes hopped a train from Grand Central Station to help their former tenants out of trouble, a new excuse had to be found for reuniting the quartet on a permanent basis. This time, the situation was reversed—the Ricardos becoming landlords as well as employers to the Mertzes. The older couple move into the guest cottage to take care of the chickens, a new business sideline that the Ricardos have been unable to manage on their own. Many of the gags were inspired by the Arnazes' long-ago experiences with raising livestock on their ranch in the San Fernando Valley.

Still being filmed in front of a studio audience, *I Love Lucy* provoked the longest outburst of laughter in its six-year history during production of the 172nd episode, which aired in March 1957, and dealt with Lucy's efforts to encourage the hens to lay more eggs. Ricky has threatened to get rid of them after discovering that their meager output so far has cost the Ricardos eighteen dollars per egg in terms of feed and upkeep.

To fool Ricky, Lucy and Ethel buy dozens of eggs in a grocery and intend to pass them off as the Ricardos' own. When Ricky arrives unexpectedly before they have a chance to plant the eggs in the henhouse, the women hide them inside their blouses. Unluckily for Lucy, Ricky wants to rehearse a tango number that they're supposed to perform at a school PTA show. Lucy manages to evade catastrophe until the final clinch, when the sequestered eggs get crunched and explode within her garments.

Sound engineer Cameron McCulloch clocked sustained audience hysteria of a minute and five seconds as Lucille Ball milked the messy situation for everything it was worth. To make her reactions as spontaneous as possible, she'd insisted on using hard-boiled eggs during rehearsals of the scene. The slimy raw eggs—seventy-two in number—were like a plate of oysters dumped down her bodice. When they dripped into her underwear and down her legs, she moved as if on fire.

Watching such hilarious high jinks, no one would have suspected that *I Love Lucy* was nearing the end of its sixth and final season on the air. But problems were developing behind the scenes that would make it impossible for Lucy and Desi to keep up the frantic pace much longer.

Earlier in the year, Desi had to be hospitalized when he tore some ligaments in his back while working on the set. It was no laughing matter when Lucy accidentally fell on top of him; she weighed almost as much as he did.

While undergoing treatment, Desi discovered that he had the beginnings of diverticulitis, a disease of the colon fairly common among high-strung executive types and alcoholics. If he didn't stop the boozing and get more relaxation, he might require a colostomy. The prospect of spending the rest of his life attached to a plastic bag for the elimination of feces was horrifying enough to cause him to follow the doctors' advice.

While resting up at their beach house in Del Mar, Lucy and Desi did some hard thinking about the future. Desi saw *I Love Lucy* as the main obstacle to his recovery. He would be much happier if they ended the stressful weekly series so that he could concentrate exclusively on running Desilu. Lucy balked, but she didn't want to send Desi to an early grave either. Knowing how much work meant to her, he promised to develop a series that she could star in by herself.

Desi flew to New York to discuss the matter with William Paley, chairman of the board of CBS, who blew his stack over the possibility of losing the top-rated program on all of television. Had it not been for Desi's bad health, Paley would have taken legal action to force him to continue *I Love Lucy,* so they ended up hammering out a deal that satisfied both sides.

For the 1957–58 season, Desilu would produce five hour-long specials featuring the usual format and characters of *I Love Lucy,* with guest appearances by top Hollywood stars. The programs would be telecast once a month, starting in November 1957 and continuing through March 1958. Hopefully, a new weekly program starring Lucille Ball sans Desi Arnaz would be ready in time for the 1958–59 season.

On April 4, 1957, the Arnazes filmed the 179th and final half-hour episode of *I Love Lucy.* Since it was their last chance to do so, they finally permitted Lucie, now five and a half, and Desi, four, to appear on the program. The kids had been bugging their parents ever since they started to talk. Lucy and Desi hoped that it would satisfy them, as well as silence the chums and schoolmates who kept teasing them for not being on the show regularly like Richard Keith was.

It seemed predestined that Lucie and Desi would be performers like their parents. "The children used to study everything we did on the program," Lucy recalled. "They'd look at the clock and say 'They're on again' and rush to the TV. After it was over, they'd get up and do the whole thing, word for word. At that impressionable age they could learn. They did the songs, the dances. We loved it and encouraged it, not just to prepare them for show business, but to teach them to express themselves. We built a little theater for them out in the garage where they put on shows with their friends."

So they wouldn't get swollen heads, Lucy insisted that the kids should make their professional acting debuts in the same way that she did almost twenty-five years earlier—as background extras. Their brief moment of glory came in the final minutes of the story entitled "The Ricardos Dedicate a Statue," which finds Lucy impersonating a sculpture of a Revolutionary War hero after she accidentally smashes the original.

During the unveiling ceremony in the town square, Lucie and Desi are part of the crowd of onlookers. The camera focuses on them for a second when Ethel Mertz, standing adjacent, asks the little boy, "Are you having a good time, honey?" and receives a nod of the head in reply.

The official end to *I Love Lucy* as a half-hour series came with the telecast of May 6, 1957. An estimated 35 million people watched as Lucy's stone-faced Minute Man disguise is undone by the wet kisses of the curious family pooch.

By this time, CBS had received thousands of letters and telephone calls protesting the termination of the weekly program. It was a night of national mourning for many viewers, who felt like they were losing their best friends.

Monday night at nine would no longer be *I Love Lucy* time in millions of households. In the autumn of 1957, CBS gave that prime weekly slot to another long-run Desilu success, *The Danny Thomas Show*, which had previously been carried by ABC under the title of *Make Room for Daddy*. Desilu still had a firm hold on the entire hour, with *December Bride* following on CBS at 9:30 P.M.

Ford Motor Company bought sponsorship of the five monthly *Lucy* specials. Budgeted at $350,000 each, the one-hour shows would be far more elaborate than any half-hour *I Love Lucy* episodes, the first of which cost $25,000 back in 1951. Filming would still be done in front of a studio audience and in black-and-white. Regularly scheduled color broadcasting was still years away because of the bitter rivalry between CBS and NBC, which had developed incompatible technology that required different types of receiving sets.

Since *I Love Lucy* continued to be rerun in non–prime time, Desilu had to select a new title for the specials. *The Lucy and Desi Comedy Hour* may not have been as clever, but it still satisfied the ego requirements of both stars. It also narrowed the already thin line that divided the Arnazes and the Ricardos in the minds of the public. To avoid that confusion, *The Lucy and Ricky Hour* might have been a better choice.

For the first special, the scriptwriters fell back on a plot device that had never been used in stories about the Ricardos—a flashback to events preceding their marriage. "Lucy Takes a Cruise to Havana" would reveal how the couple first met. Never mind that Lucy and Desi were no longer in the blush of youth. Wonders could be worked with lighting, soft-focus lenses, and body corsets to create a reasonable facsimile of what they looked like twenty years ago.

The scenario overlapped with another very popular Desilu series, *Private Secretary,* in which Ann Sothern portrayed a character named Susie MacNamara. What if Susie just happened to have been Lucy McGillicuddy's best friend when they were starting out in the business world as secretaries? The premise was too good to resist. Sothern and Lucy had been pals since their starlet days in real life.

"Lucy Takes a Cruise to Havana" provided a rare glimpse into the Ricardos' past, but for a change it borrowed little from the Arnazes' real-life experiences. While vacationing in the Cuban capital, Lucy and Susie hire horse-and-buggy driver Ricky Ricardo and his buddy Carlos Garcia (portrayed by guest star Cesar Romero) to take them sightseeing. Romance blossoms, and when the two men confess an ambition to go to the United States to become musicians, the girls try to get them jobs with singing bandleader (and second guest star) Rudy Vallee, whom they'd met on the cruise ship.

The story presented a challenge for the inclusion of the Mertzes, who, of course, were a long way from becoming the Ricardos' landlords at that time. But they turned up anyway as newlywed vaudevillians on their honeymoon. Fred still had a full head of hair then, and introduced Ethel as his "charming child bride of 1934."

"Lucy Takes a Cruise" holds a unique place in television history as the only one-hour special to run seventy-five minutes. The show had an excess of singing and dancing that Desi refused to cut to sixty-minute length (actually even less due to commercial breaks). William Paley was furious. Prime-time television then had half-hour, full-hour, hour-and-a-half, and sometimes even two-hour programs, but an hour and a quarter was heretofore unheard of.

Rather than trim the special, Desi wanted Paley to comandeer fifteen minutes from the program that followed, *The United States Steel Hour.* Paley refused to go head-to-head with the most powerful corporation in America, so Desi phoned its board chairman himself and explained the advantages of *Steel Hour* relinquishing the time. Although a favorite of TV critics, the dramatic anthology series had never been a big hit with viewers. But with the highly publicized premiere of *The Lucy and Desi Comedy Hour* as lead-in, the program would undoubtedly get the highest rating in its four-year history.

Desi shrewdly pointed out that viewers were unlikely to switch to another channel at 10:15 P.M., when competing programs were already well in progress. He sealed the deal by promising to make a speech at the end of his own show, thanking U.S. Steel for giving up some of its time and commending the company for its contributions toward high-quality programming.

Meanwhile, Lucy had gotten into a tizzy over preparations for the next special in the series. For years, she'd longed for an opportunity to work opposite her onetime drama school colleague Bette Davis. By this time, their careers had done a flip-flop. After two decades of minor fame in movies, Lucille Ball had become one of the biggest stars in all of show business. Bette Davis, now forty-nine and considered too mature for the romantic leads that made her a Hollywood legend, had been reduced to playing character parts (such as Debbie Reynolds's mother in *A Catered Affair*) if she worked at all.

Without making it seem like charity, Lucy thought that she could do Davis a favor by hiring her for a guest appearance. The scriptwriters would build an entire program around Davis as a vacationing celebrity who rents a house next door to the Ricardos in Westport, Connecticut. Although Davis's phone wasn't exactly ringing off the hook with job offers, she drove a hard bargain, demanding a fee of $50,000 and equal billing in the credits with Lucy and Desi.

Lucy was so keen on signing Davis that she agreed, but fate intervened. While horseback riding one day, Davis got thrown from her mount and broke an arm. There was no way that the injury would heal in time for her to do the program, so a replacement had to be found. Amusingly, it turned out to be Bette Davis's archrival, Tallulah Bankhead. They'd been feuding for years, ever since Davis won the lead in the movie of Bankhead's stage triumph, *The Little Foxes*. Davis's cutting semi-impersonation of Bankhead in *All About Eve* didn't improve relations between the two women.

Although Lucy herself had once spoofed Tallulah in an episode of *I Love Lucy*, the latter apparently bore her no grudge and accepted the guest star offer with alacrity. But filming of "The Celebrity Next Door" became a nightmare, thanks to Tallulah's shocking state of health, caused by a lifetime of addiction to alcohol, tobacco, and drugs.

Lucy's senior by only nine years, Bankhead sans makeup looked old enough to be her grandmother. With a crotchety nature to match, she infuriated everybody with her behavior, which included calling Desi a "fat pig" and spitting at director Jerry Thorpe for suggesting shtick that she considered beneath her dignity as a Great Lady of the American Theater.

To avoid a cat fight, Lucy kept away from Tallulah when they weren't working or rehearsing. No fur flew except before the cameras, when at one point in the action Tallulah snapped venomously at Lucy, "Remove yourself before I pull out that pink hair and expose the black roots underneath!" Although straight from the script, the line sounded like something that Tallulah might easily have spouted herself in the heat of the moment.

During the preparation of "The Celebrity Next Door," Desi was negotiating a monumental business deal that he decided to keep secret from his wife. "Lucy was having enough trouble with Miss Bankhead on the show," he recalled. "Tallulah was half crocked all the time and would never give us a good rehearsal. Lucy, being the perfectionist that she was, hated that, so I didn't want to give her any more problems than she already had."

Fantastic though it seemed, Desi had been given first crack at purchasing the production facilities of RKO Radio Pictures, the Arnazes' alma mater and the place where they first met back in 1940. Daniel O'Shea, a longtime friend and industry executive, thought of them immediately when General Tire & Rubber Company delegated him to sell the property, which it acquired from Howard Hughes in 1955.

O'Shea gave Desi twenty-four hours to make a decision. For $6.5 million, Desilu could acquire all of RKO's assets except the backlog of about 700 feature movies, which a subsidiary of General Tire would retain for TV distribution. The package included two fully equipped studios and the underlying land, which amounted to sixty-five acres of prime real estate in Hollywood and Culver City.

It seemed a bargain by any standards, made possible by the fact that General Tire had a tax crisis and needed a quick capital loss to offset some of its profits. Desi sought counsel from RKO's previous owner, Howard Hughes, who in his playboy phase had frequently dropped in to hear the Desi Arnaz orchestra during its engagements at Ciro's nightclub.

Not yet the total recluse that he would become in later years, the eccentric billionaire returned Desi's phone call almost immediately and urged him to make the acquisition.

"Grab it! Even if you tear the studios down and turn them into parking lots, you've gotta make money," Hughes said.

Desilu was still paying off the notes on its purchase of the controlling interest in Motion Picture Center, so where could Desi raise the required down payment of $2 million by the next day? He phoned William Paley to ask if CBS would be interested in becoming Desilu's equal partner in the RKO studios.

"I don't want any part of brick and mortar," Paley told Desi. "You buy them and we'll rent space from you."

Forced into going it alone, Desi called the Bank of America, which had financed the Motion Picture Center deal. A bank vice-president gasped at the request of a $2 million loan, but immediately approved one after Desi explained what he needed it for. Astonished that he had raised the money so easily, Desi decided to test his luck by trying to swing a more advantageous deal with General Tire & Rubber.

Pretending that he was having a tough time arranging financing, Desi asked GT&R to make it an even $6 million rather than $6.5 million. Middleman Daniel O'Shea refused, but by the end of nine hours of negotiation, Desi had chipped him down to $6.15 million. For that amount, Desi had persuaded O'Shea to throw in RKO's "stock" library, which contained millions of feet of clips from movies, newsreels, and travelogues that could be inserted into theatrical and TV films to establish locale, atmosphere, et cetera.

Before the deal could be finalized, General Tire's tax lawyers decided that the most that the company could accept from Desilu that year was $500,000 down, instead of the original $2 million. Because of the smaller payment, Daniel O'Shea wanted to push the total purchase price back to $6.5 million, but Desi exploded with rage.

"Like hell it will," Desi said. "We made a deal for six-one-five-zero. You wanted two million down, and you've got it in your pocket. I couldn't care less what Mr. General Tire can or cannot do with his two-million check. He can cash it, tear it up or wipe his ass with it, but the sale price is not going to change."

It was an incredible break for Desilu when Mr. G.T. (aka Thomas O'Neil) buckled under. Desi wrote a new check for $500,000 and put the remaining $1.5 million into ten-year notes earning 6 percent. The interest of $900,000 meant that Desilu had acquired the RKO package for nearly a million dollars less than the original asking price!

With the acquisition of the two RKO plants, Desilu now had a total of thirty-five soundstages, plus an outdoor backlot of more than forty acres, making it the largest motion picture and television facility in the world at that time. Bigger now than giants of Hollywood's golden age like MGM and 20th Century–Fox, which had been forced to sell big chunks of their domains to real estate developers to stay alive.

Since Desi had kept Lucy in the dark about the negotiations to buy RKO, she couldn't believe it when he told her that the deal had gone through. "We just bought *what?*" she croaked.

"We bought RKO Gower, where we used to work, and RKO Culver, where Selznick made *Gone With the Wind*," Desi said.

"I know where the RKO studios are, but do we have enough money to buy them?" Lucy replied.

"No, but we bought 'em," Desi said. "It's a hell of a deal and the Bank of America agrees. They're lending us the money, so don't worry. If worse comes to worst, we'll get our money back by selling the land. The cemetery next to RKO Gower would love to buy it because they're running out of space to put the stiffs."

19

The End of a Love Affair

LUCY was home in bed recuperating from her ordeal with Tallulah Bankhead when she received a phone call from Desi to rush over to his office at Culver City. Newspaper photographers wanted the new owners of the RKO studios to pose for pictures.

"That was the last thing I wanted to do," Lucy remembered. "I had no makeup on, and my hair was in curlers. I looked a mess, but Desi insisted. He said that if I didn't show up, they'd think there was trouble between us. We had to keep up a front. I could get my makeup and hair done at the studio."

Lucy hadn't driven to the Culver City lot since auditioning for *Gone With the Wind* nearly twenty years earlier, so she quickly got lost. Finally she pulled up to the studio entrance, but the security guard refused to admit her. She was unrecognizable in a babushka and dark glasses.

Lucy took off the shades and fluttered her lashes at the guard. His eyes bulged as he realized that he was face to face with one of his new bosses. Not sure whether he should address her as Mrs. Arnaz or Miss Ball, he waved her through the gate with a diplomatic "Go right in, Miss Arzballs!"

Nineteen fifty-seven turned out to be a banner year for Desilu Productions. To raise capital for expansion, Desi sold all 179 half-hour episodes of *I Love Lucy* to CBS in perpetuity for $4.3 million. The first fifty-two episodes were previously leased for $1.6 million for once-only repeats on CBS under the sponsorship of Lehn and Fink, so Desilu had earned a whopping $5.9 million just from reruns of the series.

Attempting diversification, Desilu entered the hostelry business with the opening of Desi Arnaz's Western Hills Resort in Indian Wells, California, about fifteen miles southeast of Palm Springs, where the Arnazes owned a vacation home. Desi sank $750,000 into building the streamlined two-story hotel, one of the first in the nation to boast of a TV set in every room. The fifty studio apartments overlooked a swimming pool and a nine-hole golf course. Desi also planned to turn the hotel's 250-seat dining room into a nightclub where he would lead the resident band whenever he came to town.

With all the couple's business commitments, the whole family was together only on weekends, vacations, or school holidays. Whether that made for an abnormal childhood for Lucie and Desi is debatable, but it was typical for most offspring of hardworking celebrities.

Since Desi had the more demanding and unpredictable schedule, Lucy became the dominant parent at home, which again was not unusual, except that she tended to overdo it. "My sister and I came along pretty late in my mother's life, so when we arrived it was almost like a miracle to her. I think this increased her normal protective instinct about a thousand percent, to the point where it was almost like a living thing within her," Desi Jr. recalled.

Lucy fans may have thought that the real Lucy would be a laugh riot to have as a mother, but she was deadly serious about raising her children. "Mom was very strict about everything," Lucie remembered. "She drilled manners into us, insisted that we show respect to our elders, and taught us that words can hurt. When we did something she didn't approve of, we were grounded and sent to our rooms. My mother must be the all-time champion grounder. You could say I spent two years of my childhood in solitary!"

Early on, Lucy seemed to take out her animosities toward her husband on young Desi. He was always the "bad" child and tended to behave that way. On the other hand, Lucie was jealous of the chubby Desi because he could play the drums. She called him "Blubberbags" and once punched holes in his bongos. The two were always fighting, with Lucy ranting and raving at them until they stopped. "She was really tough," Desi recalled. "She used to say, 'The first one who gets hurt, gets hit.' "

In November 1957, when the new *Lucy and Desi Comedy Hour* premiered on CBS with the story of the Ricardos' first meeting in

Havana, the program was seen by an estimated 50 million people and placed fifth in the American Research Bureau audience ratings for that month. The switch to irregular once-a-month telecasts cost the Arnazes their perennial number-one position. But it was an impressive showing nonetheless, because the four programs that outranked theirs —*Perry Mason, Person to Person, Gunsmoke,* and *Playhouse 90*— all had the cumulative advantage of weekly airings.

The hour-long escapades of the Ricardos and the Mertzes were self-contained stories that did not continue on to the next installment. After their encounter with next-door neighbor Tallulah Bankhead, the two couples traveled to Las Vegas for a nightclub engagement of Ricky's band. Collectors of *Lucy* trivia will remember the episode as the one in which Lucille Ball changed her upswept hairstyle for a longer, wavier look that she kept throughout the rest of her television career.

"Lucy Hunts Uranium" was the first of two episodes featuring actual Hollywood couples as guest stars. While prospecting in the mountains outside Las Vegas, Lucy Ricardo drags the vacationing Fred MacMurray and his wife, June Haver, into her get-rich-quick scheme. In real life, the Arnazes were close friends with the Mac-Murrays, who were wed in 1954 after a long and unusual acquaintance. The actor and the blonde singer-dancer fell in love while making a movie together in 1945, but he was married and devoted to his wife, who eventually died of cancer in 1952. In the meanwhile, Haver quit moviemaking and spent some time in a Catholic convent preparing to become a nun!

The next show, "Lucy Wins a Racehorse," contained some amusing echoes from the Arnazes' past. Betty Grable, one of Desi's ex-flames as well as Lucy's professional rival during their starlet days at RKO, made a guest appearance on the program in tandem with hubby Harry James, the jazz trumpeter and bandleader.

In years gone by, Lucy had been extremely jealous of the bleached blonde who'd been Hollywood's box-office queen and top pinup girl for the Army, Navy, and Marines during the World War II era, but now the tables were turned and the two could finally be friends. Five years younger than Lucy, Grable had gone into semiretirement after a string of flops, while the older woman was probably the most popular female entertainer in America at that time.

Both now middle-aged mothers of two, Lucy and Grable had more in common than just their growing children. Harry James was Desi's equal when it came to philandering, boozing, and gambling. Yet as far as the public knew, the Arnazes and the Jameses were two of the happiest married couples in Hollywood.

Fernando Lamas, an Argentinian who mangled the English language almost as well as Desi did, appeared as guest star in the season closer, "Lucy Goes to Sun Valley." Lucy hired Lamas as a favor to her close friend Esther Williams, who was having an affair with the actor and eventually married him.

Despite high ratings, *The Lucy and Desi Comedy Hour* lasted only one season. Because of the colossal failure of the Edsel, a new car developed at a cost of $250 million as competition to GM's Oldsmobile, Ford Motor Company had to end sponsorship of the program after the broadcast of the fifth monthly special in April 1958.

Surprisingly, Desi couldn't have been happier. The cancellation enabled him to proceed with a project that he'd been dreaming about for years, a weekly hour-long anthology series entitled *Desilu Playhouse*. Potential sponsors had been resistant to his idea for a mix of original dramas, mysteries, and adventures, but he could now make the package more attractive by adding some new *Lucy and Ricky* comedies to the format.

Desilu Playhouse promised to be a gigantic project, designed to keep the company's studio facilities humming for at least two years, the minimum deal that Desi would accept. Budgeted at $12 million, the package would include forty one-hour plays and eight *Lucy and Ricky* specials. Desi would introduce all programs as the series host. He and Lucy also hoped to perform individually in some of the plays, in roles outside their usual characters.

Westinghouse Electric decided to sponsor *Desilu Playhouse* as a replacement for *Studio One*, the highly acclaimed dramatic anthology series that CBS had been broadcasting live from New York since 1948. Always more of a prestige item than a popular hit, *Studio One* had sunk to the very bottom of the audience ratings, but the production budget of $6 million was only half what it would be for *Desilu Playhouse*. In order to persuade Westinghouse to switch, Desi promised the company's board of directors that *Desilu Playhouse* would double the sales of Westinghouse products by the end of the first season.

When the deal was closed, Mark Cresap Jr., president of Westinghouse, took Desi to one of the company's warehouses to impress upon him the need to keep that pledge. The huge interior was packed wall-to-wall, floor-to-ceiling with radios, TV sets, refrigerators, and washing machines. The two men had to walk sideways as they toured the narrow passages between the piles of merchandise. Desi seemed to get the message when Cresap told him, "I'd like to give a dance here next New Year's Eve for our employees."

Desilu Playhouse took over *Studio One*'s traditional CBS slot of Monday nights at ten o'clock. It was becoming pretty much a Desilu evening; the studio's *Danny Thomas Show* still occupied the 9 P.M. slot vacated by *I Love Lucy,* followed at 9:30 by the new *Ann Sothern Show* (private secretary Susie MacNamara transformed into assistant hotel manager Katy O'Connor).

To insure a top rating, *Desilu Playhouse* premiered on October 6, 1958, with its biggest guns: the Ricardos and the Mertzes. "Lucy Goes to Mexico," the first of four comedy specials to be included in the series that season, featured seventy-year-old Maurice Chevalier as guest star. Desi idolized Chevalier and had wanted to work with him for years.

Mexico may have seemed an unlikely place for the great French entertainer to turn up, but he and Ricky Ricardo were preparing to put on a show for the crew of a U.S. aircraft carrier in San Diego Bay. They're hastily summoned to nearby Tijuana when sightseers Lucy, Fred, and Ethel are arrested and jailed for allegedly trying to smuggle a little Mexican boy across the border in the trunk of their car.

The scriptwriters, of course, couldn't send Lucy Ricardo to Mexico without tossing her into a bullfighting ring before the end of the trip. Never mind how the plot got her there, but for the filming of the scene, the real Lucy had to confront a live 3,500-pound bull with foot-long horns. The script called for her to stop the charging beast in his tracks with a wave of a handkerchief drenched with perfume.

Fortunately, the bull was not only well trained, but also well sedated, so Lucy had nothing to fear. But in shooting some subsequent close-ups, she wasn't so lucky.

"They put a fake bull's head on the front of the camera and ran it down a very long track at high speed," Lucy remembered. "The damned thing jumped the track and came right at me, with four guys behind it. Thank God that one of them hit me and knocked me down, or I'd have been killed instantly. As it was, I still got gored. Oh, God, the blood!"

Collapsing in agony, Lucy was rushed to a nearby hospital to be stitched up. "It was the worst thing that had happened to me since that early episode with William Holden when my fake nose went up in flames and I came close to being disfigured for life," she recalled.

Lucille Ball was nowhere in sight when *Desilu Playhouse* switched gears to present its first dramatic program on October 13. Viewers accustomed to watching Desi in the guise of Ricky Ricardo were startled when he stepped out of character to introduce the historical play *Bernadette,* based on the life of a French peasant girl who claimed to have had visions of the Virgin Mary.

The story of Saint Bernadette of Lourdes had already been the basis for a hit movie in 1943, winning newcomer Jennifer Jones the Best Actress Oscar for her performance. This time around, Desi selected Pier Angeli, the delicate Italian beauty originally imported to Hollywood by MGM, to portray the pious heroine.

Westinghouse wanted to inject some action and thrills into the series, so Desi obliged with a two-part drama entitled "The Untouchables," inspired by the real-life exploits of U.S. Treasury agent Eliot Ness in mobster-dominated Chicago during the Depression era. Without realizing it, Desi had come across the idea for the show—a future gold mine—in a load of unproduced scripts that the floundering Warner Brothers tried to sell to Desilu. Desi couldn't afford to buy the whole package, and WB refused to break it up, so Desilu's lawyers did some investigating and learned that Warners' option on the property had expired. Desi snapped it up for $2,500. He even had his heart set on portraying Eliot Ness!

"It seemed insane, but he was the boss," Desilu vice-president Martin Leeds recalled. "Desi wanted to break out of the Ricky Ricardo stereotype and be accepted as a real actor. Lucy read him the riot act and told him to forget it. 'Even if you learn to talk like Edward R. Murrow, you'd never pass for anything but a spic,' she said."

Desi begrudgingly suggested his favorite actor, Van Heflin, for the Ness role, but Heflin had other commitments. Lucy proposed another Van, the couple's longtime friend Van Johnson, who'd risen from the chorus line of *Too Many Girls* to top stardom at MGM for nearly a decade. Johnson's career had nosedived since he was fired by a new studio regime. Lucy felt obligated to help him; he'd been a pillar of strength during her own turbulent association with MGM.

Lucy's solicitude backfired, giving the Arnazes a painful lesson in the old adage, "Don't do business with friends." Van Johnson hadn't worked in months and was delighted with Desilu's offer of $10,000 for the two-hour play. But Johnson's wife, Evie, who also served as his agent-manager, wasn't so happy. Since "The Untouchables" would be broadcast in two parts on successive weeks to suit the hour format of *Desilu Playhouse,* she reckoned that her husband should be paid twice as much—$20,000 instead of $10,000.

Lucy and Desi considered that unconscionable and told the Johnsons so. Later, when "The Untouchables" became the basis for a hit series, Van blamed Evie for causing him to lose a fortune in salary and residuals. They were divorced in 1963, ending one of Hollywood's most bizarre relationships; Evie had previously been married to Van's best friend, Keenan Wynn, who dumped her when she got pregnant during an affair with Johnson.

While thumbing through casting directories for a replacement for Van Johnson, Desi found another potential Eliot Ness in Robert Stack, a second-string romantic lead who'd been on the Hollywood scene since 1939 and was best known for giving teenaged singing sensation Deanna Durbin her first screen kiss. Independently wealthy, Stack needed exposure more than he did money, so he leaped at Desi's offer of $10,000 for the two-hour play *plus* $7,500 per episode if "The Untouchables" should ever be extended into a series.

Focusing on the Treasury Department's battle to wipe out mobsters Al Capone and Frank Nitti, the two-part "Untouchables" created a sensation when aired on *Desilu Playhouse* in the spring of 1959. While highly impressed by the ratings, CBS rejected turning the program into a series. "Once you've gotten rid of the Capone-Nitti gang, what the hell are you going to do for an encore?" William Paley asked.

"Don't you know how many crooks you had in this country? We can go on forever telling the stories about all the gangsters," Desi said. His answer failed to convince Paley, but Leonard Goldenson, president of the American Broadcasting Company, proved more receptive. ABC ordered twenty-six one-hour episodes of *The Untouchables* for the 1959–60 season.

The Untouchables caused a brouhaha between the Arnazes when producer Quinn Martin suggested hiring Walter Winchell to narrate the series. Desi agreed that the newscaster's crackling voice would provide an authenticity that was essential to the show, but Lucy had never forgiven Winchell for starting the Communist scandal that nearly wrecked her career.

Lucy blew her stack when Desi announced that he intended to sign Winchell to a contract at $25,000 per episode. She tried to talk him out of it, but Desi prevailed. "Look, honey, this is business, so let bygones be bygones," he told her.

By the time of the launching of *Desilu Playhouse*, Lucy and Desi had moved into new production headquarters at the former RKO studio at the intersection of Gower Street and Melrose Avenue in Hollywood. Except for the famous roof sign that replicated a flashing radio tower atop the world, all traces of the former ownership had been replaced with the Desilu insignia. *Daily Variety* reported that Desilu now housed more production activity than its larger next-door neighbor, Paramount Pictures, which had fallen on hard times under a decrepit management headed by eighty-five-year-old Adolph Zukor and seventy-year-old Barney Balaban.

Lucy took over the palatial dressing suite occupied by Ginger Rogers during her reign as "Queen of the Lot" circa 1934–42. The two former RKO contractees had kept up their friendship, but something of a chill had developed on the part of the envious Rogers, who'd been reduced to playing glamorous moms in exploitation movies like *Teen-Age Rebel* if she worked at all.

Ironically, Desi now had the office suite used by Lucy's ex-lover Pandro Berman when he headed production at RKO. At one time or another, the office had also been occupied by such notable production executives as David O. Selznick, Dore Schary, and Merian C. Cooper, so they were prestigious surroundings for the onetime cleaner of canary cages.

Desi took special delight in acquiring the keys to the studio warehouses, which contained a huge accumulation of props and materials saved since silent movie days. "Desi made a new discovery every week. 'It's another treasure trove,' he used to say," Vivian Vance recalled. "He found a building filled with dozens of pianos and offered to give them away to anyone who wanted them. When he came across a million rolls of wallpaper, he said 'We'll never have to buy wallpaper for the rest of our lives.' "

Based on a tip from a watchman who'd worked there for years, Desi started prospecting for oil on the Culver City lot. Drillers eventually hit a gusher that converted into a well pumping 120 barrels a day. Desi intended to use the proceeds for theatrical movies, which would be produced at slack times when Desilu stages were not being used for TV shows.

Lucy and Desi each had an electric-powered golf cart to drive themselves around the premises. Reduced to working in only five *Lucy* specials a year, the redhead found other activities to keep herself busy. Preferring to leave the administrative side of Desilu to her husband, she formed the Desilu Workshop, another throwback to the Ginger Rogers era at RKO. Lucy, of course, had received most of her professional training at RKO's talent school, then run by Ginger's mother, Lela Rogers.

Since the onslaught of television, the major movie studios had nearly eliminated the prohibitively expensive custom of maintaining contract rosters. No one was doing much to train the young actors and actresses who might become the stars of the future. Having ripened under that system, Lucy decided it was time to do something.

Lucy asked longtime production aide Maury Thompson to help her select the first batch of trainees. About 1,700 applications were considered, from which sixty-two people were invited to audition. Twenty-two were finally accepted.

Besides giving Lucy something to occupy her spare time, the workshop was intended to provide a pool of talent for Desilu productions. The trainees received the Actors Equity minimum salary of sixty dollars per week and were free to accept outside offers if any came along. The long-shuttered 200-seat playhouse on the backlot (where Lucy and Desi arranged their first date during rehearsals for *Too Many Girls*) was completely done over with a larger stage, more dressing rooms, and teaching labs for lessons in makeup and wardrobe.

Friends and associates wondered why Lucy chose to spend so much time at Desilu when she might just as easily have stayed home with the children during the production lulls between *Lucy* specials. But Lucie was now eight years old, Desi, six and a half, and both were at school for the better part of the day, leaving their mother with a lot of free time.

Working before the cameras or not, at the studio Lucy could also keep her husband under surveillance. Spies told her that when he stayed late at the office on corporate business, he often arranged for call girls to keep him company. There wasn't much that she could do to stop Desi from burning the midnight oil, but she wasn't about to let him get away with any hanky-panky while she was on the premises.

Desi's drinking was another major concern for Lucy. He frequently arrived home in the wee hours of the morning with a police escort, courtesy of the Beverly Hills P.D. Thanks to a sympathetic desk sergeant, patrol cars were on the alert to guide Desi to his driveway if they spotted his customized Cadillac weaving recklessly through the streets.

"When Desi was drinking a lot, Lucy would call me in the middle of the night and say, 'Get the priest. Do something, Ann, do something,' " Ann Sothern recalled.

"Desi was really a great guy when he wasn't drinking, but as kids we'd definitely stay away from him when he was drunk," the onetime Little Ricky Keith Thibodeaux remembered. "Once I was sleeping over when he heard that one of the hired help had called Desi Jr. a spoiled brat. That night, we were awakened by a fistfight. Big Desi caught the guy entertaining a girl in the living room and beat the hell out of him. Desi Jr. and I were so scared that we hid in the maid's quarters."

It may or may not have been the effect of alcohol when Desi turned down an offer from Texas oil billionaire Clint Murchison to purchase Desilu for $15 million. Murchison wanted the Arnazes to continue running the company, but Desi balked at the prospect of having to answer to an absentee owner. Instead, he became more determined than ever to turn Desilu into a showbiz empire that encompassed not only television but movies, recordings, and music publishing as well.

To make that possible, Desilu Productions went public on the American Stock Exchange in December 1958. The Arnazes kept half of the one million shares for themselves. Offered at ten dollars per share, the price zoomed as high as twenty-nine dollars owing to the couple's fame and popularity. On paper at least, Lucy and Desi's holdings were worth nearly $15 million. It was a far cry from when they started shooting *I Love Lucy* in 1951, when they had trouble raising the $18,000 required to produce the pilot episode.

In reel life, nothing quite that spectacular had happened to the Ricardos, but there'd been no misfortunes either. In the special entitled "Lucy Makes Room for Danny," the couple finally had a run-in with Danny Thomas and Kathy Williams, the leading characters from Desilu's *Danny Thomas Show*. Lucy and Desi had been trying to work Danny and co-star Marjorie Lord into a *Lucy* story for years, but a conflict in sponsors (rival cigarette manufacturers) had prevented it up to now.

Red Skelton, whose own TV show was filmed by Desilu, turned up as guest star in an Alaskan caper that permitted Lucy Ricardo to appear in a sketch with Skelton's inimitable Freddie the Freeloader character. In another story, Mrs. Ricardo got tired of her life as housewife and mother and applied for a job as girl Friday on movie star Paul Douglas's morning TV program. The final special of the season found the Ricardos borrowing a friend's mountain hideaway for their summer vacation, only to discover that Hollywood marrieds Ida Lupino and Howard Duff have booked for the same time and that the two couples will have to share the accommodations.

Although the Mertzes were still involved in the Ricardos' escapades, the introduction of guest stars into the specials meant that Fred and Ethel had less to do. William Frawley, now past seventy, welcomed the cutback, but Vivian Vance resented it and threatened to quit. To pacify her, Desi promised to develop a series that she could star in on her own.

Madelyn Pugh and Bob Carroll, by this time editorial advisers on all Desilu projects, saw a potential Vivian Vance series in *Guestward Ho!*, a novel about a western dude ranch by Patrick *(Auntie Mame)* Dennis and Barbara Hooton. Desi had no trouble selling the idea to ABC, which commissioned a pilot to be directed by Ralph Levy, maker of the original *I Love Lucy* audition film.

The project proved a heartbreaking experience for Vance, who found herself lost without Lucille Ball. "On the first take, I yelled 'action' and Vivian just stood there frozen" Ralph Levy recalled. "On the second and third takes, the same thing happened. I finally took her aside to find out if she was all right. Viv said, 'This is the first time in eight years I've been in my own light,' meaning, of course, that after being in the shadow of Lucille all that time, she was finding it difficult going it alone. It was a big change for her."

The pilot failed to impress ABC, which advised Desi to find another star for the series. Lucy rallied to her friend's side and helped her to get over the disappointment. As luck would have it, Vance's marriage was as troubled as Lucy's, so the two women found plenty to commiserate about.

Lucy's problems with Desi's drinking and philandering paled by comparison to Vance's problems with Philip Ober, an unsuccessful actor who resented his wife's fame and treated her with contempt. Vance often came to work sporting black-and-blue marks from Ober's beatings, according to makeup artist Hal King.

With encouragement from Lucy, Vance finally sued Ober for divorce in March 1959, charging mental and physical cruelty. The couple had been married eighteen years (presumably happily until *I Love Lucy* came along in 1951) and divided community property valued at $250,000. Claiming that most of it came from her *Lucy* earnings, Vance vowed never to marry again.

The news of the Vance-Ober divorce caused a flurry of rumors that Lucy and Desi were also on the verge of splitting up. With at least another year of *Lucy* specials contracted for, that seemed unlikely. To counteract the gossip, Lucy persuaded Desi to take the whole family on a cruise to Europe for their summer vacation. What better way of publicly demonstrating the couple's togetherness?

The four Arnazes took a plane to New York to connect with the SS *Liberté*, a luxury liner that catered to the celebrity trade. The family had forty pieces of luggage, plus two steamer trunks, crammed with clothing and necessities. They obviously didn't believe in traveling light.

The eastward crossing had overtones of a sitcom, but Lucy didn't find them very amusing. She experienced a late and violent reaction to her smallpox vaccination, which caused her left arm to swell up like a balloon. She stubbed a previously broken big toe and had a partial cast on her left foot.

"I always get such romantic ailments. What a helluva way to descend on Paris," Lucy said in a note that she dashed off to columnist friend Hedda Hopper.

Matters got progressively worse when the Arnazes started their sightseeing rounds of France and Italy. Desi kept disappearing. Lucy guessed where, but she couldn't very well tell the children. They managed as best they could without him.

"Desi was so out of it, he didn't know if we were in Pisa or Pittsburgh," Lucy recalled. "We went to stay with Maurice Chevalier at his home outside of Paris. What a wonderful man he was. He knew we were in a lot of trouble. He told me the end of a love affair is more painful than anything on earth except for staying in a love affair that had no love left. He was like a father telling me it was all right to let go."

Cutting the vacation short, the Arnazes sailed for New York on the legendary *Ile de France*. "It was the last trip for the ship, which was being retired from service. It was also the last trip for all of us," Lucy recalled.

Back in Hollywood, Lucy and Desi had to keep up a happy and united front as they prepared to film another season of comedy specials for showcasing on *Desilu Playhouse*. Westinghouse had moved the program from Monday nights at ten o'clock to Friday at nine to escape competition from NBC's new variety program with multitalented Steve Allen, the original host of the late-hour *Tonight Show*. Except for the *Lucy* specials and the two-part "Untouchables," *Desilu Playhouse* had failed to deliver top ratings. CBS hoped it would do better in its new slot, opposite ABC's *77 Sunset Strip* and NBC's highbrow *Bell Telephone Hour*.

For their 1959–60 opener, the Arnazes selected none other than "Mister Television" himself, Milton Berle, for guest star. Since Berle had an exclusive thirty-year contract with NBC, hiring him for a CBS program required Lucy and Desi to reciprocate by appearing on one of his shows in their Ricardo characters, the first time they ever did so outside their own programs.

In the *Desilu Playhouse* episode, Berle agrees to emcee a PTA show at Little Ricky's school if the Ricardos will let him use their house as a hideout from fans while he's writing a book. Remembering that Berle and Lucille were romantically involved during their contract days at RKO Radio Pictures, Desi decided to direct the program to make sure that they didn't get up to any of their old tricks.

When not acting in scenes himself, Desi rarely stayed in his direc- tor's chair. He was all over the set, squinting through his viewer, shouting orders at everyone, conferring with the lighting men and other technicians. One instant he was up a ladder; the next he was on his hands and knees showing where he wanted a gravel pathway put down. Working with the actors, he hopped in and out of the field of action, placing them forcibly in position, showing them where to walk, sometimes even twisting his face into the expressions he wanted theirs to assume.

Notorious for running his own programs like a dictator, Milton Berle was astonished by Desi's skill and invited him to direct a show for him. "He's got a tremendous flair for comedy; there's almost nobody like him," Berle said at the time. "Desi's a driver, a perfection- ist, and he usually knows 95 percent of what he wants. I have great respect for his ability to handle people and for his knowledge of what plays and what doesn't. Look what he's done for Lucy. She's the greatest comedienne in the world because she's one of the greatest actresses. Desi saw that in her and helped to bring it out."

In the next special, the Ricardos went to Japan on a tour with Ricky's band, but the Arnazes never traveled farther than the studio backlot for the filming. Robert Cummings (like Lucille Ball an expert comedian who never achieved major success until switching from movies to a weekly TV series) turned up as guest star in a farfetched plot that gave Lucy and Ethel an opportunity to masquerade as Japa- nese geisha girls.

Right after completing the show, Desi took off for Europe again, this time strictly on his own. He told curious reporters that it was simply to scout location sites for upcoming Desilu projects, but he really intended to regroup with a few lady friends for a Mediterranean cruise.

In the meantime, Lucy tried to fill the void by preparing for the Christmas edition of *Desilu Playhouse,* which would be an original revue with sketches and musical numbers featuring the twenty-two students from her Desilu Workshop. Hopefully, Desi would be back from Europe in time to join her on the show. She lined up Vivian

Vance, William Frawley, Hedda Hopper, Ann Sothern, Hugh O'Brian, Spring Byington, Rory Calhoun, William Demarest, George Murphy, and even the trained collie Lassie, to make cameo appearances.

When Desi returned from abroad, he had so much corporate business to attend to that he asked Lucy to take over directing the revue. "It seemed we were doomed to have a flop on our hands," Hedda Hopper recalled. "As director, Lucy was lost without Desi, and the whole show was going to pieces. Finally, during dress rehearsal, Desi said, 'Lucy, dear, will you let me see if I can pull this thing together for you?'

"Lucy snapped back at him with blood in her eye, 'Okay, try it!' In ten minutes, Desi had the revue ticking like a fine clock."

"The Desilu Revue" proved to be the swan song of Lucy's talent workshop. After two years, she decided it was too much for her. "I gave my time and my heart to those kids, and you can't do everything for them," she said later. "I found myself caring too much about each one. They drained me dry, turned me into a lay psychiatrist. I figured that if I wanted to go on working as an actress, I'd better conclude it."

Although the Arnazes had announced intentions to occasionally break up the team to star separately on *Desilu Playhouse,* each did it only once. Lucy played the title role in "K.O. Kitty," a comedy about a dancing teacher who adapts her skills to training boxers. Madelyn Pugh and Bob Carroll wrote the script, hoping to develop it into a series if Lucy ever decided to make one on her own.

Desi tackled a serious role in a melodrama entitled "So Tender, So Profane." In his portrayal of a Cuban factory worker struggling to keep a younger sister off the primrose path, TV critics said that he held his own against his more experienced co-stars—Barbara Luna, Pedro Armendariz and single-named Margo (wife of actor Eddie Albert).

Up to now, Desi's heavy drinking had been kept secret from the public, but a couple of unpleasant episodes suddenly landed him in newspaper headlines. A middle-aged character actor named David McCall sued for $100,000, claiming that a "grossly intoxicated" Desi had viciously assaulted him without provocation on a studio set. To avert the notoriety of a trial, the case was settled privately, reportedly for $25,000 plus reimbursement of McCall's medical bills.

In the early hours of September 19, 1959, two plainclothes policemen found Desi nearly falling down drunk on Vista Street, center for a number of disreputable nightspots known as "hooker joints." With a chauffeured limousine waiting nearby, he'd apparently been trying to make a pickup. The officers offered to help Desi to his car, but he became so abusive that they arrested him and hauled him off to the Hollywood station house. He spent thirty minutes locked in a cell while awaiting the arrival of a Desilu lawyer to post bail, which amounted to the rather demeaning sum (for a TV mogul, anyway) of twenty-one dollars.

Realizing that reporters and photographers would be out in full force, Desi failed to appear at the court hearing before municipal judge Charles Carns. The automatic forfeiture of twenty-one dollars was a small price to pay to keep Desi's face off the front pages. Since he had no previous convictions, no further action was taken against him.

Deeply concerned over Desi's drinking, Lucy blamed it on the pressures of business. She told columnist Louella Parsons: "Desi meets everything head on. He's working much, much too hard—twelve and often sixteen hours a day. It's taken its toll, as I knew it would."

Lucy could only go so far in her public pronouncements. Pride and the moral conventions of the time kept her from admitting that Desi no longer found her sexually attractive or that their disintegrating marriage was just as much to blame for his hitting the bottle.

The couple had reached a stage where they couldn't go out together socially without getting into an argument. One night they were invited to a party at the home of singer Dean Martin. Before starting out, Lucy wanted Desi to promise that it wouldn't turn into one of those all-night drinking bouts where the Arnazes were always the last couple to depart.

Desi exploded: "For Crissakes, Lucy, we haven't even left the fucking driveway yet and you're worrying about whether we're going to be the last ones to leave the party. I've *got* to be the last one to leave the party now. There ain't no way I can miss. In Cuba, when we have a party and it doesn't wind up with everybody having breakfast the next morning, we consider it a lousy party. And now, if I'm having fun and want to stay a little longer than other people, you consider me an asshole."

Although she'd purchased a new Don Loper dress for the occasion, Lucy decided to stay home that night. "I loved to go to parties with Desi, but he'd always get drunk and I'd always get embarrassed," she recalled. "I prayed that the drinking would stop, but it only increased, as did his absences. A time came when I didn't leave the house. I got invited, but didn't go. I literally became a recluse, because I couldn't go out with my husband anymore. It was impossible. I don't know where Desi went, but I certainly was alone."

Lucy might have found her husband on their luxurious power cruiser *Desilu,* which he kept docked at Balboa for weekend "fishing expeditions." He also maintained a rented bungalow in the Hollywood Hills for trysting purposes. Lucy eventually found out about it and spitefully transferred his phone calls there when he wasn't home to take them.

To keep Lucy company while Desi was out carousing, her mother often came to visit and stayed overnight, sometimes bringing friends along for a slumber party. "Mom would bunk with me, and we'd put her friends in the guest house," Lucy said. "One night, Desi came home so loaded that I wouldn't let him upstairs. I told him he'd have to sleep on the couch in the living room, but instead he went out to the guest house and tried to crawl into bed with my mother's friends. These seventy-year-old women. God, you should have heard the screams!"

Lucy started consulting family, friends, priests, and doctors for help. At one point, she flew to New York to talk with Norman Vincent Peale, whom she'd never met personally up to then. After attending one of his services at Marble Collegiate Church, she chatted for an hour with him in his study, the beginning of a lifetime friendship between them.

"I started off by telling Dr. Peale how much I'd gotten from his writings," Lucy recalled. "He interrupted by telling *me* how much *I* was appreciated for giving laughter and happiness to so many millions of people. Then I told him that what I really came to talk about was Desi and the things he did. Dr. Peale said, 'Put a capital H on the He and you have the answer to your problems. Put yourself in the hands of God—and you have the answer to your life.' "

While Lucy may have achieved some inner peace from the minister's advice, the marriage appeared doomed. Although Desi claimed it was against his Catholic beliefs, he agreed to see a psychiatrist, but the sessions proved too upsetting and he stopped after several visits. "The doctor told Desi that he had a great deal of anger toward the destruction of his early life. His fall from prince to pauper made it impossible for him to settle down, to domesticate, to win and to hold on to his winnings," a friend recalled.

Meetings with a marriage counselor were even more traumatic. "Desi and I would scream and yell in front of the doctor because we weren't screaming and yelling in front of the children. I felt sorry for the poor guy. He'd ask a question, and the two of us would jump down his throat, and the war was on," Lucy said later.

Although divorce seemed inevitable, she kept giving Desi chance after chance to redeem himself. "I thought if we got away from it all, it might help, so we packed up the kids and went off to Hawaii. Desi couldn't relax, but he sure could drink. That's all he did. He couldn't see straight half the time. Some vacation," Lucy remembered.

The day before they were due to go home, the couple started quarreling on the beach and Desi extricated himself by dashing into the ocean. A gigantic wave knocked him down, and for a moment Lucy thought that he'd drowned. Desi finally bobbed up unharmed, but he'd lost the gold neck chain on which he wore his wedding ring and a St. Christopher medal.

"It was kind of symbolic," Lucy reflected. "Our marriage was gone, so why shouldn't his ring be, too?"

20

Adios, Ricardos

UNBEKNOWN to either Lucy or Desi, plans already were under way to terminate their marriage—not through divorce but by grisly means. The Cosa Nostra, the American branch of the Italian Mafia, intended to assassinate Desi in retaliation for producing *The Untouchables,* which had struck some tender nerves since premiering as a weekly ABC-TV series in October 1959.

Not that Desi wasn't given fair warning to cancel the program. Frank Sinatra, who leased office space at Desilu Gower, moved his production company off the lot, claiming that *The Untouchables* viciously insulted his fellow Italian-Americans. The mobster-infested Teamsters' Union applied pressure by delaying shipments of products advertised on the program.

Desi also received a phone call from childhood friend and ex-schoolmate Sonny Capone, who objected to Neville Brand's blood-curdling portrayal of his father in *The Untouchables.* Al Junior threatened to sue Desilu for $10 million for defaming the Capone family. Desi laughed and wished him luck. Capone did keep his promise, but the suit was eventually thrown out of court for lack of merit.

Desi's refusals to buckle under, coupled with the soaring popularity ratings of *The Untouchables,* finally caused some of the mob *capos* to take more decisive action. In a meeting at the Mafia-owned Rancho La Costa resort hotel near San Diego, they commissioned Aladena Fratianno, known in the underworld as "Jimmy the Weasel," to carry out Desi's murder.

Fratianno, who eventually turned against organized crime and became a star witness in federal investigations, once testified that he'd already killed five men for the Cosa Nostra by the time that he took on the Desi Arnaz hit. He named Sam Giancana, head of the Chicago mob as well as a key figure in the Las Vegas underworld, as the man who wanted Desi bumped off.

Needless to say, that never happened. Sam Giancana was overruled by two of his elders in the Cosa Nostra, Paul ("The Waiter") Ricca and Tony ("Big Tuna") Accardo. Neither had much trust in Giancana, whose fiery temper and grandiose schemes had earned him the nickname "Mooney" (mob lingo for loony). Surely murdering the executive producer of *The Untouchables* would be no solution to the Mafia's image problem. Quite the contrary.

The booming Desilu Productions had reported gross earnings of $20.4 million for its latest fiscal year, as compared to $4.6 million five years earlier. But because of soaring production costs, which had quadrupled since the pioneer days of television, profits were only $250,000 for the year. Desi thought it might be time for the couple to quit while they were ahead. They could easily get $15 million for Desilu, perhaps more if lucky.

Lucy opposed the idea. "Desi wanted to sell everything and retire," she recalled. "Just the thought alone sent chills through my body. I loved working. I didn't want to retire ever. I told him that. I felt we didn't have a marriage anymore. Desi wasn't about to give up booze and broads, so I didn't see any reason to give up my work. I wanted to slow down, yes. But I didn't want to stop."

The vicious cycle continued. "The more frustrating and impractical the business became, the more difficult my job became," Desi said later. "The more our love life deteriorated, the more we fought, the less sex we had. The more unhappy we were, the more I worked, and the more I drank."

A near-tragedy finally convinced Lucy to seek a divorce. The Arnazes were spending a weekend with the two children at their beach house at Del Mar. Joining them were comedian friend Jimmy Durante and his much younger wife, Marge, a former show girl at New York's Copacabana. As usual, Desi and Durante spent the afternoon at the racetrack. By the time they returned, Desi was so drunk that he had to hold on to the apparently still sober Durante for support.

As Lucy remembered it: "Desi changed into his trunks and insisted on taking Little Desi for a swim. At first they stayed close to the shore, but Big Desi started to swim further out, and Little Desi watched him go. His dad goaded him on to join him. Little Desi was petrified but didn't want to say no to his father.

"Durante rushed over to me and said they were in trouble. Little Desi was close to his dad and they kept going out further and further. If anything happened, Big Desi was in no shape to save anyone. I went down to the shore and started screaming. Little Lucie started crying. The two Desis finally got back to the beach, but the poor kid was exhausted and coughing up water. I wanted to kill his father right there in front of everyone."

The Arnazes cut the weekend short and returned to their house in Beverly Hills. As luck would have it, a water pipe had burst during their absence. Desi went berserk when he saw the flood damage.

"He carried on about it for two days," Lucy said later. "He blamed everybody and everything. By Desi's count, there were sixteen people at fault. He was hysterical, screaming and raving about it. I was scared for my life. That did it. I couldn't take any more."

As so often happened throughout the Arnazes' marriage, business became the primary consideration when they decided to divorce. CBS and Westinghouse could sue them for breach of contract if they failed to complete the current season of *Lucy* specials for *Desilu Playhouse*. And the scandal over the breakup of one of America's most admired couples was bound to have a negative affect on TV ratings, as well as on the stock market trading in Desilu Productions.

To avoid any mudslinging in public, Desi told Lucy that he would not contest the divorce. The case turned out to be one of the most amicable in the annals of celebrity breakups; the same attorney, Milton Rudin, represented both sides.

While the preliminary paperwork proceeded, Lucy and Desi tried to put up a united front. For the sake of the children, they celebrated Christmas Day together, but for the balance of the 1959–60 holiday they went their separate ways. Lucy took the kids to Sun Valley, Idaho, where Ann Sothern put them up at her skiing lodge. Desi did a bit of golfing in Palm Springs, which during the winter season just happened to be a mecca for attractive women from colder climes.

Their parents' problems were starting to affect the children. "With Desi away from us most of the time, I knew that Lucie and Little Desi felt deserted. Kindhearted, as all children are, they never said a word," Lucy recalled.

Obviously, Lucy was only stalling for time. When she and Desi finally decided to divorce, they realized it was up to both parents to break the news to the children before it became public knowledge.

The shock of Lucie and/or Desi first learning about it while watching the news on television would have been devastating.

The Arnazes took the children to their house in Palm Springs for the weekend. Lucy lost her nerve and asked Desi to do the talking while she sat and listened. "He began by saying that Mommy and Daddy were not getting along," Lucy recalled. "Lucie asked, 'But you won't get a divorce?'

"Desi explained that perhaps we would. The kids got very quiet, put their heads down and didn't want to look at us. Desi said a little more about how we would see each other often and that he loved them very much. Finally, Little Desi looked up and said, 'But Daddy, a divorce? Isn't there some way you can take it all back?' That was almost more than we could take."

On the surface at least, Lucie and Desi took the news better than their parents expected. "They were very hip kids for their age," Lucy said later. "They had friends and schoolmates whose parents had broken up. They knew of parents who had practically killed each other over a divorce. They were afraid that would happen to us. Desi and I promised them that we would remain friends, but said that we couldn't stay married. The kids cried for a week. I cried for a month."

On March 2, 1960, which just happened to be Desi's forty-third birthday, the Arnazes filmed the hour-long special entitled "Lucy Meets the Mustache," with comedian Ernie Kovacs and his singer wife Edie Adams as guest stars. Since Lucy and Desi were still being secretive about their divorce, the studio audience was unaware of TV history being made. There would be no more adventures of the Ricardos and Mertzes after this one. *I Love Lucy* was being put to rest after 179 half-hour episodes, thirteen one-hour specials, and nine years on the air.

Under the circumstances, "Lucy Meets the Mustache" gave no hint of it being the last story in the series. The episode ended with Ricky forgiving Lucy for yet another of her loony schemes. Unlike the Arnazes, the Ricardos presumably lived happily ever after. In that never-never land where sitcoms spin on forever, Lucy and Ricky are probably still kissing and making up. Fred and Ethel Mertz may have died of old age, but their namesakes, Fred and Ethel Ricardo (the children of Little Ricky) fill the void.

With the final special in the can, the Arnazes wasted no time in revealing their secret to the world. The very next day, Lucy filed divorce papers in Santa Monica Superior Court, charging "mental cruelty." Contacted by reporters, she refused to elaborate. Desi, however, issued the following statement:

"We deeply regret that after long serious consideration we have not been able to work out our problems and have decided to separate. Our divorce will be completely amicable, and there will be no contest. Lucy will pursue her career on television, and I will continue my work as head of Desilu Productions."

The divorce news came as a bombshell to millions of Lucy and Desi fans. From the onset of *I Love Lucy* in 1951, no celebrity marriage had seemed happier or was more admired. Now it proved to have been an illusion. The darlings of the 1950s became the first casualties of the '60s.

When broadcast on April 1, 1960 (coincidentally All Fools' Day), "Lucy Meets the Mustache" seemed an anticlimax and registered the lowest rating in the series' history. Not surprisingly, Westinghouse decided to cancel *Desilu Playhouse* at the end of the season. Except for the *Lucy* specials and the original two-part "Untouchables," the program had failed to sell enough electrical appliances and light bulbs to satisfy the sponsor.

Although the Arnazes had hoped to avoid a public spectacle, reporters, photographers, and TV cameramen were blocking the entrance to Santa Monica Superior Court when Lucy arrived for the divorce hearing on May 4. Dressed in an elegant two-piece suit of black-and-white checkered silk, she playfully cleared a path through the crowd with a few parries of her tightly rolled umbrella, a seemingly unnecessary accessory for that sunny day.

As he promised, Desi did not show up in court to challenge Lucy's case. She was represented by attorney Milton Rudin. Cleo Morgan, Lucy's cousin and near sister, served as corroborating witness.

Lucy started to lose her composure when she took the stand before Judge Orlando Rhodes. Under Rudin's questioning about Desi's alleged cruelties, her chin began to quiver and her eyes turned misty. She was only nodding her answers until the judge got annoyed and told her to speak loudly and distinctly.

"My husband would frequently have temper outbursts in front of the children and this was very bad," Lucy testified. "It was so bad I thought it was better if we were apart.

"It was a Jekyll and Hyde sort of thing. There was no discussing anything with him. He would have tantrums in front of friends and relatives, and we could have no social life for the last three to four years. I couldn't bear to be at parties when he would blow up. I preferred the privacy of our home when the battles started."

Lucy claimed that it had been extremely difficult to work with Desi for the past nine years "with this sort of thing going on." That was the nearest she got to alluding to Desi's boozing and philandering, which were left out of her complaint to protect his reputation as well as the feelings of their two children.

When Rudin asked her on the witness stand if she tried to work things out with Desi, Lucy replied, "There's no discussing anything with him. He doesn't discuss very well."

Judge Rhodes wasted no time in granting the divorce. The entire hearing took less than an hour. While leaving the courtroom, Lucy bumped into a veteran reporter who reminded her that fourteen years earlier the Arnazes had gone through a so-called first divorce that lasted less than twenty-four hours.

"Will there be a reconciliation this time?" the reporter asked.

"Nope," Lucy snapped.

In the divorce settlement, Lucy received full-time custody of Lucie and Desi, but their father had unrestricted visitation rights. Although Lucy had demanded no alimony, the judge ruled that Desi must pay her $450 a month—$900 in total—toward each child's support.

According to California's community property law, Lucy and Desi's holdings were split down the middle. Lucy kept the Beverly Hills house, while Desi received their beach property at Del Mar. The Palm Springs home would be sold or leased, with the proceeds used to expand their Indian Wells Resort Hotel. Income from the hotel would be equally divided until 1966, when the property would be sold to create trust funds for the children.

The settlement also required Lucy and Desi to divide their 50 percent interest in Desilu Productions. Consequently, each wound up with a 25 percent ownership, or 282,800 shares. At that time, Desilu stock was selling for twelve dollars per share. On paper at least, Lucy and Desi's holdings were worth nearly $3.4 million apiece. To protect Desilu against corporate raiders, Lucy and Desi agreed that if either one of them ever decided to sell their stock, then the other would have first call on purchasing it. In that way, they could keep Desilu a family-owned business for generations to come.

The cancellation of Desilu Playhouse left Lucy and Desi without a showcase for their performing talents. Desi couldn't have been happier, because he could now concentrate solely on running Desilu. Lucy, however, felt lost. She'd worked long and hard for her success, and although she was nearly fifty years old, she had no intention of retiring from acting.

As the so-called Queen of Television, Lucy could easily have another series with one phone call to William Paley, but there was a hitch to it. She had an exclusive contract with Desilu that prevented her from working for other television companies. Any new program that Lucy did would mean having Desi as her boss, which hardly seemed advisable while the divorce was still an open wound for both of them.

Although Lucy hadn't made a theatrical movie in five years and none without Desi since 1951, she decided to return to that arena for lack of any alternatives. Unfortunately, Lucy's popularity on television did not guarantee that the public would rush to pay to see her on the big screen. Also, the major studios considered her over the hill in comparison to the younger generation of stars like Elizabeth Taylor, Marlon Brando, Marilyn Monroe, Paul Newman, Audrey Hepburn, Elvis Presley, Shirley MacLaine, and Natalie Wood.

Lucy finally wound up in *The Facts of Life*, which sounded like a wry comment on her situation at that time but was actually a script that had been peddled around the various studios for years without a taker. Lucy envisioned the comedy-drama as a co-starring vehicle with Bob Hope, with whom she'd worked successfully in the past. United Artists agreed to distribute the movie, with Desilu providing half the financing as well as the production facilities. To keep the peace, Desi himself would have no active participation in the project.

Focusing on two middle-aged marrieds who leave their spouses to have an affair that never gets consummated, *The Facts of Life* landed Lucy in the hospital during the movie's production. While trying to board a boat in the studio's artificial lake, she lost her balance and fell into the water, which was only three feet deep. She cut a deep gash in her right leg and was knocked unconscious. Several members of the technical crew rushed her by car to Cedars of Lebanon Hospital, where doctors found that she had suffered a slight concussion.

Desi rushed to Lucy's bedside when he heard the news. He stayed at the hospital for ninety minutes, starting press rumors that a reconciliation was in the offing. The gossip continued when Desi returned several days later to take Lucy and the children to his beach house at Del Mar while she recuperated.

It looked like a replay of an old scenario. Reporters camping at the front door wanted to know if Lucy and Desi were cohabiting again. Ken Morgan, Desilu's publicity director and part of the family via marriage to Lucy's cousin Cleo, finally stepped outside to deny it.

After returning to work, Lucy herself tried to put an end to the rumors by telling Hedda Hopper, "Desi and I will never be together again."

Nobody seemed to believe her. Since the divorce, Lucy had received about 8,000 letters from the public and read most of them. "I couldn't answer them all, of course," she recalled. "They asked me to reconsider. People just could not endure a breakup. I guess they thought we really were Lucy and Ricky. The general tone was 'Isn't there *something* that you can do?' They didn't know I had been trying to do it for years."

Meanwhile, Desi had a bad case of post-divorce blues, drinking heavily and losing a bundle at the Las Vegas casinos. After being thrown out of the Desert Inn for starting a fistfight with another guest, he had enough sense to check into a private hospital to dry out. The cure was short-lived.

"Desi wouldn't admit, especially to himself, how hard the divorce hit him," a friend recalled. "But he really took it deeply and unwisely. He rented a penthouse sumptuous enough for King Farouk. He flashed around town in big cars. There were girls, girls, and more girls. He had a suite of offices, including a bedroom, at all three Desilu studios. Sometimes he lived there. But wherever he happened to be, he was restless and unhappy."

Business kept closing in on him. Desilu had two new series on ABC that weren't doing well: *Guestward Ho!* (originally earmarked for Vivian Vance) with Joanne Dru and Mark Miller as city slickers trying to run a dude ranch in New Mexico; and *Harrigan and Son,* a self-explanatory sitcom starring Pat O'Brien and Roger Perry as law partners. While trying to salvage those programs, Desi discovered that one of his top executives was secretly trying to gain control of Desilu by purchasing large blocks of stock. Desi fired the man and took over his job as well.

Not too astutely, Lucy took the attitude that Desilu's problems were Desi's province and not hers. Between raising the children and attending to her career, she had more than enough to worry about.

However well *The Facts of Life* turned out, Lucy realized that it would be difficult, if not impossible, to continue working regularly in movies. It was a painful truth that had already been faced by such contemporaries as Bette Davis, Joan Crawford, Ginger Rogers, Katharine Hepburn, and Barbara Stanwyck. Unless you wanted to portray ax murderers or eccentric grannies—which Lucy definitely did not—there were no big starring roles being written for women over forty.

Lucy surprised everybody, herself included, when she agreed to star in a Broadway musical entitled *Wildcat.* Never mind that Lucille Ball had never been much of a singer *or* dancer. If she pulled it off and the show became a hit, she could kiss television and movies goodbye and concentrate on stage and nightclub appearances.

Working on Broadway would also enable Lucy to burn some of her bridges behind her. "I needed a change of scenery. Hollywood held too many bitter memories. I'd hit the bottom of despair. I hate failure, and the divorce was the number-one failure in my eyes. I'd been humiliated, and that's not easy for a woman to cope with. I wanted to pack up the kids and make a fresh start," she remembered.

21

Changing Partners

ALTHOUGH the marriage of nearly twenty years had ended, Lucy and Desi were still bound to each other, not only through their two children but also by way of their separate but equal stakes in Desilu Productions. The romantic flame may have died, but the relationship still had a long way to go.

Without too much arm-twisting from Lucy, Desi agreed that Desilu should invest $450,000 in the Broadway production of *Wildcat*. If the musical became a hit, Desilu would earn a fortune and also control the movie rights.

How could it miss? The farcical period piece about the rough-and-ready pioneers of the oil industry seemed an ideal vehicle for Lucille Ball. She would portray a fast-talking prospector named Wildcat Jackson, who bamboozles the residents of a western town into believing that she owns the drilling rights to the underlying land.

Mary Martin had been the first choice for *Wildcat*, but she wouldn't risk working with composers Sammy Cahn and Jimmy Van Heusen, who were well established in movies but had never done a successful Broadway show. But Lucy admired the team's catalogue of standards (which included one of her favorite songs, "All the Way") and was equally impressed by the other participants. Michael Kidd, the multi-Tony-Award-winning choreographer, would direct *Wildcat*. N. Richard Nash—whose play *The Rainmaker* was a memorable showcase for Geraldine Page on Broadway and for Katharine Hepburn in the film version—wrote the book.

Lucy committed herself to a run-of-the-play contract, which could mean living in New York for several years if *Wildcat* became a hit. Betting that it would, she signed a $50,000 lease on a seven-room apartment in Imperial House, a new East Side high-rise recommended to her by Joan Crawford, one of its charter residents. Coincidentally, Lucy's new address would be 150 East 69th Street, just a skip and a jump from the fictitious Ricardo-Mertz residence at 623 East 68th Street (somewhere in the East River if you tried to find it).

Grandma DeDe Ball came along to help with the children, who, of course, would be living with Lucy during the run of *Wildcat*. Lucy didn't want anybody feeling homesick, so she did her best to transform the New York digs into a facsimile of their residences in California. Four huge vans were required for the cross-country move. In addition to clothing, linens, draperies, rugs, and kitchen requisites, Lucy shipped furniture from the house in Palm Springs, five television sets, a grand piano, paintings and knicknacks, whole cabinets of books and phonograph records, and enough toys and playthings to stock a branch of F. A. O. Schwarz.

As a star-struck teenager, Lucy had dreamed of triumphing on the Broadway stage. Finally, at nearly fifty, her goal seemed within reach, if only in her imagination. Singing and dancing were never Lucy's strong points. And while she'd survived twenty-eight years of grinding work in movies and television, could she cope with the physical demands of live performance, which meant giving eight three-hour shows per week, including two on Wednesdays and Saturdays?

In movies, Lucy's vocal shortcomings were compensated for by dubbing, a form of electronic trickery considered unethical in theater and concert performances. To get her husky voice into condition, she took several months of daily lessons with Carlo Menotti, a singing coach almost as famous as the composer of similar name. Lucy also sought help from Kay Thompson, a much-admired singer-dancer best known for her work as coach to Judy Garland and other MGM stars in the heyday of Arthur Freed and Vincente Minnelli musicals.

"The minute that Kay saw me do something that worked, she would say, 'Do that again and remember it.' It's an authority. It doesn't matter so much how you sing, but how much authority you sing with," Lucy recalled.

But *Wildcat* got off to an unsteady start. No sooner had Lucy moved to New York than Sammy Cahn and Jimmy Van Heusen quit the show in a dispute over song royalties. Cahn and Van Heusen also took with them most of the musical's investors, so Lucy, or rather Desilu, ended up funding the entire $750,000 production budget. Two promising young songwriters, composer Cy Coleman and lyricist Carolyn Leigh, neither of whom had done a complete Broadway score before, were hurriedly hired to replace Cahn and Van Heusen.

Wildcat Jackson's love interest was a swaggering driller foreman named Joe Dynamite. Lucy wanted Stephen Boyd for the part, but the muscular sensation of the recent Hollywood remake of *Ben Hur* had conflicting movie commitments. She had to settle for Keith Andes, another hunk best known for playing the police chief hero of the short-lived TV series *This Man Dawson*.

By the time *Wildcat* started its tryout run in Philadelphia on Thanksgiving Day 1960, Lucy found herself in deep trouble. "Michael Kidd didn't direct me into the show, he directed the show around me. I had to rely on the kids in the chorus for guidance," she recalled. "Nothing that the revered Mr. Nash wrote got any laughs, so I started doing Lucy Ricardo shtick to get the reaction I was looking for. I was getting desperate, and Kidd didn't tell me not to, so I did."

Besides doing eight shows a week in Philadelphia, Lucy had to spend all but a few sleeping hours in rehearsals. Her health began to fail owing to the strains on her voice and the pummeling she took as Keith Andes and his cohorts tossed her all over the stage in the dance routines. The leg injury that she suffered during the filming of *Facts of Life* flared anew.

Stoked up with painkillers, Lucy began muffing her lines and forgetting some lyrics. Whenever that happened, she would stop the performance cold and beg the audience's indulgence while she started over. Rather than ask for their money back, people cheered her on. This was the Lucy they'd come to see, not the tough and conniving tomboy she portrayed in the play.

Lucy's fears that the divorce may have alienated her fans proved to be groundless. *Wildcat* opened to the biggest advance sale in the thirty-eight-year history of New York's Alvin Theatre. By 1991 standards, ticket buyers got a real bargain: the best seats in the house sold for $8.60 on weekday nights, $9.40 on Friday and Saturday evenings, and $5.40 at matinees.

Desi flew in from Los Angeles to attend the December 15 premiere, starting a new wave of reconciliation rumors. But that was the last thing on his mind. He knew that Lucy would need his moral support during one of the most trying times in her professional life. He also had to make sure that Desilu's investment in the show wasn't being squandered.

Mother Nature just happened to dump a blizzard on New York on the opening night of *Wildcat,* but that was nothing compared to the next morning's blitzkrieg from the town's most influential drama critics. " 'Wildcat' went prospecting for Broadway oil but drilled a dry hole," said Howard Taubman in the *New York Times.* "Everybody wanted to love Lucille Ball, but her show didn't make it easy. The new musical with which she arrived last night had as much spirit and excitement as a tame old tabby."

Taubman noted that "Miss Ball worked hard, singing and dancing with zest and reading her lines with an expert's timing, but 'Wildcat' did not seem to test her full capacities as a performer."

Walter Kerr of the *New York Herald Tribune* started his review, "Naturally, in the case of 'Wildcat,' what you really want to know about is Lucille Ball. So do I. I want to know why that bonny and talented and ever so bright girl isn't present—in person—on the Alvin stage.

"Miss Ball is up there, all right, doing all of the spectacular and animated and energetic and deliriously accomplished things she can do, but what happened? Is it simply the unsmiling libretto of N. Richard Nash that makes her seem to be performing by proxy?"

Despite the critical barbs, *Wildcat* became an immediate hit. Lucy's popularity overcame all obstacles. From the moment that she strutted on stage in form-fitting blue denim and singing "Hey, Look Me Over," the audience was on its feet cheering.

"We had SRO business and I couldn't have been happier," Lucy recalled. "But I soon realized they wanted the TV Lucy, not Wildcat Jackson. So I gave 'em Lucy, which was fine with me. I loved Lucy, doing her. Loved the mugging. Ad-libbing to a character onstage: 'Say, do you know a fellow named Fred Mertz?' They ate it up. I had a ball. Did what I liked."

During the final curtain calls, Lucy would do a solo bit, thanking the audience for coming and performing a few bumps and grinds to comedy sound effects by the orchestra's drummer. She would then call for another chorus of "Hey, Look Me Over" and invite the audience to join in the singing.

One night, a little Yorkshire terrier in the cast happened to defecate on stage. Lucy stopped the show cold, shouted into the wings for a mop and bucket, and proceeded to wipe up the mess. The audience howled when she announced, "It's in the small print of my contract. I have to clean up the dog shit!"

Between the physical stress of the show and New York's coldest winter in a decade, Lucy's health started to break down. Although she had an understudy, what was *Wildcat* without Lucille Ball? Performances had to be canceled while she recuperated from colds, torn muscles, and nervous exhaustion. By February, Lucy had been out so much that doctors advised her to take a vacation in a warmer climate. *Wildcat* was shut down for two weeks while she jetted to Jamaica with the two children.

"A holiday in the sun was supposed to help me, but it almost killed me," Lucy said later. "The humidity nearly put me away, and nobody warned me that Jamaica had a revolution going on at the time. Wow!"

Returning to *Wildcat* anything but rested, Lucy put up a valiant effort to keep the show running. It was a matter of professional pride, as well as a need to protect Desilu's $750,000 investment. But during the second of her two performances on Saturday, April 22, Lucy fainted on stage. Edith King, an actress performing with her at the moment, caught Lucy and broke the fall, but in the process fractured her own wrist.

In the best show business tradition, the musical went on anyway after Lucy and King were carted off. Since it was the middle of the last act, Lucy's understudy had already gone home, so assistant choreographer Shelah Hackett, who also danced in the chorus, filled in for the star.

By the following Monday, Lucy and King were both back at work. But a month later, Lucy collapsed on stage again. Reluctantly, she decided to suspend *Wildcat* for a summer vacation. By that time, the musical had given 171 performances.

An ad in the June 4 issue of the *New York Times* announced that *Wildcat* would resume on August 7, but it never did. Lucy and her ex-husband decided it would be too costly for Desilu. The actors' and musicians' unions were demanding full pay for their members during the show's unexpected nine-week hiatus.

Desilu not only lost $750,000 on *Wildcat*, but also had to refund $165,000 to the public for tickets purchased in advance. *Variety* claimed it was the largest payback in Broadway history up to that time.

Not surprisingly, Lucy badmouthed *Wildcat* for the rest of her life. "When I left the show, I was so sick they almost carried me out in a coffin," she once told an interviewer. "I had lost twenty-two pounds and my doctor refused to be responsible anymore with the insurance company. I don't think I'll ever do another play. Most of the work is at night, which means you lose the days and have little contact with the outer world."

Caught short, Lucy had no plans for the future. She still had years to go on the lease to the New York apartment, but the children weren't too happy about the living arrangements.

"My mother was very protective and never allowed us to go anywhere," Lucie Arnaz remembered. "We lived at the Imperial House, *inside*. We never got a chance to even play in Central Park, which was only a few blocks away. Mom was absolutely petrified of Central Park. We went everywhere in a chauffeured limousine, which embarrassed me and reminded me of funerals.

"The only place that Mom seemed comfortable was at Sardi's restaurant, where she could be with other show business people. She wouldn't go out shopping for fear of being recognized and starting a mob scene. People would bring clothes and things to the house for her to pick out."

During their summer vacation, Lucy took Lucie and Desi on another tour of Europe. Not eager to resume working either in Hollywood or on Broadway, she considered buying a chalet in Switzerland and settling there permanently with the children.

By this time, the divorce had become final. Lucy was free to marry again, but at age fifty did she really want to? The question suddenly became a burning issue when she found herself being swept off her feet by vaudeville and nightclub comedian Gary Morton.

The couple first met through the connivance of mutual friends, comedian Jack Carter and his fiancée Paula Stewart, who portrayed Lucy's kid sister in *Wildcat*. "Lucy had been going out every night with stage-door johnnies, rich guys, boring people," Jack Carter recalled. "She loved fun, so we brought Gary around. We went to a pizza parlor on Third Avenue and they just kept staring at each other. For days, she kept calling him 'That kid, what's his name, that guy, you know . . .' They were inseparable after that."

Not immediately. Morton was working in the stage show at Radio City Music Hall at the time and played some out-of-town bookings after that. The romance didn't blossom until *Wildcat* closed and Lucy found herself with time on her hands.

Son of a Bronx truck driver, Gary Morton (born Morton Goldapper) was a throwback to the rough-hewn Mack Grey–Broderick Crawford types that Lucy dated before she married Desi Arnaz. Tall and husky, Morton wore a toupee and claimed to be forty-two, which made him eight years younger than Lucy. He started his career during

World War II in USO shows, spent the 1950s as a wisecracking emcee in vaudeville, and became a minor celebrity on the Borscht Circuit of resorts and nightclubs that catered to a Jewish clientele in the Catskills and Miami Beach.

During a brief and discouraging attempt to establish himself in Hollywood, Morton married actress Jacqueline Inmoor, but the union ended in an annulment after six months. Wary of Morton's checkered past, Lucy took her time about getting seriously involved with him. She had to make sure that he wasn't just a fortune hunter in pursuit of her wealth and prestige. He had a great deal to gain, both monetarily and in what becoming "Mr. Lucille Ball" could mean to his career.

For his part, Morton confessed to knowing next to nothing about Lucy's professional past. He remembered her as a gorgeous movie star, but he'd never seen even one episode of *I Love Lucy* because he was always performing on stage somewhere when the programs aired. That admission endeared him to Lucy, as did the fact that he seemed very much his own man, dedicated to his work. He was also an avid golfer and an expert on vintage automobiles.

Not surprisingly, Lucie and young Desi disapproved of the new man on the scene. The children apparently had fallen under the spell of the Walt Disney film *The Parent Trap*, in which twin sisters (both enacted by Hayley Mills) succeed in reuniting their long-divorced parents.

"Gary was a nice man, but he was no father figure, and my kids weren't about to accept him without a battle," Lucy recalled. "Lucie and Desi thought that if they took me to see this movie often enough, I'd get the idea. I must have sat through it five or six times! But I kept telling them that their daddy and I would never get together again and that we'd all be happier if they just let us get on with our lives."

As the start of another school year approached, Lucy decided to pull up stakes and move back to Beverly Hills. She had no real reason for remaining in New York, and the children missed their friends and especially their father, who rarely had time to fly east to visit them.

Lucy was extremely worried about young Desi. "He was unhappy, he'd put on a lot of weight, and the Catholic nuns he had for teachers spoiled and pampered him rotten," she said later. Upon their return to California, Lucy enrolled him in St. John's Military Academy to learn some discipline. His sister, meanwhile, resumed her studies at Immaculate Heart School for Girls.

Gary Morton followed Lucy west, ostensibly for nightclub engagements in Las Vegas and Lake Tahoe. Morton's career was one of the last impediments to their getting married. Lucy still had painful memories of the long separations from Desi during his years of traveling with the band. She did not want another part-time husband.

It would have made no sense for Lucy to join Morton's nomadic life, so she offered to help him get started in the television business if he gave up his road career. She also wanted him to sign a prenuptial agreement covering his rights to her estate. Such are the rules of the game when a wealthy star marries a nobody. In the worst case, she had to protect herself and the children in the event of another divorce.

"I didn't really want to get married again. At my age, I didn't think it was necessary," Lucy recalled. "But my mother said, 'Look, the children will grow up and leave you, and you'll be all alone. You don't want to be alone, do you?' I said I didn't, and then she said, 'Well, Gary's a very nice man. We like him.' So that settled it. I liked him, too. I enjoyed his nonstop humor. His jokes tickled me. It was good to be able to laugh again after all I'd been through with Desi."

Before accepting Morton's proposal, Lucy insisted on introducing him to her ex-husband. "Desi was still too much a part of my life *not* to be consulted," she recalled. "I suppose it was a bit like asking Big Daddy for his blessing, but I wouldn't have had it any other way. Happily, Desi liked Gary immediately, and they were always very friendly."

Desi did not, however, attend the wedding, which took place in New York on November 19, 1961 (just eleven days prior to what would have been the twenty-first anniversary of the Arnaz nuptials). Lucy had traveled east again to appear with Henry Fonda and Mort Sahl in "The Good Years," a ninety-minute CBS special about the bucolic era that preceded America's entry into World War I. Since she still had the apartment at Imperial House, she brought the children and her California relatives to town for the marriage ceremony at Marble Collegiate Church on lower Fifth Avenue. Gary Morton's relations came in via subway from the Bronx and Long Island.

Norman Vincent Peale, Lucy's longtime confidant, conducted the Reformed Protestant service. Still reeling from her recent nomination to Earl Blackwell's list of the worst-dressed women in America, Lucy splurged on an exquisite bridal costume at Bergdorf Goodman: a sleeveless blue-green dress of windowpane silk and a matching tulle headdress. The tuxedo-clad groom sported a new hairpiece for the occasion.

Jack Carter and Paula Stewart, the couple's matchmakers and now Mr. and Mrs. themselves, served as best man and matron of honor. Although Lucy and Gary had tried to keep the wedding private, several thousand people were assembled outside Marble Collegiate

Church when the couple arrived together in a chauffeured Rolls-Royce. Policemen had to form a wedge to get them through the mob of well-wishers, many of whom were chanting, "We love Lucy," over and over again.

There was no honeymoon. After a small reception at Lucy's digs in Imperial House, the newlyweds stayed on in New York until she finished taping "The Good Years." Afterward, they took off for Palm Springs, where Morton had a booking at the Chi Chi Club, one of several he'd contracted for prior to promising Lucy he'd quit.

In an interview with columnist Earl Wilson, Lucy made it plain that she did not intend to become a Gary Morton groupie: "I won't make a practice of going to Gary's nightclub openings. Because if you go, people mistake the reason. They don't believe you would go just to be with someone you love. They think you go to hype business. They said it about Eddie Fisher and Elizabeth Taylor, but they're not going to say it about Gary and me."

Lucy scoffed at rumors of a "Lucy and Gary" comedy team. "We have no plans or even thoughts of working together," she said. "Frankly, I think it would horrify the millions of *Lucy* fans who are still waiting for Lucy and Ricky to kiss and make up."

Except for "The Good Years," broadcast in January 1961, Lucy hadn't appeared on prime-time television since the final "Lucy and Ricky" installment of *Desilu Playhouse* in the spring of 1960. It seemed about time to reconsider a return to the medium where she was most appreciated. In the interim, she signed on for yet another movie with Bob Hope—their fourth together and the seventy-first effort in Lucy's screen career.

The Technicolor comedy entitled *Critic's Choice* proved to be anything but, although the original play by Ira Levin had been a moderate success on Broadway with Henry Fonda and Georgann Johnson in the leads. Reportedly inspired by the real-life marriage of Jean and Walter Kerr, the story stretched the limits of credulity by casting Lucille Ball as an aspiring playwright and Bob Hope as an astringent drama critic who just happens to be her husband and must review her first Broadway effort. Audience reactions at previews were so negative that Warner Brothers shelved the movie for a year, finally releasing it in the spring of 1963 to disastrous results.

By that time, Lucy had already made a triumphant return to television in a weekly CBS series entitled *The Lucy Show*. While making *Critic's Choice*, she saw the handwriting on the wall and realized that she'd have to concentrate on television if she wanted to continue working with any regularity. To a ticket-buying public with a median age of twenty-three, stars like Bob Hope and Lucille Ball were dinosaurs.

The Lucy Show was also designed to rejuvenate Desilu Productions, which now drew most of its revenues from *The Untouchables* and the rental of studio facilities. As head of production, Desi didn't have much luck with short-lived series like *Guestward Ho!*, *Harrigan and Son*, and *Fair Exchange*. He was partly to blame, spending more time drinking, gambling, and skirt chasing than he did attending to business.

"After the divorce, Desi really fell apart," a friend recalled. "He drank even more, he was depressed, he hid from everybody. Lucy decided it was up to her to help him. By insisting that he become the executive producer of the new series, she could make sure he toed the mark. Of course, she was thinking of herself as well. She was scared shitless that the show would be a disaster without Desi's input."

In showbiz parlance, everybody knew that *I Love Lucy* would be a tough act to follow. Despite its title, *The Lucy Show* was not a continuation of that series, although daffy heroine Lucy Carmichael could easily pass for Lucy Ricardo's twin sister. Marilyn Pugh and Bob Carroll, who wrote *I Love Lucy* from its inception, derived their new format from a novel by Irene Kamp entitled *Life Without George*. Casting their star as a widow who worried more about her children than about finding another husband seemed preferable to pairing her with a steady leading man who would have to contend with viewers' indissoluble memories of the Lucy and Desi partnership.

Lucy wisely decided that she couldn't do the new series without Vivian Vance, who by this time had married literary agent John Dodds and retired to their home in Connecticut. Fed up with being taken for Ethel Mertz in real life, Vance drove a hard bargain before she accepted. She demanded co-star billing, a glamorous wardrobe, and the character name of "Viv" so that she could break loose of her dowdy image from *I Love Lucy*. She also refused to be reunited with William Frawley, an impossibility anyway, because he now had a co-starring role in Fred MacMurray's *My Three Sons* series.

Last but not least, Vance demanded a whopping pay increase. Lucy approved it, but told Desi that she didn't want to know how much. "The figure will only make me angry," she said, speaking as co-owner of Desilu. "But whatever it is, Viv deserves every penny."

On the first day of production of *The Lucy Show*, Desi turned up on the set to welcome his ex-wife back to work. He kissed Lucy on the cheek and handed her a good luck charm from Van Cleef & Arpels

—a tiny four-leaf clover made of antique emerald jade. As she embraced him, they both started to cry.

Later that morning, Vivian Vance bumped into Desi while he was watching rehearsals, and they, too, shared some tears. "Like me," Vance remembered, "Desi was thinking back to when we all started *I Love Lucy*—him and Lucy and Bill Frawley and me, and how it was then. All the newness, all the anticipation and the hope, all the fun. And here we were, starting again, only this time Desi was on the outside looking in and it wasn't fun anymore. He wasn't acting in the show. He was divorced. I'd been divorced, but I was married again. And Lucy was married again. So much had happened to so many people, but most of all to Desi, leaving him alone and a little sad, although he tried to hide it."

Lucy and Desi's only public appearances as a team now were at the annual stockholders meetings of Desilu Productions. The one in August 1962 generated enough laughs for the *Los Angeles Times* to comment the next day: "Desilu may have missed a good bet in not filming the proceedings. It unquestionably was the year's brightest, liveliest and earthiest corporate function.

"Co-starring Desi Arnaz as a $156,000-per-annum president and Lucille Ball as vice-president at $25,000 (not counting her contract acting income), it was Hollywood's uncut, unrehearsed version of 'How to Succeed in Business by Really Trying.' "

Ironically, the meeting was held in the onetime RKO Little Theatre, where Lucy and Desi made their first date in the midst of rehearsals for *Too Many Girls*. Twenty-two years later, Desi barely resembled that sexy young conga drummer. His hair had turned almost totally gray, he wore thick horn-rimmed glasses, and the figure beneath the dark business suit had grown thick and stoop-shouldered.

Time had been kinder to Lucy. Despite the heavily made up face, she still gave an impression of youthful vitality as she bounced in from the set of *The Lucy Show* wearing a yellow blouse, green slacks, and white loafers. She took a seat on the dais next to Desi and listened while he read a speech detailing Desilu's prospects and activities.

Desi painted a rosy picture of the company's future, predicting it would earn its first million-dollar profit in the next fiscal year. He said the Desilu studios were operating at 87 percent of capacity and that with the new *Lucy Show*, the company would have four series of its own on the air. The syndication of old programs was bringing in $1.75 million a year. Desilu also intended to expand into the theatrical market, starting with a feature movie entitled *The Scarface Mob,* an adaptation of the first two segments of "The Untouchables" that were shown on *Desilu Playhouse* in 1959.

Lucy pulled a Charlie Chaplin and spoke hardly a word as Desi started to field questions from the seventy-five or so shareholders in the audience. Many were angry about a recent drop in the price of Desilu stock, precipitated by the board's decision to suspend the fifteen-cent quarterly dividend and retain earnings for corporate expansion. A woman blurted out that her broker told her that she'd be a fool to increase her holdings. Desi countered: "Give me your broker's name. He's probably in league with my ex-boss Xavier Cugat."

The inevitable question was raised by a peroxide blonde who claimed she was an unemployed actress and would rather have a job than dividends: "Why don't you and Miss Ball do another series together?"

Desi turned to Lucy for comment, but she just stared at him with her best stone face. Desi shrugged and said diplomatically, "I love working with Lucy, but I am producing her new show, and with my other duties, I don't think I will be able to."

The Lucy Show was a hit from its first CBS telecast on October 1, 1962, and demolished its direct competition, NBC's *Saints and Sinners* and ABC's *The Rifleman*. In its first full season on the air, *The Lucy Show* ranked fifth on the Nielsen list of America's most-watched programs. Number one was another newcomer, *The Beverly Hillbillies,* followed by the long-established *Candid Camera, The Red Skelton Show,* and *Bonanza.*

"Coming back on the air in a series without Desi had to be the biggest challenge of Lucy's career," said Mike Dann, then head of programming for CBS. "The whole program staff was fifty-fifty whether she would be successful, let alone as successful as she had been with Desi. There was absolute amazement when she became just as big a star as before."

Like *I Love Lucy,* the half-hour episodes of *The Lucy Show* were filmed in black-and-white in front of a studio audience, but the similarities ended there. Without Ricky Ricardo and his links to show business, the new program was closer to the traditional family-next-door sitcom. The widowed Lucy Carmichael worked as a secretary at the First National Bank in Danfield, Connecticut. Her best friend and neighbor, Vivian Bagley, was a divorcée. Their children and Lucy's cantankerous boss, Mr. Barnsdahl, caused most of the plot complications.

This "Lucy" had two kids instead of one, a boy and a girl, but the star resisted a natural temptation to cast the parts with her own brood. "Lucie and Desi were still in shock over the divorce, and I didn't want to interrupt their education again. There's just so much that children can take at one time," she said later.

Trivial Pursuit players can score bonus points by naming the young actors who portrayed Jerry and Chris Carmichael (Jimmy Garrett and Candy Moore). Ralph Hart played Vivian's son, Sherman Bagley. The part of the grouchy boss went to Charles Lane, a stern-faced character actor who'd known Lucy since her days as a Goldwyn Girl and had over 300 movies to his credit.

The implementation of *The Lucy Show* caused a flare-up of bickering and bad feelings between its star and her executive producer. Although Lucy and Desi tried to stay out of each other's personal lives except where the children were concerned, daily contact at the studio became a tribulation, not only for them but for everybody who had to work with them.

"Lucy had become such a perfectionist that she didn't trust anyone anymore, not even Desi," executive Edward Holly recalled. "Lucy wanted to do everything herself, from directing the shows to selecting the costumes and set decorations. Of course, her demanding ways were understandable. If *The Lucy Show* flopped, she would have been humiliated."

Although Lucy had previously given Desi a free hand in running Desilu, she started getting involved in that as well. "Lucy questioned a lot of his decisions, and you just couldn't do that with Desi. He had to be BOSS, in capital letters," Holly said.

As soon as *The Lucy Show* landed in the Top Ten ratings, Desi stunned Lucy by deciding to quit the business. "Desilu had gotten to be a monster," he recalled. "In the beginning, it was fun. But when you're in charge of three studios, with 3,000 employees and thirty-five soundstages working all the time, the fun is long gone.

"The things that got me where I was were the things I couldn't do anymore. I couldn't perform, I couldn't direct, I couldn't work with the writers, I couldn't do anything but be a tycoon. I had bankers and stockholders breathing down my neck. I even had the FCC on my tail over *The Untouchables*. By that time, the show had gangsters of every ethnic group, including Chinese and Jews, so complaints were coming in from all over."

To keep Desilu in the family, Lucy exercised her right to purchase Desi's interest in the company. With financing from the City National Bank of Beverly Hills, she bought his 300,350 shares for $2,552,975, figured at the current market price of $8.50 per share. Lucy wound up with 600,700 shares—52 percent of Desilu's outstanding stock. On paper at least, her holdings were worth $5,105,950.

In November 1962, the board of directors elected Lucille Ball to the presidency of Desilu Productions. In the process, Lucy made showbiz history by becoming the first woman to run one of Hollywood's major production entities. Only Mary Pickford, "America's Sweetheart" of silent days, had come close to that achievement as one of the founders (together with Douglas Fairbanks, Charles Chaplin, and D. W. Griffith) of United Artists Corporation.

After more than a decade as one of the most visible celebrities in America, Desi dropped from public view and bought a forty-five acre horse-breeding farm in Corona, California, about fifty miles southeast of Los Angeles. At one time or another, he had as many as forty racehorses in his stable, including Soldier Girl, a longtime record holder for fillies at Del Mar, and Amerigo's Fancy, a gorgeous chestnut with four white legs. The prize of his collection was the retired racing champion Nashville, which Desi purchased for $300,000 and offered for stud at $6,000 per live foal.

Desi also built a lavish vacation hideaway at Las Cruces in Baja California, on the Pacific coast of Mexico just below the U.S. border. It was about as close as Desi could get to his native roots without returning to Cuba, then under blockade by the United States government for permitting Soviet missiles and bomber bases on its shores.

Desi designed his swimming pool in the shape of a Spanish guitar. "If Liberace can have a piano-shaped pool, why not?" he often said.

At age forty-five and with millions in the bank, Desi had become one of Hollywood's most eligible bachelors. Between his Roman Catholic conscience and the many women who had their traps set for him, it was inevitable that he would marry again. Temporary housekeeper Lolita Arnaz kept telling her only child that she would not die happy unless she saw him settled down with a wife who would take care of him for the rest of his life.

Desi would never give up his tomcat habits with prostitutes and pickups, but since the divorce he'd been keeping company with someone from his early Hollywood past.

This "someone" was Edith McSkiming, a onetime cigarette girl at Santa Anita racetrack with whom he'd had a brief flirtation before marrying Lucy. Years later, Edie turned up as one of the Arnazes' neighbors in Del Mar. By that time she was the wife of Clement Hirsch, a multimillionaire who owned thoroughbred racing stables and originally made his fortune manufacturing Calcan Dog Food (a bizarre combination of interests if one stops to think about it).

After Lucy and Desi were divorced in 1960, Edie stepped into the picture; another redhead, except that she looked more like Doris Day than Lucille Ball and was the same age as Desi. Both were horse-aholics. Desi nicknamed her "Speedy Edie." They attended all the racing meets and horse auctions together.

In August 1962, Edie divorced Clement Hirsch and received custody of their five-year-old son. The circumstances of the breakup were kept secret, but friends of the couple describe it as amicable on both sides. Hirsch apparently had a new love as well, so he was happy to grant Edie her freedom. As a condition, however, she had to surrender all claims to Hirsch's millions except for child support.

Since Lucie and young Desi had known Edie for years and were playmates of Greg Hirsch, the coupling of the two divorced parents seemed a natural. But just as Lucy did with Gary Morton, Desi first sought approval from his ex-wife. Lucy was delighted and gave her blessing. She'd always liked Edie and believed she'd make a good stepmother.

Desi and Edie were married at the Sands Hotel in Las Vegas on March 2, 1963, which just happened to be his forty-sixth birthday. The civil ceremony was performed by Judge David Zenoff, with only the Jimmy Durantes and several other friends from the Del Mar crowd in attendance. Frank Sinatra, one of the owners of the hotel, supplied the wedding cake. Since Desi had severed his connection with Desilu and *The Untouchables,* the two had become friends again.

At her own request, Lucy was not invited to the wedding. She still carried a torch for Desi. It would have been too painful to watch him marrying anyone, even a woman she approved of. But she did send the two racing fanatics a huge floral arrangement in the shape of a horseshoe. The message on the satin sash read "Congratulations on both of you picking a winner."

The newlyweds honeymooned at the Indian Wells Country Club near Palm Springs. The Arnaz-owned hotel had been neglected while Desi ran Desilu, but he hoped to revive it by spending more time there and making it a mecca for conventions and golf tournaments.

Between Indian Wells, the horse ranch at Corona, and the beach properties in Del Mar and Baja California, Desi and Edie had plenty to occupy them and lots of time to enjoy the good life that went with it. Rather quickly, Desi Arnaz disappeared from the celebrity limelight and became a forgotten man except to his friends and loved ones.

22

Time Marches On

AFTER Desi's departure from Desilu, Lucille Ball adapted easily to her new role as Madame President. She made few changes in Desilu's executive slate, but hired Oscar Katz, a CBS executive she'd known since the days of *My Favorite Husband,* to be her adviser on business affairs.

"It really didn't seem like a *terribly* big deal for me to be running a studio," Lucy recalled. "Of course, it *was* a big deal, but I had all these marvelous people around me, and I really was in great hands. I just had to make the final decisions, sign the papers, and attend a lot of meetings. I didn't understand many things at first, but I learned fast."

So fast that friends noticed her turning into something frightening. "She's so tough, you think you're talking to a man," said columnist Sheilah Graham.

"Without Desi, Lucy has to be in charge both in front of and behind the cameras. It's hard to see yourself correctly in both situations," director Jerry Thorpe said.

Lucy laughed off such criticism. "If I was going to turn into a man, I would have done it ages ago," she said at the time. "When I took over this job, I decided to do it my way. My ability comes from fairness and a knowledge of people. The rules were here before I took over. I never wanted to be an executive, but when Desi left, I couldn't just walk away from my obligations and say forget it."

Lucy's first corporate crisis was ABC's cancellation of *The Untouchables,* which finally ran out of ethnic gangsters to revile after four controversial years on the air. As a replacement, Desilu came up with *The Greatest Show on Earth,* a spinoff of the Cecil B. DeMille epic in which Lucy nearly starred back in 1951. With Jack Palance as the circus boss and Stuart Erwin as his business manager, the hour-long stories gave Lucy an opportunity to find work for no-longer-in-demand friends like Buster Keaton and Ruby Keeler as guest stars. To hype the ratings, Lucy herself appeared in one episode as a lonely performer who adopts an orphaned boy, but the series never became a hit. ABC dropped it after one full season.

Lucy also authorized pilots for series built around stars who, in her opinion, had been unjustly neglected by television: Ethel Merman, Donald O'Connor, and Glynis Johns. Of the three series, only *Glynis,* a sitcom about a novelist turned amateur detective, got on the air, but CBS pulled it after three months because of low ratings.

Lucy was intensely loyal to people she admired or who had been kind to her in the past, and she found work for them whenever possible. In the case of long-ago lover George Raft, she also helped out financially when the IRS sued him for tax evasion. She became the main support of hard-drinking character actress Barbara Pepper and her children after the ex–Goldwyn Girl's husband was killed in an automobile accident.

Since Lucy had her own weekly series to contend with, she could spend only an hour or two a day in the president's chair. For the second season of *The Lucy Show,* she needed to make a major change in the cast when Charles Lane quit for a more lucrative assignment on *Petticoat Junction.*

Gale Gordon came aboard as Lucy Carmichael's new boss, Theodore J. Mooney. Lucy had been waiting years to work with Gordon again, and it proved well worth it. They had first acted together on radio in *My Favorite Husband.* Gordon was Lucy's original choice for Fred Mertz in *I Love Lucy,* but he'd already signed for the TV version of *Our Miss Brooks* and did that series instead, followed by *The Brothers, Pete and Gladys,* and *Dennis the Menace.*

Another new addition to *The Lucy Show* could be seen only by the studio audience. Lucy wanted Gary Morton to learn the ins and outs of the television business, so he began by doing what he did best—warming up the crowd with jokes and banter prior to each filming. Desi, of course, had initiated the practice with *I Love Lucy,* but it had ended when the couple divorced.

Morton also scouted material for new series, sat in on executive meetings, and generally served as Lucy's third and fourth hand. He had no official title, but those who resented his station as the boss's husband referred to him behind his back as "Mr. Balls" or "the man who lights Lucy's cigarettes."

The Mortons were about to celebrate their second wedding anniversary, putting to rest predictions that the marriage wouldn't last six months. Friends believed that Lucy would have stayed with Gary even if he turned out to be a scoundrel. She did not want to be cast in the role of failed wife ever again, or to go through the public embarrassment of a second divorce.

When she married Morton, Lucy made a clean sweep by completely redecorating the house on North Roxbury Drive, getting rid of the Early American furniture of the Arnaz era and replacing it with a mixture of contemporary designs and French provincial. Morton joked that his contribution was to rid the kitchen of tortillas and to bring in bagels.

Asked to compare her two husbands, Lucy once said, "Gary is more home-oriented, truly concerned with the welfare of his family. Desi *talked* a lot about the value of the family, but he did nothing about it. He gave us many houses to live in, but he was never home to share them with us."

Morton also made for a compassionate full-time father figure at a time when the children desperately needed one. "In between the marriages, Mom got super-strict. Whenever she told us to do something, there was no arguing with her. We could try, but she'd rant and rave and slam doors until she got her way," Desi Jr. recalled.

"But Gary knew how to handle her and became the peacemaker whenever we got into a fight. He was easygoing and kind. We could relate to him, even though he came from a completely different background—a Jewish neighborhood in the Bronx—than anything we'd ever known."

As if Lucy didn't have enough on her slate between her TV show and running Desilu, she started a daily CBS radio program in the summer of 1964. *Let's Tell It to Lucy* was another project designed to keep her husband busy. Gary Morton served as executive producer and handled all the logistics for the ten-minute talk sessions, in which Lucy interviewed stars like Bing Crosby, Barbra Streisand, Dean Martin, Jack Benny, and Danny Kaye.

By this time, Lucille Ball had become such an institution that the news media and the public rarely called her anything but just "Lucy," whether they were referring to the real person or the TV character. Never before in showbiz history had there been such a phenomenon.

Close friend Phyllis McGuire (of the singing sisters) recalled going shopping with Lucy one day. "People kept coming up and saying, 'Oh, Lucy, we love you!' I asked how it felt to be called Lucy. She said, 'It always gives me a thrill. I don't know how I could even answer if they called me Miss Ball.'"

In August 1964, the New York World's Fair celebrated "Lucy Day." More than 100,000 people turned out to cheer as Lucy and Gary Morton were given a grand tour of the exhibits.

Throughout her TV career, viewers had been deprived of one of Lucy's trademarks, the blazing red hair, which they saw in black-and-white. But in 1965, *The Lucy Show* switched to filming in color, and the star emerged in all her hennaed glory. All the top programs were being broadcast in color by that time, as the result of an industry-wide decision to adopt a single system, the one developed by RCA.

Lucy was now fifty-four. What she would have looked like if she stopped dyeing her hair is anybody's guess, but there seemed slight chance of that happening. To protect herself from running out, she had pounds of henna stored in a disaster-proof safe, enough to last her to age 110 at least. The dye was imported from Egypt and reputed to be manufactured from the same formula that Cleopatra used in ancient times.

Whether the switch to color broadcasting helped or not, *The Lucy Show* increased its audience share considerably and reached number three in the ratings for the 1965–66 season, just behind *Bonanza* and *Gomer Pyle, U.S.M.C.* By this time, Vivian Vance, tired of commuting between Hollywood and her home in Connecticut, had quit the show so she could spend more time with her husband.

To compensate for Viv's disappearance from the stories, *The Lucy Show* underwent another change. Lucy Carmichael sent her children to boarding school and moved to California to resume her secretarial job with bank president Theodore J. Mooney, who'd been transferred there. Except for boss Gale Gordon, all the original supporting characters were dropped. The new format included frequent guest-star appearances by the likes of Jack Benny, Dean Martin, Ann Sothern, Danny Thomas, George Burns, John Wayne, Phil Silvers, and Carol Burnett.

Meanwhile, showbiz saw the emergence of a new star in Desi Arnaz Jr. Just for the fun of it, the chubby twelve-year-old drummer had formed a rock group with two guitar-playing buddies, Dino Martin, thirteen, and Billy Hinsche, fourteen. To supplement their weekly allowances, the trio began playing at friends' parties for five dollars a night. Lucy let them perform—without pay—at some of her audience warm-ups to gain experience.

Surprisingly, neither Lucy nor Desi had much influence on what happened next in their son's "career." Frank Sinatra, the best friend of Dino Martin's father, heard the boys performing and signed them to a contract with his Reprise Records label. The novelty of three sons of Hollywood royalty (Hinsche's father was a top executive in the business) banding together seemed enough to garner reams of publicity and a hit single or two. Their "I'm a Fool" became a monster hit and the basis for an album. Papa Dino featured them as guests on one of his NBC variety hours and their success snowballed. They were soon getting $4,000 a shot on *The Ed Sullivan Show* and *Hollywood Palace*. They formed a music publishing company to handle their self-written songs, and found themselves mobbed when they went on tour. Girls chased them down the streets and camped outside their hotels.

Desi's parents found themselves at odds over his sudden emergence as a teen sex symbol. Except for the lad's shoulder-length hair (all the fashion then), Big Desi approved and was delighted at the prospect of the Arnaz name carrying over into the next generation of show business. Lucy saw danger signs but said nothing, to avoid being branded a spoilsport.

By the time he was thirteen, Desi had developed a dependence on alcohol. "I started drinking as an alternative to dealing with my fears and resentments from childhood," he said later. "Most of my friends were drinking heavily too. It was socially acceptable, but that didn't mean it was right."

But instead of facing his alcohol abuse, Desi began experimenting with drugs. "I'd want to start drinking as soon as I woke up in the morning, but I knew that wasn't right. So I started to smoke marijuana instead. Soon I was drinking and smoking pot at the same time. Then I tried amphetamines and barbiturates. Nobody noticed. If I behaved a little erratic or crazy sometimes, that was supposed to be part of being a teenager," he said.

Meanwhile, three years of retirement didn't agree with Desi Arnaz, who started to get bored with his bucolic pursuits and missed the excitement of show business. Marriage to Edie turned into a replay of the one to Lucy, except that his new wife seemed to take a more tolerant attitude toward his philandering.

"Edie knew that Desi would never change," one of her friends recalled. "They had an understanding that Desi could come and go as he pleased so long as he kept Edie in the style she was accustomed to in her previous marriage. Desi gave her $5,000 a month to cover everyday expenses and another $5,000 to gamble on horses. 'Stingy' was never an adjective that applied to Desi Arnaz."

In August 1966, Desi made scandalous headlines when he went on a drunken rampage and got arrested for firing a gun at some young people who were partying in the vacant lot next to his beach house at Del Mar. Desi insisted that the .38 revolver, originally given to him as a souvenir by the production crew of *The Untouchables,* had been loaded with blanks. One of the youths claimed it contained real bullets and that Desi threatened to blast away the tires of their car if they didn't clear out.

By this time the gun had been emptied, so police couldn't decide who was telling the truth. But they took Desi to the sheriff's office and booked him for assault with a deadly weapon. He spent three hours in jail before Edie arrived with a lawyer and paid the $1,100 bail.

In an unrelated but far more serious incident, Desi happened to be sitting on the veranda of his house in Baja California when the floor collapsed under him. He was impaled on the jagged stump of a tree, which tore into his side, caused severe hemorrhaging and resulted in several blood clots. For lack of medical facilities in the area, he had to be flown by helicopter to the Scripps Clinic in La Jolla. An operation saved his life, but friends claim that Desi's health never returned to normal after the accident.

With not much to do with his time except feel sorry for himself, Desi fell into a deep depression. To snap him out of it, Edie and friends kept badgering him to get back into show business. If not television, nightclubs. His pal Jimmy Durante suggested teaming up for a tour of the Las Vegas–Lake Tahoe circuit.

Desi chose neither. After reading a detective thriller entitled *Without Consent,* he thought it would make a terrific movie and decided to produce it himself. While trying to raise the financing, he got a call from a peeved William Paley, who thought that with his expertise in television, Desi should be working for CBS rather than trying to break into the much riskier theatrical field.

In the end, CBS paid Desi $50,000 to develop some ideas for series. Two fell by the wayside (*The Carol Channing Show* and *Land's End*), but Desi excited interest with a sitcom entitled *The Mothers-in-Law,* written by his *I Love Lucy* cohorts, Madelyn Pugh and Bob Carroll.

Desi insisted on 50 percent ownership of the show, with CBS and sponsor Procter & Gamble splitting the other half between them.

In a bizarre twist, Desi's ex-wife and corporate partner became his landlady when he rented production space at the Desilu studio in Culver City. "I may as well give the business to mama. Of course I don't mean that literally," Desi said at the time.

CBS had a long-term contract with Eve Arden, who'd been floundering since the demise of *Our Miss Brooks,* so she became one of the two Mothers-in-Law. For the co-starring role, Desi selected Kaye Ballard, a stage and nightclub entertainer who came highly recommended by their mutual friend Jimmy Durante.

The series focused on next-door neighbors Eve Hubbard and Kaye Buell and the marriage between Eve's daughter and Kaye's son. The supporting cast had the expected complement of relatives and friends, with Desi making occasional appearances as a retired bullfighter named Raphael del Gado.

Desi directed the first episode of *The Mothers-in-Law,* but a screening failed to impress CBS programming head Fred Friendly, who shrugged his shoulders and said, "Who cares about mothers-in-law?"

"Everybody who has ever had one or is about to have one, which includes most of the human race," Desi responded, but to no avail. CBS canceled the project and wished him luck in placing it elsewhere.

"It was my first experience with big-time television, and I was absolutely appalled by the ruthlessness of it," Kaye Ballard recalled. "CBS showed no loyalty to Desi or to Eve Arden, who had both made so much money for the network in the past. Even though the sponsor loved the show, CBS said no. I loathe people who are not loyal."

Desi quickly resold the program to NBC, but he had to settle for the so-called Death Valley slot of eight-thirty on Sunday nights. That meant competing against two very popular programs, CBS's *Ed Sullivan Show* and ABC's *The FBI,* both of which had the extra advantage of starting at eight and running a full hour.

Surprisingly, *The Mothers-in-Law* survived the test, probably due to the fact that it was sandwiched between two of NBC's top-rated programs—*Walt Disney's World of Color* and *Bonanza*—and had similar appeal to family audiences. Although it never came anywhere near to equaling the success of *I Love Lucy, The Mothers-in-Law* developed a loyal following and proved that Desi Arnaz hadn't lost his producer's touch.

Of course Desi was now only small potatoes compared to Lucy, who'd entered her fourth year as president of Desilu Productions.

Between its own programs and the lease-out of facilities, the company was doing a gross annual business of $30 million. Lucy had just signed a $12 million deal with CBS, which contracted for another season of *The Lucy Show* as well as the rerun rights to the entire series.

In the 1966–67 television season, Desilu introduced two series that were slow to capture sizable audiences but eventually exceeded anyone's wildest expectations: *Mission Impossible* on CBS and *Star Trek* on NBC. Desilu's sales force had a tough time persuading the networks to take the adventure thrillers, which were considered too far-out for that time. If it hadn't been for Lucy's considerable clout, neither program might have gotten on the air.

Like Desi before her, President Lucy relied heavily on the creative and administrative input of her executive staff. Her personal contributions to Desilu's successes beyond *The Lucy Show* tended to be greatly exaggerated by the news media, which treated Desilu as if it were a one-woman organization.

As a consequence, Lucy took a lot of flak from minority shareholders who blamed *her* for the company's continuing no-dividend policy. At one of the annual meetings, she was accused of being another Evita Peron who was milking the company dry by paying herself an "exorbitant and illegal" salary. In 1966, she received $350,000 for *The Lucy Show* and an additional $75,000 as president of Desilu.

Lucy didn't know it, but her corporate days were numbered. In the autumn of 1966, Gulf + Western Industries, a gigantic mercantile conglomerate headed by Austrian immigrant Charles Bluhdorn, took over Paramount Pictures Corporation. Once the largest and most successful movie company in the world, Paramount had been on the skids since the 1950s, but Bluhdorn intended to rejuvenate it with new management and make it the nucleus of G + W's expansion into the leisure-time field.

Since the Desilu studio in central Hollywood just happened to be right next door to Paramount's slightly larger spread, it seemed likely that Bluhdorn would eventually want to purchase the property. By simply breaking down the dividing wall, Paramount could double its production facilities and office space.

Rumors to that effect circulated for months, but Lucy shrugged her shoulders. If Bluhdorn did make a reasonable offer, she'd be a fool to reject it. Desilu would still have plenty of space of its own at the Cahuenga and Culver City studios, and she could use some of the proceeds to pay back the balance of the $3 million she had borrowed to buy Desi's interest in the company.

In February 1967, Charles Bluhdorn finally made a bid, but it knocked Lucy for a loop. Gulf + Western not only wanted to buy the Gower Street studio, but Desilu Productions in its entirety. Up to then, Paramount Pictures had never been a major force in television production, but with Desilu under its wing it could become one instantaneously.

Bluhdorn gave Lucy seventy-two hours to consider his offer. In total, the deal would be for $17 million in Gulf + Western stock. As the largest and controlling stockholder in Desilu, Lucy's share would be worth about $10 million.

Lucy tried to stall for time while she made up her mind. Claiming that she needed to confer with Jackie Gleason about a project they had in the works, she took off with Gary Morton to visit "The Great One" at his home in Miami Beach. When she did not return phone calls, Milton ("Mickey") Rudin, Desilu's chief counsel, finally had to fly to Miami himself to pin her down.

As Lucy remembered it: "Panic! By this time, Mickey said we only had twenty-four hours or we'd blow the deal. We went through the whole thing over and over again. Mickey kept telling me that a company like Desilu couldn't survive on its own in the current market. 'You have to make twenty pilots to get three. How do you amortize that?' "

Lucy's instincts told her that G + W might turn the Desilu studios into housing developments or shopping malls. She worried that once Paramount took over, it might fire many of the executives and workers who had been so loyal to her over the years. And after years of being boss, she would not relish becoming just a paid employee again.

"I started to cry. I pleaded for another hour," she recalled. "Finally I said, 'Do you know, Mickey, I haven't even met this Mr. Bluhdorn.' Mickey said he'd get him on the phone so I could talk to him, but I said no. 'I like to see a man's eyes, shake his hand.' "

Rudin placed the call anyway. "Do you know what Bluhdorn said? He said, 'Miss Ball, one of the things I am prepared to like about you is that you care.' I cried again. Then I said yes," Lucy remembered.

The deal finally went through in July 1967. By that time, Lucy had started production on Desilu's first theatrical movie, with herself, not surprisingly, as one of its stars. Before Paramount made the bid for Desilu, Lucy had already signed a distribution deal for the film with United Artists, so Yours, Mine and Ours became a trailblazer in the new Hollywood that was emerging from the ashes of the old studios. Though UA would still release the movie, Paramount would take in a tidy share of the profits through its ownership of Desilu.

Lucy had originally hoped to make a TV series of Yours, Mine and

Ours, but had never been able to come up with a workable format despite the best efforts of her longtime scriptwriters Madelyn Pugh and Bob Carroll. Although it happened to be based on a real situation, the idea of a marriage between a middle-aged widow and widower who had eighteen children between them seemed too farfetched even for the looniest of sitcoms.

Melville Shavelson, a writer-director who'd made some hit family-oriented movies with the likes of Cary Grant, Bob Hope, and Danny Kaye, took over the project and hired Frank and Helen Beardsley, the couple whose story the script was based on, as consultants. Between them, they conjured up a warmhearted comedy that flowed from true experiences rather than contrived slapstick.

Lucy wanted Fred MacMurray for leading man, but he had a conflict with his *My Three Sons* TV series, and she happily settled for Henry Fonda. Lucy and Fonda hadn't made a movie together since *The Big Street* in 1941, but they'd kept up a friendship over the years and were devoted to each other.

On the first day of filming *Yours, Mine and Ours,* the two stars couldn't help reminiscing about their brief courtship back in the days even before *The Big Street,* when both were just starting out in Hollywood. "Just think," Fonda said. "If we'd gotten married, this studio might be known today as Fondalu instead of Desilu."

The seventy-second movie of Lucille Ball's screen career, *Yours, Mine and Ours* became the most successful by far, earning nearly $12 million in rentals after its release in the spring of 1968. Ordinarily, such a smash hit would have encouraged Lucy to make another movie immediately, but it soured her on the film business for years to come.

It seems that everybody made a fortune on *Yours, Mine and Ours* except Lucy. Unprepared for the success of the movie, her accountants failed to provide a tax shelter for her share of the profits. Most of the $2 million that Lucy earned went to the Internal Revenue Service. Furthermore, another $2 million share that would have gone to Desilu went to Gulf + Western instead, thus paying back a nice chunk of the conglomerate's purchase price for the company.

To no one's surprise, Lucy did not remain in the G + W fold beyond the year that remained on her contract with Desilu for *The Lucy Show.* Charles Bluhdorn hired John Reynolds, a hard-nosed CBS executive who'd never been one of Lucy's favorites, to take charge of the television division. With both of its founders no longer involved, Desilu was renamed Paramount Television. Who could have guessed that one of Desilu's principal assets, *Star Trek,* would eventually be turned into a series of Paramount theatrical movies that would earn about ten times what G + W originally paid for Paramount Pictures *and* Desilu Productions combined?

In their separate ways, Lucy and Desi both turned a bit misty-eyed over the retirement of the Desilu signature. Originally dreamed up in 1942 as a name for their first home, it had become synonymous with their marriage as well as with their professional collaboration.

Even when Lucy and Desi divorced and were no longer working together, mere mention of the word "Desilu" evoked memories of their relationship and kept it alive. Now, five years later, the disappearance of Desilu from the entertainment scene seemed to be official notice that Lucy and Desi would never get together again. It was over for good.

23

Growing Pains

LUCY and Desi continued to use the onetime Desilu studio facilities for their various production projects, but that was the extent of their contact with their former empire. Desi's *The Mothers-in-Law* did well enough in its first season to be renewed for a second by NBC. *The Lucy Show* ended in June 1968, but after a summer hiatus, the star returned to CBS in a new though not radically different series entitled *Here's Lucy*.

The newest *Lucy* was the first effort of Lucille Ball Productions, which had Lucy as president and her husband as executive producer. By this time, Gary Morton's comedic performing was limited to warming up the audiences of Lucy's shows. Otherwise he pretty much ran the company so that Lucy wouldn't be distracted from her job as the star and guiding force of its sole enterprise of the moment.

Here's Lucy turned into a real family affair when she decided to put both of her children into the series. From their births, it had seemed inevitable that Lucie and Desi would eventually land in one or another of the *Lucy* projects. But now it became a matter of urgency because of their parents' concern over their education and welfare.

"They weren't working up to their potential at school, and all the kids around them were in trouble. It was the so-called Swinging Sixties—drugs, booze, and girls getting pregnant. I told their father, 'Let's get them away from that,' and he agreed," Lucy said later.

She made it plain, however, that her children would get no preferential treatment on the set. "Mom told us straight out that if we weren't good enough, we wouldn't be on a second season. She said she'd find a way to write us out of the show, and she really meant it," Lucie recalled.

At fifteen and a half, Desi was already washed up as a rock star, but he longed to become an actor and had recently appeared in an episode of his father's series *The Mothers-in-Law*. Seventeen-year-old Lucie's professional experience had been limited to an occasional appearance in *The Lucy Show*, but she was a good singer and mimic. Big Lucy thought her daughter had real potential if she could overcome her extreme shyness, which may have been the result of growing up with a celebrity mother.

As minors, Lucie and Desi could drop out of school provided they spent so many hours per week with private tutors. To keep them from getting swell-headed, Lucy showed no partiality and paid them union scale. Separate three-year contracts, which had to be approved by the Los Angeles Superior Court, provided for a salary for each child of $17,600 in the first year, $20,400 for the second, and $25,200 for the third. Twenty percent of their earnings had to be invested in U.S. government bonds and deposited with the county clerk until the kids turned twenty-one.

After nearly twenty years of collaborating with Madelyn Pugh and Bob Carroll, Lucy decided she needed a change and hired Milt Josefsberg, a longtime associate of Jack Benny and Burns and Allen, as head writer of *Here's Lucy*. Josefsberg, however, didn't believe in tinkering with success, and the series was largely a replay of *The Lucy Show* with different characters.

This time around, our heroine became Lucy Carter, a widowed secretary working in a Los Angeles employment agency. Interestingly, no Lucy since Lucy Ricardo had a living husband. The image of Lucy and Ricky was still too strong to contend with. While Lucille Ball could make movies with the likes of Bob Hope and Henry Fonda, when she played the TV Lucy she knew that her fans would never accept her in the arms of anybody but Desi Arnaz.

For an obvious reason, Lucie and young Desi could not use their real first names as characters in *Here's Lucy*, so they were called Kim and Craig in the episodes. Lucy tried desperately to talk Vivian Vance into becoming her second banana again, but Vance would only agree to an occasional guest appearance. Gale Gordon took over the bulk of the support work. This time, as Harrison Otis Carter, head of the Unique Employment Agency, Gordon was not only Lucy's boss but her brother-in-law as well.

Here's Lucy premiered on CBS on September 23, 1968, with Lucy

Carter scheming to get her talented teenagers hired as entertainers at a posh birthday party. At the last minute, Kim loses her voice and Lucy substitutes as the vocalist with Craig's band. Not much had changed since the time of *I Love Lucy*.

On the day of the broadcast, Desi Arnaz took full-page ads in *Daily Variety* and the *Hollywood Reporter* with an open letter of congratulations to his two children on their "splendid debut." In a post script, he noted, "That red-headed gal playing your mother is the greatest."

In its sixth and final season (1967–68), *The Lucy Show* had been the second most popular program on the air, topped in the Nielsen ratings only by *The Andy Griffith Show*. The first season of *Here's Lucy,* however, found the series in ninth place, suggesting that viewers didn't care for the new format or were just getting tired of Lucille Ball, who'd been on the tube now for seventeen years.

Reviews were extremely mixed. The *New York Times* enthused that "the Arnaz youngsters know how to trade lines with the veteran star. And Miss Ball should have a ball trying to bridge the generation gap." But Cleveland Amory of *TV Guide* said, "While we loved 'I Love Lucy,' we can't even make friends with this show. It's the old Lucy all right, and she does her zany darnedest to make you give a damn, but the trouble is, you don't." Part of the trouble seemed to be Lucie and Desi, whom critic Rex Reed described a bit intemperately as "totally talentless." Once they found their feet as actors and responded to their mother's prodding, *Here's Lucy* improved and the ratings along with it.

Putting Lucie and Desi on the program created more problems than it solved. "Mom worked us harder than anyone," Lucie recalled. "A lot of people thought that because we were Lucille Ball's kids we had it made. But on the set, we might as well have been strangers. She was extremely demanding, because she expected more out of us than anyone else."

Lucie and Desi looked forward to escaping from their mother on the weekends, which they usually spent with their father at his ranch or at the beach. Both children had grown especially close to their stepmother and found that they could talk to her about anything, which they couldn't do with Lucy.

Lucy resented the times that the children spent with their father, but there wasn't much she could do about it. "I suddenly became the meany," she recalled. "I never got to spend the holidays or weekends with them. I was always the one who had to say, 'Do your homework' or 'It's past your bedtime.' And their father was always saying, 'What do you guys want to do now, have a picnic, go horseback riding?' He got the better end of it."

By the end of the first season of *Here's Lucy*, the children were ready to mutiny and quit the show. "Lucie and I had two quite different relationships with my mother: parent-child at home and employer-employee at the studio. It wasn't a very good arrangement," Desi recalled.

"Mom would treat us—rightfully so—as cast members at work, but we would still take things personally that probably weren't intended that way. When most people are hassled at work, they can blow off steam when they get home. But it didn't work that way for us, because we just continued the same arguments when we got home."

Gary Morton became the mediator and restored peace for a time. The children liked and respected him, and he had a knack for being able to control Lucy's dominating ways with his prickly Jewish humor.

Another crisis developed in July 1969 when Lucie turned eighteen and decided to leave home. Lucy ranted and raved for several weeks, but finally consented after visiting Lucie's intended apartment and making sure that the building was in a good neighborhood and securely protected.

Lucie's departure from the homestead left Desi to bear the brunt of his mother's nagging and intervention. Not surprisingly, he had started boozing again, and was also dabbling in all the fashionable drugs of the time—mescaline, cocaine, and Quaaludes.

The real-life dramas in Lucy's family bore slight resemblance to what was happening between Lucy Carter and her children in *Here's Lucy* at the time; the show's most serious tiffs were over adopting a dog and buying a second car for the kids to use. Otherwise Lucie and Desi were just accessories to their mother's zany capers, which often involved guest stars like Jack Benny, Shelley Winters, Wayne Newton, Ernie Ford, Eva Gabor, Wally Cox, Carol Burnett, and Johnny Carson.

By this time, Lucy's domineering behavior behind the camera had earned her the reputation of "The Wicked Witch of the West" among her peers. Actors often turned down her bids to appear on the show because she abused her power. "She even tells people like Jack Benny where to stand and how to deliver a line. There is a place where professionalism stops and tyranny begins," said Jack Lemmon.

Tony Randall recalled that "a lot of people found Lucy very, very tough to work with. She bossed everybody around and didn't spare anybody's feelings. But I didn't mind that, because she knew what she was doing. If someone just says, 'Do this!' it's awful if they're wrong. If they're right, it saves a lot of time. And Lucy was *always* right."

Joan Rivers remembered: "I was working with her one time when she stopped a shot and said, 'The camera angle is three inches off.' They said, 'Oh, no, Lucy, it's not.' And she said, 'Measure.' It was."

Shelley Winters said that Lucy even knew the inventory of the props warehouse: "We were shooting a scene and suddenly needed a certain type of table. The art director said, 'Well, I'll try to find one, but it will take quite a while.' Lucy said, 'Go down the second aisle, in the fourth bin, up on the second shelf.' "

Jack Carter pitied Lucy's directors. "Directing Lucy was like trying to flag down the Super Chief with a Zippo lighter," the comedian said. "You had to keep the traffic moving and stay out of her way. Any good director who lasted with her, like Jack Donohue, knew how to roll with the punches. When she screamed at him, he'd turn to the crew and say, 'Did the redhead say something? Did she yell at me? I could have *sworn* I heard her say something.' "

Of all the guest stars who paraded through *Here's Lucy,* none created more of a sensation than Elizabeth Taylor and Richard Burton. The Burtons were then so high up in the celebrity stratosphere that it never even occurred to Lucy to invite them on anything so mundane as a half-hour TV sitcom. But when the couple personally requested it as longtime *Lucy* fans, a script was hurriedly written for them built around the awesome sixty-nine-carat diamond ring that Burton bought for Taylor at Cartier's for $1.1 million. (It gets stuck on Lucy's finger just before Liz is due to model it at a press conference.)

Unintimidated by Burton's reputation as one of the world's greatest actors, Lucy thought during rehearsals that he missed many opportunities to get laughs, so she kept stopping to teach him how to improve his performance. Burton got furious. He was the sort of actor who waited for his gift to materialize; if it didn't, he just slammed through. Lucy, on the other hand, worked on her talent like an engineer, rehearsing and reshaping until she achieved a mechanical perfection.

After four exhausting days of rehearsals, Burton wrote in his diary: "Those who had told us that Lucille Ball was 'very wearing' were not exaggerating. She is not 'wearing' to us because I suppose we refuse to be worn. She lives entirely on that weekly show which she has been doing and successfully doing for nineteen years. Nineteen solid years of double-takes and pratfalls and desperate up-staging and nervously watching the 'ratings' as she does so."

Perhaps out of pity, Lucy trod easily around Elizabeth Taylor, who had a severe case of hemorrhoids and was scheduled to go into the hospital for surgery several days later. Although she'd known the actress since their MGM days, she addressed her either as Miss Taylor or Mrs. Burton. The star's husband was Your Highness or Mr. Burton, and sometimes Mia. Lucy started calling Burton that after Taylor told her that since he started dieting, sleeping with him had become like sleeping with pencil-thin Mia Farrow.

"Lucy Meets the Burtons" launched the 1970–71 season of *Here's Lucy* and achieved one of the highest audience ratings (52 percent) of any of the various *Lucy* programs since the birth of Little Ricky back in 1953. Even without the Burtons, the series consistently outpointed its direct competition—NBC's *Laugh-In,* which had been the number-one show of the previous season but fell to number twelve in 1970–71. *Here's Lucy,* meanwhile, jumped from number six in 1969–70 to number three in 1970–71. Clearly the public still loved Lucy and would go on loving her for a long time to come.

Behind the scenes, problems with the children continued. Lucie had fallen in love with Phil Vandervort, an aspiring actor-director seven years older than she. Big Lucy claimed that Vandervort was courting Lucie mainly to further his career. The more she tried to break up the couple, the closer they became. When they started living together, no one could be sure if it was out of passion or to defy Lucy.

Young Desi, meanwhile, seemed headed for a crisis. Between the drinking and the drugs, he gained and lost weight rapidly, lacked energy, and suffered from headaches and depression. He had difficulty doing things that had always been easy for him.

"I was supposed to do a drum solo on *Here's Lucy,* but I'd been drinking and taking pills and I was so high I couldn't coordinate my arm movements. I did it over and over again in front of the audience, but couldn't get it right until long after they left the studio," Desi recalled.

Desi finally begged his mother for help. The family physician advised sending him to a detoxification clinic. But as soon as he left the hospital, Desi went right back to his former habits.

By this time, Desi had also developed quite a reputation as a Casanova, first as a rock star and then as a TV celebrity; women found him irresistible. He had numerous affairs by the age of seventeen, when he fell seriously in love with twenty-three-year-old Patty Duke, the onetime child star who won an Oscar for her portrayal of young Helen Keller in *The Miracle Worker*.

Desi became entranced when he saw Patty being interviewed on television on *The Merv Griffin Show*. Fearing that she might reject him as too young, he got her phone number and arranged a meeting on the pretext that he was forming a record company and interested in signing her to a contract.

From the time that Desi started sending her roomfuls of flowers and calling her his "sweet Irish leprechaun," Patty knew that he had something more than a business deal on his mind. An affair ignited after their first date. The press was soon comparing them to Eddie Fisher and Debbie Reynolds in their happier days: two young icons who had a lot in common professionally and seemed to be made for each other. But somehow the "America's Sweethearts" image never took hold, because of an unwholesome element: At seventeen, Desi qualified as "jailbait," while Patty was separated but not yet divorced from TV director Harry Falk.

Not unexpectedly, Desi's parents had opposing views on the coupling. Big Desi welcomed Patty into the fold and hoped she would have a steadying influence on his son. The age difference didn't bother him. After all, hadn't he been six years younger than Lucy?

For Lucy, however, it was the final straw. She had enough problems coping with her son's drinking and drug taking. Now he was running around with an older woman who had a reputed history of mental instability. If Desi didn't drop Patty immediately, Lucy threatened to kick him out of the house, disinherit him, and get the law after Patty for corrupting a minor.

The couple tried cooling it for a time, but were soon back together. When Lucy found out, she retaliated by firing Desi from *Here's Lucy*. Without telling him in advance, she also sent him packing from 1000 North Roxbury Drive.

"I was visiting my best friend, Dino Martin, when my clothes were suddenly delivered to me," Desi said later. "Shoes, everything, my whole closet was there. A guy from the studio transportation department brought it, so I said, 'I don't want to move out of the house. Take it all back.' So he did." But when Desi went home a few hours later, he found an empty house. To avoid a confrontation, his mother and stepfather had gone to Palm Springs, and he found his clothes still packed in the delivery cartons.

The worst was yet to come. In June 1970, Patty Duke turned out to be pregnant. Was Desi responsible? It appeared so, except that during the time when the couple suspended the affair to appease his mother, Patty had a secret fling with married actor John Astin.

The scenario became even more bizarre when Patty cracked up under the tension. A diagnosed manic-depressive, she fell into one of her manic phases, and before it ended she found herself with a new husband she barely knew. Rock promoter Michael Tell somehow wormed his way into her confidence, and they were married in Las Vegas on June 24, 1970. With $14,000 of Patty's money, they chartered a Learjet to fly them and her two dogs to New York for a honeymoon. While there, Patty accepted an invite to appear on *The Dick Cavett Show*, where she promptly announced her pregnant condition to about 25 million TV viewers.

If Patty married Mike Tell just to provide a substitute father for the baby, she changed her mind after concerned friends persuaded her to check into a psychiatric hospital for treatment. When reason returned, she filed for an annulment, claiming that the marriage had never been consummated.

Patty's on-air confession to Dick Cavett unleashed a scandal of epic proportions in the fan magazines and weekly tabloids. Who but Desi Arnaz Jr. could be the father of her child? The affair was celebrated, and in addition, Desi had superstar parents who could be dragged into the headlines, whether they deserved to be there or not. The baby promised to be the first grandchild of Lucy and Desi, and illegitimate to boot.

Ironically, the affair that caused it all had nearly burned itself out by this time. At the immature age of seventeen, Desi had never given any consideration to marriage or parenthood. Of course he was still a minor and needed his parents' consent to get married. He knew that he could get it from his father, who was thrilled at the prospect of the Arnaz name being perpetuated for another generation, but his mother would kill rather than have Patty Duke for a daughter-in-law.

The boy whose birth had made headlines throughout the world turned eighteen on January 19, 1971. Big Desi threw a lavish family party at the Luau, a celebrity watering hole in Beverly Hills. Practically everybody attended, including Patty Duke and Gary Morton, but Lucille Ball was conspicuous by her absence.

"Patty was almost due by that time, expecting at any moment," a friend recalled. "Lucy was afraid that with her luck the baby might be born then and there. No way would she risk being involved in such an embarrassing situation."

Lucy had nothing to fear on that score. Patty went on for another month before her doctor became concerned over the baby's heartbeat and opted for a cesarean delivery. Sean Duke, as his mother chose to call him, arrived on February 25, 1971. Weighing a scant five pounds, he spent his first three days in an incubator.

Desi rushed to visit mother and child, telling reporters afterwards, "It was an incredible sensation. The baby looks just like me."

Needless to say, Lucille Ball never went to the hospital, but Desi and Edie Arnaz did, as well as Lucie Arnaz and Gary Morton. Patty was estranged from her own family at the time, so she appreciated the visits. "Given the sordidness of the circumstances and the fact that there were reporters literally camped out in the stairwells, it was a very brave and gracious thing for them to do," she recalled.

When Sean was two months old, Desi finally persuaded Lucy to invite Patty and their son to her house, but the meeting accomplished nothing. To please her son, Lucy hugged the baby, fed it, and even changed its diaper, but she refused to acknowledge it as her grandchild. "It was just an adorable baby. I didn't think of it as anything else. Nothing that its mother said or did ever made any sense to me, so I never believed it was Desi's child," Lucy recalled.

While the controversy ground on, there was another surprise development in the Arnaz family. A wedding would take place, but between Lucie Arnaz and Phil Vandervort. Despite her mother's prodding her to date other men, Lucie had been going steady with Vandervort for four years, so it seemed about time to legitimize the affair.

Lucie still appeared with her mother in *Here's Lucy,* with her role considerably expanded since her brother left the series. Once Lucy decided to accept the twenty-nine-year-old Vandervort as a son-in-law, she gave him a job in her production company, where he served as an assistant to Gary Morton. Presumably, couples that worked together stayed together, though it had proved otherwise in the case of Lucie's parents.

Lucie chose to be married on July 17, 1971, which just happened to be her twentieth birthday. The ceremony was held outdoors at dusk before 300 guests in the backyard at 1000 North Roxbury Drive. The arrival of celebrity friends like Jimmy Durante, Carol Burnett, Lloyd Bridges, and Buddy Hackett attracted so many gawkers that neighboring householders turned on their sprinklers to keep the crowds off their lawns.

"It was almost like a *Lucy* sketch," guest Jack Carter recalled. "Lucy had sold Desilu for umpteeen millions, but she had cold cuts and paper plates. She had no knowledge of the correct, chic thing to do."

Desi Sr., of course, gave the bride away. Lucy's secretary, Wanda Clark, who'd been like a third mother to Lucie over the years, was maid of honor. Phil Vandervort's best friend, actor Dick Gautier, served as best man. Desi Jr. was an usher. Not surprisingly, Patty Duke and her baby were not invited.

During the dancing, everybody applauded when Lucy and Desi paired up for the first time since their divorce. When Gary Morton finally cut in, Desi quipped, "That's the second time you've cut in on me."

Lucie's marriage provided a temporary diversion from the Desi-Patty mess, which never had a happy outcome. To this day the identity of Sean's real father remains a mystery. John Astin eventually married Patty Duke in 1974 and adopted Sean Duke as his own son.

Lucy breathed a sigh of relief when Desi moved on to someone nearer his age, twenty-five-year-old Liza Minnelli. The two had grown up in the same Hollywood orbit, but no sparks were ignited until Desi happened to attend one of Liza's dynamic concert performances. Soon, she and Desi were making happy sounds together. A mutual fondness for cocaine and marijuana added zing to the affair.

Liza had just finished making the screen version of *Cabaret* and seemed on the verge of stardom. While not in that league, Desi was receiving lots of movie offers and getting ready to go to Japan to star in a musical about young Marco Polo. Theirs was another of those proverbial "made in heaven" matches that the news media could milk for all it was worth—plenty in this case due to the parentages on both sides. The couple exchanged gold rings to symbolize their mutual devotion, but marriage would be impossible until Liza's long-pending divorce from Australian singer Peter Allen became final.

Since she'd known and adored Liza since birth, Lucy took a more tolerant attitude toward her son's latest romance than she did with Patty Duke. "Long before Judy died, Liza had to take on the responsibility of raising her half sister and brother, so she tends to fuss over Desi like a mother hen," Lucy said at the time. "They're very good for each other, and I couldn't be happier."

In January 1972, the Mortons took Desi and Liza for a skiing holiday near Aspen, Colorado. At sixty-one years old, Lucy had suddenly caught ski fever and purchased a condominium on Snowmass Mountain, an intermediate slope considered safe enough for children and beginners. She talked of retiring there after another season or two of *Here's Lucy,* but nobody believed her.

One morning, while Lucy was gathering courage to make a descent, another skier crashed into her and knocked her down. Though she heard her leg crack, she tried to tell herself it was nothing more than a sprain. But after she was taken to the hospital on a toboggan stretcher, X rays revealed a multiple fracture.

"The leg was broken in four places," Lucy recalled. "I had to be hospitalized five times. It took weeks of bed rest and a whole year to get over the accident. At first they had me right up to the waist in a plaster cast. I took the heaviest thing I could find, the detachable handle used for raising and lowering the bed, and broke the damned cast all the way down to the calf three times before they finally gave me what I wanted: a cast I could move in a little.

"I kinda got used to it, but it was still hell. Jesus, the antibiotics, the drugs. I'd wake up screaming and find myself encased. I'd pound at the cast and cry out like a maniac, and the doctors and nurses would come runnning in."

When the cast was finally removed, Lucy's leg proved to be permanently damaged. Four pins would enable her to walk on it again, but she would need to wear a brace until she could learn to do without one.

Gary Morton took Lucy to their house in Palm Springs to recuperate. Depression settled in. She lost interest in her appearance. She threatened to cancel her television series. "I'll never work again. To hell with it. To hell with it all," she told friends.

But Lucille Ball spending the rest of her life as an invalid was unlikely if she had any control over the matter. Efforts were soon under way to insure another season of *Here's Lucy*. Scripts were hastily rewritten so that the TV Lucy would also be convalescing from a broken leg. The strenuous slapstick would be assigned to Lucie Arnaz until her mother was strong enough to handle it. As a consequence, plans for Lucie to do a spinoff series as her *Here's Lucy* character had to be canceled.

Prior to the accident, Lucy had been on the verge of signing a contract for the movie version of the Broadway musical smash *Mame*. Neither Warner Brothers nor producer Robert Fryer seemed bothered by the fact that Lucille Ball had flopped miserably in her one fling at Broadway stardom or that she was not musically talented. The eccentric Auntie Mame Dennis had to be portrayed by a mature dynamo, but there were few around who were considered big enough box-office names to fit the bill.

Angela Lansbury, the stage auntie, had never been a major Hollywood star, and she had done two flop Broadway musicals since

Mame. Were it a decade later, Lansbury undoubtedly would have gotten the part on the strength of her hit TV series *Murder, She Wrote.* But at the time, Lucille Ball's TV following clinched the deal. The American Broadcasting Company owned a big piece of *Mame* and stood to clobber its competitors when the movie eventually had its TV premiere.

With a broken leg, not even a workhorse like Lucille Ball could make a full season of television programs and a $12 million movie spectacular simultaneously. Since she obviously couldn't leave CBS with a hole in its schedule, *Here's Lucy* took priority. Warner Brothers wanted her so much that instead of hiring another star, it opted to postpone *Mame* until Lucy was fully recovered.

The opening of the fifth season of *Here's Lucy* found Lucy Carter in a hospital bed with her leg in traction. Subsequent episodes dealt with her recuperation at home, a stint in a motorized wheelchair, and eventual recovery. To take some of the work load off his sister, who now appeared in every show, young Desi returned for one episode that featured footballer Joe Namath as guest star.

Desi and Liza Minnelli were still very much a hot item, but Lucie Arnaz had suddenly overtaken them in the tabloid headlines. Three weeks short of her first wedding anniversary, she left Phil Vandervort and filed for divorce. Rumors circulated that the real reason for the breakup was that Vandervort was a homosexual—rumors for which there was no substantiation but which made Lucie's next infatuation seem even more bizarre. She met twenty-six-year-old Jim Bailey, a female impersonator, while he was doing his version of Phyllis Diller in one of the *Lucy* episodes.

"After I separated from Phil," Lucie recalled, "I fell into tremendous depression. I didn't want to be alone, and Jim was wonderful company. I could fly off to New York or Las Vegas and watch him perform. It took my mind off a lot of things. It was fun for a long time, but the press made it into a big romance, which you couldn't stop if you tried."

Lucie's mother eventually got disgusted with the situation and intervened. "My daughter had no romance with Jim Bailey," Lucy recalled in an interview. "Jim needed publicity and he got it at Lucie's expense. I dig talent. I saw Jim's nightclub act and I was so impressed that I had a part specially written for him on one of my shows. Then he grabbed on to Lucie and started getting his name in the papers.

"But I called him on it. I said, 'Cut it out,' and that was the end of it. They were just having a lot of fun together, dressing up the same."

In January 1973, a full year after breaking her leg, Lucy finally started working on *Mame,* which had a nineteen-week shooting schedule and became the worst ordeal of her career. For months she had been in training with choreographer Onna White to walk normally. But she'd become so dependent on her leg brace that she made slight progress until White ordered her to get rid of it. Within weeks, Lucy was kicking high enough that she could have qualified for that long-disbanded troupe of dancing grandmothers known as the "Hollywood Elderlovelies."

At age sixty-one, Lucy had taken on a role that Angela Lansbury enacted at forty and Rosalind Russell (in the original non-musical play *Auntie Mame)* at forty-nine. There were snide reports that the tab for concealing Lucy's wrinkles and jowls ran well into six figures. At the end of production, her longtime makeup artist, Hal King, was so unstrung by her demands that he vowed never to work for her again.

When she first signed for *Mame,* Lucy insisted that Bea Arthur be hired to re-create her original Broadway role of bosom buddy Vera Charles. During the filming delay, however, Arthur had suddenly become the new queen of prime-time television with the series *Maude,* which ranked number four in the season's Nielsen ratings, far ahead of *Here's Lucy* at number fifteen.

Fearing that Arthur might steal her thunder in *Mame,* Lucy considered having her replaced, but that would have caused an even more serious problem. Director Gene Saks, who also helmed the original stage production, was Bea Arthur's adoring husband and unlikely to stand for her dismissal.

Although she'd relied on dubbers throughout her career, Lucy insisted on doing her own singing in *Mame.* When Lucy tackled the hit ballad "If He Walked into My Life," composer Jerry Herman, who happened to be in the recording booth, tore off his earphones in horror.

Lucy got upset if anyone criticized her singing. She told an interviewer, "Auntie Mame drank and stayed up all night. Was she supposed to sound like Julie Andrews? Come on!"

Fretting over her injured leg, wizened looks, and musical deficiencies, Lucy drove co-workers to distraction with her demands and perfectionism. Although she had to tolerate Bea Arthur, she wouldn't accept Madeline Kahn, a promising actress-singer who'd been signed for the role of dumpy secretary Agnes Gooch.

"Lucy wanted the movie to be exactly like the Broadway show," Gene Saks recalled. "During the first day of rehearsals, she turned on

Madeline and started criticizing her voice and walk. 'Excuse me, Madeline,' she said, 'but just when are we going to see your interpretation of Gooch, dear?'

"Madeline grinned icily back at her. 'You *are* seeing her, dear.' Lucy just said, 'Oh,' then asked if she could talk to me privately. We went to my office and Lucy started to weep, saying 'I swore I wasn't going to cry.' She was so manipulative, so controlling that she absolutely wouldn't have Madeline, who was too young and too pretty. Lucy insisted that we replace her with the stage Gooch, Jane Connell, who by that time was probably fifty and really too old for the part."

Warner Brothers rush-edited *Mame* in order to secure the coveted Easter holiday booking at New York's Radio City Music Hall in March 1974. Lucille Ball in the movie of a Broadway smash might have seemed a natural for the "Showplace of the Nation," except that times had changed. Traditional musicals like *Mame* and *Hello, Dolly* had lost favor to free-form rock epics such as *Hair* and *Jesus Christ Superstar*. The Music Hall, now the only theater in New York with a stage-and-screen policy, had been operating in the red for years and was threatened with demolition.

The Music Hall's traditional Christmas and Easter pageants were an exception and had a loyal following, whatever the screen attraction. Box-office records may have been broken during the run of *Mame,* but nobody could tell whether the movie or the total entertainment package was the reason. When *Mame* went into general release on its own, it did moderate business but never reached hit status. Warner Brothers reportedly lost $25 million on the project, which included the print and marketing costs.

Mame was Lucille Ball's seventy-third movie and also her last. Although it has gone down in film history as a Golden Turkey, one can't help admiring it for Lucy's ultraglamorous appearance. Wearing one breathtaking Theadora van Runkle ensemble after another, she never photographed more beautifully.

While working in *Mame,* Lucy decided she'd reached her limits and decided to quit the grind of a weekly television series. Her contract with CBS required her to do a sixth season of *Here's Lucy,* but after that she would only be available for occasional hour-long specials.

Because of the four pins in her leg, Lucy had lost her lateral movement and could no longer do physical comedy with ease or grace. But she was too proud to admit it when she announced her semi-retirement and attributed it to other reasons.

By its final season, *Here's Lucy* had dropped out of the Top Twenty ratings, the first time ever that a Lucille Ball series was off the charts. Lucy had apparently worn out her welcome, and she knew it.

"I think people got tired of the same formula over and over," she recalled. "My writers had run out of ideas. And frankly, I couldn't figure out why, at my age, I was still kicking up my heels and hanging from chandeliers. Besides, I wasn't making that much money, being in such a high income tax bracket."

Here's Lucy had its last broadcast on March 18, 1974, appropriately enough with a pie-throwing finale in which Gale Gordon gets hit in the face and sighs to the camera, "I *knew* it would end like this."

TV Guide soon noted that Lucille Ball had completed twenty-three years on network television, an industry record. She had made 492 regularly scheduled programs, including 179 episodes of *I Love Lucy*, thirteen of *The Lucy and Desi Comedy Hour*, 156 of *The Lucy Show*, and 144 of *Here's Lucy*. If shown nonstop around the clock, the total viewing time would be nearly eleven days!

24

Silver Anniversary

IRONICALLY, in the same week that *Here's Lucy* went off the air, Desi Arnaz turned up in an episode of NBC's *Ironside,* the San Francisco crime series that starred Raymond Burr as a paraplegic detective in a wheelchair.

Desi's guest stint was intended to serve as a pilot for a series built around the character he portrayed, a small-town general practitioner named Dr. Domingo, who supplements his income by serving as the local coroner and medical examiner. "He's a cross between Marcus Welby and Columbo," Desi said at the time.

Now fifty-seven, Desi had not been involved in TV production since the demise of *The Mothers-in-Law* in 1969, but he occasionally acted or performed on the shows of friends like Danny Thomas and Dean Martin. In 1971, he had another severe attack of diverticulitis, which seemed to become an "in" disease for celebrities after the highly publicized case of President Lyndon Johnson.

"What with various operations and aftereffects, it put me out of action for several years," Desi recalled. "But it was worth it. I shot up to 205 pounds before the operation and felt terrible. Afterwards, I returned to my normal weight of 175 and got my old seven handicap at golf back again."

Between the medical bills, gambling losses, and the costs of maintaining his racing stable and various homes, Desi was no longer a multimillionaire, but he still had reserves in the bank. "I'm O.K. if I don't live too long," he joked at the time.

At a party, Desi ran into his former agent Lew Wasserman, now head of MCA-Universal, who told him he was too young to be retired and should be back in the TV business. Knowing Desi's aversion to administrative details, Wasserman persuaded him to sign a development deal where he would only be concerned with the creative end.

As luck would have it, Desi's new office at Universal Studios was just around the corner from that of Lucille Ball Productions, which moved there after she split from Paramount. Besides *Dr. Domingo*, Desi had a comedy series under development entitled *Chairman of the Board*, starring Elke Sommer as a lady executive bucking the big-business establishment. Desi had been toying with the idea for years, originally as a vehicle for his ex-wife when they ended *I Love Lucy*.

Except for the *Ironside* episode featuring Dr. Domingo, Desi never succeeded in making a deal for either series. Network disinterest was the main reason, but he also got involved in a project that took up the better part of two years.

Without really considering the implications, Desi let his agent, Marvin Moss, talk him into writing an autobiography, but he insisted on doing it himself, without assistance from a ghost writer. Moss knew that Desi would still need input from an expert editor, so he first offered the book to William Morrow's Howard Cady, who specialized in celebrity memoirs and had just finished working on Rex Harrison's. After meeting with Desi and hearing what he intended to cover in the book, Cady bought it for an advance of $125,000, a hefty sum for that time.

Left to his own devices, Desi never got further than making some penciled notes and going through scores of old scrapbooks and files with Ken Morgan, his longtime friend and press agent. Howard Cady finally had to fly out from New York to try to rescue the project.

"Desi put me up at a motel near Del Mar racetrack. Every day for a week, we spent hours in my room tape-recording our conversations. Ken Morgan would fire questions at Desi to jog his memory. We hired a couple of secretaries to transcribe everything to paper so that Desi could have something to take home and study overnight," Cady said.

Work went smoothly until the discussions of Desi's breakup with Lucy. "It was apparent that he still loved her very much. He would get very emotional as he realized that he'd been a rotten husband and had not treated her well. Desi became extremely tense and increasingly nutty, in the sense that he would get desperate for a drink or female companionship. When he imported a floozy from Baja California and installed her in the same motel, everything sort of fell to pieces, but we got an awful lot done before that," Cady said.

The "floozy" was actually a young woman who lived with Desi at his Las Cruces hideaway and looked after it in his absence. "Edie Arnaz knew about the arrangement and never went there," a friend said. "Edie took the attitude that Desi was going through a stage where he had to prove he wasn't too old to cut the mustard, so she let him have his flings. Both were approaching sixty, the marriage had worked out well in other respects, so what would have been the sense in Edie leaving him or suing for divorce?"

Meanwhile, the marriage between Lucille Ball and Gary Morton seemed to lack such problems. Lucy kept Morton on an extremely tight leash. She wasn't kidding when she once told a reporter, "We have an arrangement. Gary loves to collect cars, so I let him buy whatever he wants. But if I ever catch him with a woman, I'll kill him!"

Morton seemingly kept to his part of the bargain. He had a Rolls-Royce (which Lucy purchased from the estate of her great friend Hedda Hopper), two Karman Ghias, a Mercedes 300-SS, a Mark II Lincoln, a vintage Stutz Bearcat, and a Model-T Ford stored in various garages around town.

Lucy had all the wealth, but Morton ruled the roost. The monogram "M" predominated everywhere in their home, from the front doormat to the cocktail glasses and the bath towels. Although there wasn't anything he could do about her mother, Morton reportedly caused Lucy to break with the rest of her family, whom he claimed had been sponging off her for most of their lives.

Twice-married Fred Ball, who once managed the Arnaz-owned resort hotel in Indian Wells, got pensioned off to Cottonwood, Arizona, where Lucy bought a motel for him and his wife to run. Cousin and near-sister Cleo, who worked as Lucy's associate producer in between broken marriages to radio comedian Artie Auerbach and publicist Ken Morgan, moved to Mexico when her third husband, Cecil Smith, retired as broadcasting critic for the *Los Angeles Times*.

After the shutdown of *Here's Lucy,* Lucille Ball didn't exactly disappear from TV screens. All three of her series, and especially *I Love Lucy,* turned up at some hour of the day or night in syndicated reruns. And beginning with the prime-time 1974–75 season, she had a contract with CBS for two one-hour specials per year.

In the first, "Happy Anniversary and Goodbye," she departed from her traditional *Lucy* character by co-starring with Art Carney in a farce about a couple who decide to separate after twenty-five years of marriage. In "Lucy Gets Lucky," she returned to her usual scatter-brain role for a Las Vegas casino caper that featured Dean Martin as guest star.

By this time, Lucy had spent over forty years working steadily, week after week, in TV and movies, so the cutback in activities sent her into a deep depression. "It was one of the most traumatic events in my life," she recalled. "It was a terrible thing for me—the loss of my creative arena. I lost not only the pleasure of being with my friends every day on the set, but also my identity. Being *Lucy* gave me a built-in intimacy with the public. I loved being her. I loved the antics and the gags. I enjoyed my work."

Friends tried to cheer her up, but nothing worked. "Lucy just sat there alone all day in that big house with the blinds drawn and felt sorry for herself," Vivian Vance recalled.

After a while, Lucy decided that a hobby might help. After brief forays into golfing and horseback riding, neither of which agreed with her weak leg, she settled on backgammon. The venerable two-person board game had suddenly become the rage of the Hollywood celebrity circuit. A private club in Beverly Hills called Pips packed them in night and day.

Backgammon appealed to Lucy because it was played sitting down and could be much more exciting than chess or cards; winning depended as much on luck and the roll of the dice as it did on skill and strategy. In a place like Pips, she not only had a wide range of expert partners to choose from, but could also queen it up a bit for the spectators in the crowd.

Lucy's obsession with the game turned her home into what resembled a branch of Pips, with a backgammon table in nearly every room and several clustered around the swimming pool in the backyard. She even started sponsoring backgammon tournaments to raise funds for charities such as the March of Dimes and the Los Angeles Children's Hospital.

Backgammon also helped to steady Lucy's nerves in her ongoing travails with Lucie and young Desi. Her generally disapproving attitude toward the children was the direct opposite of their father's. "Desi loved those kids so much that they could do nothing wrong. And because of all the indiscretions in his own past, he tended to be far more tolerant than most fathers," a friend said.

Lucie Arnaz had moved on from Jim Bailey to thirty-eight-year-old Burt Reynolds, ex-lover of one of her mother's best friends, Dinah Shore. Needless to say, the two older women were outraged by the affair, but there wasn't much that Lucy could do to stop it now that her daughter had totally flown the coop. Since the demise of *Here's Lucy,* Lucie had been supporting herself by acting in summer stock and with regional theater groups. She played one of the leads in the West Coast edition of the off-Broadway hit *Vanities,* and then co-starred with John Gavin and Tommy Tune in the national touring company of the Broadway musical smash *Seesaw.*

Lucie also starred in her first telemovie, *Who Is the Black Dahlia?* based on a brutal murder in 1947 Los Angeles that remains unsolved to this day. The film caused some friction between mother and daughter when NBC ran it on March 1, 1975, directly opposite Lucille Ball's special with Dean Martin, "Lucy Gets Lucky." Guess who got the higher rating?

Young Desi, meanwhile, suffered severe damage to his image when Liza Minnelli dumped him for middle-aged Peter Sellers. He quickly found a new flame in Victoria Principal, but he seemed to be luckier in romance than with his career. *Marco,* the movie musical that he made in Japan with Zero Mostel co-starring as Kublai Khan, turned out such a turkey that it barely got released.

Like his parents, Desi would find his niche in television, but he got more than he bargained for while making ABC's "Having Babies," a melodrama about four couples enrolled in a natural birth program. Desi fell in love with his blonde co-star, Linda Purl. A long and passionate affair developed, punctuated by frequent breakups and reconciliations caused by Purl's unhappiness with Desi's fast-lane lifestyle.

Nineteen seventy-six not only marked the American bicentennial, but also the twenty-fifth anniversary of the launching of *I Love Lucy.* This seemed the appropriate time for William Morrow to finally publish Desi Arnaz's autobiography, which, for lack of a better title (Lucy acidly suggested *Too Many Girls*), was simply called *A Book.*

By publication date, editor Howard Cady had made several more trips to California to work with Desi, who reciprocated by traveling to New York to correct the galley proofs. "In the end, we had to get rid of the whole last third of the book because it got so depressing and sad when Desi started reflecting on his life after *I Love Lucy,*" Cady recalled.

As a consequence, *A Book* starts with Desi's childhood memories and concludes abruptly with the filming of the final Lucy and Ricky episode. As might be expected, no hard feelings were expressed toward Lucille Ball.

In an epilogue in which he thanks everybody from his parents to current wife Edie for their love and understanding, Desi wrote: "As for Lucy herself, all I can say is that I loved her very much and, in my own and perhaps peculiar way, I will always love her. We spent twenty years together; many happy moments and many unhappy moments came and went during that time. It is a precious God-given gift that I most remember the happy ones. I hope she was given the same gift."

In conclusion, Desi said, "The success of *I Love Lucy* is something that only happens once in a lifetime, if you are fortunate enough to have it happen at all. If we hadn't done anything else but bring that half hour of fun, pleasure and relaxation to most of the world, a world in such dire need of even that short time-out from its problems and sorrows, we should be content. But we did more. With God's help we also created Lucie and Desi."

To promote the book, Desi agreed to host an edition of NBC's *Saturday Night Live,* the audacious ninety-minute comedy revue that proved how permissive network television had become since the innocent days of *I Love Lucy.* Desi had fears of not being able to keep up with much younger and glibber clowns like Chevy Chase, Dan Aykroyd, and Gilda Radner, so he brought along Desi Jr. to serve as his co-host and moral support.

As it turned out, Desi Sr. loved the improvisational nature of *SNL,* and producer Lorne Michaels had problems keeping him from taking over the whole program. Father and son joined the "Not Ready for Prime Time Players" in a spoof of the Desilu warhorse *The Untouchables.* In another sketch, Desi Sr. portrayed a lunatic acupuncturist who used Cuban cigars instead of needles on a jittery John Belushi.

Later in 1976, the silver jubilee of *I Love Lucy* was officially commemorated with a two-hour television spectacular entitled "CBS Salutes Lucy: The First 25 Years." The program was produced by Gary Morton for Lucille Ball Productions, which explains why it became an overview of Lucy's entire TV career up to then, rather than just a tribute to the series that made it possible.

Desi made a token appearance by introducing the proceedings and giving an affectionate tribute to his ex-wife. It marked the first time that Lucy and Desi had appeared together on television in the sixteen years since their divorce. Time seemed to have taken its toll on both of them as Desi presented clips of their younger selves from the original *I Love Lucy* pilot (which had never been televised up to that time), and the most-watched episode dealing with Little Ricky's birth.

To hype the ratings, the extravaganza featured testimonials from many of Lucy's guest stars over the years, including Carol Burnett, Dean Martin, Johnny Carson, Bob Hope, Danny Kaye, Milton Berle, John Wayne, and Danny Thomas. Lucie and young Desi recalled the pleasanter side of working with their mother. Second bananas Vivian Vance and Gale Gordon also turned up. William Frawley, who dropped dead of a stroke while strolling on Hollywood Boulevard in 1966, did not.

William Paley, still very much the head of CBS (by dint of declaring himself immune to its mandatory retirement rule), said that he could hardly wait for Lucy's fiftieth anniversary celebration, but in truth her future with the network seemed in doubt. Her most recent specials, "Three for Two" with Jackie Gleason, and "What Now, Catherine Curtis?" with Art Carney, had bombed, probably owing to the fact that in neither of those mixed bags of comedy and drama did she play the madcap Lucy that her fans loved the most.

In July 1977, Lucy suffered a severe depression over the death of her mother, who succumbed to a stroke at the rather ripe age of eighty-five. Always her daughter's number-one fan, DeDe Ball had become something of a Hollywood legend for her quarter century of perfect attendance at the filming of all of Lucy's TV shows. Her loud cackle stood out above the audience laughter on the soundtracks.

"Lucy always treated her mother like a queen," longtime friend Kay Vaughan said. "After marrying Gary Morton, she bought her a lovely house in Brentwood. On taping days, she sent DeDe to the beauty parlor for the full glamour treatment. That night, DeDe and some of her friends were taken to and from the studio in a chauffeured car. Before the show, Lucy would acknowledge her mother's presence and ask her to stand up and take a bow. DeDe just thrived on all the attention."

Lucy nursed a considerable amount of guilt over her mother's passing. She felt that she'd pulled the plug by depriving DeDe of her greatest joy in life. It was nonsense, of course, but it added fuel to Lucy's need to go on working. She knew that her mother would have wanted it, but at the same time she realized that she would have to stop eventually and probably soon. She'd gotten too old for roles in which she played childish pranks and got screamed at by bossy types like Gale Gordon.

Lucy's first CBS special after DeDe's death turned out to be her last. To make up for the disappointing ratings of her collaborations with Jackie Gleason and Art Carney, she came up with the idea for a *Lucy* reunion with her two favorite sidekicks, Vivian Vance and Gale Gordon. The script, entitled "Lucy Calls the President," dealt with her efforts to persuade Jimmy Carter to stay at her house during one of his frequent get-acquainted visits to grassroots America.

Sadness hung over the filming, not only because of DeDe Ball's absence from the studio audience, but also because of Vivian Vance's ill health. Having suffered a stroke several months earlier, Vance still showed signs of paralysis, and only the right side of her face could be photographed. Since that also happened to be Lucy's better side, it made for some weird camera setups when the two women had to be in the same shot.

It turned out to be their final program together. Vance died of cancer two years later at age sixty-seven. Lucy visited her in her last days and said afterwards, "I couldn't believe how very beautiful she looked after all the pain she must have suffered."

The combined age of Lucille Ball, Vivian Vance, and Gale Gordon in 1977 was 203 years, which probably explains why CBS took one glance at the low ratings for "Lucy Calls the President" and decided to end the series of specials. In recent seasons, the network had lost its long dominance of the Nielsen ratings to ABC, which had hits like *Laverne and Shirley, Happy Days, Three's Company,* and *Charlie's Angels.* To compete effectively against such youth-oriented programming, CBS needed to change its image, and Lucille Ball was too much a reminder of the old one.

In lieu of her own specials, Lucy hit the guest-star circuit, even appearing on several programs on NBC, a sure sign that CBS no longer considered her one of its top drawing cards. In November 1978, she starred in a CBS variety show entitled "Lucy Comes to Nashville," merely serving as emcee to a flock of country-and-western performers. It turned out to be the last program of her CBS contract.

While Lucy's TV career seemed to have reached its nadir, things were definitely picking up for her two children. ABC was so delighted by the ratings for "Having Babies" that it reteamed young Desi and Linda Purl in "Black Market Baby," this time as unmarried lovers who sell their unborn child to finance their college tuitions. Desi also starred in two NBC features and Robert Altman's theatrical movie, *A Wedding.*

In January 1979, just days before his twenty-eighth birthday, Desi finally legalized his long-term affair with Linda Purl. Though neither was Jewish, they were married at the Simon Weis Temple in Bel Air after every church that they contacted refused to permit them to write their own version of traditional wedding services.

It was an intimate affair, with only relatives and close friends attending. Greg Hirsch, Desi's stepbrother, served as best man, with Linda Purl's sister Mara as maid-of-honor. Dino Martin and Tony Martin Jr. were ushers, Lucie Arnaz a bridesmaid. Lucy wasn't obligated to pick up the tab this time, and as a consequence the reception was held at the ultrachic Le Bistro in Beverly Hills.

Lucy and Desi Sr. were delighted by the prodigal son's decision to settle down, which came after another siege of drug-related problems. In an interview at the time, Lucy described her new twenty-three-year-old daughter-in-law as "a real Barbie doll, just adorable. Desi's father came up to me at the wedding and said, 'How lucky can we get?' Here's a girl who's a planner, an organizer. Our son can't even organize himself to get out of bed in the morning."

No wedding was on the immediate horizon for Lucie Arnaz, who became involved with TV talk show host Bill Boggs after Burt Reynolds dumped her for Sally Field. Seemingly more interested in her career than romance, Lucie was on the verge of a major breakthrough in the one arena where her mother had failed—musical comedy.

Ironically, it was Vivian Vance rather than Lucille Ball who inspired Lucie to broaden her talent. "During the six years that I did *Here's Lucy,* Viv encouraged me to work in summer stock during the vacation breaks. Speaking from her own experience, she told me that I would have to get out from Mom's shadow if I wanted a career of my own. I had to prove that I could do other things besides playing Lucy's straight man," she recalled. After touring around the country in revivals of *Cabaret* and *Annie Get Your Gun,* Lucie was picked to co-star with comedian Robert Klein in the Broadway musical *They're Playing Our Song*.

Lucy and Desi put on a united front by flying in from California with Gary Morton and Edie Arnaz for Lucie's premiere, which coincidentally took place at the same theater where Desi Sr. made his Broadway debut in *Too Many Girls* nearly forty years before. Asked afterward to comment on her daughter's peformance, Lucy said, "She told me to take notes of anything she did wrong, but I have no criticism. I'm in awe of her, she puts me away."

Desi was even more flabbergasted, telling a reporter, "I always knew my son would make it in show business, but Lucie was always so stiff and shy when she was little that I never thought she'd become a performer. I just told her mother, 'If we never did anything else, tonight makes it all worthwhile.' And she agreed." Critics declared that Broadway had a bright new star, comparing Lucie Arnaz to Ethel

Merman and Barbra Streisand for matching a big voice with meaning and feeling.

Lucie's triumph may have sparked something of a jealous reaction in her mother, who suddenly signed a new production deal with the National Broadcasting Company. Lucille Ball had been a CBS luminary for more than thirty years, so the move shocked the broadcasting industry. But it seemed inevitable if Lucy intended to continue working on a regular basis.

Fred Silverman, NBC's wunderkind president, wanted Lucy to star in a series of specials, as well as to develop new programs and talent via Lucille Ball Productions. Ironically, Lucy and Silverman had frequently clashed during his previous tenure as programming vice-president at CBS, but mutual necessity often breeds strange bedfellows.

A much-heralded special entitled "Lucy Moves to NBC" inaugurated the new deal on February 9, 1980. Amazingly, Lucille Ball's career now spanned six decades of show business, and from the look of it, she would go on forever. Divided into two parts, the ninety-minute extravaganza was one of her most unusual efforts, showcasing her talents as a comedian and as a production impresario.

In the first hour, Lucy and Gale Gordon portrayed themselves in a backstage comedy in which Fred Silverman (played by Gary Imhoff) hires them away from CBS to develop a series for NBC. While putting together a pilot entitled *Coogan's Music Mart*, Lucy and Gordon have run-ins with some of their new NBC compatriots, including Bob Hope, Johnny Carson, Jack Klugman, and pint-sized Gary Coleman.

In its last half hour, "Lucy Moves to NBC" switched over to a screening of the pilot, which actually was one of the projects that Lucille Ball Productions hoped to sell to the network. The series about a music shop run by a retired song-and-dance team would star Donald O'Connor and Gloria DeHaven, talented movie has-beens whom Lucy thought deserved a second chance. Madame Producer kept her hand in by making an unbilled guest appearance in a character role.

Lucille Ball may have moved to NBC, but upon arrival she didn't go very far. The network didn't know what to do with a sixty-eight-year-old comedian any more than CBS did, so she wound up making an occasional guest appearance on other people's specials. Fred Silverman also rejected *Coogan's Music Mart* and everything else that Lucille Ball Productions proposed. It became plain that Silverman's main interest had been in Lucy's prestige value. Just having the "Queen of Television" on the NBC roster impressed the business community and served as a lure to other stars and producers at a time when the network was battling for its very existence against top dogs ABC and CBS.

Meanwhile, the new decade started ominously for Desi Arnaz Jr., whose marriage to Linda Purl lasted a few days short of one year. Linda filed for divorce on January 3, 1980, citing "irreconcilable differences" that were unspecified to spare Desi public embarrassment but had to do with his abuse of drugs and alcohol. The split-up sent Desi on a bender that left him unemployable and more addicted than ever.

Both Arnaz children were now batting zero at matrimony, but Lucie was getting ready to try again, this time with stage actor Laurence Luckinbill, her senior by seventeen years and thus old enough to be her father. The couple were introduced by playwright Neil Simon. Luckinbill was going through the throes of a divorce from soap-opera star Robin Strasser, with whom he had two sons, so the romance developed slowly at first.

Soon enough, however, Lucie Arnaz had become a very pregnant Mrs. Laurence Luckinbill. She was already in her third month when the couple were married in June of that year. Whether it was a shotgun wedding or pure romance only the two involved know for certain, but it was probably a combination of both. With Lucie's strict Catholic upbringing, an abortion was out of the question. And she seemed genuinely smitten with Luckinbill, not only as a lover but also as a mentor.

No one could have foreseen it at the time, but the wedding turned out to be the last happy gathering of the dynasty propagated by Lucille Ball and Desi Arnaz. Coincidentally, the affair was held near Kingston, New York, about 250 miles from Lucy's native Jamestown. Supreme Court Justice Aaron Klein officiated at the outdoor ceremony, held on the grounds of a seventy-acre farm that belonged to Luckinbill's attorney.

At the end of the service, someone asked Desi if he wasn't bothered by the fact that he'd just given his daughter away in marriage for the second time. "Not at all," Desi said within earshot of the bride. "I'm going to keep on doing it until she gets a husband she's happy with."

When Lucie shouted, "Stop it, Daddy!" he added "I'm sure that Larry's the one."

At Lucie's request, Desi performed the title song from *Forever, Darling*. While he sang, it was plain that Desi meant the tender lyrics as much for his ex-wife as he did for his daughter. Lucy broke down in tears and kissed and hugged him afterwards. It made for a better fade-out clinch than the one in their flop movie.

In lieu of a honeymoon, the newlyweds embarked on a national stage tour in *Whose Life Is It, Anyway?* the critically acclaimed black comedy dealing with euthanasia. The Luckinbills clearly had ambitions toward becoming a serious acting team. This particular play gave them an opportunity to demonstrate their versatility by alternating in the leading roles. Lucie would portray the incurable patient and Luckinbill the doctor, or vice versa. Like her mother before her, the pregnant Lucie kept on working for as long as her health permitted.

In December 1980, Lucille Ball and Desi Arnaz became grandparents for either the first or second time, depending on whether or not Sean Astin can be counted as Desi Jr.'s child. In any case, the arrival of Simon Luckinbill (named in honor of his parents' matchmaker, Neil Simon) was a joyous occasion, dampened only by Desi's disappointment that he still had no grandson to perpetuate the Arnaz name. Although she was nearly seventy, Lucy hated the family label of "Grandma" and insisted on being known as "Nana," which took years off her ego if not her appearance.

Lucy and Desi's son-in-law was a stage-reared actor who hated the whole Hollywood scene, so the Luckinbills resided in New York in an apartment on Central Park West. Not exactly conducive to regular visits by Simon's California grandparents, but Lucy eventually made it easier for herself by renting a home away from home on the more fashionable east side of the park. After all, when you're one of the richest women in America, why let money stand in the way of happiness? *Forbes* magazine estimated Lucy's fortune to be at least $65 million at the time, based just on the market value of her holdings in Gulf + Western Industries.

Although her fortune was vast, work was less plentiful, and the 1980s shaped up as prime-time television's first Lucyless decade. But in November 1981, she reached a milestone that did not pass unnoticed—the twentieth anniversary of her marriage to Gary Morton.

"I now have more time in with her than Desi did," Morton boasted to an interviewer. "Desi and Lucy were married nineteen years. I kid him about it all the time. Through the kids, we've become great friends. I call him my husband-in-law."

Now seventy, Lucy was beginning to sound a bit like Gary's mother when she said, "This boy takes such good care of me. He gives me protection. He's steady, patient, has a great sense of humor. I'd like to tell the whole world how intelligent, how knowledgeable, and how wonderful he is." In his usual jocular way, Morton said, "We're very compatible. We even sing in the same octave."

Desi Arnaz, meanwhile, seemed content in his retirement and rarely strayed from his homes in Del Mar and Baja California.

"Desi had an enormous capacity for enjoying life and having a good time," a longtime friend recalled. "He was a superb yachtsman, a tireless fisherman with the big game fish. He raised blooded horses and delighted in watching them race. He was a gourmet cook of Cuban dishes. His rice and black bean casserole was legendary."

His children found him a much happier man than he was when they were growing up. Desi Jr. said, "My dad should have stayed in Cuba and had a little house and boat. On the way up, he lost sight of the things that were really meaningful to him, so there was a bad period when his values were all scrambled. But now he's found himself again. Now he can admit his own mistakes. He has a new way of life and a wife geared to those attitudes. He'll never let himself be consumed by business again, and that's the way it has to be with him."

Unluckily, Desi's problems with diverticulitis and other intestinal problems were far from over. He was in and out of hospitals for treatment and therapy. Against the advice of doctors, he continued smoking four or five huge Cuban cigars per day.

In March 1982, Desi was well enough to accept an invitation to be guest of honor at Carnival Miami, a festival staged at the famed Orange Bowl for the city's huge Hispanic community. The crowd of 30,000 roared its approval as Desi Sr. bounded on stage as well as any convalescing sixty-five-year-old could, pounding a conga drum and singing "Cumba, Cumba, Cumba, Cumbachero." Lucie and young Desi joined him for a rousing production number that saluted Havana's legendary Tropicana Club. Courtesy of her mother, Lucie was garbed in the same shimmering sequined dress that Lucy once wore in her Sally Sweet duets with Desi's Cuban Pete.

While his health permitted, Desi accepted another intriguing invitation. Francis Ford Coppola of *Godfather* fame wanted him for a character role in *The Escape Artist,* which Coppola was producing for his Zoetrope Films with promising newcomer Caleb Deschanel as director. Desi knew it might well be his last chance to appear in a major movie, and he couldn't resist playing a crooked politician who seemed straight out of an episode of *The Untouchables*. He didn't seem to mind that Coppola chose him mainly for his Hispanic heritage, which made him an ideal father for the film's chief villain, Puerto Rico–born Raul Julia.

The Warner Brothers release didn't change Desi Arnaz's luck as far as his movie career was concerned (forty-two years had passed since he made his first). The critical and box-office disaster also contributed to the eventual bankruptcy of Coppola's Zoetrope empire.

If *The Escape Artist* is remembered at all, it will be as the movie in which Desi Arnaz received curious billing as Desiderio Arnaz. In future, he wanted to be known professionally under his full name so that the younger Desi Arnaz, now in his thirties, would no longer have to be lumbered with the tag of Junior. The gallant gesture went unheeded by the news media, which continued to refer to the elder as Desi Arnaz and to paint the junior as his parents' perennial bad boy.

By the spring of 1982, young Desi hadn't made a movie or TV film in nearly four years because of his drug taking and drinking. In April, he found himself in Las Vegas for a charity tennis tournament, during which he snorted so much cocaine that he didn't sleep for a week. Returning to Los Angeles, Desi sought help from his parents and landed in Scripps Memorial Hospital in La Jolla, where he was enrolled in the Chemical Dependency Center.

While the whole family pulled together to rescue Desi, they still had their own lives and problems to contend with. Fed up with being ignored by the NBC brass, Lucy and Gary Morton moved Lucille Ball Productions to 20th Century–Fox in February 1983. The tottering Hollywood giant had been taken over by the Mortons' close friend, oil tycoon Marvin Davis, who wanted them to produce theatrical movies as well as TV programs.

The deal got under way with the $5.6 million *All the Right Moves,* one of the first films to star a promising young actor named Tom Cruise. When the drama about a high school football team received an R rating for its rough language, Lucy had her name removed from the credits for fear it would ruin her reputation as a purveyor of wholesome family entertainment.

Although experience should have told her otherwise, Lucy was also considering a return to the Broadway stage in a musical adaptation of *The Solid Gold Cadillac*. Though best remembered for the movie version with Judy Holliday, the play about a minority stockholder's war against a giant corporation had originally been written for the elderly character star Josephine Hull. At seventy-two, Lucy seemed to have nothing going for her in the song-and-dance role but age. The project never got off the drawing board.

By this time, Lucy and Desi had become grandparents again with the arrival of Joseph Henry Luckinbill on the last day of 1982. "Both my grandsons were born in December," Desi told columnist Earl Wilson. "I yelled at Lucie and said, 'What's going on? Do you and Larry only make love in the spring?'"

Desi Jr., in the meantime, had "graduated" from the Scripps drug dependency program and had become deeply involved with the New Life Foundation, a non-profit organization run by Vernon Howard, a prominent author and lecturer in the controversial field of "inner health." Apparently, Desi found something in Howard's teachings about self-awareness and "success without stress" that replaced drugs and booze as his way of coping with life's problems. With no tempting showbiz offers coming his way, Desi started traveling around the country as a spokesman for the New Life Foundation and trying to help people recovering from problems similar to his own.

Lucille Ball, meanwhile, had a cause of her own to pursue. She was threatening to sue the Rolling Stones for using an unflattering portrait of her in the gallery of women on the cover of their *Some Girls* album. Obviously, Lucy had gotten bored with retirement and needed diversion and attention. In 1984, she became active in charitable endeavors, helping to raise money for the Motion Picture and Television Relief Fund, Variety Clubs International, and the March of Dimes. Denver-based tycoon Marvin Davis, owner of 20th Century–Fox, founded the Lucille Ball Diabetes Research Center in that city.

In April 1984, it seemed only fitting that the "Queen of Television" should be honored by the new Museum of Broadcasting in New York City, a project made possible by the vision and generosity of her former boss William S. Paley. With a library, two auditoriums, and individual video and audio devices, the museum marked the first time that the public would have access to the radio and television programs of the past.

The five-month retrospective entitled *First Lady of Comedy* featured screenings of eighty hours of choice moments from all of Lucy's series and specials. The Mortons flew in from California for the gala opening night, restricted to VIPs from the broadcasting industry. The next day, Lucy threw caution to the wind and met her fans head-on in a seminar that was videotaped for the museum's archives. Thousands of people had to be turned away, since the auditorium seated only 225.

Wearing tinted glasses to conceal the bags under her eyes and sounding huskier than Tallulah Bankhead, Lucy fielded questions on everything from the real contents of the Vitameatavegamin bottle (apple pectin) to what advice she gave to Cher when the latter broke up with Sonny Bono (none, since she barely knew her). At one point, Lucy had a bit of a fright when a woman came up from the audience to shake her hand and gripped her in a bear hug instead. Lucy quickly broke away, gasping for breath.

The inevitable query about a possible comeback with a new TV series brought a mournful reply: "I'm not going to try alone now what I've done with partners in the past. Gale Gordon, God bless him, is even older than I am, and Vivian Vance and Bill Frawley are both in heaven."

Lucy said she had plenty to occupy her between running homes in Beverly Hills and Palm Springs and making frequent trips to New York to visit her two grandchildren. That total swelled to three in January 1985, with the birth of Kate Desiree Luckinbill, named for Lucy's longtime friend Katharine Hepburn and the baby's great-grandmother DeDe Ball.

Lucie, in the meantime, made another attempt at a TV series generically titled *The Lucie Arnaz Show,* which premiered for a limited season on CBS in May 1985. Based on the extremely popular British sitcom *Agony,* which starred Maureen Lipman as an "agony aunt" (the British expression for a press columnist specializing in advice to the lovelorn and troubled). Six episodes of *The Lucie Arnaz Show* were aired before CBS decided to cancel the series; drained of all the outrageous satire and sexual explicitness of *Agony,* it had failed to please either critics or viewers. The two Arnaz children were obviously not destined to inherit their parents' TV success.

Surprisingly, while *The Lucie Arnaz Show* was airing, the star's mother decided to take herself out of retirement by making a CBS TV movie in New York. Whether it was out of competitiveness, boredom, or just for the excuse to be near her grandchildren, Lucy shocked everybody by agreeing to take on an atypical dramatic role as a derelict bag lady in *Stone Pillow.* At the time, Lucy claimed that she couldn't resist the opportunity to work with George Schaefer, one of television's most revered directors, or scriptwriter Rose Leiman Goldemberg, whose harrowing *The Burning Bed,* with Farrah Fawcett as a battered wife, was one of the highest-rated TV movies ever.

The feisty hag known as "Florabelle" (named in honor of Lucy's maternal grandmother) was about as distant as Lucille Ball could get from her usual *Lucy* character. Discontented with the regimen of living in a women's shelter, Florabelle takes off on her own, sleeping in abandoned buildings, relieving herself in back alleys, and fending off rats and stray dogs.

Now nearly seventy-four, Lucy certainly could pass for an old crone, even though her enormous wealth hardly marked her as a candidate for the ranks of the homeless. For the sake of realism, she insisted on wearing a minimum of makeup and going on a diet to lose twenty-five pounds. During four years of professional inactivity, she had acquired considerable girth and a double chin, neither of which suited someone who supposedly lived on pickings from garbage cans.

Although *Stone Pillow* registered a huge audience rating when broadcast in November 1985, the filming proved a near-disaster for Lucy and left her in frail health for the rest of her life. Having spent her entire career laboring in the controlled environment of Hollywood studios, she never took into account what she'd have to contend with while working on location on the streets of Manhattan during a May heat wave. To make matters worse, the action of *Stone Pillow* took place in winter, which meant padding herself with extra layers of whatever bag ladies wear to protect themselves against the cold.

During the six-week shooting schedule, Lucy injured a shoulder, sprained her already damaged leg, lost her appetite, and frequently collapsed under the intensity of the ninety-degree weather. By the time she returned to Los Angeles, she was so seriously dehydrated that she had to be hospitalized for two weeks.

Hospital tests also revealed Lucy to be allergic to cigarettes, so she was ordered to stop smoking. Since she'd been a chain-smoker from the age of fifteen, doctors marveled that she was still alive to talk about it, but she claimed it was because she never inhaled.

Lucy's hospitalization started rumors that she was terminally ill and could be in her grave by the time that *Stone Pillow* reached the airwaves. But by the autumn, she was out drumbeating the movie on all the major talk shows and even joking about her advanced age.

During a guest appearance on NBC's *Tonight,* Johnny Carson's substitute host Joan Rivers wished her at least another twenty-five years on the tube. Lucy started counting on her fingers and cracked, "Please, I hope not. Do you know how old I'll be in another twenty-five years?"

25

Forever Darling

LUCY and Ricky Ricardo will live forever, or at least for as long as the films of their exploits are preserved. Lucille Ball and Desi Arnaz had no such luck, but they were only human.

For both, death seemed to be lurking impatiently in the wings from 1985 onward. Not long before Lucy's ordeal of *Stone Pillow*, Desi's wife, Edie, died of cancer after a three-year siege. Happily, she was able to lead a fairly normal life up to the final months, but the end of their twenty-two-year marriage shattered Desi and affected his own frail health.

Although the couple had many problems initially due to Desi's drinking and philandering, friends claim that the relationship mellowed and became tenderly romantic as they advanced into their senior years. No doubt their health problems also gave them a common bond, each becoming a support for the other to lean upon.

By the time of Edie's death, Desi had sold his horse-breeding ranch and other properties to keep up with the medical bills, which between the two of them were quite staggering. He still had the beach house at Del Mar, but living there on his own was not a pleasant prospect. His mother, Lolita, now well into her eighties, tried to help out, but she was getting feeble and hardly able to care for herself.

In his grief, Desi accelerated his boozing, which he'd never given up despite all the doctors' warnings. Young Desi, now something of an expert on alcoholism because of his own history and cure, tried to get his father to quit, but soon realized that he had waited too long.

"You can't undo a lifetime of alcohol abuse," Desi Jr. recalled. "Even if Dad stopped immediately, the damage to his system had been done. The best we could hope for was that by cutting back on the drinking he might be able to go on a bit longer."

At the pleading of both children, Lucy took Desi under her wing for a brief spell and gave the new widower the use of the guest cottage in her backyard. It made for a bizarre reunion of the couple that once shared the main house.

Desi's plight seemed to pull the whole family closer together. Lucie made frequent flying visits from New York with the three grandchildren while trying to persuade her husband to uproot to Los Angeles. The five Luckinbills had already given up their cramped Manhattan apartment and moved to a small farm about eighty miles north of the city in Rhinebeck, New York.

Now married five years, Lucie and her husband were going through their first major crisis—an inevitable conflict of careers. Their attempt at a performing partnership fizzled out, due as much to a shortage of suitable vehicles as to the nearly twenty-year age difference between them. Furthermore, at fifty-one, Laurence Luckinbill wasn't receiving many acting offers at all, so he started a second career writing articles on theater and the arts for magazines like *Esquire* and *Cosmopolitan*.

Born with showbiz in her veins, Lucie Arnaz could take only so much of being a rural housewife. In December 1985, she joined longtime friend Tommy Tune for a four-month stage tour in *My One and Only,* the Tony Award–winning Gershwin musical that had been a smash hit on Broadway with Tune and Britisher Leslie Hornby (better known as Twiggy).

Lucie not only proved that she was no longer the pudgy teenager of her mother's TV series, but that she could sing and dance with the best of them, something that Lucille Ball never could.

Ironically, Lucie and Luckinbill now found themselves facing the same predicament that her parents had when Desi was away from home touring with the band. More trusting of her husband than Lucy was of Desi, Lucie didn't run up huge phone bills the way her mother did. Friends claim that if Lucie had anything to worry about, it wasn't romantic competition but Luckinbill's fondness for alcohol, which got worse with the decline in his acting career.

Nineteen eighty-six began ominously when Desi Arnaz was diagnosed with lung cancer and had to be hospitalized several times at Scripps Memorial in La Jolla. Doctors saw slight hope of his recovering, but started radiation and chemotherapy treatments regardless.

It was almost thirty-five years since the premiere of *I Love Lucy.*

The likelihood of either of its co-stars turning up again in a new television series seemed remote if not impossible, especially in Desi's case. But Lucy surprised everybody—herself included—by signing with the American Broadcasting Company for a weekly half-hour frolic entitled *Life With Lucy*.

Wags were quick to wonder what life could be left in Lucille Ball at nearly seventy-five. Her decision to unretire again was more a matter of being unable to say no than of a compulsion to prove that she could still do it. ABC, which started its long climb to being the number-one network with Desilu's *The Untouchables* oh so many years ago, had fallen to number three behind NBC and CBS. Impressed by the high ratings of *Stone Pillow,* which seemed to confirm that the star still had a loyal following, ABC envisioned *Life With Lucy* as the nuclear weapon that could blast NBC's *Bill Cosby Show* and *The Golden Girls* from their perches as the most popular sitcoms on the air.

Life With Lucy would be a joint effort between Lucille Ball Productions and producer Aaron Spelling, an ex-actor who'd once worked in an episode of *I Love Lucy* but had gone on to become ABC's top source of programming with series like *Dynasty, Hotel, Hart to Hart,* and *The Love Boat.* Gary Morton took on the assignment of executive producer as well as his usual job of warming up the studio audience with jokes before each taping.

With her professional track record, Lucy refused to make a pilot, so ABC had to buy a full season of *Life With Lucy* sight unseen. Interestingly, each of the twenty-two episodes would cost roughly $650,000 to produce. The first installments of *I Love Lucy* averaged about $18,000!

Twelve years had passed since Lucy's last weekly series, *Here's Lucy,* but she decided to stick to her traditional zany character rather than attempt a new one that might be more suited to a septuagenarian. Always working best when surrounded by people she knew and trusted, she persuaded Gale Gordon to be her co-star and the original *I Love Lucy* team of Madelyn Pugh and Bob Carroll Jr. to write the scripts.

The format that the writers came up with bore a certain resemblance to one that they devised for Desi Arnaz when he produced *The Mothers-in-Law.* Widowers both, Lucy and Gordon ran a hardware store together and had children who were married to each other. "The Partners-in-Law" might have been a more appropriate title than *Life With Lucy.*

At a press conference just before production began, Lucy showed up wearing black trousers and a sequined top, turning misty-eyed and emotional whenever reporters delved into the sensitive areas of age and retirement.

"It's terrible to retire," Lucy said. "It's the last thing in the world I ever wanted to do. Backgammon and travel and playing with your grandchildren are dandy—if you've got nothing better to do! I never considered myself retired, but then I was. It just happened. Anyway, I'm glad that I'm back."

Asked if she intended to do strenuous slapstick in the new series, Lucy replied, "You bet your double bippy! I'm working out every day, the same things I've always done. I do my bendovers and my barre work and my swimming. I don't jog, but I'm a walker. I ride a bicycle. I try to eat right to keep my weight down."

But at age seventy-five, with four pins in one leg and still in a generally weakened condition from dehydration, Lucy was obviously exaggerating her robustness. As production progressed, she developed what's known in the acting profession as a "stamina problem." She tired easily, frequently flubbed her lines, and needed extra rehearsals. When she collapsed while dancing a jazzy Big Apple with guest star Peter Graves, Aaron Spelling ordered a rewrite of the scripts to delete any situations that might land her in sickbay.

Life With Lucy lasted less than two months on ABC and probably took a few years off Lucille Ball's own life, given the physical strain and psychological suffering it caused her. Critics loathed the thirty-fifth anniversary version of *Lucy,* and the public seemed to agree. The series landed in the bottom ten of the Nielsen ratings for all prime-time programming. ABC's cancellation caused a flurry of "The Queen Is Dead" headlines in the television press.

"Lucy called me on the phone after her final show," said lifelong friend Ann Sothern. "She was crying. 'Ann, I've been fired. ABC's let me go. They don't want to see me as an old grandma. They want me as the Lucy I was.' It was hard for her to have to stop working. She brought so much happiness to people, but I don't think she really knew how much people loved her."

Another close friend, onetime singer Lillian Briggs Winograd, said that Lucy was devastated by the bad press: "That hurt her more than anyone can know. She kept saying, 'I should never have done it.' The effect was awful. She couldn't understand why her type of comedy didn't seem to work anymore."

Lucy also felt terrible about causing the unemployment of so many people, most of whom had been with her for years. They'd been promised at least a full season's work, but found themselves jobless after six weeks.

The afternoon that Lucy and Gary Morton moved out of their office at Burbank Studios was one of the most upsetting of her lifetime. "I had some scripts in my arms and Gary was carrying a portable typewriter. As we walked out to the parking lot, people would just turn away," she recalled. "They treated us like lepers. Some *seemed* like they were on the verge of saying they were sorry or something, but most of them looked at us and looked away. I felt as if we were stealing, like we were trying to get the stuff to the car without being caught. God, it was awful. I cried for three days."

Sadly, while Lucy was closing down what eventually proved to be her last television series, Desi Arnaz happened to be on the brink of death. Hospitalized off and on since the beginning of the year, he'd finally returned to his ocean-front home in Del Mar to await the inevitable. Daughter Lucie took leave of her family and career to care for him.

Desi had turned sixty-nine in February. In recent months, his weight had dropped to below a hundred pounds and he'd gone nearly bald due to chemotherapy. He didn't want to be seen by anyone, least of all by his ex-wife, the great love of his life. He enjoyed talking to her on the phone whenever she called, which was several times a day, but he ordered her to stay away.

When Lucy heard that the priests had been alerted, she drove to Del Mar anyway, hoping that Desi would relent. No luck. He would only talk to her through the closed door of his bedroom. Lucy screamed and hollered and finally got her way. Seeing her former husband in such a pathetic condition must have been traumatic, but she stayed for several hours. What they chatted and perhaps laughed about is unknown, but Lucy and Desi had played their final scene together.

Three weeks later, Desi lapsed into a coma and never regained consciousness. He died peacefully in his daughter's arms on December 2, 1986.

According to his physician, Bruce Campbell, Desi died of lung cancer. "It was from smoking those Cuban cigars. That's the truth," Campbell said.

As luck would have it, Lucy was taping a guest appearance on the TV game show *Password* when she received the news.

Actress Betty White, also on the program, recalled the experience:

"Lucy was being real funny on camera, but during a break she said 'You know, it's the damnedest thing. Goddamn it, I didn't think I'd get this upset. There he goes.' It was a funny feeling, kind of a lovely, private moment."

Besieged by reporters for comment, Lucy issued a statement through her press representative: "Desi had been ill with cancer for many months, and my family and I have been praying for his release from this terrible ordeal. Our relationship had remained very close, very amiable over the years, and now I'm grateful to God that Desi's suffering is over."

Lucie Arnaz was more forthright, describing Desi as "a good daddy, but a lonely man at times, one who chose a difficult path. He was so bright, a genius, and had so much emotion, he was like an open wound. We were prepared for this for months, but I still dreaded it. What helped me through was a book called *Deathing* by Anya Foos Graber. It instructs you on how to help a person make the transition into the next life. I kept telling Dad to go to the light."

Although he remained an old-fashioned Catholic to the end, Desi left instructions to be cremated. He considered the traditional open display of the deceased to be ghoulish, so there was no casket in evidence at the funeral service. Only a photograph of Desi Arnaz at his handsomest graced the altar.

Lucie and Desi Jr. handled all the arrangements; it hardly seemed proper for their mother to do so, even though she may have wanted to. Nearly a hundred friends and relatives attended the private memorial mass, which was held at Desi's home parish of St. James Roman Catholic Church in Solana Beach. Danny Thomas, star of one of Desilu's most successful series, delivered the eulogy.

"I will never ever, ever forget Desi's tremendous help to me. And I speak not only about what he did for me, but what he has done for the entire industry," Thomas said. "Television owes him a tremendous debt of gratitude. No one but no one has ever come close to the kind of TV Desi brought with Lucy to this industry."

Escorted by Gary Morton, Lucy had to put up with being taken for the widow, even if she wasn't dressed like one in a light-colored suit and blouse. During the service, she had to remove her sunglasses to more easily wipe the tears from her eyes.

Outside the church, hundreds of people had gathered, many driving from Los Angeles and San Diego to pay tribute. When Lucy finally emerged, the crowd cheered and a young girl ran over to hand her a single red rose. As far as their fans were concerned, it seemed that neither divorce nor death could separate Lucy and Desi. In that sense, they would always be married.

Only in death did Desi Arnaz receive recognition as one of the most important figures in the history of television. *Variety* described him as "the architect of the couple's great success. He possessed a keen business acumen and inherent knack for showmanship that guided Desilu from a one-series production company to the preeminent Hollywood independent."

The *New York Times* hailed Desi for his production innovations and dubbed him father of the rerun, noting that *I Love Lucy* could still be seen twenty-four hours a day, "if not in English, then in Greek, Portuguese or Bantu." The *Los Angeles Times* said that "Desi Arnaz bestrode the flickering world of television like a colossus. It's well to remember that every evening that we spend watching television, we are exposed to his influence."

Although obituaries cited the multimillions that Desi earned over the years, he apparently died less than a millionaire. Friends claim that he went through everything with his gambling and high-flying lifestyle, not to mention the professional inactivity and illnesses of his last decade. In his will, he left Lucie and Desi the houses in Del Mar and Las Cruces, but both properties were believed to be heavily mortgaged.

The children also took over responsibility for their grandmother, Lolita Arnaz. Senile and living in a nursing home, she died nearly three years later at age ninety-one, never knowing that her only child had predeceased her.

Less than a week after Desi's death, Lucy received one of the highest cultural awards that her country can bestow, the Kennedy Center Honors for Achievement in the Performing Arts. The organizers had originally wanted Desi to emcee Lucy's portion of the televised ceremonies, which would have made for a highly emotional reunion of TV's favorite lovebirds. But when Desi's health prevented that, they chose Robert Stack, who'd never acted with Lucy but did have a definite connection as star of Desilu's second most popular series, *The Untouchables.*

Lucy and Gary Morton flew to Washington, D.C. for the proceedings, which covered a weekend of activities at the White House and the Kennedy Center Opera House. President Reagan and wife Nancy started things off with a private dinner for all the honorees, who also included violinist Yehudi Menuhin, married actors Hume Cronyn and Jessica Tandy, ballet dancer/choreographer Antony Tudor, and blues singer/pianist Ray Charles.

Events reached their zenith with a glittering two-hour extravaganza at the Kennedy Opera House, which CBS-TV taped for broadcast later in the month as one of its Yuletide specials. Despite the ravages of age, Lucy never looked more stunningly regal than she did with the golden Kennedy Medal hanging from her neck in a garland of red, white, and blue ribbons. She and the other honorees sat in box seats next to the President and First Lady while friends and colleagues saluted their artistry with verbal and visual bouquets.

The segment devoted to Lucy's career couldn't help becoming a tribute to Desi Arnaz as well due to an emphasis on classic clips from *I Love Lucy*. One can only guess at Lucy's feelings as she watched them for what must have been the first time since Desi's death.

The Kennedy Honors turned out to be an unofficial capping off to Lucille Ball's fifty-three years in the public spotlight. A comic actress rather than a comedian, she needed a full-blown vehicle to carry her, but how many were being written for septuagenarians? Had she been a stand-up jokester like the even older Bob Hope, Milton Berle, or George Burns, she might have gone on indefinitely fronting TV specials and making nightclub and theater tours.

Like it or not, Lucy's future public appearances would be mainly for awards and testimonials, and she seemed to be running out of those. By that time, she'd won her share of Emmys and been elected to the Broadcasting Hall of Fame. An honorary Oscar for her long but disappointing movie career appeared unlikely.

Perhaps it was just as well. "I really do appreciate the acclaim," she told a friend, "but it makes me feel old. It's like having to listen to your own obituary."

In the interests of marital harmony, Lucy kept her production company running, mainly so that Gary Morton would have a job to go to every day. Lucille Ball Productions was now mainly a clearing house for fan mail and requests on Lucy's charity, but it left her husband with less time to hang out at the Friars' Club and other trouble spots.

After the cancellation of *Life With Lucy*, friends noticed a definite decline in Lucy's spirits. "She wanted people like me around, anybody who could be up and bright and keep her from getting depressed. She would always say, 'I miss my work,' " Lillian Winograd recalled.

Still, Lucy's sense of humor never seemed completely lost. One day she asked Winograd to accompany her to the dentist while she had two molars extracted. "She came out bleeding, and her mouth was filled with cotton," Winograd remembered. "I told her, 'Come on, Lucy, let's go home and take a nice nap.' Through the cotton she said, 'I wanna play backgammon.' I tried to talk her out of it, but when we got back to the house she insisted on 'just one game.' She rolls her dice and it turns out they were the two molars! She was in pain, bleeding, but all she wanted to do was pull that joke on me. She was *hysterical.*"

The death of one parent often strengthens the bond between the surviving parent and their children. In the case of the Arnaz offspring, that applied more to Lucie than to Desi. After her father died, Lucie seemed to realize that her mother might not be around much longer either. To facilitate togetherness, the Luckinbills sold their farm in upstate New York and bought a house in the upper reaches of Beverly Hills, just a short drive from Nana's place in the flatlands.

Lucie and Laurence Luckinbill were still having problems but trying to avoid a divorce for the sake of three young children. It appeared to be a fairly common case of a young wife being far more successful than her considerably older husband, compounded by his heavy drinking. Both were in psychotherapy in hopes of exorcising the demons.

Meanwhile, Desi Arnaz Jr. had quit show business entirely and moved to Boulder City, Nevada, headquarters for the New Life Foundation. Due in part to its proximity to Las Vegas, the organization was widely regarded as a racket, a New Age cult that preyed on wealthy but confused individuals who didn't know what to do with their money. Rumors said that Vernon Howard, NLF's reclusive "Invisible Pope," had his sights set on the millions that Desi stood to inherit when his mother died.

Desi himself scoffed at the gossip and continued to crusade for NLF as its national spokesman. Fraud or not, it seemed to be keeping him out of trouble. Another factor in his rehabilitation was the tragic death of his best friend, Dino Martin, in a plane crash in March 1987. Only thirty-five when he died, Dean Martin's eldest child would be remembered mainly as a dissolute playboy who never amounted to anything despite all the advantages; Desi decided it wasn't going to happen to him.

While working in behalf of the New Life Foundation, Desi fell in love with another of its disciples, an ex–Las Vegas ballerina named Amy Bargiel, who ran a children's dance studio in Boulder City. A year younger than Desi, Bargiel had also been briefly married and divorced and had a daughter who lived with her.

The relationship blossomed into a ready-made family when Desi and Amy were married in October 1987. The Mortons and the Luckinbills made the 350-mile trip to Boulder City for the ceremony, the first gathering of the clan since Big Desi's death. The strict Catholic probably would have been appalled by the unorthodox service, which was conducted by a lay minister from the New Life Foundation.

If Lucy had any doubts about NLF, she kept them to herself. "I'm so proud of Desi," she tearfully told a reporter afterward. "This boy missed two-thirds of his life, but he's finally come back. He's even giving seminars to help other people with their problems. It's a pleasure to know him after all these years."

Amazingly, 1988 would mark Lucille Ball's fifty-fifth anniversary in show business. After the debacle of *Life With Lucy,* she kept insisting that she would never work as an actress again. When gossip columnist Liz Smith reported her to be a prime candidate for the movie version of *Driving Miss Daisy,* Lucy phoned the producers and declared herself out of the running. Jessica Tandy later won an Oscar for the same role.

But Lucy couldn't resist another opportunity to work with one of her favorite co-stars, Bob Hope, on the NBC television special honoring his eighty-fifth birthday in May 1988. The guest appearance suggested that Lucy was starting to lose her grip.

"Lucy had a wonderful dancing and singing sketch, but there hadn't been much time to rehearse, and it was difficult for her to match her steps to the orchestration," said fellow guest star Brooke Shields. "She reminded me of a little girl—frustrated, embarrassed that she was having trouble with the steps."

About a week later, Lucy collapsed at home and had to be rushed to Cedars-Sinai Medical Center in nearby West Hollywood. News bulletins soon had Lucy on her deathbed, but Gary Morton qualified her condition as a minor heart attack and stroke.

Lucy hated hospitals. After several days of rest and a successful angiogram, she checked herself out and returned to 1000 North Roxbury Drive to continue her recuperation. Her right side was partially paralyzed, making it difficult to speak and eat. She required a full-time nurse, but seemed determined to make a full recovery. As soon as she was allowed out of bed, she started physical therapy with choreographer friend Onna White, who had helped her through the broken-leg crisis of *Mame.*

Within three months, Lucy was strong enough to take early morning strolls to Rodeo Drive with Gary Morton to look in the boutique windows. She still tired easily and tended to drool when she spoke, but those impairments all but vanished with time.

In September 1988, Lucy couldn't resist an invitation to be a week-long guest star on one of her favorite game shows, *Super Password*, hosted by Bert Convy. With Carol Channing, Betty White, and Dick Martin as the other players, she taped all five shows in one night. The cheering and laughter of the studio audience apparently energized her enough to get through, but she was completely exhausted by the end of the grueling seven-hour session.

Lucy must have known that her days were numbered. Not long afterward, she summoned her longtime makeup artist Hal King to the house for a reconciliation luncheon. Lucy had blamed King for some of the fiasco of *Mame* and hadn't spoken to him in fourteen years. But now she delegated him to be her cosmetician in death, giving him detailed instructions on how she wanted to look in her casket.

Lucy's professional activity seemed over (*Super Password* turned out to be her last appearance on a TV series). She filled her time playing backgammon, baby-sitting with her three grandchildren, and watching *Password* and her other favorite, *Hollywood Squares*. When superagent Irving Lazar told her that he could get a seven-figure advance for her autobiography, she agreed to write one, provided that she didn't have to dish any dirt about her life with Desi Arnaz. Desi treated her with kid gloves in his book, and she intended to return the favor.

In February 1989, Lucy received a call from the producers of moviedom's annual Academy Awards spectacular asking if she'd team up with Bob Hope on the next telecast. The two "Living Legends" would introduce a big production number featuring young performers who might well become the legends of the future. Having encouraged new talent during her Desilu Workshop days, it was an offer she couldn't refuse.

Whether she sensed it or not, Lucy treated the occasion as if it would be her grand farewell appearance before the world. The Oscar show was a perennial number one special, watched by hundreds of millions in sixty-five countries. To give them something to remember her by, Lucy ordered an evening dress a size too small and then went on a strict diet to enable herself to squeeze into it.

Designed by Bob Mackie associate Ret Turner, the black beaded gown had a gold sequined collar that complemented Lucy's flaming red hair. The dress weighed a ton and nearly dragged her down, but it did have its compensations. The skirt was split up one side nearly to the hip, revealing that she still had the shapely gams of a Goldwyn Girl.

Whether it was out of affection or just plain astonishment at their combined 162 years of longevity, Lucille Ball and Bob Hope received a standing ovation when they strolled out on the stage of the Chandler Pavilion on the night of March 29. Although it went unnoticed by the audience and TV viewers, Hope had an inkling that Lucy was unwell.

"Her hand felt clammy and she seemed a bit wobbly," Hope recalled. "When we finished, Gary grabbed her and took her right out. So I wondered to myself, 'Gee, I hope she's all right.'"

When Bob Hope phoned the next day to ask how she felt, Lucy claimed to be fine. Encouraged, Hope offered the Mortons an all-expenses-paid trip to Paris so that Lucy could appear on his next TV special, which would be filmed in the French capital. Lucy cursed her luck. She'd already made other commitments and couldn't cancel them. She had to fly to her native Jamestown, New York, to accept an honorary degree from the local community college.

Lucy never made it back to Jamestown. Three weeks after the Oscar telecast, she was just finishing breakfast when she felt stabbing pains in her chest and began sweating profusely. Gary Morton phoned the doctor, who told him to drive her to Cedars-Sinai Medical Center immediately.

Lucy refused. She said after her last experience at Cedars-Sinai that she'd never go back. "Gary was in total panic," a friend recalled. "He didn't know what to do, so he phoned Lucie and she came flying over from her house. The two of them had tears rolling down their faces as they pleaded with Lucy to go to the hospital. Finally she agreed, provided that she could get fully dressed and put on her makeup!"

Just after twelve noon, Lucy arrived at the Cedars-Sinai emergency room. "She looked awful, huddled over in a wheelchair," a nurse recalled. "She was white as a sheet and gasping for breath, wearing a sweater and blue slacks, with a shawl in her lap. They rushed her to the cardiac unit on the sixth floor. By 12:45, she was in the operating theater."

A surgical team headed by Dr. Robert Kass opened Lucy's chest and discovered that her entire aorta, the main artery carrying blood from the heart to the rest of the body, was fatally damaged. Although the chances of saving Lucy's life were next to zero, the doctors made an attempt by replacing a section of the aorta with pieces from a heart donor. Lucy's own heart had to be stopped during the seven hours and forty minutes she was on the operating table. She required nearly a dozen blood transfusions.

That Lucy even survived such an ordeal was encouraging. After spending an uneventful night in intensive care, she awoke at 9:45 the next morning and seemed to be alert and making significant progress, a hospital spokesman said. When Gary Morton popped in to see her, the first thing she asked him was "How's Tinky?" referring to their three-year-old white poodle.

Lucy's crisis unleashed the greatest outpouring of public sympathy since Elizabeth Taylor's near-fatal double pneumonia in 1961. Cedars-Sinai received over 5,000 phone calls from around the world on the first day. At the family's request, hundreds of floral tributes were rerouted to children's hospitals and senior citizen centers. A shopping mall opposite Cedars-Sinai hung a huge "We Love Lucy" banner on the roof in the hope that she'd be able to see it.

Ironically, two days after the operation, one of Lucy's closest friends, Ruth (Mrs. Milton) Berle, died of cancer only a few rooms away in the same hospital. The news was kept from Lucy for fear the shock would kill her.

As far as the world knew, Lucille Ball was getting progressively better, but it turned out to be a ruse to keep her spirits up. On Monday, April 24, she was still in the intensive care unit, but had been moved from the critical section. Following a visit, Gary Morton told reporters, "Her Irish eyes are smiling." Lucie Luckinbill said that her mother was upset over the hospital's refusal to permit a beautician to come in and set her hair.

At five in the morning on April 26, Lucy suffered a full cardiac arrest. "Doctors immediately began working on her, using state-of-the-art techniques," according to hospital spokesman Ron Wise. "For an hour, they struggled feverishly to get her heart started again, but it was to no avail. She was declared dead at 6:04 A.M."

Cardiologist Yuri Busi said that Lucy's aorta had ruptured again at a site fairly distant from the point of the operation. "I don't think she had enough time to know what was happening to her," Busi said.

"Lucille Ball: Dead at 77." Seldom has a news flash caused more shock or tears. President George Bush said in a statement, "Lucille Ball possessed the gift of laughter. But she also embodied an even greater treasure—the gift of love. She appealed to the gentler impulses of the human spirit. She was not merely an actress or a comedian. She was 'Lucy' and she was loved."

Inevitably, the tributes were as much for Desi Arnaz as they were for Lucy. In an editorial, the *New York Times* said, " 'I Love Lucy' ran for only six years, from 1951 to 1957, and Lucille Ball starred in a lot of good TV shows, in films and on Broadway after that. But if she had ended her career when 'I Love Lucy' ended its run, she'd still have died famous.

"One reason has to do with timing: Lucille Ball helped inaugurate the age of television just as surely as Charlie Chaplin helped inaugurate the age of movies. A second reason has to do with timelessness: nowhere is 'I Love Lucy' more honored than in its enduringly popular reruns. The shenanigans of Lucy, Desi and their best friends and neighbors, Fred and Ethel, are as fresh and funny today to their third generation of viewers as they were to their first."

As soon as the news broke, fans began flocking to Lucy's house in Beverly Hills to say a quiet prayer or to drop flowers outside the front door. Hired guards were hurriedly posted to protect against vandalism and to keep traffic flowing.

Longtime friend and rival funnylady Carol Burnett, who turned fifty-six on the same day that Lucy died, said, "I don't think any public figure—politician or movie star—has ever affected people like this. It's like having someone in the family die. Anybody who ever watched TV felt that Lucy was part of the family. I don't know if that was or ever will be duplicated."

Most extraordinary of all was the action surrounding Lucille Ball's brass and coral terazzo star on The Walk of Fame, which honors about 1,800 celebrities up and down both sides of Hollywood Boulevard in the heart of the entertainment capital. Within hours of Lucy's death, the Hollywood Chamber of Commerce placed an easel with her photo and a wreath of flowers on the spot and started collecting signatures to send to her family. The continuous scroll of white parchment eventually extended up a full block of Hollywood Boulevard, from Lucy's star at the corner of Wilcox Avenue to the next intersection at Cahuenga Boulevard.

To avoid the circus of a public funeral, Lucille Ball had none. Her body was cremated, the ashes buried in the family plot that she bought at Forest Lawn Cemetery during her starlet days. Gary Morton, her two children, and their spouses were the only witnesses to the interment, which was kept secret from the press to insure privacy.

The settlement of Lucy's estate has also been kept private, leaving some unanswered questions about her wealth and who inherited it. Her fortune may have been worth as much as $350 million if she held on to the Gulf + Western stock she received for Desilu, which went through many splits and conversions over the years. (G + W is now known as Paramount Communications.) Her house at 1000 North Roxbury Drive was estimated to be worth $7.5 million, but at the start of 1991 it remained unsold due to the real estate recession, and brokers rated it a steal at $5 million.

Many people assumed that the bulk of Lucy's estate would go to her two children, but that might not have been the case. Some friends claim that her main beneficiary was Gary Morton, that Lucie and Desi were amply provided for with trust funds set up decades ago when their parents were still married. Others say that Morton received the Beverly Hills house and that the children and grandchildren inherited everything else.

Lucie and Desi have reportedly formed a company called "Desilu, too" to handle the complicated business of sorting out ownership rights to both of their parents' various enterprises, which may take years.

One thing is certain about Lucille Ball's will. She left detailed instructions for a memorial gathering, which Lucie and Desi honored a month after her death, appropriately enough on Mother's Day. The affair was more a picnic than a wake, held outdoors on what had once been Robert Taylor's ranch in Mandeville Canyon, an unspoiled reminder of Lucy's beloved Desilu in Chatsworth, long parceled into housing developments.

About fifty relatives and close friends came to honor Lucy and to dine on the favorite foods of her Jamestown childhood: baked ham and beans, potato salad, cole slaw, and watermelon. No eulogies were delivered. Everybody exchanged memories of Lucy while her favorite record album, *Bobby Darin at the Copa,* blasted from loudspeakers.

The tributes were far from over. The children and Gary Morton received so many requests for some kind of public remembrance that special memorial masses were held simultaneously at St. Monica's Catholic Church in Los Angeles, St. Ignatius Loyola in New York, and Old St. Patrick's in Chicago on the night of May 8. It was, of course, a Monday, which had always been the night for *I Love Lucy* in millions of households. Those who couldn't make it to the three churches, which meant most of the nation, were urged to observe a moment of silence at the traditional *Lucy* airing time of 9 P.M.

Hours before the services started, the waiting lines outside the churches far exceeded the seating capacities, so loudspeakers were set up in the streets to enable the overflow to participate.

Cuban immigrant Elisa Maria de Llanos was one of the lucky thousand to get into the Los Angeles mass. Afterwards she told a reporter, "When I came to this country in 1956, Lucy and Desi were the first people I saw on television. I never felt homesick, because watching them made me laugh. I don't feel sad now that they're both gone. They left something to make people happy forever."

In Seattle, psychic Delilah Cornet claimed that Lucille Ball and Desi

Arnaz had been reunited in the spirit world, not as themselves but as Lucy and Ricky Ricardo. During a séance, Lucy allegedly told the medium that she and Desi got along so much better in a heavenly re-creation of *I Love Lucy* that they were remarried in a simple ceremony in the Ricardos' living room, with Fred Mertz as best man and Ethel Mertz as maid-of-honor.

Whether one believes in an afterlife or not, there is no question that Lucille Ball and Desi Arnaz will go on forever in the hearts of those who have seen *I Love Lucy* or who will watch it in future generations. Because of the long reach of television, no couple has ever brought more laughter to the world. Their humor is universal and timeless, and inevitably—owing to the dearth of original comedy in the field today—their work will seem even funnier as time goes on. They left us a legacy that puts a happy ending to their story after all.

Acknowledgments

I would like to express my gratitude to the following people who kindly shared memories and information with me: George Abbott, the late Harry Ackerman, Edie Adams, Jack Aldworth, the late Eve Arden, William Asher, James Bacon, Kaye Ballard, Art Barron, the late Joan Bennett, Milton Berle, the late Tom Bodley, William Boerst, the late Howard Cady, Jack Carter, Marge Champion, Dane Clark, Wanda Clark, Dr. William Clark, the late Xavier Cugat, Marge Durante, Kurt Frings, the late Lud Gluskin, Greg Hirsch, Bob Hope, Van Johnson, Hal King, Emmett Lavery, Martin Leeds, Pauline Lopus, Phyllis McGuire, Virginia Carroll McLean, Frances Mercer, Ann Miller, the late Jess Oppenheimer, Charles Pomerantz, Marcella Rabwin, Jill Winkler Rath, Marco Rizo, Joan Rivers, Maxine Jennings Saltenstall, Jay Sandrich, Red Skelton, Ann Sothern, Robert Stack, Keith Thibodeaux, the late Danny Thomas, Jerry Thorpe, Marion Strong Van Vlack, Kay Vaughan, Betty White, and Lillian Briggs Winograd. Numerous other friends and professional associates of Lucille Ball, Desi Arnaz, Lucie Arnaz and Desi Arnaz Jr. also participated, but names have been withheld at their request.

My thanks also go to the staffs of the following research centers for their splendid assistance: the Margaret Herrick Library of the Motion Picture Academy of Arts & Sciences, Los Angeles; the American Film Institute Library, Los Angeles; the Performing Arts Library at Lincoln Center, New York City; and the Museum of Broadcasting, New York

City. Background information was also provided by the Fenton Historical Center, Jamestown, New York; and the Center for Cuban Studies, New York City.

Jerry Silverstein was especially helpful during my work in Los Angeles. A further note of gratitude to counselor Janet Klosko and my agent, Dan Strone, as well as to editor Bob Bender and his assistant, Johanna Li, for shepherding me through the most challenging project of my writing career. For their encouragement and good cheer, heartfelt thanks to my relatives and friends, especially all the Harrises, Spratts, Isbys, and Martoranas, Jerrold Weitzman, Georgina Hale, Evelyn Seeff, Eva Franklin, Nen Roeterdink, George Bester, Ron Samuels, Jay Watnick and the late Alan Hobbs.

Index